T5-CCK-201

Database Management Systems

Understanding and Applying Database Technology

Books and Training Products From QED

Database

Data Analysis: The Key to Data Base Design
The Data Dictionary: Concepts and Uses
DB2: The Complete Guide to Implementation and Use
Logical Data Base Design
DB2 Design Review Guidelines
DB2: Maximizing Performance of Online Production Systems
Entity-Relationship Approach to Logical Data Base Design
How to Use ORACLE SQL*PLUS
ORACLE: Building High Performance Online Systems
Embedded SQL for DB2: Application Design and Programming
Introduction to Data and Activity Analysis
ORACLE Design Review Guidelines
Using DB2 to Build Decision Support Systems
IMS Design and Implementation Techniques
SQL for DB2 and SQL/DS Application Developers
Using ORACLE to Build Decision Support Systems
Database Management Systems: Understanding and Applying Database Technology
Effective DSS Processing with Teradata

Systems Engineering

Handbook of Screen Format Design
Managing Software Projects: Selecting and Using PC-Based Project Management Systems
The Complete Guide to Software Testing
A User's Guide for Defining Software Requirements
A Structured Approach to Systems Testing
Storyboard Prototyping: A New Approach to User Requirements Analysis
The Software Factory: Managing Software Development and Maintenance
Data Architecture: The Information Paradigm
Advanced Topics in Information Engineering
Software Engineering with Formal Software Metrics
Data Architecture: An Information Systems Strategy (Video)

Management

CASE: The Potential and the Pitfalls
Strategic and Operational Planning for Information Services
The Management Handbook for Information Center and End-User Computing

Management (cont'd)

Winning the Change Game
Information Systems Planning for Competitive Advantage
Critical Issues in Information Processing Management and Technology
Developing the World Class Information Systems Organization
How to Automate Your Computer Center: Achieving Unattended Operations
Ethical Conflicts in Information and Computer Science, Technology, and Business
Mind Your Business: Managing the Impact of End-User Computing
Controlling the Future: Managing Technology-Driven Change

Data Communications

Data Communications: Concepts and Solutions
Designing and Implementing Ethernet Networks
Network Concepts and Architectures
Open Systems: The Guide to OSI and its Implementation

IBM Mainframe Series

How to Use CICS to Create On-Line Applications: Methods and Solutions
DOS/VSE/SP Guide for Systems Programming: Concepts, Programs, Macros, Subroutines
Systems Programmer's Problem Solver
VSAM: Guide to Optimization and Design
MVS/TSO: Mastering CLISTS
MVS/TSO: Mastering Native Mode and ISPF
Advanced VSE System Programming Techniques
REXX in the TSO Environment
DOS/VSE: Introduction to the Operating System

Self-Paced Training

SQL as a Second Language
Building Online Production Systems with DB2 (Video)
Introduction to UNIX (CBT)
Building Production Applications with ORACLE (Video)

Programming

C Language for Programmers, Second Edition
VAX/VMS: Mastering DCL Commands and Utilities

Database Management Systems

Understanding and Applying
Database Technology

QED Information Sciences, Inc.
Wellesley, Massachusetts • Montreal

170 Linden Street
Wellesley, Massachusetts 02181

Library of Congress Number: 89-70144

International Standard Book Number: 0-89435-323-3

Printed in the United States of America

91 92 93 10 9 8 7 6 5 4 3 2 1

Library of Congress Cataloging-in-Publication Data

Gorman, Michael M.
Database Management Systems: understanding and applying database technology/ Michael M. Gorman
p. cm.
ISBN: 0-89435-323-3

I. Data base management. I. Title.
QA76.9.D3G6668 1990
005.74--dc20

89-70144
CIP

To: Don Deutsch, Phil Shaw, Jim Melton and Len Gallagher

There is no measure to the debt the DBMS community owes to Don Deutsch of General Electric, Phil Shaw of IBM, Jim Melton of DEC, and Len Gallagher of NIST (formerly National Bureau of Standards). They are clearly the unsung heros of DBMS.

Don Deutsch has been the chairman of X3H2 for eleven of its thirteen years. While on the committee, Don also managed the DBMS standards work of the U.S. National Institute of Standards and Technology (NIST, formerly the U.S. National Bureau of Standards), and for the last several years, he has worked on the vendor side of the DBMS community at General Electric. Don has managed the committee superbly. The committee has had over 100 different corporate and individual members, and about 2500 technical papers have been presented. Don not only crafts the agendas and manages the meetings, he has also managed to bring to the market the first two DBMS standards: NDL and SQL. Under Don's chairmanship, X3H2 has finished two additional SQL standards: one for referential integrity, and the other for the interface specifications between SQL and six different programming languages (Ada, COBOL, C, Fortran, Pascal, and PL/I), and is starting on the home stretch of the SQL2 standard, a robust extension to the original SQL standard. Work on the next SQL standard, currently called SQL3, has already started. The quality of X3H2's work is a direct result of Don's leadership, patience, and persistence.

Phil Shaw has been the IBM representative to X3H2 since the first meeting in 1978. Phil provided the vast majority of the technical papers for the network data language standard, NDL, and because of Phil, NDL is a very high quality specification. While much is said in the press and on the lecture and seminar circuit, of the work of the originators of the SQL language, they are its fathers in name only, because it has been Phil Shaw, over the years, without notice or attention, who has toiled days, weeks, and years drafting, redrafting, and wordsmithing the ANSI SQL/86 standard. And, once the American NDL and SQL/86 standards were finished, it was Phil who was the key American representative to the International Standards Organization (ISO), enabling both NDL and SQL/86 to become international standards.

Jim Melton of Digital has been the editor of the SQL/2 (about 1992) base document since 1987. It serves both ANSI/X3H2 and the ISO Database Languages rapporteur group. This document has grown from a little over 100 pages (SQL/86) to well over 600 pages (SQL2 and SQL3). Jim spends 40 to 60 hours every week integrating the results of each ANSI/X3H2 meeting (six per year) and of the three ISO meetings. The progress of X3H2 and the ISO/DBL groups is a direct consequence of Jim's work.

Len Gallagher of the NIST is both the international representative from X3H2 to the International Standards Organization (ISO), and the convener of the ISO database languages rapporteur group. Len's ISO group consists of representatives from about a dozen countries, who must review proposals and then arrive at a consensus. Under Len's stewardship, the ISO/DBL rapporteur group has managed to avoid confrontation and the development of nationalistic fractions.

Phil and Jim also attend every ISO meeting as representatives of X3H2, making the American group one of the strongest. Notwithstanding, Len ensures that all countries are heard, and that consensus, not dominance, moves the agenda.

And finally, thanks to GE, IBM, DEC, and NIST for their strong support of Don, Phil, Jim, and Len in the database standards effort.

CONTENTS

PREFACE

The next DBMS generation is here. It contains DBMSs that look alike--on the outside. That is, they conform to ANSI/SQL, or ANSI/NDL, or to a combination of ANSI/NDL and ANSI/SQL. This does not mean all DBMSs are the same--on the inside. On the inside, DBMSs perform very differently: some slow, others fast; some rudimentary, others advanced. To buy a DBMS solely because it is ANSI standard is to also believe that all automobiles are the same. This book is about the critical DBMS differences.

Database management systems (DBMSs) have evolved a great deal over the last 30 years. The first systems were created in the early 1960s. Through the years there have been several major technology mergers. Almost all of these mergers were the direct result of market pressures. The first evolution resulted from the merger of the capabilities of the host language DBMSs and the self-contained language DBMSs. The resulting DBMSs were almost all based on embedded, interrecord-type relationship mechanisms, known in this book as static relationships. Then there arose the dynamic relationship mechanism DBMSs (shared data element values in different record type instances). The first such systems were servicing hundreds of production databases in the late 1960s, years before the first papers *discovering* relational DBMSs were published. Throughout the late 1960s and 1970s, static and dynamic relationship DBMSs were installed and used with great success.

The second merger began around 1984. Some DBMS vendors discovered that the majority of the facilities contained in their respective products were independent of data model and independent of technology. Thus, they made their products support both network (static) and relational (dynamic) facilities and also be implemented on a variety of hardware types, that is, microcomputers, minicomputers, and mainframes. Consequently, this book addresses both network and relational DBMSs that operate on mainframes, minicomputers, and microcomputers.

The author first encountered a DBMS in 1969. It was an inverted access, hierarchical data model, natural language DBMS that became operational in the middle 1960s. This DBMS's maximum database size was about 1 million characters. It supported between 50 and 100 concurrent users and the computer required to support it filled a room. Today's room-sized computers support databases 10,000 times larger and service thousands of concurrent users. Today's desk top computers support databases 10 to 25 times larger than the 1969 database and service from 20 to 30 concurrent users.

If this book were written in 1969, its contents would be valid only for mainframe computers. Due to today's miniaturization and the increased sophistication of *personal* software, almost all of today's mainframe DBMS characteristics are found in today's micro- and minicomputer DBMSs. Thus this book is also valid for DBMSs operating on mini- and microcomputers.

In many ways, DBMSs are the same today as they were years ago. The same data models still exist, as do the types of natural and host language interfaces. Today, however, it is even more necessary to have storage efficient databases that can load, update, and retrieve data rapidly because database sizes have grown from millions of characters to tens of billions of characters. And it is even more necessary to provide security, audit trails, and multiple user access.

Whether you are selecting a micro-, mini-, or mainframe DBMS, to be sophisticated means that the DBMS supports screen generators, query languages, host language access, indexes, concurrent access, and multiple data model support, etc. These are all needed regardless of the hardware technology or the application.

Not everything has stayed the same, however. Since 1969, there has been an increase in the use of on-line facilities (screen generators, etc.) and of DBMSs for a wider range of applications. There is also a much better understanding of the fundamental aspects of a data model. Most important has been the realization that data model implementations are for the most part independent of their specification. This means that DBMSs of the same data model can have very different implementations, some substandard, most only acceptable, and a few of high quality.

Furthermore, the years since 1969 have seen an effort to specify standards for common DBMS facilities. The first of these efforts were by CODASYL. Starting in the early 1970s, ANSI/SPARC began an effort to standardize DBMS facilities by developing a framework from which sprang three standards: NDL, SQL, and the IRDS. NDL is for network databases, SQL for relational databases, and the IRDS for storing and manipulating metadata.

The ANSI standards process did not fix features, rather it standardized interfaces. An organization is now free to select various products that produce syntax conforming to an interface, or that can read conforming syntax. The real value of ANSI database standards is that the days of being locked in by a vendor are now over. For example, a company can purchase a sophisticated menu-driven report writer that produces interactive NDL or SQL data manipulation language. This NDL or SQL is read by the DBMS, which obtains the data records and passes them across the standard interface for final formatting by the report writer.

The next DBMS generation has been *born* and contains DBMSs that look alike, on the outside. That is, there are classes of DBMSs that conform to SQL, NDL, or to a combination of facilities from NDL and SQL. But these DBMSs are not all the same, any more than all paintings done with oils are the same. Clearly, it is possible to design a DBMS that fits the standards but is of poor quality nonetheless. Just as there is more to a quality painting than choosing paints, there is more to a quality DBMS design than following standards.

This book goes to considerable length to detail the components of a sophisticated DBMS and to provide the information DBMS users or evaluators need to look critically at DBMS products.

I would like to acknowledge the help of those who made this book possible. First there is my family, all of whom showed great understanding during the time it took to finish the book. Thanks go especially to my son, Michael, who spent hundreds of hours reading, editing, and pointing out the many areas of the book that needed to be reworked. I am grateful to Ruth Jennings for her many hours work on the over 200 figures contained in the book. Thanks go to Hal Stull and Jerry Hoffman for reading the final manuscript to catch the *one last error*.

Thanks are owed to the members of the ANSI/X3H2 committee, whose members, at this book's publishing, number over 40. The committee meets six times yearly for four-day meetings at which 75 to 100 papers are presented. Ideas are presented and then subjected to intense review by implementors and users. In this way, standards progress one syntax and general rule at a time. Initially, standards' progress is quick, but as months and years pass, the task becomes more and more complex, and the work slows. To acknowledge the X3H2 members who performed the work would take pages. Consequently, they shall remain named only in the actual NDL and SQL standards.

Finally, I am grateful to the staff at QED for their constructive editing and book formatting suggestions.

1

ANSI DATABASE STANDARDS

A database management system (DBMS) is a very popular class of software (sometimes even hardware) rivaling word processors and spread sheets. DBMSs were first developed for large mainframes in the early 1960s. Shortly after the emergence of minicomputers and microcomputers, DBMSs began to appear on them too. Today there are probably over 200 different DBMS developers. DBMSs have been used on almost every imaginable type of database application--for example, medical, industrial, government, financial, personnel, educational, and engineering.

A database is not a technology. Rather, it is an expression of organization, clarity, and precision. It may or may not be computerized. If it is, it may exist on a microcomputer, a minicomputer, or a large mainframe. Finally, a database may or may not be centralized. However a database is implemented and operated, success is impossible without the codification of and adherence to data semantics, which are the rules for meaning, validity, and usage.

When a database is computerized, it represents the automation of the knowledge component of a business, which is manifest through the business's quality operation, planning, and management. With a successful database, the managers of a business can research the past, organize the present, and plan for the future.

When a class of software becomes as widely accepted as have DBMSs, standards must be established so there can be portability. While portability is important for moving database applications from one computer and DBMS to the next, the most important class of portability is staff. Today's staff must be mobile as there is such a diversity of hardware and DBMSs. When standards exist, database design, application implementation, and maintenance strategies can be taught at the University and be presumed knowledge when an employee is hired. Companies then have only to concentrate on application-specific training.

1.1 IN THE BEGINNING . . .

In the middle 1960s, the Systems Committee of CODASYL (Committee On Data Systems and Languages) undertook two surveys of existing DBMSs. The CODASYL organization then created several committees to develop specifications for a network DBMS. The American National Standards Institute (ANSI) reviewed the CODASYL work and in the early 1970s began the database standards process by developing a reference model. The process to standardize syntax and semantics of DBMS began with the establishment of the committee X3H2 in 1978, which developed the NDL and SQL standards: NDL is for network databases, SQL for relational databases. Another ANSI committee, X3H4, developed the Information

Resource Dictionary System (IRDS) standard for storing the metadata so critical for effective data processing (including database) environments.

This chapter presents an overview of reference models and of the three ANSI standards.

1.2 REFERENCE MODELS

A reference model is a mechanism or framework for describing a database management system in terms of its interfaces, processing functions, and the flow of data through the DBMS. An early reference model was partially defined and presented through an ad hoc study committee of the ANSI Standards Planning and Requirements Committee (SPARC). This incomplete model was published in 1975 and became known as the ANSI/SPARC reference model. The complete reference model was never finished, and the ad hoc study committee was disbanded in 1975. While this 1975 partial model was a necessary first step for ANSI's creation of DBMS standards, it is now only of historical interest, as its architecture no longer relates to a modern, sophisticated DBMS, and it has been completely replaced by the IEC/ISO/TC1 reference model.

The most significant contribution of the ANSI/SPARC architecture was the recognition of the need for an organization to have a conceptual schema, which is an institutionalized information resource dictionary system (IRDS), to serve as a repository for information requirements of the business. This IRDS can be used to show where, how, and by whom information is used throughout an enterprise.

1.2.1 The 1975 ANSI Reference Model

ANSI is divided into a number of committees. One, X3, the Computers and Information Processing Committee, commissioned a study by its Standards Planning and Requirements (sub)Committee (SPARC) in the Autumn of 1972 to determine whether technical committees should be established to create database (really DBMS) standards. From 1972 to early 1975, the ad hoc committee set up by ANSI/X3/SPARC met to resolve this question. The membership of this committee included Honeywell, IBM, Eastman Kodak, Equitable Life, Boeing Computing Services, Sperry Univac, Deere and Company, NCR, University of Maryland, Exxon Corporation, Columbia University, and RAND. The following is the ANSI/SPARC committee's own summary description of its work:

> There are three realms of interest in the philosophy of information. These realms are: real world, ideas about the real world existing in the minds of men, and symbols on paper or other (storage) medium representing these ideas.
>
> In addition, there are several realms of interest in data processing, the manipulation of the symbols representing these ideas. Three of these realms have special significance ... These realms are: external, including a simplified model of the real world as seen by one or more applications; conceptual, including the limited model of the real world maintained for all applications;

and internal, including the data in computer storage representing the limited model of the real world. (1)

While the committee identified three realms, they chose to use the more technical term *schema*. In addition to using the word *schema* to mean *realm*, the committee used the word *interface* to mean *schema*. That change of terminology is not so bad, in that an interface can also be called a schema since it is a framework of reference, or an outline that is output by one processor in order to be input to the next processor.

As for the identified schemas themselves, the ANSI/SPARC architecture study actually identified 42. Some of the schema definitions were merely titles, while others were whole sections of text. Since the committee recognized that an explanation of 42 separate interfaces would certainly have turned the ANSI/SPARC data architecture report into volumes, three main classes of interfaces, cited above and analogous to the realms, were presented: external, conceptual, and internal. The committee's original names for these three interfaces were subschema, super-schema, and schema. As described in an edited version of the draft ANSI/SPARC report, the three schema are:

- An external schema that contains the specifications of the external objects, the associations and structures in which they are related, operations permitted upon these objects, and administrative matters
- A conceptual schema that includes the specification of the conceptual objects, and their properties and relationships, operations permitted on these objects, consistency, integrity, security, recovery, and administrative matters.
- An internal schema that includes the specifications of the internal objects, indices, pointers, and other implementation mechanisms, other parameters affecting (optimizing) the economics of internal data storage, integrity, security, recovery, and administrative matters. (2)

The ANSI/SPARC committee saw the conceptual schema as a super-sized interface between all the different external schemas and the one or more internal schemas. Because of advances both in technology and in understanding, however, that role of the conceptual schema is seen as being too narrow.

The purpose of the ANSI/SPARC study was to identify areas for ANSI to standardize, rather than to define the standards. This is evident from the name SPARC--Standards Planning and Requirements Committee--which implies that the purpose of the committee's work was to plan for standards activities. The introductory section of the draft ANSI/SPARC report supports this assertion by stating that:

> Among the responsibilities of the Standards Planning and Requirements Committee (SPARC) of the American National Standards Committee on Computers and Information Processing (ANSI/X3) is the generation of recommendations for action by the parent Committee on appropriate areas for the initiation of standard development efforts. (3)

X3 allowed ANSI/SPARC to convene another ad hoc database study group in 1982. One of the many goals accomplished by this ad hoc study committee was to review the 1975 draft reference model and issue a report providing corrections, revisions, and expansions. Among the many items addressed by the committee were problems left untouched by the 1975 draft report:

- Is metadata different from data?
- Are metadata and data stored separately?
- Are metadata and data described in terms of different data models?
- Is there a schema for metadata--a metaschema?
- Are there also external and internal metaschema?
- Are the interfaces used to retrieve and change metadata different from those used to retrieve and change data?
- Can a schema be changed on-line?
- How would on-line schema changes affect the data? (4)

During the process of answering these questions, many new ones arose. For example, it was determined that the 1975 draft reference model was too simplistic, as it did not address:

- Distributed schemas that may result from distributed database processing
- Open systems architecture
- Establishment of a unified concurrency model (teleprocessing and database interactions)
- Operating system (O/S) based security and privacy

The results of the 1982 ANSI/SPARC Reference Model subgroup have been incorporated in the work effort of the reference model subgroup of the IEC/ISO/JTC1/SC21/WG3 committee (Joint Technical Committee 1 (JTC 1) from both ISO (International Standards Organization) and IEC (International Electrical Committee), Standing Committee 21 (SC 21, Information Processing Systems), Working Group 3 (WG3, data management).

If the three ANSI database standards produced in the 1986-1988 time frame were forcibly mapped to the ANSI/SPARC three-schema architecture that was produced in 1975, then X3H4 (IRDS) would be standardizing some parts of the conceptual schema, while X3H2 (SQL and NDL) would be standardizing other aspects of the conceptual schema, as well as the DBMS side of the internal schema and the entire external schema. No ANSI committee is working on a computer side of the internal schema, as computer technology changes faster than it can be standardized.

1.2.2 The ISO Reference Model

The ANSI/SPARC reference model was created before there were any DBMS standards. Consequently, the developers of that 1975 reference model could only hypothesize what the interfaces should be and how they should be interconnected. Since that early work, three database standards, NDL, SQL, and IRDS, have been developed. The ISO reference model thus reflects what was learned by those standards committees.

The purpose of the IEC/ISO/JTC1 reference model is to provide a common basis for the coordination of standards development.

The IEC/ISO/JTC1 reference model is a framework for existing (NDL, SQL, IRDS, and RDA) and future data management standards. The reference model does not specify services or protocols for data management, nor does it specify implementation strategies, nor does it serve as a basis for appraising the conformance of implementations. The reference model, however, does define the common terminology and concepts pertinent to all data held within database applications. These concepts are then used by the individual database management and dictionary management committees to define their respective standards.

The IEC/ISO/JTC1 reference model is only concerned with the abstracted specification of the types of interfaces, across which the various DBMS components operate. The reference model specifies neither the actual interface, that is, its syntax and semantics, nor its components that are on either side of the interface. Both the specification of the interface and the components on either side of the interface are the responsibility of the ISO (ANSI) committees specifying the DBMS service.

As stated in the IEC/ISO/JTC1 reference model document, the objective of the reference model is to provide a framework for the following:

- The identification of interfaces
- The positioning of all such interfaces relative to each other
- The identification of facilities provided at each interface
- The identification of the process and, where appropriate, specific data which supports each interface
- The positioning of the use of the interfaces in terms of an information systems life cycle

- The identification of the binding alternatives associated with each appropriate identified interface(5)

In IEC/ISO/JTC1, the reference model specifies the types and kinds of services that are to be available from a DBMS. The six services identified by the IEC/ISO/JTC1 reference model are

- **Dictionary Definition**: the specification of the types of data that an organization requires in its dictionary system. This provides the schema for the dictionary database, referred to as the dictionary schema.
- **Dictionary Use**: the storage and retrieval of dictionary data relating to all aspects of other information systems with special dictionary capabilities, such as keeping many versions of data. The dictionary database includes the data definitions for application databases.
- **Application Schema Definition**: the specification of the schema in the form appropriate to the DBMS. Depending on support for the DBMS provided by an IRDS, the dictionary system may provide the schema based on its data descriptions.
- **Application Database Use**: the storage and retrieval of data from an arbitrary database structure.
- **Database Creation**: the establishment of a database.
- **Database Maintenance**: the changes to a database required as a result of changes to its schema. (6)

Through the definition of these six services, the IEC/ISO/JTC1 reference model defines the framework for coordinating the development of existing and future standards. The existing standards included in this data management reference model are: NDL, SQL, IRDS, and RDAP (remote data access protocol).

1.2.2.1 Levels of Abstraction

The IEC/ISO/JTC1 reference model is presented first at an abstract level, identifying only the essential features of the system being modelled and ignoring everything else not directly relevant. Thus, the IEC/ISO/JTC1 reference model at the highest level of abstraction is the same for both the IRDS and the DBMS. At the DBMS level, the NDL and the SQL are the same. At the NDL level, all NDL compliant DBMSs are the same. The reference model thus contains only the specification of the highest level model as it is the responsibility of the IRDS and the DBMS (NDL and SQL) committees to define their respective reference models. (7)

The reference model document states that a DBMS and/or IRDS would be conforming in any of the alternatives for either of the two interface types: user and processing. A user interface is the interface between the end-user and the facility providing the service. A processing interface is the interface between two software and/or hardware components. The user interface alternatives are:

- Panels (abstract screen formats)
- Language syntax, concrete or abstract

The alternatives for processing language interfaces are:

- Procedure calls
- Syntax (execution time interpretation)
- Service conventions
- Protocols which define permitted interactions

While all seven forms satisfies the IEC/ISO/JTC1 reference model, each lower level standard (SQL, for example) has its own conformance section specifying a more detailed conformance requirement.

1.2.2.2 Levels of Data

Data exists in two forms: values and representations of values. TELEPHONE NUMBER is the semantic representation of the value 212-555-1234. In this regard, the following pairs of terms stand in this relationship: data record type and data record instance, data record element and value, metadata and data. This kind of representation does not take place on only one level. For example, a data record type includes the definitions of element types. The IEC/ISO/JTC1 reference model describes four common levels of representation:

- Fundamental
- Dictionary definition
- Dictionary
- Application

Figure 1.1 illustrates the four levels, the databases associated with each level, and the schemas required to represent the contents. In the complete database environment, these four levels must all exist.

At the fundamental level, the IRDS itself is defined, resulting in the IRDS' own schema and the associated data, editing, and validation rules, etc. necessary to establish an IRDS.

The dictionary definition level is employed to define the data stored in the data dictionary and the constructions that represent data stored in the dictionary. Data instances at this level are values such as DATA RECORD, DATA RECORD ELEMENT, RELATIONSHIP, and the like. Second, after the IRDS is established,

Fundamental Level			Dictionary Definition Schema
Dictionary Definition Level		Dictionary Schema	Dictionary Definition Database
Dictionary Level	Application Schema	Dictionary Database	
Application Level	Application Database		
	Application Level Pair	Dictionary Level Pair	Dictionary Definition Pair

Figure 1.1 Data Levels and Level Pairs

individual databases can come into existence, each with its own schemas, data, editing and validation rules that are to serve all data represented in the database. It is at this level that individual data models exist.

The dictionary level is employed to receive a request and to determine whether the data record element names are correctly referenced. To the dictionary, the data are the data record element names, SALARY or EMPLOYEE. Other data at the dictionary level can refer to the name of the program (for validation), schemas or views, referential integrity rules, table look-ups, proper subschemas, terminal identifiers, and the like.

Once the individual database is brought into existence, the fourth level, *application*, can exist. Of course, there may be many applications operating against a database that serve different purposes and are programmed in different languages. Each application program contains its own schematic of data (subschemas or views) and has its own set of data, editing, and validation rules that it controls whenever services are requested of the application. (8)

Figure 1.2 illustrates the interaction of these four levels.

1.2.2.3 Generalized Reference Model

The IEC/ISO/JTC1 committee defined a generalized version of the reference model that is independent of any of the particulars necessary to view the individually bound components of the models. Figure 1.3 illustrates this model. It consists of the following five components:

- User
- User request processor
- Database controller

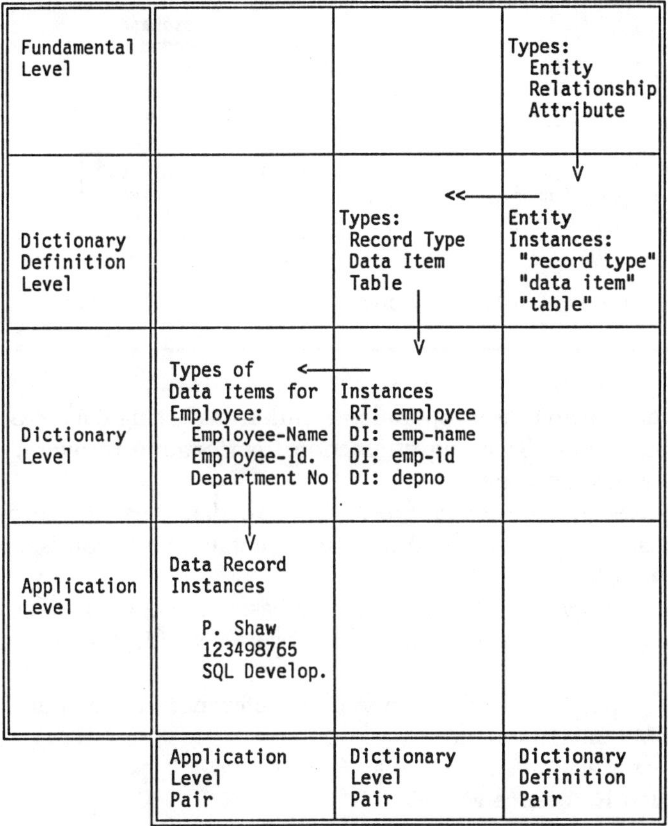

Note: RT means record type
DI means data item

Figure 1.2 Data Levels and Level Pairs

- Block server
- Schema server

User identifies the person requesting services from the user request processor. The request is accepted upon satisfactory identification.

The user request processor receives the user request and verifies that the service request is valid by checking the database schema server (through a subschema or view).

The database controller performs the largest component of work. It is tasked with establishing a session; noting the processing intent; performing database

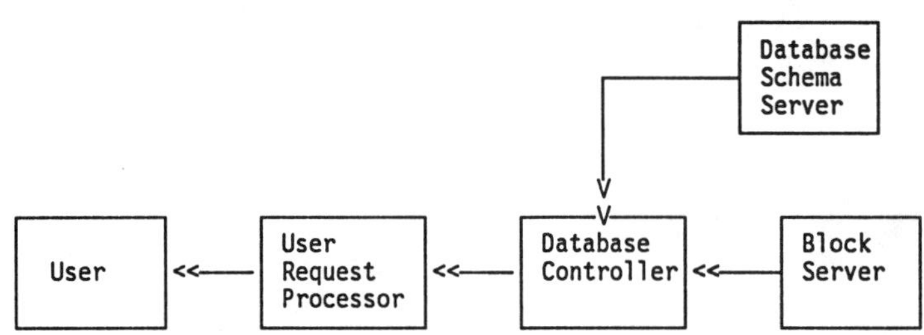

Figure 1.3 Simplified Diagram of the Abstract Reference Model

select, store, delete, and insert operations; bulk transferring data to and from the database; initiating and stopping transactions; performing recovery; performing database reorganization, etc.

The block servers stores and receives blocks of data (DBMS records), maintain recovery and activity journals, and restore the database to a consistent state after a rollback or crash.

The schema server, whether it is database or blocks of data, stores and retrieves parts of a schema that are needed for user verification, data translation, etc.

These components of the generalized reference model interact to be a complete DBMS environment.

1.2.2.4 Detailed Reference Models

The generalized reference model is intended to be a general representation of any detailed reference model. In this way, any of the following DBMS use scenarios can be modelled:

- Application access
- Proprietary DBMS vendor language access
- Application program use of an IRDS access
- IRDS definition access
- Multiple data model support access

In each of these cases, the user interacts with the named component (e.g., application program), which in turn accesses the IRDS schema and database if applicable and, in turn, accesses the block server to perform the data service request. (9)

1.2.2.5 ISO Reference Model Summary

Included in the many products generated by the IEC/ISO/JTC1 reference model committee were answers to the questions left over from the ANSI/SPARC 1975 three schema effort. That is, the IEC/ISO/JTC1 reference model incorporates work from the IRDS, NDL, and SQL. Thus, it clearly resolves the metadata questions.

The IEC/ISO/JTC1 reference model not only supports the 1975 recommendation that there should be support for multiple data models, but also illustrates multiple data model usage.

Finally, the ISO model also indicates that a database environment should support multiple databases within a single session, as well as data from distributed processing.

1.3 ANSI DATABASE COMMITTEES: X3H2 AND X3H4

As previously stated, the 1975 ANSI/SPARC data architecture ad hoc study group did not intend their three schemas (conceptual, external, and internal) to be definitive, but illustrative, as these three schemas were merely the committee's shorthand way of discussing the three different subgroupings of the 42 different interfaces (schemas) that it had identified. As support for that statement, consider that each ANSI standard consists of five main components: conformance statements, field of applicability, (syntax) format, general rules, and syntax rules. The ANSI/SPARC study group produced, at best, the field of applicability section. If the remaining sections had been completed, then the report would have covered many thousands of pages.

As final evidence that the 1975 ANSI/SPARC committee was never created to produce standards, SPARC dissolved its ad hoc reference model subcommittee in 1975 and chose to create the ANSI committees, X3H2 and X3H4, with the expressed purpose of creating database standards.

1.4 THE BATTLE OVER DATA MODELS

The ANSI/SPARC committee in 1972 addressed the battle concerning data models with the following statement:

> There is continuing argument on the appropriate data model: e.g., relational, network, hierarchical. If, indeed, this debate is as it seems, then it follows that the correct answer to this question of which data model to use is necessarily *all of the above.* (10)

The 1975 ANSI/SPARC committee saw, as confirmed by the IEC/ISO/JTC1 reference model committee in 1988, that a data model is merely a formalized method of defining data record types, data record elements, the relationships among the data record types, and the operations that are allowable on those data record elements, data record types, and relationships. Today, there are four popular data models: network, hierarchical, independent logical file, and relational. X3H2, the ANSI database languages committee, has created NDL to manipulate network data model databases and SQL to manipulate relational data model databases. These four data models are presented in Chapter 3.

In the two years following the 1972-75 ANSI/SPARC committee's work, ANSI/X3, SPARC's parent committee, decided to establish a database standards committee, named X3H2. Its first meeting was in June 1978, and its initial charter was to develop an NDL standard. In 1981, X3H2's charter was expanded to include the development of an SQL standard. In addition to standardizing the data definition language (DDL) and the data manipulation language (DML) for NDL and SQL, X3H2 has standardized the use of these database facilities from the ANSI standard languages: COBOL, FORTRAN, PASCAL, PL/I, Ada, and C.

In addition to the DBMS standards work of X3H2, X3 established the X3H4 committee to create a standard for Information Resource Dictionary System (IRDS).

In sum, the ANSI database standards process began with SPARC, which identified the need for database standards through the definition of a draft reference model (1975). They recommended the establishment of a database standards committee (X3H2) to draft the standards NDL and SQL, and recommended the establishment of X3H4 to develop the IRDS. To ensure that these standards work together, X3H2 maintains liaisons with the IRDS committee, X3H4, and the various language development committees, such as PL/I (X3J1), BASIC (X3J2), Fortran (X3J3), COBOL (X3J4), Pascal (X3J9), and C (X3J11). Since there is currently no ANSI committee for Ada, liaison is conducted with the U.S. Department of Defense's Ada Joint Program Office in Washington, D.C. The liaison with these committees consists of shared organizational memberships, exchange of documents, occasional joint meetings, and joint votes on critical issues.

1.5 DBMS STANDARDS

During 1986, ANSI ratified two database standards, one for the network data model, called NDL (network database language), and another for SQL (formerly meaning structured query language). ANSI/X3H2, the authoring committee of these two standards, is composed of individual experts from DBMS vendors, government agencies, corporations, and consulting organizations.

NDL was derived from the CODASYL data model, which had been implemented on computers from almost all major hardware vendors and by a few software vendors. The CODASYL 1978 specification was used as NDL's initial base document, and over a four-year period, the specification was streamlined until all physical aspects were removed. For example, the concept of AREA was removed because it is a technique for partitioning data record instances and has been implemented by DBMS vendors in very different ways. Over the four years the actual elapsed meeting time was less than five work months.

NDL has been substantively implemented by Digital (DEC). Their DBMS is quite logical, easy to implement, and cost effective to operate.

The other standard, SQL, founded on IBM's SQL, has been implemented on almost every brand of hardware and all three hardware tiers: micro-computers, mini-computers, and mainframes. X3H2 was initially chartered to develop a relational database standard by X3 in 1982. X3H2 determined that it is more expedient to develop a standard based on an existing product, rather than create a DBMS standard from scratch. The X3H2 member from IBM, Phil Shaw, created an SQL technical specification document at the request of the committee.

The two ANSI database standards are based on different data models: network and relational. The relationships in NDL are not required to be value-based. NDL relationships are defined in the data definition language, and data record instances which belong to a specific relationship instance can have their order (with respect to the relationship instance) specified. NDL can explicitly declare almost all the types of relationships. Referential integrity in NDL is defined through a set of clauses that govern data record insertion and retention.

SQL relationships must be value-based, with the definition of the relationship occurring in the application program's view of data or in programming logic. Data record orderings are requested by the application program and are performed by the DBMS prior to their presentation to the program. SQL can declare only one relationship type, but users can accomplish most of the others through application program logic. Finally, SQL has referential integrity to control insertion and retention.

These two standards are not conflicting but complementary. Any DBMS vendor could implement NDL, SQL, or both, either as separate DBMSs or as a combined set within one DBMS. During any database application implementation, there should be a DBMS selection step. If an application is an add-on to existing data already installed under a DBMS, then the choice is already made. If however, the application is for a completely different type of processing, for example, decision support rather than transaction processing, the DBMS selection and evaluation should focus first on the selection of data model, and then on the selection of accessories, and finally on performance.

A DBMS really consists of two classes of products: the database control system (DBCS), and accessories. The DBCS is the product that stores, selects, and manages the DBMS records. An accessory tool may be a vendor's natural language that interfaces with the DBCS, a third generation language interfaced through a language embedding, or an application package that is implemented either through natural languages or language embeddings. ANSI committees have standardized the syntax and semantics of the third generation languages, that is, COBOL, FORTRAN, PL/I, Ada, C, and Pascal.

The ANSI process standardized the external specifications of two types of DBCSs: NDL and SQL. Each standard specifies the syntax and semantics of the language that communicates the database's structure to the DBCS. Each standard also specifies the semantics of the operations that an accessory tool must use whenever it communicates with a standard DBCS to store, retrieve, and update data. Finally, each standard specifies the syntax appropriate for embedded language interface.

An organization is now free to select the DBCS for each application based on the DBCS' ability to select, store, and manage data record instances for the company's transaction processing (possibly NDL) or decision support needs (possibly SQL) without fear that all accessory tools will have to be relearned.

Independent of the decision on the DBCS, an organization can select, on the basis of individual requirements or styles of applications, accessory tools that interact with the DBCS through standard interfaces. Accessory products that have standard interfaces can operate against any DBCS that can *read* the interface language. If the interface is not generated, then the accessory product will not be as portable as an ANSI standard language run-unit (e.g., COBOL, FORTRAN, etc.). Once these products are selected and installed, data can be collected and stored by the accessory tools suited for that purpose, while other tools can be used for selecting and reporting data in tabular forms and graphics.

An application package is an accessory tool. It represents a *canned* database structure, various load and update programs, and an array of reports. These packages are affected by ANSI standards in that vendors can now concentrate on developing product features rather than nonstandard DBMS interfaces. This benefits application package users as well, since they have a broader set of standard products from which to select.

Both ANSI standards were created to be independent of the method of physical implementation. Traditionally, the physical implementation of NDL data has been through O/S files so that each file stores data record instances from multiple data record types. Traditionally, the physical implementation of SQL data has been through O/S files so that each file stores data record instances (rows) from only one data record type (table).

Now that there are ANSI standard specifications for the interfaces, vendors are free to experiment with different physical implementation strategies to achieve different performances. While there have been traditional methods of physically implementing data models, a data model neither requires nor specifies a particular method of implementation. For example, the ANSI/NDL (network) data model has traditionally been implemented through embedded relative record addresses with the data records from one or more data record types stored on one O/S file. Also traditionally, the SQL data model has been implemented by storing each relation in its own O/S file. Today, however, there are ANSI/NDL-like DBMSs with value based relationships and each data record type in its own physical file. And there are ANSI/SQL (relational) DBMSs that allow rows from different tables to be stored together to improve performance.

Today, sophisticated DBMS vendors recognize the value of both ANSI/NDL and ANSI/SQL, and allow database system designers to freely mix these types of relationships in a single database design. Furthermore, these DBMS vendors recognize that physical database design is, for the most part, independent of data model. Thus, physical database design can be tailored to meet the needs of flexibility or of high volume and performance. This tailoring can be directed to a database as a whole or to just one set of data record types within a database.

In analyzing database applications, an organization may find that it needs different DBCSs adhering to the same data model, but with different physical implementations, as well as DBCSs supporting different data models. Since all the DBCSs adhering to ANSI standards would be interacting through standard interfaces, different DBCSs can be selected, installed, and changed without having to reprogram existing ANSI standard language applications. If, however, an application's data model must be changed, say from NDL to SQL, then application programming logic has to be changed as well unless there is a sophisticated view facility in place (see Chapter 5).

Another very important benefit of these standard interfaces is that applications can be developed on a mainframe and ported to minicomputers or to microcomputers, providing that the applications on those computers use ANSI standard languages.

1.6 ANSI/NDL

NDL, the network database language, contains the syntax and semantics for defining data record types, data record elements, and five different types of relationships. The relationships can define explicit network structures. NDL also defines the basic operations on those structures. Finally, NDL provides functional capabilities for designing, accessing, maintaining, controlling, and protecting the database. A high level DBMS reference model that illustrates the NDL interface languages is contained in Figure 1.4.

Each NDL data record type can contain data record elements that are either single-valued or multi-dimensioned. A single-valued data record element are for data like SOCIAL SECURITY NUMBER. Multi-dimensioned data record elements is for data like MONTHLY SALES (one dimension), or MONTHLY SALES BY YEAR (two dimensions).

NDL also allows for the definition of five classes of relationships:

- Owner single member
- Owner multiple member
- Singular single member
- Singular multiple member
- Recursive

The owner single member relationship is the most common, and defines the relationship between a DEPARTMENT and its EMPLOYEES.

The owner multiple member relationship is less common, but quite useful. For example, for TERRITORY, the owner data record type is DISTRICT OFFICE, and the member data record types are SALESPERSON and CUSTOMER.

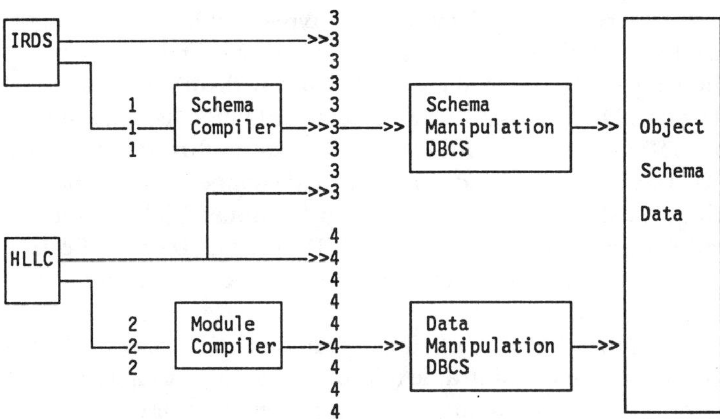

Legend:

```
   1 = Schema Definition Language
   2 = Procedural Language
   3 = Schema Manipulation Language
   4 = Data Manipulation Language
IRDS = Information Resource Dictionary System
HLLC = High Level Language Compiler, e.g., Cobol, Query, POL
```

Figure 1.4 NDL Reference Model (1982)

A singular relationship is a relationship in which there is no defined owner data record type. If there is a need to maintain a list of top salespersons, then the singular set TOP-SALESPERSONS can be defined, involving only the data record type SALESPERSON.

An example of a singular relationship with multiple record types is the relationship among all employees by year of earliest hire. If there are two types of employees, full-time, and part-time, the relationship is EMPLOYEES BY START YEAR, and the members are FULL-TIME EMPLOYEES and PART-TIME EMPLOYEES.

The final NDL relationship type is recursive. A recursive relationship is one in which the owner and member data record type are defined to be the same data record type. For example, in an organization chart or a bill-of-materials, both the parent and the member are person and part respectively. Examples of these different relationships are explained in greater detail in Chapter 3.

Sort clauses can be included in all the NDL relationship clauses. Thus, as a data record instance is added to the database, it is placed in its proper sort order with respect to other data record instances already stored in the database.

NDL allows for the definition of integrity clauses on the element, the data record type, and the relationship. These rules control whether data record instances are allowed to be stored in the database at all. One kind of NDL referential integrity rule declares that a data record instance can be stored only if an owner data record instance is already present. Another NDL referential integrity rule prohibits owner data record instance deletions whenever there are member data record instances. A third NDL referential integrity rule automatically deletes all member data record instances whenever the owner data record instance is deleted. Because these integrity clauses are defined in the data definition language, they are enforced on all languages that interact with NDL database.

NDL also specifies a module procedure language that can be employed by developers of NDL systems. This language specifies all the rules and regulations that must be followed if an NDL database is accessed through COBOL, FORTRAN, or any other type of language, such as report writers and query-update languages.

NDL is a complete specification of the DBCS component of the DBMS. It specifies neither the types of language that can interface, nor any mode of DBCS implementation. The components of DBMS that are standardized by NDL are identified in Figure 1.5.

To help understand the evolution of NDL, a review of its development history is appropriate. The Database Task Group (DBTG) of the CODASYL programming language committee delivered its 1970 report that served as the basis for several DBMS implementations (e.g., Honeywell's IDS and Cullinet's IDMS). The DBTG committee then split into two groups. The Data Description Language Committee (DDLC) took over the task of specifying the syntax and semantics of the data definition language portion of the CODASYL database specification. The Database Language Task Group (DBLTG) was a subordinate group within CODASYL COBOL. The DBLTG's function was to define the syntax and semantics for the subschema language and the data manipulation language (DML).

During the period 1971 to 1978, several DDLC documents, called journals of development (JOD) were issued. A JOD is more a working document than a strict implementable specification. For example, the CODASYL concept of AREA has been implemented somewhat differently in every CODASYL DBMS. In one CODASYL DBMS, an AREA is a collection of O/S files. In another, multiple AREAs are contained in a single O/S file, and in at least one other, an AREA means one O/S file.

Famous among the JODs are the 1973 and the 1978 issues. During this time, several more DBMS vendors implemented DBMSs based on these JODs, for example, NCR, Data General, Digital, and PRIME.

In the 1976-1978 time frame, ANSI/SPARC determined that the CODASYL approach should be standardized since there had been so many successful implementations. The ANSI committee X3H2 was formed to undertake the task. What was to be the relationship between the CODASYL DDLC committee and the ANSI/X3H2 committee? In the development and standardization of the language COBOL, there exists a relationship between CODASYL and ANSI: the CODASYL COBOL committee develops and the ANSI X3J4 committee standardizes. That means that no COBOL language development is performed within the ANSI X3J4

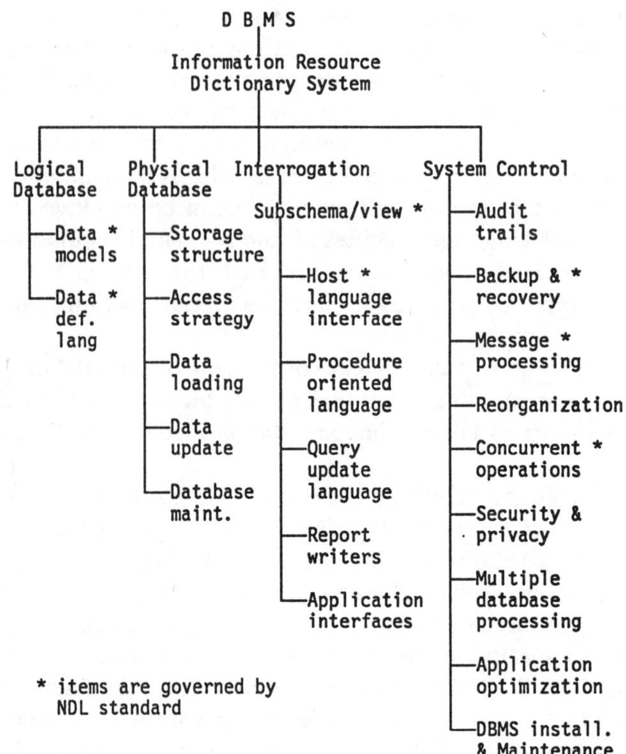

Figure 1.5 Database Management System Components Addressed by ANSI/NDL

committee. For example, if a facility of COBOL is determined deficient by the ANSI X3J4 committee, the only option for ANSI is to drop the facility until the CODASYL COBOL committee fixes the problem. That fix can take one or more years.

X3H2 found that approach unacceptable for database, and from its first official committee meeting (the meeting after the charter formation meeting), decided to do its own development. To implement this decision, X3H2 voted to *consider any proposal submitted by its own members.* The vote was 17 to 2 in favor! The relationship with CODASYL was also addressed in a motion that stated . . . *CODASYL Data Description Language Committee (DDLC) is the development authority for the DDL and the CODASYL Journal of Development (JOD) is the only source* . . . The vote was 17 to 2 against!

X3H2 began its database standardization efforts in July 1978 by adopting the CODASYL DDLC 1978 JOD as its base document. During the first six months of

X3H2's work, almost half of this document was deleted, either because the facilities were poorly specified or because they were not portable from one machine environment to another. These deletions were for more than academic reasons. X3H2 felt that if the deleted facilities were implemented as formed, bad function would result. The respective CODASYL vendors saw this too, as each implemented these under-specified functions in different way. Since there was no standards committee to keep the various CODASYL implementors together, different versions of CODASYL systems were created from the same *standard*.

During the next several years, X3H2 added, deleted, and modified DDL facilities. Since X3H2 had reserved development authority to itself, the CODASYL DDLC committee found itself without much to do and was disbanded in 1982.

The CODASYL COBOL committee's corresponding ANSI committee, X3J4, had a subcommittee, X3J4.1. This committee was charged with standardizing the syntax and semantics of the subschema and the data manipulation language. Their work ceased by 1980 for two reasons. First, X3J4 members were not greatly interested in database, especially since the committee's mission was COBOL. Second, the CODASYL DDLC committee, which passed its JOD to CODASYL COBOL for their use in defining the syntax and semantics of the subschema and DML, ceased to exist. Thus, CODASYL COBOL no longer had a DDL source for standardizing development.

Beginning in 1980, X3H2 petitioned ANSI to broaden its charter to not only define the syntax and semantics for the data definition language, but also define the syntax and semantics for the subschema language and the semantics of the DML operations. That petition was approved. X3H2 then modified its base document to include the new areas and, during the summer of 1983, the document was approved.

After a base document is approved by the committee, it becomes a dpANS (draft proposed American National Standard) and is subject to a four month public review. If the public review is successful the document is voted by X3, and if the vote is successful, it is voted again by ANSI. If the ANSI vote is successful the dpans becomes an American National Standard. Generally, the committee's work takes about three years, and the X3 and ANSI review and their votes take another two years.

The final steps of standardizing the NDL were delayed about six months so X3H2 could finish work on SQL. That enabled both NDL and SQL to be released together. In August 1986, both NDL and SQL were accepted as ANSI standards.

Once NDL was stabilized, X3J4 created an ad hoc committee to create a DML specification for COBOL that was issued as an X3J4 information bulletin.

To summarize NDL's development history:

- CODASYL produced JODs in 1971, 1973, 1978, and 1980. The 1980 JOD reflected ANSI's NDL deletions.
- All but one of the CODASYL DBMSs were implemented during the 1970s. Only DEC's NDL is based on the 1980 NDL dpans.

- Most CODASYL DBMSs differed from each other in areas critically important to portability. NDL does not contain those nonportable features.
- The portable components of the *CODASYL standard* really are the ANSI/NDL standard. Thus, the NDL is the ONLY network DBCS specification that supports portability.

Figures 1.6a through Figure 1.6d presents a comparison of three popular DBMSs--CA's IDMS/DB, Unisys' DMS/1100, and the DEC's VAX-DBMS as a way of illustrating that these three DBMSs compare favorably to NDL. Figure 1.6a presents a comparison of ANSI/NDL schema language clauses for schema, data record type, and data record element. Figure 1.6b compares the set (relationship) clause. Figure 1.6c compares the subschema (view) clauses. Figure 1.6d compares the data manipulation language clauses. It must be noted, however, that the comparison was made only to the extent of general functional and command purpose. No attempt was made to determine exact syntax, or semantic compatibility.

ANSI/NDL Facility	Addressed by		
	IDMS/R	VAX-DBMS	DMS-1100
Schema Declaration	Yes	Yes	Yes
Record Definition	Yes	Yes	Yes
Record Clause	Yes	Yes	Yes
Location Mode Clause	Yes	No	Yes
Record Check Clause	No	Yes	Yes
Element Definition	Yes	Yes	Yes
Element Types	Yes	Yes	Yes
Defaults	Yes	Yes	No
Complex Elements	Yes	Yes	Yes
Occurs	Yes	Yes	Yes

Figure 1.6a ANSI/NDL versus IDMS/R, VAX-DBMS, & DMS1100 Facilities Schema Compariosn

ANSI/NDL Facility	Addressed by		
	IDMS/R	VAX-DBMS	DMS-1100
Set definition	Yes	Yes	Yes
Set Name Clause	Yes	Yes	Yes
Set Order Clause	Yes	No	Yes
Owner Clause	Yes	Yes	Yes
Owner is System Clause	Yes	Yes	No
Member Clause	Yes	Yes	Yes
Retention Clause	Yes	Yes	Yes
Insertion Clause	Yes	Yes	Yes
Order Clause	Yes	Yes	Yes
Member Check Clause	No	Yes	No
Member Uniqueness Clause	No	No	No

Figure 1.6b ANSI/NDL versus IDMS/R, VAX-DBMS, & DMS1100 Facilities
Set Definition Comparison

ANSI/NDL Facility	Addressed by		
	IDMS/R	VAX-DBMS	DMS-1100
Subschema Definition	Yes	Yes	Yes
Subschema Clause	Yes	Yes	Yes
Schema Reference	Yes	Yes	Yes
Record Definition	Yes	Yes	Yes
Record Name Clause	Yes	Yes	Yes
Element Definition	Yes	Yes	Yes
Schema Set	Yes	Yes	Yes
Set Names	Yes	Yes	Yes

Figure 1.6c ANSI/NDL versus IDMS/R, VAX-DBMS, & DMS1100 Facilities
Subschema Comparison

ANSI/NDL Facility	Addressed by		
	IDMS/R	VAX-DBMS	DMS-1100
Control Statements	Yes	Yes	Yes
Ready	Yes	Yes	Yes
If	Yes	Yes	Yes
Commit	Yes	Yes	No
Rollback	Yes	Yes	No
Nullify	No	No	No
Find/Obtain Current	Yes	Yes	Yes
Find/Obtain Within Set	Yes	Yes	Yes
Find/Obtain Owner	Yes	Yes	Yes
Find/Obtain Within Set Using Key	Yes	Yes	Yes
Get	Yes	Yes	Yes
Using/Where Clause	LRF	Yes	Yes
Retaining Clause	No	Yes	Yes
Store	Yes	Yes	Yes
Modify	Yes	Yes	Yes
Connect	Yes	Yes	Yes
Disconnect	Yes	Yes	Yes
Erase	Yes	Yes	Yes
Reconnect	No	Yes	No

Figure 1.6d ANSI/NDL versus IDMS/R, VAX-DBMS, & DMS1100 Facilities Control Statement Comparison

1.7 ANSI/SQL

In 1981, X3 assigned X3H2 another project. It was to create a standard language for relationally structured databases. Phil Shaw from IBM created a Backus Naur Form (BNF) specification for IBM's SQL product and submitted it to the committee as a proposed base document for the relational language. Appendix A illustrates BNF. The SQL specification was accepted as the base document, and the language was called RDL (relational data language). The DBMS reference model

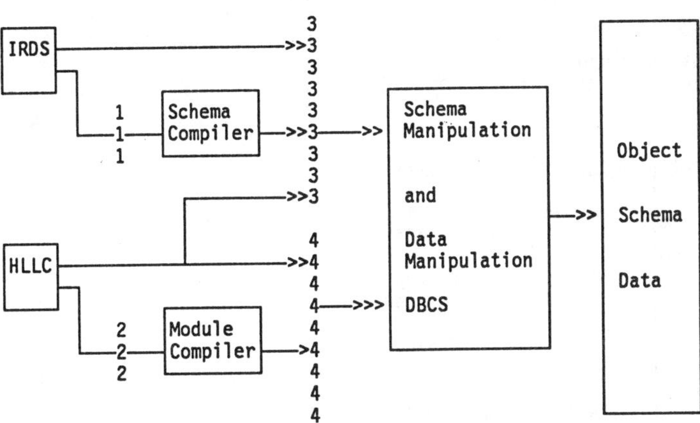

Legend:

1 = Schema Definition Language
2 = Procedural Language
3 = Schema Manipulation Language
4 = Data Manipulation Language
IRDS = Information Resource Dictionary System
HLLC = High Level Language Compiler, e.g., Cobol, Query, POL

Figure 1.7 SQL Reference Model (1988)

that applies to the resultant standard, ANSI/SQL, is illustrated in Figure 1.7. The components of DBMS that are standardized by ANSI/SQL are identified in Figure 1.8

The relational standards effort concentrated on IBM's SQL work. Since many vendors had already implemented their own version of IBM's effort, X3H2 developed an SQL baseline standard, so that all vendors could work together to develop further evolutions together.

The original RDL specification was modified throughout 1982 and 1983. It included, for example, a schema manipulation language and referential integrity. In 1984, the members of X3H2 determined that RDL had moved too far from existing SQL implementations, that is, too far from IBM, Data General, Digital, Oracle, UNISYS, and others. The committee decided to remove these incompatibilities and name the standard SQL rather than RDL. By 1985, SQL was accepted by X3H2.

Once the baseline SQL was completed, X3H2 immediately began to develop an extended SQL, calling it SQL2. Knowing that the development of SQL2 would take years, X3H2 also began development of two interim SQL extensions: Addendum-1, and Embedded SQL. Addendum-1 contains a basic set of referential integrity clauses and actions. Embedded SQL contains the specifications for

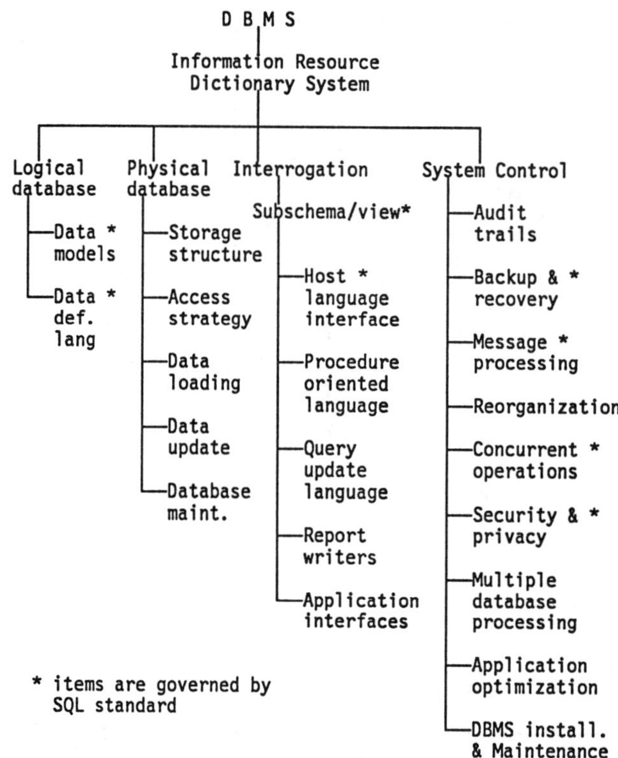

Figure 1.8 Database Management System Components Addressed by ANSI/SQL

binding SQL to the programming languages COBOL, FORTRAN, PL/I, PASCAL, C, and Ada. Both Addendum-1 and Embedded SQL became ANSI standards in 1989. SQL/86 with referential integrity along with minor corrections and clarifications is now known as SQL/89.

The SQL2 project will be technically complete during the first half of 1991, and become an ANSI standard by late 1992, and will take the name SQL/92. SQL2 contains both relaxations and *repairs* to the specifications contained in SQL/86, Addendum-1, and Embedded SQL. In addition, there are extensions in the following areas:

- Datetimes and intervals
- Derived tables in FROM clause
- Dynamic SQL
- Intersection/Difference

- Multiple module support
- NULLIF and IFNULL/COALESCE
- Outer join
- PRIMARY KEY implies NOT NULL
- Query expressions in views
- Referential actions such as cascade delete
- Relaxed UNION compatibility rules
- Renaming columns in the select list
- Row expressions
- Schema manipulation language
- Schema information tables
- Self-referencing deletes
- Self-referencing updates
- SQLSTATE
- Subquery in value expressions
- Substrings and concatenation
- Variable length character strings

In general, SQL/89 permits the definition of data as two-dimensional tables and defines the basic operations on these tables. The single valued data record elements are the columns, and the data record instances are the rows. Furthermore, SQL/89 provides functional capabilities for designing, accessing, maintaining, controlling, and protecting the database.

SQL/89 contains clauses for the definition of schemas and tables belonging to those schemas. Each table contains column (data record element) definitions. Each column may contain the definition of default values and table constraints for uniqueness, referential integrity, and various check clauses.

The data manipulation language for SQL/89 includes the traditional relational operations such as select, project, and join.

1.8 THE ANSI/IRDS

The information resource dictionary system (IRDS) is designed to be an organization's repository of metadata. Uses of the IRDS include the following:

- A documentation tool
- A software life cycle and project management tool

- A data element standardization and management system
- An organizational planning tool
- A tool to support database administration, document administration, information resource management and data administration
- A tool for supporting a distributed processing and database environment
- A source and object library management system
- A configuration management facility
- The storage location for NDL & SQL schema and subschemas (views)

To handle such a broad set of requirements, the IRDS is not actually all those facilities. Rather, it is a core set of facilities with the ability to define and expand into the areas for which explicit definitions have not been provided.

The architecture of the IRDS contains four levels. The top level is implementation-defined. It is the actual software provided by an IRDS vendor to define, store, and operate on the data in the information resource dictionary system.

The second level defines the objects that comprise an IRDS schema. This level also holds definitions of the various control mechanisms, including naming rules, defaults, and validation information for the information resource dictionary contents.

The third level is for the dictionary. This level describes the environment being modelled. It describes the objects in the environment and the associations among the objects.

The fourth level, not described in the IRDS, is actual instances of the objects in the dictionary.

The minimum set of objects in the IRDS is specified in the IRDS part 2, Basic Functional Schema. It contains the following eight objects:

- data element
- data record
- document
- file
- module
- program
- system
- user

Also included in the IRDS are four types of relationships to interconnect the IRD objects:

- One to many
- One to one
- Many to many
- Recursion

The following are illustrative combinations of objects and allowed relationships:

- Document contains document
- Document contains data element
- Document contains data record
- Document derived from document
- Document derived from file
- Document derived from data record

The IRDS also contains access control specifications for extending and modifying the objects contained in an IRD. The IRDS contains a complete language for manipulating the IRD contents. Typical verbs are DO, IF, CASE, and RETURN.

The ANSI IRDS does not specify any method of implementation. Thus, it may be an extension to a DBMS's data dictionary (NDL or SQL), or a completely stand alone product. In the former case it is active and in the later case it is passive.

1.9 DATABASE STANDARDS SUMMARY

The ANSI database standards process started in the mid-1970s and continues today. Its milestones and achievements include:

1975	Creation of the Draft Reference Model (three schema)
1978	Establishment of X3H2 (NDL charter)
1979	Establishment of X3H4 (IRDS)
1981	Extension of X3H2's Charter extended for SQL
1983	Replacement of the ANSI/SPARC 1975 Reference Model
1986	Approval of the ANSI/NDL database standard
1986	Approval of the ANSI/SQL database standard (i.e., SQL/86)
1986	Development of the ISO Reference model (replaces 1983 model)

1988	Approval of the ANSI/IRDS standard
1989	Approval of ANSI/SQL Addendum-1 (i.e., SQL/89)
1988	Development of the IEC/ISO/TC1 Reference model (replaces 1986 model)
1989	Approval of ANSI/SQL (embedded SQL language support)
1992	Completion of ANSI/SQL2 (probably SQL/92)

	Year (19--)									
ANSI/X3H2 Event	78	80	82	84	86	88	90	92	94	96
Start of X3H2	X									
NDL-DDL development	X==	==X								
NDL-DML development		X==	==X							
NDL processing			X==	====	==X					
RDL development			X==	==X						
Change RDL to SQL				X						
SQL Development				X=X						
SQL processing					X=X					
SQL referential integrity revision					X==	==X				
SQL embedded language standard					X==	==X				
SQL2 development					X==	====	=X			
SQL2 processing							X==	==X		
SQL3 development							X==	====	==X	
SQL3 processing									X==	==X
	78	80	82	84	86	88	90	92	94	96

Figure 1.9 ANSI/X3H2 Standards Activity
Past, Present, and Predictions

The specific milestones of X3H2 are portrayed in Figure 1.9. The dates for the start of the processing of SQL2 and the development and processing of SQL3 are estimated.

This book does not address IRDS other than to indicate its place in the set of database standards. Rather, this book concentrates on DBMS, and the effects ANSI/NDL and ANSI/SQL have on DBMS products.

The benefits derived from SQL and NDL standards are principally in two areas. First, database design efforts can proceed in the direction of either SQL or NDL confident that resulting products will not be locked into a particular vendor's products. Further, in the case of SQL or NDL, database management systems that *read* SQL or NDL data definition language can compile database structures directly, rather than just conceptually.

Second, products that produce either or both of these two languages as their output can be procured safely. For example, if a company offers a screen-oriented, menu-driven product for producing database structures, it can be procured knowing that the syntax and semantics of the language it produces are governed by an ANSI standard rather than by a vendor who might change his side of the interface to force out competition.

The next DBMS generation is already here and contains DBMSs that look alike, superficially. That is, there are DBMSs that conform to SQL, or NDL, or to a combination of NDL and SQL. But this does not mean that they are the same. There are differences in taste, and dramatic differences in quality. Choosing one DBMS over another is becoming more and more difficult, as the real differences lie beyond simple conformity or non-conformity to ANSI standard syntax. Consequently, the remaining chapters of this book deal, not with syntax conformity, but with real DBMS discriminators.

References

1. FDT, The Bulletin of ACM--SIGMOD, The Special Interest Group on Management of Data, Volume 7, Number 2, 1975, ANSI/X3/SPARC Study Group on Data Base Management Systems, Interim Report, 75-02-08, page II-1.

2. The ANSI/X3/SPARC DBMS Framework, Report of the Study Group on Database Management Systems, Tsichritzis and Klug, University of Toronto, Toronto, Canada, AFIPS Press 210 Summit Ave, Montvale, New Jersey 07645, page 9.

3. FDT, The Bulletin of ACM--SIGMOD, The Special Interest Group on Management of Data, Volume 7, Number 2, 1975, ANSI/X3/SPARC Study Group on Data Base Management Systems, Interim Report, 75-02-08, page I-1.

4. ACM's SIGMOD RECORD, Vol 15, Number 1, March, 1985, page 27.

5. IEC/ISO/JTC1/SC21/WG3/N2641, project 97.21.30 Reference Model of Data Management, Version 9, March, 1988, page 2.

6. IEC/ISO/JTC1/SC21/WG3/N2641, project 97.21.30 Reference Model of Data Management, Version 9, March, 1988, page 13.

7. IEC/ISO/JTC1/SC21/WG3/N2641, project 97.21.30 Reference Model of Data Management, Version 9, March, 1988, page 16.

8. IEC/ISO/JTC1/SC21/WG3/N2641, project 97.21.30 Reference Model of Data Management, Version 9, March, 1988, pages 18-21.

9. IEC/ISO/JTC1/SC21/WG3/N2641, project 97.21.30 Reference Model of Data Management, Version 9, March, 1988, pages 39-45.

10. FDT, The Bulletin of ACM--SIGMOD, The Special Interest Group on Management of Data, Volume 7, Number 2, 1975, ANSI/X3/SPARC Study Group on Data Base Management Systems, Interim Report, 75-02-08, page I-1.

2

DBMS APPLICATIONS AND COMPONENTS

A DBMS is a large collection of computer processes that can be entirely software or firmware that operate in a generalized or specialized computer that provides languages or mechanisms to:

- Define the logical database component of a specific database either directly or through reference to the IRDS metadata, that is, the data record types, data record elements, and relationships.
- Define the physical component of a specific database, that is, the storage structure definition, and the techniques for access strategies, data loading and updates, and database backup.
- Specify interrogations that access data through one or more types of languages such as host languages like COBOL or FORTRAN, and/or natural languages like query-update, report writers, or procedure-oriented.
- Specify system control facilities, that is, audit trails, backup and recovery, concurrent operations, and the like.

This chapter provides an overview of the affects and characteristics of static and dynamic relationship applications. In addition, it contains an explanation of these DBMS components and how they interrelate in today's DBMSs. This chapter also explains how database management *issues* arise that lead to confusion on the part of evaluators. Finally, this chapter compares database applications with DBMS to show that they are inextricably linked.

2.1 APPLICATION CLASSIFICATIONS

Applications can be classified in many ways. For example, applications can be classified by their major use, such as accounting, engineering, or personnel. Or, they can be classified by the types of audiences they serve: operations, support and control, or high-level MIS. For DBMS purposes, the real difference in applications is whether their design is constant or is variable.

DBMS facilities too can be classified in many ways, for example, host language or self-contained, network or hierarchical, embedded pointers or indexed based relationships, and so forth. While the third of these classifications hints at a major difference, the real difference in DBMSs is how they handle the differences in applications. One type of DBMS serves applications that are constant and unchanging, and another type of DBMS serves applications that are variable and changing.

2.2 STATIC AND DYNAMIC RELATIONSHIPS

Either static or dynamic relationships dominate a database application. Seldom is there an application in which the quantity of relationship types is evenly divided. Figure 2.1 shows the critical differences between static and dynamic relationship applications.

If the application is based on static relationships, then the relationships among data record types are normally well-defined, stable, and seldom-changing. Static relationship applications also tend to be production-oriented, with large transaction

Application Characteristic	Relationships	
	Static	Dynamic
Fundamental orientation	Corporate	Project
Required DBA orientation	Centralized	Decentral-ized
Database design effort	Significant	Casual
Frequency of design changes	Low	High
Design change control	Strict	Lax
Design change effects	Profound	Trivial
Typical data volume	Large	Small
Application and database design interdependence	High	Low
Predominant interrogation language	Cobol	Query-like

Figure 2.1 Static-Dynamic Relationship Application Characteristics

volumes that require high velocities. The principal access languages for static relationship applications are languages like COBOL.

A dynamic relationship application, in contrast, tends to have relationships that change almost as often as the data. The orientation of the application is MIS (management information system). These applications often typically have less data, lower transaction volumes, and consequently require lower velocities than the static relationship applications. The principal access languages for dynamic relationship applications are natural languages like query-update, procedure-oriented, and report writer.

A static relationship DBMS's DDL contains formally defined relationship clauses with all their attendant integrity, data record storage, and retrieval subclauses. Data record instances are often stored in the order loaded, and are maintained in DDL defined ordering; or they are stored and maintained in the order of the value from a data record instance's primary key. Data record instances are selected and presented according to the order implied by the primary key value or as specified in the DDL.

A dynamic relationship DBMS's DDL usually does not contain formally defined relationship clauses. Data record instances are often stored in the order presented and maintained in any order, or they are stored and maintained in the order of the data record's primary key. The user of a dynamic database has sort clauses as a fundamental part of every access language. Data record instances are selected and sorted before presentation. Once presented, the data record instances can be re-sorted and re-presented. In most DBMSs, the data record instances are not actually sorted, their address identifiers are.

The effect of having a dynamically related set of data record instances is the inverse of having a statically related set of data record instances. With dynamic relationships, each interrogation has an equal chance of retrieval and update efficiency. There is no bias to the processing. Often there are no restrictive relationship integrity clauses. The burden of maintaining relationship integrity is placed on the user because the dynamic database has undefined data record interrelationships. Thus it follows that the integrity clauses governing the interrelationships may also be undefined.

This lack of relationship integrity has prompted the builders of some dynamic relationship DBMSs to borrow a concept, inherent in static relationship DBMSs, called referential integrity. This is a two-part concept. First, it is the specification of the rules that relate two data record instances from two different types, and second, it is the automatic enforcement of the rules by the DBMS. This simple concept is, however, fraught with pitfalls, and must be carefully implemented. Referential integrity is covered in Chapter 3.

Knowledge of a DBMS's data model is important, but not as important as knowing whether the DBMS creates static or dynamic relationships. If the DBMS's relationships are static and the application is dynamic, application failure is almost always the outcome. If the DBMS's relationships are dynamic and the application is static, then the application will run, but the production performance will normally fall far below achievable levels.

2.3 THE NATURE OF A STATIC RELATIONSHIP APPLICATION

How many times since the creation of data processing has a bill of materials (BOM) system's design been substantively changed? Few times if ever. The reason is simple: the process's design is static. For this kind of production application, the software is written once and runs for years. And because it runs for years, and with voluminous transactions, the software written to process BOMs is *very close to the machine*. This software must be well designed and expertly implemented. A very large effort is justified because the design changes are few, and because the through-put required is very high.

Static relationship database applications are similar to BOM, in that they are less prone to change than others, and require very high through-put over a static set of relationships. These applications thrive on a certain kind of DBMS. Database benchmarks principally based on static relationship processing have, over the years, shown this assertion to be true. These DBMSs are designed to handle static relationships.

Applications implemented with static relationships should exhibit distinct characteristics, as enumerated in the static relationship column of Figure 2.1.

DBMS COMPONENT	RELATIONSHIP TYPE & EFFECT	
	STATIC	DYNAMIC
LOGICAL		
Record types per database	Many	Few
Relationship mechanism	Pointers	Data values
PHYSICAL		
Relationship binding	Load/Update	Retrieval
Record Keys	Single	Multiple
Data Loading	Via structure	Record by record
Relationship change	Delete & re-add	data value change
Fundamental Bias	Toward Database design or production	Neutral or ad hoc MIS-like
INTERROGATION		
Host Language	Excellent	Good
Natural Languages	Average	Excellent
SYSTEM CONTROL		
Multiple data record type Audit Trails	Easy	Hard
Reorganization		
Logical	Hard	Easy
Physical	Expensive	Reasonable
Multiple DB Processing	Acceptable	Excellent
Multiple data record locks	Easy	Hard

Figure 2.2 Static-Dynamic Relationship DBMS Characteristics

The critical characteristics of such DBMSs are cited in the static relationship column of Figure 2.2. Examples of DBMSs that contain static relationships are: DMS-1100, IDMS/R, IMS, SUPRA, and SYSTEM 2000.

2.4 THE NATURE OF A DYNAMIC RELATIONSHIP APPLICATION

In contrast to static relationship applications, there is a class of applications for which design change seems to be a way of life. Changes arise from two sources. First, there are changes that exist because the application is young and not yet completely evolved. Second, there are changes that are due to the very nature of the application. Dynamic relationship applications tend to require many changes to the data record types and the relationship types among data record instances in order to keep the applications relevant to the user's changing needs. These applications tend to contain smaller amounts of data than do static relationship applications, and tend to be better suited to a natural language environment rather than to a production COBOL environment. This is because changes are needed faster than COBOL programs can be created or changed.

Applications implemented with dynamic relationship DBMSs should exhibit distinct characteristics, as enumerated in the dynamic relationship column of Figure 2.1.

To handle such applications, there is a class of DBMSs that are designed around dynamic relationships. The characteristics of these systems are cited in the dynamic relationship column of Figure 2.2.

Examples of DBMSs that contain dynamic relationships are: ADABAS, Datacom/DB, DB/2, DMS-170, FOCUS, IDMS/R, INQUIRE, MODEL-204, NOMAD, and SUPRA.

2.5 PROBLEMS AND BENEFITS OF STATIC RELATIONSHIP DBMSs

Applications implemented with static relationships can have problems in two areas. The first occurs when it is necessary to produce a report that does not mirror the database's structural definitions. While almost any output requirement can certainly be satisfied, some are ill-suited to the database's design. Complex programs must then be created that consume large amounts of computer resources to satisfy the report requests. Eventually, if that reporting requirement is frequent enough, the database's design needs to be modified to reduce the processing resources consumed.

The second problem pertains to the database itself. Redesigning a static database usually involves great amounts of computer and human work concerning the:

- Actual redesign of the database's individual data record types
- Formal relationships among the data record types
- Programs that process data from the databases

Programs are often involved because they are usually written with the database's structure in mind. As a result, once the database design is changed, the programs that process data from it often require changes. If the programs use the DBMS's view facilities that are described in Chapter 4, the extent of program changes can be minimized.

In contrast to the problems, the benefits derived from applications implemented with static relationships are significant. Because relationships in static relationship DBMSs are most often implemented through traditional pointers, all data record types are under the control of a single schema. The DBMS then always knows all the data record types and is able to perform relationship maintenance (logical database reorganization) from this centralized point of view. Another benefit is the opportunity to build well-engineered and controlled databases. This results naturally from the data loading and maintenance process, which is performed principally through COBOL programs.

These two benefits greatly increase database integrity. As a final benefit, reports that mirror the database structure are highly efficient.

2.6 PROBLEMS AND BENEFITS OF DYNAMIC RELATIONSHIP DBMSs

Applications implemented with a dynamic relationship DBMS have almost the inverse set of problems and benefits described for the static relationship DBMS.

Database integrity can be a significant problem with a dynamic relationship DBMS. This is because the data record types are related through data record element values that are under user control. If a DBMS does not have referential integrity and the value in an owner data record element is accidentally changed, then the owner's corresponding member data record instances are lost with respect to that relationship. Members can be placed in a wrong relationship if the data value in the member is updated incorrectly.

DBMS benchmarks have shown that whenever there are production-oriented data processing-intensive interrogations, dynamic relationship DBMSs perform more slowly than static relationship DBMSs. This is because dynamic relationship DBMSs often have to access the owner data record to get the data value used to select--via secondary index searches--the member data record instances. The static relationship DBMS, on the other hand, simply follows a predefined *pointer-based* road map to another data record that may be on the same physical page.

Other difficulties associated with applications of dynamic relationship DBMSs center around the implementation of multiple data record type applications. It is the very independence of the data record types that causes the problems.

Whenever there is a need for a multiple data record type update, elaborate schemes must be implemented to ensure that all affected data record instances are updated in unison. Compounding the lock problem for the multiple data record type update, all well-designed dynamic database applications must have coordinated backup and recovery, and audit trails.

While these problems can be overcome by good user code and sophisticated techniques, they can cause concern to the application's users if not dealt with effectively.

The benefits associated with applications implemented with dynamic relationship DBMSs are just as significant as the problems. The benefits are flexibility, speed in some settings, and distributed processing. Flexibility heads this list. Data record types associated with a dynamic relationship database are often separate and independent physical files, and thus their loading and maintenance can be carried out without fear of disturbance by processes accessing other data record type instances.

Additionally, these data record types can often be processed sequentially--at great speeds--since all data record instances in the data record type's file are of the same type and format.

Finally, the greatest benefit of the dynamic relationship DBMS is that the data record types that might traditionally operate together under a static relationship schema can enjoy some of the benefits of a centralized schema without being preloaded into one static database. For example, it is possible to have multiple applications operating apart throughout the year, and then to bring them together at year's end under the control of a *virtual* schema for corporate-wide reporting.

2.7 IMPLEMENTING THE STATIC RELATIONSHIP APPLICATION

The fundamental goals of a static relationship database can be only to:

- Create a data organization that mirrors the fundamental processes in the business organization
- Impose maximum DBA control over user updating and reporting of data in the database

There cannot be different goals, because the static relationship DBMSs will not permit them to be implemented.

2.7.1 The Logical Database

The database design process should take considerable time, as the designer should become involved in an in-depth analysis to determine the *natural* organizations of data.

Looking to existing data processing systems may only throw the designer off track as these systems are typically implemented to produce ad hoc reports. As a result, these systems had ad hoc data collections and ad hoc programs to transform the collected data into the report. When another report was needed, another system was created. Finally, all the month-end systems were combined into one to reduce the multitude of file extracts, sorts, and prints. These systems were set for data processing efficiency, not the organization's efficiency. *But organizational efficiency is what database is all about.*

Once a thorough information requirements analysis is complete, the real database design effort can begin, producing first a high-level design that serves the needs of the whole organization. Then a second level set of database designs should be built, each drawn from the high level design and addressing a specific database problem that has to be solved immediately. The combined scope of the second level designs should approximate that of the high level design. Finally, the lowest level of design should be constructed in the DBMS's data definition language syntax.

The products generated during the first two design levels are all part of the business model. At the highest level the design applies to the organization as a whole, and is a requirement specification for the middle level design. The middle level design applies either to a specific application or to a division of the organization. The middle level design also serves as a requirements specification for the lowest level design. The lowest level design applies both to a specific application and to the needs of a specific DBMS.

2.7.2 The Physical Database

For static relationship DBMSs the storage structure and the data access strategy are normally very complex. Included in their design are different kinds of pointers, indexes, relationships, storage organizations, overflow tables, access techniques, and the like. These things taken together give a static relationship database its speed. And, these things taken together tightly bind static relationship database designs to their applications.

There are two other significant parts of the physical database: the data loading subsystem and the data update subsystem.

The data loading subsystem is a one-time-only application. Database integrity begins with this subsystem. A static relationship database is best suited to be a non-redundant data store for a large collection of related applications. Prior to database, even related applications often had data in different formats, lengths, code tables, and so forth. All this data had to be brought together into one common format before loading into a database. The data loading subsystem becomes the single melting pot for diverse data. The data loading subsystems' design and implementation thus take a great deal of time; and the conversion of existing and running applications to the single database takes talent, skill, and cleverness.

The data update subsystem is typically required for both batch and on-line updating. For a static relationship database, most data record instance access is through pointers that lead owner to owner, owner to member, member to member, and member to owner. This traversal process must be very carefully designed to make it efficient. Efficiency is required because the many different applications, brought together under one database, must have their formerly separate update and retrieval transactions coordinated and engineered to keep transaction response times acceptable.

2.7.3 Interrogation

Most static relationship database interrogations are through host languages like COBOL or FORTRAN. This is for two reasons:

- The database structure is often so complex that the sophistication of a COBOL-like language is typically required to make best use of it.
- A sophisticated natural language, which would allow any kind of interrogation to be formulated, traditionally operates too slowly.

A static relationship database derives its efficiency from its strict structure and pre-planned road maps of pointers. Because a sophisticated query-update language enables users to easily formulate interrogations that do not coincide with the database's design, most vendors of static relationship DBMSs have chosen not to produce very sophisticated query-update languages. They have, however, produced procedure-oriented languages, report writers, and elementary query-update languages.

2.7.4 System Control

System control covers the activities that control database, the DBMS, and the application. Figure 2.2 enumerates those system control functions that most affect static and dynamic relationship applications. Most significant to static relationship applications is reorganization. Since almost all programs are created with the database structure in mind, changing that structure is a complicated job. The process of reorganization must be very carefully planned so that the affected programs are identified and researched for the required reprogramming effort.

Whenever data is needed from several static relationship organized databases, the normal method of extraction is through host language interfaces (HLI). Most static relationship DBMSs do not permit multiple database processing capabilities for either their query-update or report writing languages.

2.7.5 Static Relationship Application Summary

The most important fact to remember about the static relationship application is that all aspects of its design should remain unchanged for as long as possible. This means that application designers should spend as much time as possible on analysis and design. If this effort is cut short, then there will be many expensive database reorganizations. But if the database is designed correctly from the start, then it will run efficiently for a long time.

2.8 IMPLEMENTING THE DYNAMIC RELATIONSHIP APPLICATION

The fundamental goals of the dynamic database environment are:

- To create databases from existing collections of data processing files or single-purpose applications
- To allow the users maximum control over the updating and reporting from their databases

User control over updating and reporting cannot be restricted as the facilities enabling user control permeate dynamic relationship DBMSs.

2.8.1 The Logical Database

Database design takes place very informally. Simple flat file-like structures can be created from any existing data processing files by coding up the DDL and submitting it to the DBMS. For dynamic relationship DBMSs, the terms *file* and *data record type* have almost the same meaning. A complex structure, in which there are several interrelated data record types, can also be created. These interrelationships are encoded either into views or DML language expressions, which are executed by the DBMS when the interrogation is submitted. Some dynamic relationship DBMSs require the connecting data record elements to be of the same type, format, kind, and value. Other than that, the database design process is quite simple.

2.8.2 The Physical Database

Many dynamic relationship DBMSs implement each data record type as a distinct operating system (O/S) file. Some allow the combination of several of these data record types into one O/S file. This is usually done to increase performance. When this is done, though, some of the flexibility of the independent O/S file approach is lost.

Most of the dynamic relationship DBMSs allow for the creation of indexes, both primary (unique value required) and secondary (non-unique values allowed). They use primary indexes to locate individual data record instances, and secondary indexes to locate sets of data record instances. Dynamic relationship DBMSs often use the primary index from one data record type as a secondary index of another data record type as a way to implement a parent-child relationship. In lieu of index connections, a dynamic relationship DBMS may merely require the user to state which two data record elements relate the data record types. The DBMS takes care of all the processing.

The data loading subsystem for a dynamic relationship application is also informal. Dynamic relationship DBMSs often provide data loading utilities that transform a data processing file into a database. If the transformation is simple, the utility works. If the transformation cannot be handled, the user must accomplish data loading through a host language interface program.

Data update is performed by the users, one data record type at a time. Since each data record type is independent of any other, it is of little concern when other users update data record instances from other data record types. Simple collections of data record types can be updated by one of the DBMS's natural languages. Complex updates are normally done through host languages.

2.8.3 Interrogation

Most dynamic relationship DBMSs are supported by very well-developed natural languages. Some of these are actually very sophisticated programming languages that allow multiple data record type access, automatic report formatting, code table look-up, branching, looping, terminal prompting, definition, and invocation of stored procedures. Dynamic relationship DBMSs that do not employ the ANSI/SQL language often have under developed host language interfaces. The reason is simple: few users ever need to use COBOL or FORTRAN to process data from the database, given the sophistication of the natural languages.

2.8.4 System Control

Reorganization is a simple process with a dynamically organized database. A utility is invoked, the data record element types are added, deleted, or changed, and the DBMS automatically reorganizes the data record type. Whenever there is a new relationship between two data record types, only one data record type is changed by incorporating the new data record element type. Following the addition of the data record element type, the user creates the update program to store values required by this new data record element for the relationship. Once valued, the basis of the relationship is in place, waiting to be used.

One drawback of a dynamically organized database application occurs when multiple data record type updates are attempted. The user or program attempting the update must acquire locks over all the data record types involved. This is difficult, because a user is normally allowed to *open-for-update* only one data record type at a time, and a data record must be opened before it can be locked.

Construction of a multiple data record type audit trail is also difficult. This is because the entries to the audit trail are usually made on a data record type basis. As a result, the integrated audit trail can only be created through the update program. When an audit trail is needed, the only safe vehicle for its creation is through a host language program. Consequently, the use of all other languages should be avoided.

2.8.5 Dynamic Relationship Application Summary

The most important fact to remember about a dynamic relationship application is that the user is in control of database definition, updating, reporting, and many of the system control activities. The dynamic relationship DBMS facility is a system where you *do your own thing*. This would be disastrous for payroll, accounts payable, and the like, but for some applications, like marketing research, it is ideal.

2.9 DBMS COMPONENTS AND SUBCOMPONENTS

Figure 2.3 illustrates how the components of a DBMS are interrelated. Any data processing product contains interfaces, capabilities, and processes. Standard interfaces enable products to *connect*. Capabilities are the tools that a product

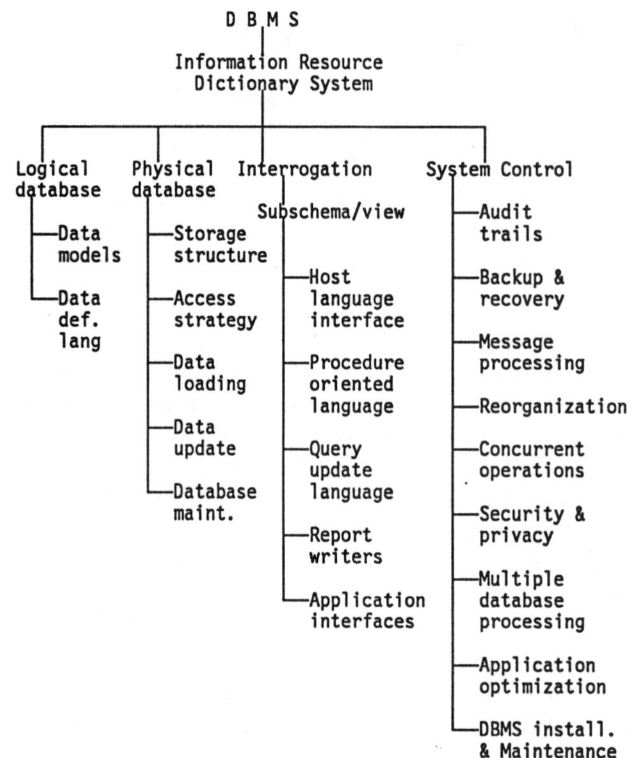

Figure 2.3 Database Management System Components

brings to the user. Processing represents the transfer of the data (input and output) with which users ultimately deal.

ANSI/SPARC, in their 1975 draft reference model report, recognized the critical importance of interfaces by stating:

> In the course of the early discussions [about a reference model], it emerged that what any standardization should treat is interfaces. There is potential disaster and little merit in developing standards that specify how components are to work. What is proper for standards specification is how the components are meshed; in other words, the interfaces. (1)

To illustrate what is meant by interfaces, there are a number of vendor products that generate COBOL source programs, for example, MAGEC by Al Lee and Associates. These products enable users to define the various aspects of a COBOL program, which the products then generate. The resultant COBOL program is an interface between the product and the COBOL compiler. If the specification (content) of the interface is IBM COBOL, the programs can not be ported to DEC computers, because IBM COBOL does not work on DEC computers. If, however, the interface is ANSI standard COBOL, then a program can be specified independent of the target computer environment, generated on either computer, and then run on both.

To illustrate what is meant by capabilities, this same program generator package might offer to interact with its users through menu-driven facilities, or through syntax input, and so on. Furthermore, the generator package might contain default capabilities, for example, that all files are VSAM, and thus might automatically generate COBOL code appropriate for VSAM. MAGEC, for example, automatically generates data access language statements to VSAM, Datacom/DB, and SQL. Interfacing to SQL means that the generated COBOL program can be used with any ANSI/SQL compliant DBMS. In comparing various types of program generator packages, various capabilities are evaluated to determine the best package. Since the purpose of a program generator is to save programmer time and produce standard bug-free code, the packages that enabled these things to be done efficiently and easily would rate highly.

To illustrate what is meant by processing, the program generator might have the same capabilities as another package, but generate COBOL code three times more slowly. All else being equal, that is, price, interface, and capabilities, the faster package would be the better buy. While DBMSs are a great deal more complicated than program generators, the ultimate selection goals are still the same. The package procured should be one that offers the most ANSI standard interfaces with the most capabilities and the most efficient processing.

2.10 THE DBMS

All fully functional DBMSs contain four distinct sets of facilities: the logical database, the physical database, interrogation, and system control. The first set supports the logical database and provides for the structuring of a database according to one or more of the four popular data models.

The DBMS's physical database facilities enable data loading, data update, various access strategies that affect storage structure design, and facilities to maintain the database, i.e., backup. Data update and database backup are included within physical database to understand their physical effect on the database.

The third set of facilities, interrogation, supports retrieval and update of the database's data record instances through a number of interrogation languages. These range from simple-to-use non-programmer facilities to sophisticated languages for professional programmers.

The fourth set of facilities, system control, provides protection to databases and database applications, and secures the DBMS and database from unwanted access. These facilities include: audit trails, backup and recovery, message processing, reorganization, concurrent operations, security and privacy, multiple database processing, DBMS installation and maintenance, and database application optimization.

2.10.1 The Logical Database

The logical database component of a DBMS enables user definition of data record types, data record elements, and explicitly defined relationships.

Data record element types include single-valued, multiple-valued, groups, and repeating groups. Data record element data types include character and numeric and fixed and variable lengths.

A defined data record type includes its name, primary key (if any), secondary keys (if any), and the various data record elements. If the data record type definition is for hierarchical or relational DBMSs then only single-valued data record elements are allowed. If the definition is for network (CODASYL or ANSI/NDL) or Independent Logical File (ILF) then, depending on the DBMS, some of the following data record elements can be defined: multi-valued, groups, repeating groups, and multi-dimensioned arrays.

Relationships are the expression of a semantic connection between data record instances from the same type, or between data record instances from two or more types. There are eight types of relationships that can be defined among data record types:

- One-to-many
- Owner-multiple-member
- Singular-one-member
- Singular-multiple-member
- Recursive
- Many-to-many
- One-to-one
- Inferential

One-to-many relationships are the most common relationship type, and are also known as owner-member. An example of this relationship type is: COMPANY has many EMPLOYEES. The single relationship type name would be EMPLOYEES, and the two data record types are COMPANY and EMPLOYEES.

An owner-multiple-member relationship is an owner-member relationship in which there are multiple-member data record types. For example, a COMPANY has PART-TIME-EMPLOYEES, FULL-TIME-EMPLOYEES, and RETIRED-EMPLOYEES. The relationship type name would be EMPLOYEES, and the four data record types participating in the one relationship are COMPANY, PART-TIME-EMPLOYEES, FULL-TIME-EMPLOYEES, and RETIRED-EMPLOYEES.

A singular-one-member relationship is so named because it is defined to contain only one data record type, a member. For example, the relationship

HIGH-PROFIT-MARGIN-COMPANIES would only contain data record instances from the one data record type, COMPANY.

A singular-multiple-member relationship has no owner, but more than one member. There may be one or more member instances of each of the members for each relationship occurrence. For example, the relationship HIGH-ACHIEVERS could be defined to have data record instances from the PART-TIME-EMPLOYEES, FULL-TIME-EMPLOYEES, and RETIRED-EMPLOYEES data record types.

Recursive relationships are those that can express owner-member relationships among data record instances that are from the same data record type. A typical example of a recursive relationship is COMPANY ORGANIZATION in which all the data record instances come from the data record type ORGANIZATIONAL UNITS. The relationship would keep track of the organization from the office of the president down to the mail room.

The many-to-many relationship type is common in database applications. This relationship, like the one-to-many relationship, involves two different data record types. The relationship, however, is one-to-many in BOTH directions. The relationship enables the first of the data record types to be the owner of the second, and also the second data record type to be the owner of the first. A common example of the two parts of the many-to-many relationship ASSIGNMENTS is:

1) Each EMPLOYEE works on many PROJECTs and

2) Each PROJECT uses many EMPLOYEEs.

There is also the one-to-one relationship. The one-to-one relationship is not employed often. It relates a single data record instance from one data record type to a single data record instance from another data record type. The most common use of this relationship type is to segment the data record elements from one data record type into two or more data record types. An example would be to segment respondent's profile information from the answers to a questionnaire. In this case, the two data record types would be RESPONDENT's PROFILE and RESPONDENT's ANSWERs.

The inferential relationship relates data record instances from two types. This relationship, however, does not involve the primary key of either data record. Rather, it involves a data record element from two different data record types that is not uniquely defined in either data record type. For example, an EMPLOYEE data record type is defined to contain the data record element ASSIGNED PROJECT. Another data record type, BUILDING, has a repeating data record element HOUSES PROJECTS. The relationship LOCATED, between the two data record types, is at best inferential as it is not known which building the employee is located in, since multiple buildings can house the same project.

In addition to having a data definition language to declare the data record types, data record elements, and relationships to the DBMS, there must also be supplemental subclauses to define sophisticated editing and validation clauses and to execute procedures during (before and/or after) data record, data record element, and relationship updating.

Not all these logical database capabilities can be implemented in all DBMSs. When a well-defined set of facilities is implemented across a number of different DBMSs, that subset is commonly referred to as a data model. There are four recognized data models: network, hierarchical, independent logical file, and relational.

2.10.2 The Physical Database

The physical database component of any DBMS, regardless of whether it supports one or several data models, specifies the storage structure and access strategy for data record types.

DBMSs allow an index to be defined for any data record element. These indexes are used in selection clauses to enhance processing. Sophisticated access strategies optimize the access of data record instances by using all the indexed elements referenced, or by ignoring the fact that a data record element is indexed when list processing is slower than data record processing.

The physical database also supports variable physical designs such as including all of a data record type's data on one O/S file, storing the data from several data record types on one O/S file, or spreading the data from one data record type across multiple O/S files. Variable physical designs enable portions of a very large database to be moved off-line when there is no need for on-line access. Additionally, sophisticated DBMSs offer alternative O/S access methods, blocking factors, and DBMS record sizes to achieve even more highly tuned performances.

The single central-version, multiple-database DBMS enables databases to be brought on- and off-line at will, and so that database and/or DBMS failures will be isolated in their effects.

2.10.3 Interrogation

Interrogation is the process of selecting and retrieving data to satisfy simple queries or complex reports. Sophisticated DBMSs offer different languages, each suitable to a class of tasks. For example, a procedure-oriented language (POL) for quick application specification, a query-update language for simple reports and/or updates, and a report-writer for complicated on-line or batch reports. Additionally, sophisticated interfaces to compiler languages such as Ada, Pascal, C, COBOL, FORTRAN, and PL/I enable the development of complex database applications.

To help users access data, sophisticated DBMS vendors provide a mechanism for reducing the amount of knowledge that users are required to have of the database's data model or physical database organization. The mechanism, called a view, is a separately defined subset of data record elements from one or more data record types. If multiple data record types are involved in a view, then its definition must also implicitly or explicitly include logic to navigate between data record instances from different data record types. Since views are simpler to comprehend, the available commands are also simplified: GET, STORE, MODIFY, and DELETE. To help users find the appropriate set of data record instances, the view should include a comprehensive set of WHERE clause facilities. Ideally, the view, its simplified commands, and the comprehensive set of select clauses is available to all the interrogation languages.

Of course, if the vendor does not provide a view capability, then access must take place through a more detailed set of commands that operate across the DBMS's data structures.

Some database operations are dependent upon the data model. For example, there are some special relational-only operations such as division, outer-join, and product. For NDL-related data record types, there are special navigational and data-data record-at-a-time operations such as GET OWNER, GET MEMBER, and GET NEXT.

2.10.4 System Control

System control capabilities provide support for controlling the database's audit trails, message processing, backup and recovery, reorganization, concurrent operations, security and privacy, multiple database processing, DBMS installation and maintenance, and database application optimization.

The DBMS's audit trails capture update transactions according to criteria such as user, data record type, date, time, and program. These transactions are selectively reportable, and available during backup and recovery operations.

Message processing facilities provide sophisticated on-line help for investigating the cause of a user, database, or DBMS error.

Backup and recovery facilities permit unaffected users to continue work while back-ups are taken of production databases and to undergo minimum interruptions while the DBMS recovers a database from a DBMS, user, or computing environment induced error.

Reorganization involves both logical changes to the database's data record element and relationship types, and physical reorganization of the database's storage structure components.

Concurrent operations enable a single run-time copy of the DBMS to support multiple concurrent update and retrieval transactions from multiple interrogation language run-units to the same or different databases without any compromise to database integrity, and with automatic detection and resolution of execution deadlock.

Quality DBMSs permit multiple databases to operate under a single central version. This allows logical database changes to be isolated and applied without affecting any of the other databases that may be running under that central version. Furthermore, if one database crashes, then only that database is affected, and while it is being recovered, the others remain operating.

Security and privacy support the definition of a comprehensive set of user, profile, and passwords to prevent and then report on illicit data access and database operations. The DBMS security provides protection at the database, data record type, and data record element level for at least update and retrieval access and ideally also for select clauses.

DBMS installation and maintenance facilities, if sophisticated, enable the generation of special run-time version that favors certain types of update or retrieval processing.

Finally, if the DBMS provides performance assessment aids, physical database designers can tune the database's logical and physical design to achieve high performance on critical applications. These DBMS application optimization facilities generate statistics on database access efficiency, overlay usage, DBMS routine invocation, and the like to guide physical and logical reorganization, or to guide the creation of a special DBMS version. A detailed presentation of the system control component is contained in Chapter 6.

2.11 DBMS ISSUES

Use of some DBMS facilities provokes argument. Each side of the argument usually has sound logic behind its position. Consider, for example, the issue of sorting. For the proponent of dynamic facilities, performing a sort of the data before it is presented to the user is a critical operation in any dynamic DBMS language. To have the DBMS maintain data record instances in a predetermined order is a waste of time, so the argument goes, since users will always want data record instances in a different order from a DBMS stored order.

On the other side of the sorting issue is the static relationship DBMS proponent who feels that if an organization has done a *proper* job of designing the database, it will rarely, if ever, be necessary to waste computer time sorting data record instances because the DBMS would have already sorted them into a *proper* order. Besides, if sorting does have to be done, the user should retrieve the data record instances and let the operating system utility sort them, relieving the DBMS of such a ridiculous and unimportant task.

The issue is actually more complicated than either of these sides allows. For example, both sides are presuming that static relationship DBMS facilities automatically maintain order among data record instances and do not allow sorting, and that dynamic DBMS facilities do not automatically maintain order among data record instances and do allow sorting. While this is generally true, SYSTEM 2000, a static relationship DBMS, does not automatically maintain data record instances in a sorted order, and does provide a sorting command to both host and natural languages. And FOCUS, a dynamic DBMS, maintains data record instances in a sorted order, and also provides sort verbs in its languages.

In other words, many issues are often founded on long-standing practices or on specific DBMS implementations, rather than on the fundamental technology of DBMS or on DBMS standards.

Nonetheless, all issues have both performance and flexibility impacts. Regrettably, performance and flexibility are almost always opposed. What you gain on one, you lose from the other.

For example, if a DBMS automatically maintains data record orders, then resources must be expended to maintain these orders. As a new data record is stored, its proper place must be found. Generally, the DBMS stores the data record without regard to sorting, then traverses the data record instances according to their sort order, locating the proper *before* data record. This data record's *next* pointer, which points to the data record's old *next* data record in the sequence, is modified to point to the newly stored data record. The newly-stored data record then has its *next* pointer modified from NULL to the value of the old *next* data record. This is a different process from merely storing the data record and leaving the problem of sorting to the retrieval program.

The benefits of data record sorting are the inverse of its drawbacks. If many different retrieval programs use data record instances, all according to the same order, then run-time sorting would not have to be performed if the data record instances were already stored in that order.

There are often two sides to issues like sorting, and flexibility and performance are typically on different sides. A two dimensional matrix occurs, like the one in Figure 2.4, can be employed to set down the differences. To select one

Issue And Consequence	DBMS Maintained Sorting	User Maintained Sorting
Flexibility	Reduces ability to create different sort orders on reports	Users can develop reports or updates different order
Performance	Slows updates but speeds reports using DBMS provided record ordering	Speeds updates, but slows reports as each run unit must perform its own record sorting

Figure 2.4 Positive and Negative Aspects of an Issue

alternative requires a detailed analysis of the database applications to identify the frequency of sorting during retrievals versus the cost of maintaining the data record instance orders during updates. Once the analysis is complete, the decision can be made.

2.12 APPLICATION COMPONENTS AND DBMS COMPONENTS

There are significant differences between the components of a database application and the components of a DBMS. Despite the differences, the application and the DBMS are inextricably linked. The differences are related to perceptions and use sequencing.

In a database project, a need is specified on behalf of an application's uses. Then the need is addressed by implementing a facility through the DBMS. Finally, the new facility is used by the application's users to meet their business needs.

The difference between the logical database component of a database application and the logical database component of a DBMS is analogous to the difference between specifying the data to be handled in a database application and implementing that specification with the DBMS. While both represent the logical database, the representations are from different viewpoints.

For example, a database application requires the data record element TELEPHONE NUMBER. When implemented in a DBMS, the TELEPHONE NUMBER may be declared to be CUST-TEL-NBR TYPE IS INTEGER 9(10). The difference may arise when the DBMS can only handle names with only 12 characters, not allowing blanks in names, and requiring a data type specification.

The difference between logical database from the application point of view and logical database from the DBMS point of view extends to data record types and relationships. A data record type, from the point of view of the application, may merely be a data record type name and the identifications of the contained data record elements. In contrast, the data record type from the DBMS point of view typically requires a name, element identifiers, access clauses, check clauses, and so on.

An application logical database relationship may only identify the data record types involved and an enumeration of the rules that specify how to determine which data record types belong to the relationship. In contrast, the DBMS relationship contains the names of the data record types, which data record type is the owner and which are the members, whether the members are to be *sorted* within the context of the owner, and any referential integrity clauses governing data record membership in these relationships.

A database application has requirements relating to the physical database, that is, an estimation of the size of each data record type, the volume and volatility of data record instances, and the nature and frequency of updates. The DBMS's requirements for the physical database relate to how these data record instances are stored, that is, fixed or variable lengths; how they are accessed, that is, through indexes and embedded pointers; and how update operations are carried out, that is, by updating in place, moving data record instances around, or splitting data record instances so that the different parts can be stored in different locations.

Interrogation, to a database application, is the identification and specification of necessary reports and queries, including their specification, life span, data volumes, and frequency of invocation. To the DBMS, interrogation relates to the various types of languages that are used to implement and produce the reports, including issues related to language sophistication, ease of use, and performance.

System control, to the database application, represents the identification of the requirements for audit trails, backup and recovery, and security and privacy. From the DBMS point of view, system control components represent the detailed specifications of how the DBMS satisfies these requirements, including issues related to sophistication, ease of use, and performance.

2.13 DBMS REQUIREMENTS SUMMARY

Sophisticated DBMSs support multiple data models. The two portable data models are ANSI/NDL (network) and ANSI/SQL (relational). Multiple data model supports enable databases to be built that are network only, hierarchical only, independent logical file only, or relational only. Today's popular combinations are network and relational (IDMS/R and SUPRA), hierarchical and relational (FOCUS), and independent logical file and relational (ADABAS and Model 204). The interface language of choice for the network and relational data models is NDL and SQL respectively. Regardless of the data model, all DBMSs must have sophisticated editing, validation, and referential integrity.

Sophisticated DBMSs also support multiple access methods for the files. Depending on the kind of performance needed, the relationships supported between data record types and files should, at a minimum, be one-to-one, one-to-many, or many-to-many.

Modern DBMSs have a variety of languages, such as query-update languages, procedure-oriented languages, and report writers, so that whole applications can be implemented without resorting to the use of host languages.

Finally, the complete DBMS has a rich set of system control facilities for backup and recovery, and audit trails. Critical to an effective environment is multiple database processing, multiple threaded operations, and the ability to manipulate the DBMS software and buffers to achieve different performance characteristics.

References

1. FDT, The Bulletin of ACM--SIGMOD, The Special Interest Group on Management of Data, Volume 7, Number 2, 1975, ANSI/X3/SPARC Study Group on Data Base Management Systems, Interim Report, 75-02-08, page I-3.

3

THE LOGICAL DATABASE

3.1 DEFINITION

The logical database is an expression of the data's organization represented in the database. The data organization is communicated to the DBMS through a data definition language (DDL). While most DBMSs, upon detailed examination, have a unique data organization, these organizations can generally be perceived as mapping to one of four main data models: network, hierarchical, independent logical file, and relational.

In addition to *plain vanilla* data model structures, quality DBMSs support the specification of various types of integrity rules and regulations. Integrity clauses govern the allowable operations on the database. These clauses can enable the execution of preprogrammed logic that can cause the acceptance or rejection data element values, the addition/deletion/modifications of the data record instance, and even cause triggering of other actions, which in turn might cause adds, deletions, or modifications of data within data record instances from other data record types.

A DBMS must have a robust set of data structuring and integrity facilities to then allow use of natural languages for updates rather than requiring all update programs to be written in COBOL. COBOL, of course, supports the syntax to accomplish these editing and validation procedures through programmer created logic. If, however, these data structuring and integrity facilities are available through schema-based DBMS facilities, then a screen update program can be created in a natural language with only one or two hours work rather than one or two weeks. That's a 40:1 improvement in programmer productivity!

Even if COBOL were as easy to use as is a natural language, it would still be very important to have editing and validation facilities as a part of the DBMS, because that way all the update clauses can be defined and maintained in one place, without having to find, change, recompile, and retest many, many COBOL programs, and without risking a loophole by failing to change all affected programs.

This chapter presents detailed definitions of the components of the logical database (Section 3.2), describes how these components are combined to make up a data model (Section 3.3), and explains the language that communicates logical database constructs to the DBMS (Section 3.4). The chapter closes with a summary.

3.2 LOGICAL DATABASE COMPONENTS

The logical organization of a database is defined through the specification of:

- Domains, which control ranges and types of data element values.

- Data elements, which represent discrete business facts.
- Data record instances, which are collections of data elements determined by the organization to have a collective business policy meaning. When data elements are assigned to data record types they are called data record elements.
- Relationships, which define connections established between data record instances of the same or different types for various reasons.
- Operations, which specify allowable actions on data record instances and on the relationships between and among data record instances.

DBMS data dictionaries and IRDS store information about all five components. Many DBMSs do not, however, distinguish data elements from data record elements; thus, within the context of a DBMS, data elements exist only within the context of a data record type. To reflect this difference within DBMSs, the phrase *data [record] element* is employed. If the DBMS distinguishes data elements from data record elements then the phrase means data elements, otherwise data record elements.

3.2.1 Domains

A domain is a method of defining the business meaning of a class of values represented by data [record] elements. A data [record] element represents discrete classes of data values. These values have physical boundaries (minimum and maximum values), and represent certain business semantics, such as WEIGHT, LENGTH, and PRICE. Because a data [record] element represents business semantics, certain combinations of data [record] elements should be permitted, while others should not. For example, DATE should not be multiplied by PRICE as the result has no common business meaning.

A domain contains the specification of the type and value characteristics that might be used by various data [record] elements in different data record types in the database. For example, sex would have the domain of male and female; salary would have the domain $3,000 to $60,000. An example of a domain appears in Figure 3.1.

Because domains control values, they are in some sense *super-data [record] elements*. Consequently, domains have definitions similar to those of data [record] elements. The characteristics that describe domains reflect whether the data represented by the domain consists of fixed- and variable-length character strings, fixed-and floating-point numbers, integers, or special data types such as date and time.

More importantly, domains are employed to specify a series of statements that govern the values that are allowed in one or more data [record] elements. Included in these rule sets are:

- Valid value ranges

- Specific valid values
- Invalid value ranges
- Specific invalid values
- Duplicates allowed or disallowed
- Default values
- Conversion rules
- Null value allowed or disallowed

```
DOMAIN IS SALARY
TYPE IS NUMERIC
PICTURE IS 99,999.99
RANGE IS 3000 TO 6000
```

Figure 3.1 Domain Salary

Finally, complete domains contain rules that define allowed interactions. For example, it might be perfectly legal to multiply a duration of time by an integer to arrive at a longer duration. But in an ordinary business situation, it would not make sense to take the square root of time. Some operations might be allowed on different domains, producing a third domain. For example, multiplying SQUARE FEET by POUNDS yields PRESSURE. These rules of engagement must be defined in the database so that when the widest possible audience is using the database through a natural language, database operations such as additions, modifications, and various combinations can be made in a manner deemed acceptable by the organization.

3.2.2 Data Elements

Data elements represent discrete instances of business data. Examples are: SOCIAL SECURITY NUMBER, RECEIPT DATE, FIRST NAME, ADDRESS, and REMAINING AMOUNT. Data elements exhibit many characteristics, all of which must be known before the data element can be fully understood. Each data element clause incorporates by reference the specifications contained in a domain specification, and possibly even augmentations to them. For example, the domain EMPLOYEE SALARY may have a value range $1 to $5,000, while the HOURLY EMPLOYEE SALARY may further restrict that range to $4 to $20. A data element consists of its name, its data type, its structural composition, and the applicable integrity clauses.

3.2.2.1 Data element Names

Among the many issues surrounding data elements, the issue of names is very important. To adopt a data element naming standard that (for example) prefixes each data element with a code indicating its use or characteristics trivializes the issue, however. Such a proposal would force the choice of a single prefix indicating that the data element is a key, or a code, or a date, or a number, and so forth. Rather there must be a fully developed IRDS to store all the rules surrounding data elements. In short, there is much more to a data element than just its name, as the following examples show.

SOCIAL SECURITY NUMBER is typically represented as a 9-digit number, but is not arithmetic in nature. Consequently, it is senseless to compute the average SOCIAL SECURITY NUMBER for a sampling of EMPLOYEES. Additionally, there are legal and illegal values for SOCIAL SECURITY NUMBER. Thus, while, its form is certainly numeric, SOCIAL SECURITY NUMBER is certainly not numeric in the conventional sense. Thus, prefixing SOCIAL SECURITY NUMBER with the data type NUMERIC would hide its true nature, looks ridiculous, and take up an additional 8 character positions in the name.

RECEIPT DATE is another numeric business data element. RECEIPT DATE has legal and illegal values and, if properly stored, can be used in some types of arithmetic logic. For example, a query might be constructed to print the DATE that is 15 days beyond a specific RECEIPT DATE. It would also make sense to compute the standard deviation, average, or median number of days elapsed from the date an invoice was issued to the date it was paid. Such a calculation involves subtraction, summing, and square roots. Multiplying two dates, on the other hand, would make no sense. So, to say that RECEIPT DATE is a number is to mislead users as to allowable operations even though it can be involved in numeric calculations. To establish a data type called DATE is a good solution, but unless it is carefully thought out as to internal storage, the variety of external representations, and the problems caused by different time zones, this would cause more problems than it would solve. To prefix RECEIPT with the data type DATE begs for the inclusion of the word *OF*, which makes the data element name four characters longer without adding any real semantic value.

FIRST NAME is most probably an alphabetic data element. Its values are restricted to a combination of the instances of LETTERS, with the first letter being in upper case. In general, numbers would probably be an indication of an error, although not always. After all, the movie *Star Wars* gave rise to C3PO and R2D2! Determining the real data element name here is difficult. After all, is NAME a part of the data element's name, or is it an indication of the type of data (character)? Thus, the data element's name could be NAME, or FIRST, or FIRST NAME, or *NAME FIRST*. Depending on how that question is answered, and presuming the domain to be CHARACTER, the following alternatives for first name are:

- CHARACTER NAME
- CHARACTER FIRST
- CHARACTER FIRST NAME
- CHARACTER NAME FIRST

Another type of data element is ADDRESS. This data element presents a different set of problems, the least of which is its data type. ADDRESS does not represent a discrete value, but a set of *lower level* data elements, each of which has a discrete value. Each of the lower level data elements may be of a different data type. For example, ADDRESS is most likely composed of EFFECTIVE DATE, STREET NUMBER, STREET NAME, CITY, STATE, ZIP, and COUNTRY. Again, each of these data elements may have rules for the types of values, and rules for specific ranges of legal values. In the case of CITY and ZIP, these two have specific instances of legal values--in combination. In the case where the country was the United States, letters would be illegal in a ZIP code, while in CANADA, an all numeric ZIP code would be illegal. So, what is the domain prefix of ADDRESS, the first data type, the mode data type, or the average (whatever that means)? Since no meaningful domain prefix can be determined, it is inappropriate for any to be assigned.

A final example of a data element is REMAINING AMOUNT. This data element is obviously computed from some other source. Furthermore, it may have certain rules about its upper and lower limits (negative not allowed, for example). This data element would probably also be subjected to rounding rules for MONEY, and be allowed to be operated upon in certain ways, but not in others. For example, the SQUARE ROOT of REMAINING AMOUNT might not be sensible, but the STANDARD DEVIATION (which involves square roots) may be. Again, identifying the data type as numeric would be misleading, as not all arithmetic operations ought to be permitted.

The point of all of these examples is that data elements conform to certain rules of behavior, some of which are implied by their obvious data type, and some of which can be mistakenly implied by their data type.

Another attribute of a data element is its use context. For example, the data element REMAINING AMOUNT might be allowed to have negative values in some situations, but not in others. In a checking account, for example, a negative REMAINING AMOUNT might be allowed, resulting in INTEREST being charged by the bank. In the case of a mortgage payoff, the amount to be paid is required to be exactly that which is due, since the REMAINING AMOUNT on a mortgage cannot be negative. And, of course, if a REMAINING AMOUNT data element were part of an INVENTORY-ON-HAND data record, not only negative numbers but also fractions would not be allowed.

It should be quite clear that a data element cannot be fully understood unless its scope, intent, rules, and other modifiers are known. These include:

- Data characteristics
- Use context
- Domain
- Valid, invalid, and range rules
- Allowable combinations of operations

As has been shown, these modifiers when applied to the same data element--in different combinations--produce different results.

The only convention that leads to understanding, rather than to misunderstanding, is to give a data element its most common business name and state all the modifiers that provide for complete definition. With this convention, data element names can be used over and over where appropriate, changing only the name of the context in which it is used.

For example, when the data element REMAINING AMOUNT is prefixed as follows, its meaning is almost obvious:

- MORTGAGE REMAINING AMOUNT
- INVENTORY REMAINING AMOUNT

But what about the issues of type, valid values, and so forth that were presented above? The answer is simple: provide the additional definition of a data element's semantics (rules of meaning and usage) outside the confines of a data element's name. With that approach, the semantics can be expressed in a form that is appropriate for the subject data element.

3.2.2.2 Data Types

The types of data represented by a data element include fixed- and variable-length character strings, integers, fixed- and floating-point numbers, and special data types such as date, time, and money.

Fixed-length character string data elements are appropriate for formatted data. Data involving paragraphs of text, comments, and addresses can benefit from variable length character strings.

Numbers are represented either exactly or approximately. Exact numbers are represented with a precision and a scale. Precision denotes the number of digits in the number. The number 346.98 has a precision of 5 because the number has five digits. Scale is the number of digits to the right of the decimal point. The number 346.98 has a scale of +2.

Integers are exact numbers with a scale of zero (0). That means that integers represent only whole numbers. The magnitude of these numbers is usually hardware-dependent. A typical hardware restriction is some number that is a power of 2, for example, 2 to the 24th power, or about 16,777,220. Some integer numbers are DBMS software-dependent. For example, FOCUS has a maximum length of 9 digits for integers. That means that an integer number can range from 0 to 999,999,999.

Fixed decimal numbers are exact numbers with a scale greater than zero. 3289.445 is an exact fixed-decimal numeric with a precision of 7 and a scale of 3.

Approximate value numbers are commonly known as either single precision or double precision floating numbers. Approximate numbers consist of a mantissa and an exponent. For example, in the number 5.87125×10^3, *5.87125* is the mantissa, and 10^3 is the exponent. Single precision implies that the mantissa can only be a certain length. Double precision implies a precision greater than single precision, usually twice as great.

Data types such as date, time, and money represent special uses of numbers. In addition to specifying the legal values for dates and time, a date-time facility also provides rules for operations. A money data type for American dollars would have the $ sign, commas, and appropriate rounding.

3.2.2.3 Data Element Structures

Structural composition clauses indicate whether a data element is single-valued, multi-valued, multi-dimensioned, a group, or a repeating group.

A single-valued data element, for example, PRODUCT-NAME, represents only one value per data record instance. Multi-valued data elements represent multiple occurrences of values, all of the same data type. Multiple-valued items have either one or more dimensions. A single-dimension, multiple-valued item is often called a vector or an array. Its values are distinguished positionally, that is, the first value, the second value, and so on. Figure 3.2 illustrates a multiple-valued item, TELEPHONE NUMBER, of a single dimension. If the multiple-valued item has more than one dimension, then a data element like SALES-BY-DISTRICT-BY-MONTH results, as depicted in Figure 3.3. It represents 120 values, 12 per year for 10 DISTRICTS, for each product record. The values in this multi-valued item are distinguished through the intersection of the *by* values. That is, the sales for *district* = <*value*> and for *year* = <*value*>.

Telephone numbers

3012495300	3012491142	7176485913	...

Figure 3.2 Multi-valued Data Elements

Some data elements are groups. A group data element has a name and a set of individually defined subordinate data elements, each with their own data element characteristics. For example, FULL-NAME might be subdefined into FIRST-NAME, MI, and LAST-NAME. A typical group data element is ADDRESS, illustrated in Figure 3.4. Within the group are subordinately defined data elements, each having its own data type specification.

The final data element type is repeating group, a group with multiple occurrences. For example, there might be a discount structure for product sales. For each DISCOUNT, there might be a QUANTITY-MINIMUM element, a QUANTITY-MAXIMUM element, and a PRICE element. In some DBMSs, a repeating group is additionally allowed to contain multi-valued data elements and other repeating group data elements. Figure 3.5 illustrates the repeating group DEPENDENT in the EMPLOYEE data record. Note that in this repeating group there is the additional repeating group data element, HOBBIES.

Sales Group Element (12X10X1)			
Dimension	12	10	1
Sub-element	Month	District	Value
Data value	JAN JAN JAN JAN JAN JAN JAN JAN JAN JAN FEB FEB FEB	1 2 3 4 5 6 7 8 9 10 1 2 3	\$2500 \$1800 \$1700 \$2900 \$1100 \$2300 \$2400 \$1600 \$1800 \$3300 \$3560 \$2200 \$3400

Figure 3.3 Multiple Dimension Data Elements

Address

Number

Street

City

State

Zip

Figure 3.4 Group Element

```
Employee-ID
  •
  •
  •
Dependents (rg)

     Name
     Sex
     Birth-date
     Hobbies (RG in Dependents)
          Hobby name
          Annual cost
```

Figure 3.5 Repeating Groups

3.2.2.4 Data Element Integrity Rules

Data elements are governed by integrity rules. These rules typically involve:

- Valid value ranges
- Specific valid values
- Invalid value ranges
- Specific invalid values
- Numbers of occurrences
- Duplicates allowed or disallowed
- Default values
- Conversion rules
- Null
- Encodes and decodes

```
ELEMENT IS JOB-TITLE, TYPE IS CHAR, LENGTH IS 10,
NULL IS NOT ALLOWED, DUPLICATES ARE ALLOWED
VALID VALUES ARE SENIOR, TRAINEE, MANAGER
```

Figure 3.6 Job-Type Data Element Definition

Figure 3.6 contains an example of the data definition language (DDL) for the data element JOB-TITLE. The only valid data element values for JOB-TITLE type are SENIOR, TRAINEE, or MANAGER. In this data element, duplicate values are allowed, but no-value (NULL) and JUNIOR are illegal.

3.2.3 Data Record Types

A data record type, in the context of a DBMS, is a collection of assigned data elements called data record elements. A DBMS allows data record instances, represented by the data record's definition, to be inserted, deleted, and sorted, and to be related to record instances of the same and different types.

From the DBMS point of view, the data record instance is just a string of data. Thus, if a data record instance is a statement of management policy, then the definition of that policy must be completed before the database application's logical database is developed.

In general, the syntax for a data record type specification consists of the clause that identifies the name of the data record, a clause identifying the primary key, clauses identifying other keys, one or more clauses enumerating the data-record-based integrity clauses, and a list of the data record elements identified as belonging to the data record.

Whenever data record elements are assigned to a data record, their role must also be defined. These roles are

- Primary key
- Secondary key
- Candidate key
- Foreign key (unique and nonunique)

3.2.3.1 Data Record Instance Name Clause

The data name clause typically consists of only the name of the data record instance and the name of the schema to which it belongs.

3.2.3.2 Data Record Instance Integrity Clauses

A data integrity clause represents a collection of computable rules that govern the acceptance or rejection of the data record instance as a whole. For example, record insertion might be denied if all the elements are not valued or if HIRE-DATE is less than the BIRTH-DATE or greater than the DEATH-DATE.

```
RECORD IS SALESPERSON;
ON STORE, CALL STORE-REC-PROC;
INDEXES ARE SSN, JOB-TITLE, REGION
DUPLICATES ARE NOT ALLOWED
FIELD IS SSN, TYPE IS ......;
FIELD IS EMPLOYEE NAME, TYPE IS....;
FIELD IS JOB-TITLE, TYPE IS .....;
FIELD IS REGION, TYPE IS ....;
.
.
.
RECORD IS.....
```

Figure 3.7 Salesperson Data Record Type Definition

In the example of the data record type EMPLOYEE, shown in Figure 3.7, the record name is EMPLOYEE; and on the data manipulation (DML) verb STORE, the procedure STORE-REC-PROC is invoked to process the record before its actual inclusion in the database. The DBMS will not allow duplicates for this data record type in the database. The DBMS is instructed by the DDL to build indexes for SSN, JOB-TITLE, and REGION. Finally, the data record elements in the data record type include SSN, EMPLOYEE-NAME, etc. The actual data represented by a data record type's definition is called a data record instance. A record instance for the data record type defined in Figure 3.7 might be

262625949¦Ed Wallish¦Manager¦North East¦. . . .

In this example, the ¦ symbol illustrates data element value separation.

3.2.3.3 Data Record Elements

When data elements are assigned to data record instances, data record elements result. When the DBMS allows only single-valued elements in each record, then its data record type is termed simple. When multi-valued elements, groups, and the like are allowed, the record structure is termed complex.

Some DBMSs allow data record types of such complexity that it is difficult to distinguish data record types from dependent structures within a data record type. For example, SYSTEM 2000's hierarchical data model permits any reasonable number of repeating groups on any level, up to 32 levels. Is the repeating group a data record type in its own right, or is it a dependent segment within a data record type? The following guideline establishes the difference:

> A data record type can be stored, retrieved, and deleted on its own, independently from others, while dependent segments need the location and context of other data record type instances for their own storage, retrieval, and deletion.

Given this guideline, SYSTEM 2000 only has one data record type per database.

A DBMS data record type almost always has a defined primary key with all dependent segments defined in subordinate roles. When a data record instance is deleted (after being selected by means of its primary key), all dependent segments are also deleted. In contrast, a dependent segment does not require a primary key of its own, especially in static relationships, because the dependent segment is accessed from within the context of a data record that has a key. Further, the dependent segment can be deleted without affecting the higher level segment instance. However, its deletion often affects lower level segments that may be defined in a subordinate relationship to the segment being deleted.

A SYSTEM 2000 implementation of the structure in Figure 3.8 results in two databases, each having one data record type. The first data record type has six segments, and the second has four. Each has only one data record type because a deletion of an instance of the COMPANY also removes all instances of the COMPANY's dependent segments. PRODUCT, PRODUCT SPECIFICATION, PRODUCT PRICE, REGION, and SALESPERSON are also deleted.

IDMS/R can implement the database illustrated in Figure 3.9 either as a single database with a set of simple independent data record types, or as a single database that contains several complex data record types along with several simple data record types. The segments that are related hierarchically can be implemented as independent simple data record types or as dependent segments with complex data record types. The database designer must define formal relationships (ANSI/NDL or CODASYL sets) to relate independent data record

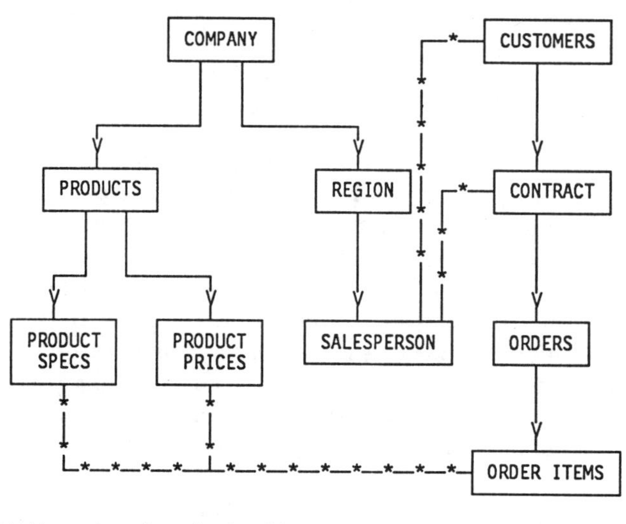

Figure 3.8 Hierarchical Data Model
Two Databases with 6 and 4 Record Types Each

types. No formal relationships have to be defined to relate dependent segments. Formally defined relationships (sets) are defined only between and among data record types, not among dependent segments.

3.2.3.4 Data Record Element Roles

All data record elements are attributes of the data record type. That is, they represent a quality or characteristic of the data record type. It is important to note that *attribute* implies a semantic affinity. Thus, it would not make much sense to assign the data record element HORSEPOWER to the data record instance EMPLOYEE.

Some of the data record elements assigned to a data record instance can serve one or more additional roles. These roles are commonly known as:

- Primary keys
- Candidate keys
- Secondary keys
- Foreign keys

In this context, a key represents a certain integrity or access characteristic.

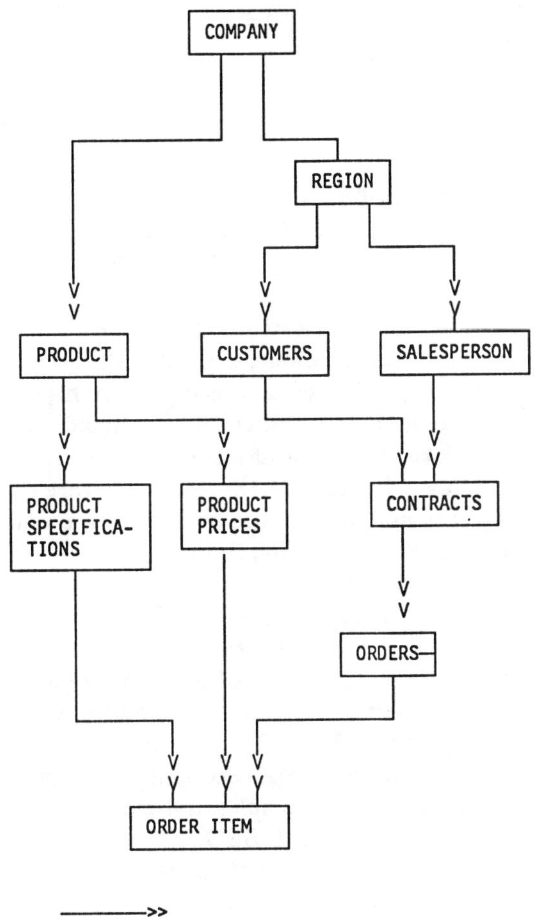

Figure 3.9 Network Data Model
One Database with Ten Record Types

When a data record element takes on the role of primary key, the value represented by the data record element uniquely identifies a data record instance. SOCIAL SECURITY NUMBER would likely be the primary key for an EMPLOYEE data record. There may be more than one data record element assigned to the primary key role. In such a case, the primary key is represented through a compound data record element. For example, the primary key for a STUDENT GRADE RECORD is likely to be the value represented by the combination of the values of five data record elements:

- STUDENT NUMBER and
- COURSE NUMBER and
- COURSE SECTION NUMBER and
- COURSE YEAR and
- SEMESTER.

The STUDENT NUMBER is the primary key of the student's data record type. The COURSE NUMBER, COURSE SECTION NUMBER, COURSE YEAR, and SEMESTER data record elements are together the primary key of the course-section data record type.

If a data record type EMPLOYEE has two data record elements representing unique values across all data record instances, for example, EMPLOYEE ID and SOCIAL SECURITY NUMBER, then only one of these data record elements can be the primary key. The other data record element is known as a candidate key. In the EMPLOYEE database, the primary key might be the combination of the two data record elements: EMPLOYEE NAME and BIRTHDATE. If this were the case, the SOCIAL SECURITY NUMBER would assume the role of a candidate key. The candidate key is a kind of alternate primary key, in that it can also be used to select a uniquely existing data record instance.

A role different from either primary or candidate key is secondary key. The secondary key role implies that the values, more often than not, appear in multiple data record instances. Thus, a query on the basis of a secondary key's value usually retrieves more than one data record. For example, a query to the EMPLOYEE data record instance on the basis of DEGREE = BA will retrieve all those employees who have been awarded the BA degree. A secondary key can be defined singly or as a compound secondary key. For example, in the STUDENT GRADE data record, COURSE NUMBER and COURSE SECTION NUMBER and COURSE YEAR and SEMESTER would be the data record elements necessary to identify the complete set of students that had enrolled in the particular course section. Both data record elements, YEAR and SEMESTER, are needed to screen out the students who had taken the same course in earlier semesters.

When a primary key is a compound data record element, one or more of the data record elements comprising the primary key may also be a secondary key.

Foreign key is the last of the types of roles that a data record element can assume. A foreign key generally takes on the characteristics of a secondary key with the additional constraint that it is the primary key of another data record. Thus, in the example of the STUDENT GRADE RECORD where the primary key is represented by the five data record elements: STUDENT NUMBER and COURSE NUMBER and COURSE SECTION NUMBER and COURSE YEAR and SEMESTER, the data record elements COURSE NUMBER, COURSE SECTION NUMBER, COURSE YEAR, and SEMESTER additionally take on the role of a compound foreign key. That is, COURSE NUMBER, COURSE

SECTION NUMBER, COURSE YEAR, and SEMESTER together, are the primary or candidate key of the data record instance COURSE SECTION. Further, within the COURSE SECTION data record type, COURSE NUMBER is a foreign key to the COURSE data record instance in which it is the primary key.

It is obvious from the foregoing presentation that a data record element can take on multiple roles. The IRDS must be able to reflect them all.

3.2.3.5 Physical Implications of Data Record Instance Structures

If a data record instance has all fixed length data record elements assigned to it, the physical effects are minimal. However, if a data record instance is complex and/or has variable length character data record elements, then the DBMS has to be quite sophisticated to handle the complexity in an acceptable manner.

A number of benefits result from having complex records. For example, if an EMPLOYEE data record instance is to be defined, most of the data record elements that relate only to the EMPLOYEE can be defined and stored in one logical unit. Along with the EMPLOYEE's basic biographical information, it is important to collect and store pre-employment interview results, prior company work experiences, education, courses attended, dependents, benefits selected, and so on. To require the definition of completely separate data record types, replete with their own primary keys and referential integrity constraints for each of these data groupings, over and above the definition of the main EMPLOYEE data record type, is to make work where none should be.

It is a perfectly good idea and discipline to specify data record types in third normal form, but it is absurd to require that data record types be implemented that way in the face of sophisticated complex data record instance capabilities. Not only does the process of definition take longer, but computer performance often suffers dramatically. In a benchmark between a relationally implemented database and an equivalent one implemented with complex data record instances, the DBMS with complex records performed 300% better.

In dynamic relationship DBMSs, data record instances are normally stored contiguously. Because of this, most dynamic relationship DBMS data record types are simple. Some are complex, but dynamic relationship DBMS vendors typically recommend only one level of repeating groups in order to have data record instances that can be stored in a computer-efficient manner. Dynamic relationship DBMSs thus have either simple data record instances or complex data record instances with only one nested level.

In some static relationship DBMSs, the data record types can have complex structures such that the segments are stored noncontiguously from the main part of the data record instance. These noncontiguous segments are connected by DBMS-generated addresses. Consequently, a complex data record type, which implies a significant amount of data (maybe 5000 characters), can be stored in a computer-efficient manner.

3.2.3.6 Data Record Instance Summary

A fully defined data record instance consists of data record type semantics, and data record elements and associated clauses containing directly and indirectly the appropriate combination of the following categories of information:

- Data record instance name
- Data record instance description
- Data record element name
- Data record element description
- Data type, length, and picture clauses
- Data record element role identifiers (primary, candidate, etc.)
- Valid value entries
- Invalid value entries
- Range value entries
- Encode/decode entries
- Referenced domain name
- Referenced domain description
- Referenced domain's valid value entries
- Referenced domain's invalid value entries
- Referenced domain's value entries

Completely defining data record types and their associated data record elements is not a simple task. To support the definitions there must be a sophisticated IRDS to store all these business semantics.

3.2.4 Relationships

A relationship is the manifestation of a business rule between two or more data record instances from the same or different data record types. As an example, a company might require that all employees be assigned to a project, or that an employee be assigned to a department, or (in the case of a University) that all teachers must belong to a college and teach at least one course. Such business rules, manifest in a database as relationships, can be either arbitrary or computed. A relationship is arbitrary when the set of rules that binds records together is not reflected in the set of values stored in one or more data record elements contained in the data record instances. A relationship is computed when the set of rules is manifest as commonly shared data record element values.

The following example illustrates both arbitrary and computed relationships. A company's regional manager determines, once each quarter, that a certain set of salespersons are the BEST SALESPERSONS.

If the relationship between the sales manager and the salespersons selected for the honor is arbitrary, then the rules determining the set of BEST SALESPERSONS might only be known to the sales manager. Once the decisions had been made, the sales manager would create the list of SALESPERSONS belonging to that category. The mechanism that relates the sales manager to all these SALESPERSONS is the relationship.

Alternatively, if the relationship between the sales manager and the SALESPERSONs selected is to be computed, then all the factors that determine the BEST SALESPERSONS category must be known to all and stored in the data record instances, so that a mathematical formula involving all the data record elements representing the factors can be created and used to find the SALESPERSONs satisfying the BEST SALESPERSONS category.

Arbitrary and computed relationships differ in one very important respect: explicit semantics. In the case of arbitrary relationships, the semantics that bind the records are known to the sales manager, personally. In the case of computed relationships, the semantics must be known to all, democratically.

Relationships are an extremely critical component of database, and cannot be fully understood until the following topics have been examined:

- Relationship types
- Relationship implementation mechanisms
- Referential integrity

3.2.4.1 Relationship Types

There are eight types of relationships that can be defined among data record instances. These are

- One-to-many
- Owner-multiple-member
- Singular-one-member
- Singular-multiple-member
- Recursive
- Many-to-many
- One-to-one
- Inferential

3.2.4.1.1 One-to-Many Relationships

The most common relationship is one-to-many, also known as owner-member. An example of this relationship type is: *COMPANY has many EMPLOYEES.* In the case of an IRDS, an example is: *Data record instance has many data record elements.* The relationship is hierarchical in nature. That is, for each owner instance, there can be one or more member instances. The relationship is graphically represented with an arrow that has two heads on one end (——>>). The point of the arrow touches the member and the shaft end touches the owner (owner ——>> member). In Figure 3.9, all the relationships, starting at the top of the figure and preceding to the bottom, are owner-member relationships.

Figure 3.10 illustrates a one-to-many relationship that exists between the two record types PARENT and CHILD. An instance of the relationship is illustrated. Note that the relationship is not the records, but the mechanism of connection between the records. Thus, in the relationship CHILDREN, there are four links that are the relationship, as well as four data record instances.

Figure 3.11 depicts an IRDS owner-member relationship that exists in an IRDS between a data element's domain and the data element. For each data element there can be only one domain, while there may be many data elements governed by one domain.

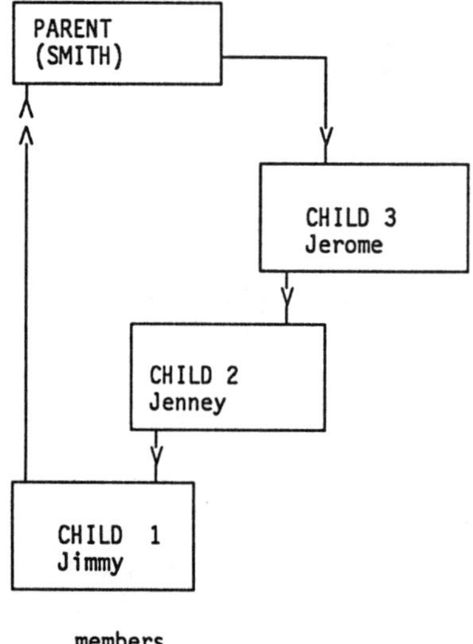

members

Figure 3.10 Regular Owner-member Set
Set type: Regular, Single Member

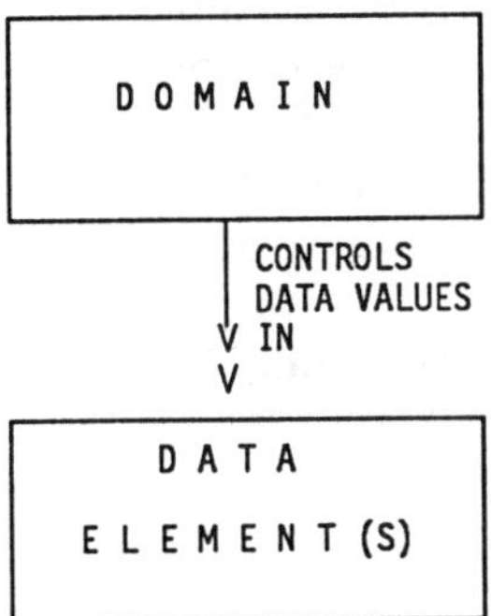

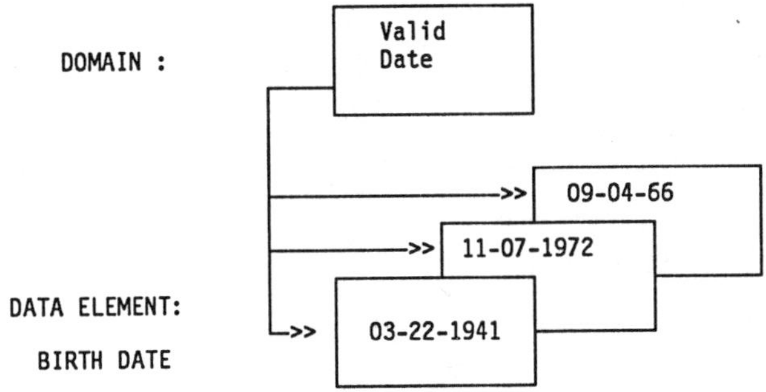

Figure 3.11 One-to-many Relationship

3.2.4.1.2 Owner-Multiple-Member Relationships

An owner-multiple-member relationship is an owner-member relationship in which there are multiple-member data record types. This type of relationship is necessary when a single relationship is expressed across multiple types of diverse data. For example, a company has different classes of employees and keeps different quantities of data for each class. To interrelate all the employees from the different classes, a single relationship is needed from COMPANY through each of the different classes. Such a relationship has COMPANY as the OWNER, and PART-TIME-EMPLOYEES, FULL-TIME-EMPLOYEES, and RETIRED-EMPLOYEES as the members.

Another use of the owner-multiple-member relationship is found in sales and marketing. Companies typically have their sales regions divided into territories, where each territory has one salesman and multiple customers. The owner-multiple-member relationship would thus have REGION as the owner, and

SALESMAN and CUSTOMER as the members. This relationship would be processed by accessing an owner record instance, for example, the San Francisco region, then accessing the salesman and each of the customers assigned to the territory.

Figure 3.12 illustrates the definition of a multiple-member relationship TERRITORY. The owner is REGION and the members are SALESPERSON and CUSTOMER.

Figure 3.13 illustrates an instance of another multiple-member relationship

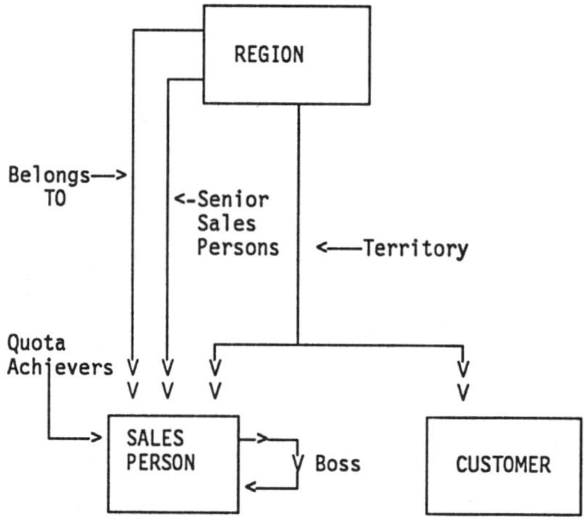

Figure 3.12 ANSI Network Data Model Relationships

in which the owner data record type is MACHINE TYPE, and the member data record types are SALESPERSON and STORE. An owner data record instance is Vending Machine, and the STORES in which vending machines are placed are the Arrowsmith Archery, the Hi Rise Bakery, and the Hard Knock Hardware Store. Finally, the SALESPERSON is Jones.

Here is a final example of multiple-member relationships. If there are separate data record types for each marketing program due to different data record elements, and if they are *owned* by a marketing campaign record, then the multiple-member relationship permits the review of all records from all members through the traversal of one relationship, rather than requiring a different relationship for each member data record type. This capability saves relationship

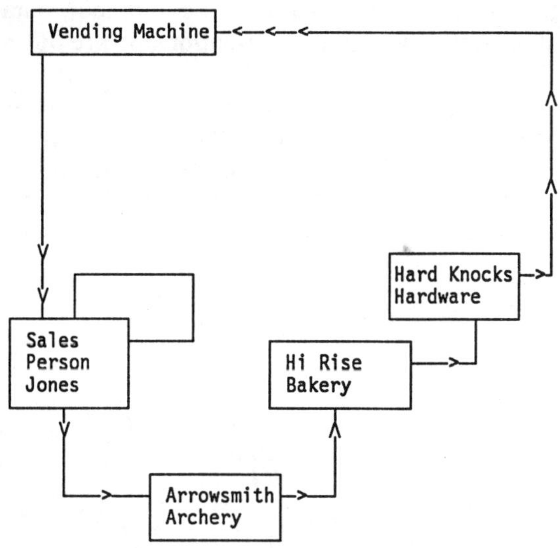

Set: Territory

Owner: Machine Type

Member: Salesperson, Store

Figure 3.13 Relationship Type: Multi-Member Set

definition time and programming time, and greatly eases report writing syntax.

Each of the records in the multiple-member relationship must be capable of standing on its own. It must have its own primary key, data record element definitions, data record element and data record check clauses, data record instance lengths, data record instance sort clauses, ability to participate in other relationships, and ability to be stored within the same or different O/S files.

3.2.4.1.3 Singular-Single-Member Relationships

A singular-single-member relationship is so named because it is defined to contain only one data record type, a member. There is no owner data record type. The need for an ownerless relationship arises when it becomes necessary to relate data record instances from the same data record type without there being a naturally existing--different--owner data record type. For example, in Figure 3.9 there is no naturally existing data record type that is the owner of the COMPANY data record type instances. The singular-single-member relationship interconnects all COMPANYs that have a profit margin above a certain percentage.

Another example of a singular relationship is all the employees who are HIGH-ACHIEVERS, where FULL-TIME-EMPLOYEES is the member data record type, and the data record instances that belong to the relationship are those determined to be high achievers.

Figure 3.14 illustrates a singular relationship of one member. The member is FAMILY MEMBER, and the relationship name is FAMILY. There is no owner. The instance of the relationship shows that the family members are shown in

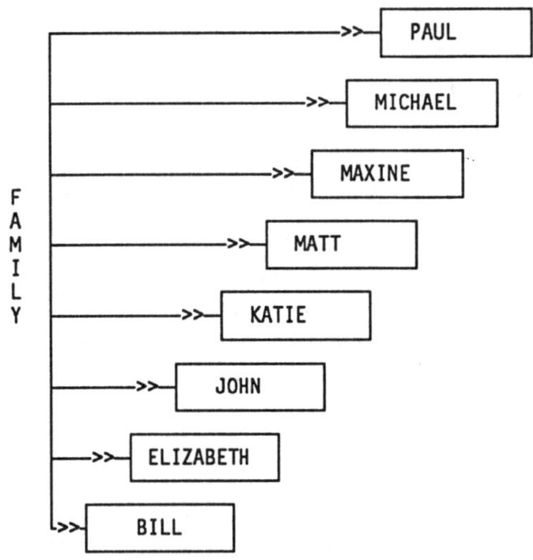

Set type: Singular, single member

Figure 3.14 Relationship Type: Singular Set

alphabetical order. From the information given in the figure, it is not possible to know whether the relationship binding mechanism is static or dynamic. If the relationship binding is static, then the data record instances were sorted by name before loading. It is also possible that the family named the children in alphabetical order in the order of their BIRTHDATES. If that were true, then an instance of the FAMILY relationship from another family would most likely not show the children's names in alphabetical order.

If the relationship binding mechanism is dynamic, then the presentation order of the data records could be alphabetic by coincidence, or else there must be a sort clause in the program that retrieves the set of data record instances belonging to the specific family.

One of the important differences between static and dynamic relationship binding is sorting. If the relationship binding is static, then the sort rules can be contained in the data definition language (DDL). As data record instances are stored in the database, the relationships that thread through the data record instances are an implementation of these ordering rules. It is important to note

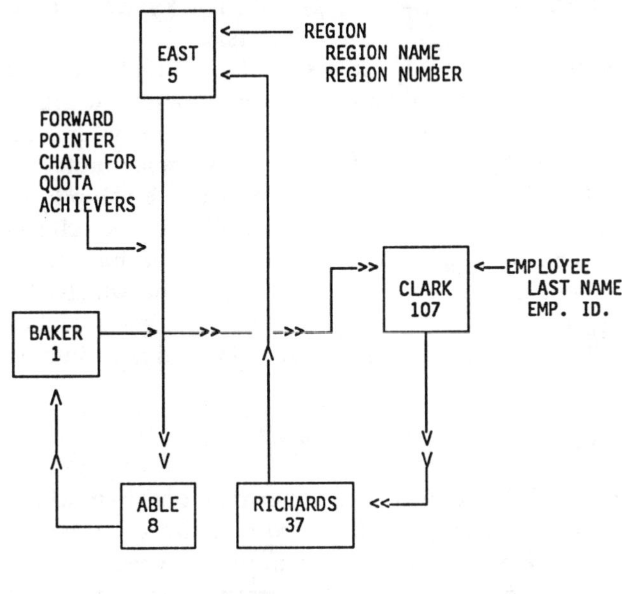

MEMBERS

Chain Represents Forward Alphabetical Order

Stored in EMPLOYEE-ID ORDER

Figure 3.15 Physical Relationship Illustration

that a DDL-based sorting clause between an owner and its members creates a logical ordering of the data record instances, not a physical ordering. Figure 3.15 illustrates this point. The EMPLOYEE data record instances are stored in EMPLOYEE-ID order. This is depicted by the increasing EMPLOYEE-ID starting with Baker to Able to Richards to Clark. There is, however, a relationship between REGION and EMPLOYEE that is ordered on LAST-NAME. Figure 3.15 illustrates this alphabetic ordering, which begins with Able, and continues through to Richards.

If the relationship is dynamic, then the ordering among the data record instances is completely controlled on the selected data record instances at retrieval time.

3.2.4.1.4 Singular-Multiple-Member Relationships

A singular-multiple-member relationship has no owner data record type, but more than one member data record type. There may be one or more member instances from each of the member data record types for each relationship occurrence. A typical example for the relationship is HIGH-ACHIEVERS, but unlike a singular relationship, all the different types of employees can participate. That is, PART-TIME-EMPLOYEES, FULL-TIME-EMPLOYEES, and RETIRED-EMPLOYEES.

A singular-multiple-member relationship is essentially multiple lists of different data record type instances. There might be different types of customer data record types, each having a different set of data record elements, but all participating in a single relationship BEST ACCOUNTS. The singular-multiple-member relationship BEST ACCOUNTS would be the list of relationship links from all the instances of the different data record types according to the criteria that made them best accounts. The definition of a *best account* does not have to be value-based. That is, there does not have to be a value upon which the relationship is based, such as TOTAL-ORDERS. If singular-multiple-member relationships were required to be value-based, then the DBMS would not conform to ANSI/NDL.

3.2.4.1.5 Recursive Relationships

Recursive relationships are a special class of owner-member relationship in which the owner data record type and the member data record type are the same. A recursive relationship exists between one instance of a data record type and other instances from the same data record type. Over the years, recursive relationships have been known as nested relationships, looped relationships, and bill-of-materials relationships. When data record instances of a given data record type are associated with other data records from the same data record type, the graphic symbol used to represent the relationship is a loop. Figure 3.16 presents the recursive relationship. Recursive relationships represent hierarchies of varying

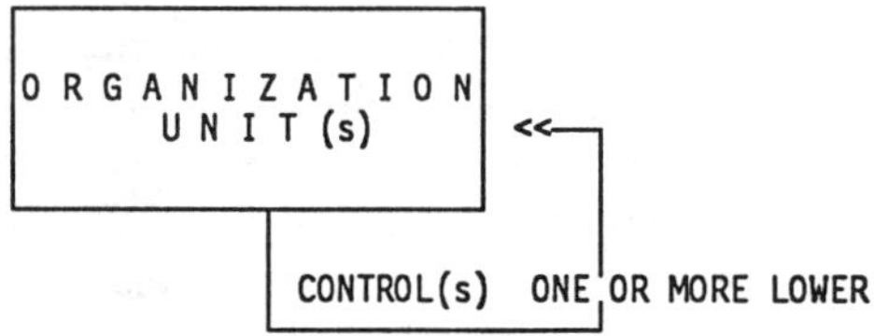

Figure 3.16 Recursive Relationship

depths within one structure. For example, within a company's chart there can be different levels, depending on the suborganizations. Figure 3.17 illustrates that very situation. A company is divided into two divisions. Each division is divided into subordinate areas. San Francisco is subdivided, and within San Francisco, the Silicon Valley is subdivided.

Prior to the *invention* of recursive relationships, a database might be hierarchically structured to represent the five levels. Each level would have to be assigned a name, indicative of its level. In the example we have been using, the levels might be as follows:

- Company
- Division
- Region
- District
- Territory

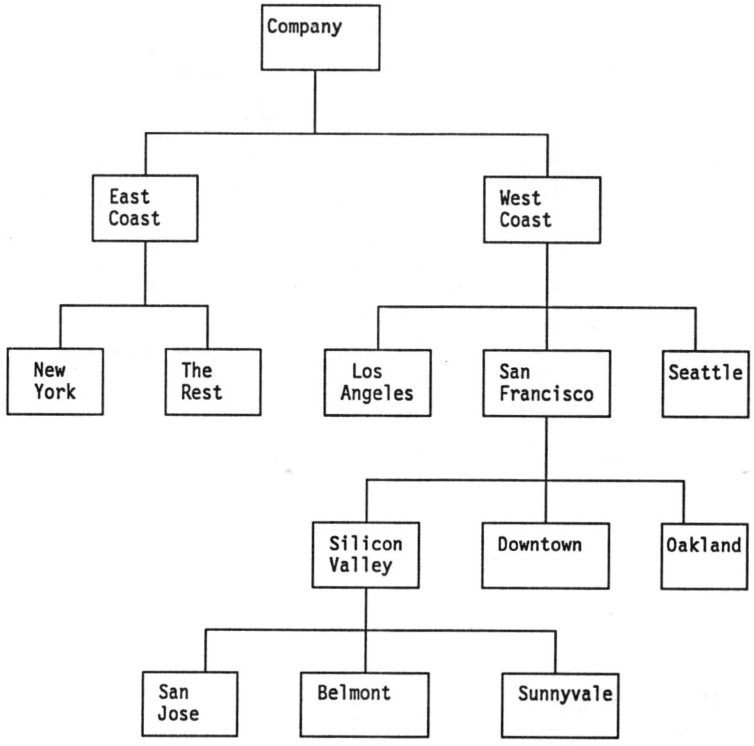

Figure 3.17 Hierarchical Layout of Company Organization Chart

The four names fit just fine: West Coast division, San Francisco Region, Silicon Valley District, and Belmont territory. But what about other cases? Is New York a region, a district, or a territory? If it is a territory, are there then phantom regions and districts between the East Coast division and New York?

In addition to these kinds of problems, there is also the negative impact of having to add an additional level. For example, suppose there was a need to divide San Jose into three subordinate units. The database would have to be restructured into six levels to reflect the organizational change. Along with the database design changes there would also be programming changes for update and retrieval.

Recursive relationships are a way to avoid this difficult situation. A DBMS that supports recursive relationships allows a relationship to be defined with the owner data record instance and the member data record instance belonging to the same data record type. In the example, the owner data record instance would be ORGANIZATIONAL UNIT, and the member data record instance would also be ORGANIZATIONAL UNIT. Some DBMSs that support recursive relationships keep a *hidden* set of pointers, maintaining the order of the organization chart, all

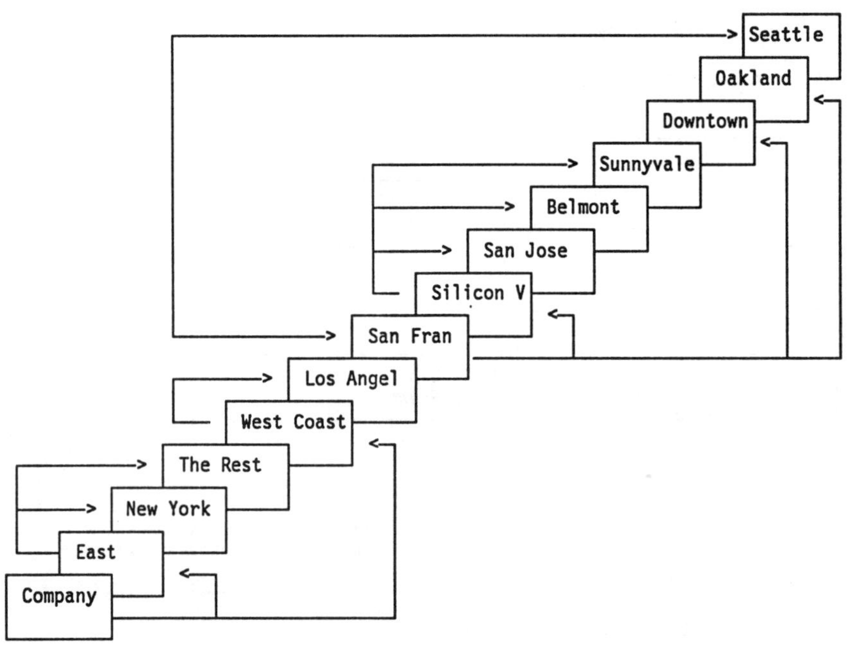

Figure 3.18 Recursive Layout of Company Organization Chart

in one data record type. Figure 3.18 illustrates the net effect of the one data record type approach to recursive relationships. Any number of offices can be added at any level, and any number of additional levels can also be added, all without any database redesign or programming changes. The ANSI NDL fully defines the recursive relationship and the data manipulation operations necessary to process the data record instance set.

Not all network DBMSs can explicitly define and process a recursive relationship. IDMS/R, for example, simulates the recursive relationship by defining and implementing two data record types. One data record type is ORGANIZATIONAL UNIT and the other is SUBORDINATE

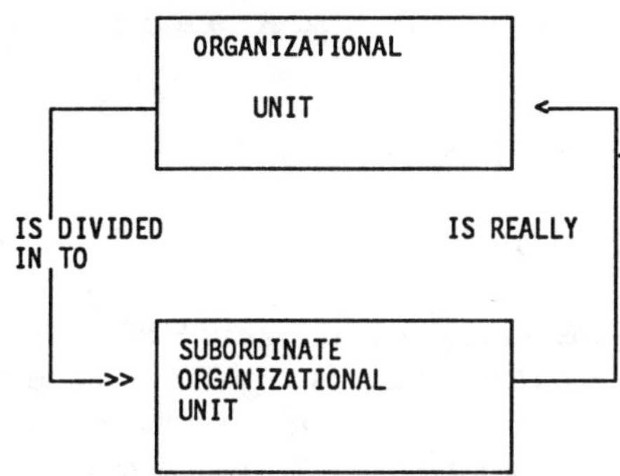

Figure 3.19a IDMS/R Method of Representing Recursive Relationships

ORGANIZATIONAL UNIT	SUBORDINATE ORGANIZATIONAL UNIT
Company	East coast, West coast
East coast	New York, the rest
West coast	Los Angeles, San Francisco, Seattle
San Francisco	Silicon Valley, Downtown, Oakland
Silicon Valley	San Jose, Belmont, Sunnyvale

Figure 3.19b Sets of Data Records Loading IDMS/R Recursive Relationship

ORGANIZATIONAL UNIT. Figure 3.19a shows these two data record types and the relationship types between them. The data record instances that are represented by this two-level hierarchy are shown in Figure 3.19b. IDMS/R requires the decomposition of the recursive relationship into two different relationships: a one-to-many and a one-to-one. The one-to-many relationship is reflected in Figure 3.19a as *COMPANY is divided into EAST COAST and WEST COAST*. The one-to-one relationship exists between the SUBORDINATE ORGANIZATIONAL UNIT and ORGANIZATIONAL UNIT. For example, WEST COAST (subordinate organizational unit) is related to WEST COAST (organizational unit).

3.2.4.1.6 Many-to-Many Relationships

A common relationship type in a database is the many-to-many relationship. This relationship, like the one-to-many relationship, involves two different data record instances. The relationship, however, is one-to-many in BOTH directions. The first of the data record types is defined as the owner of the second, and the second of the data record types is defined as the owner of the first. A common example of a many-to-many relationship is:

1) each STUDENT is taught by many TEACHERS and

2) each TEACHER teaches many STUDENTs.

An instance of this many-to-many relationship appears in Figure 3.20.

Another example of a many-to-many relationship is registered owners of automobiles. Several persons can be the registered owners of one automobile, and several automobiles can be owned by one person. Figure 3.21 illustrates instances of this many-to-many relationship.

	COURSE		
STUDENT	MATH 203	ENGLISH 701	BIOLOGY 107
JONES		YES	YES
SMITH	YES	YES	YES
JACKSON	YES		

Figure 3.20 Many-to-Many Relationships

In an IRDS database application, the many-to-many relationship is very important. Figure 3.22a presents a many-to-many relationship. Instances of this many-to-many relationship are presented in Figure 3.22b and they show that the ZIP CODE data element is contained in the EMPLOYEE and COMPANY data record types, and the COMPANY data record type contains the CITY and ZIP CODE data elements. Examples of many-to-many relationships in an IRDS include:

- Policy governs many objects, and an object reflects many policies.
- A data record element is represented in many data record types, and a data record type represents the inclusion of many data record elements.

In the event that a DBMS cannot directly support a many-to-many relationship, the many-to-many relationship must be decomposed into two one-to-many subrelationships. To accomplish the decomposition, a third data record type is created to act as the *member* that both *owners* point to. Figure 3.23a illustrates the three data record type decomposition of the two data record type many-to-many relationship illustrated in Figure 3.22. Figure 3.23b presents the instances from that three data record type decomposition.

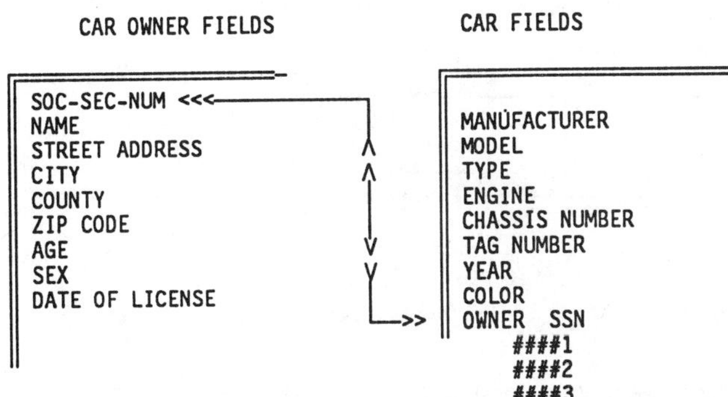

Figure 3.21 Many-to-Many Relationship Illustration

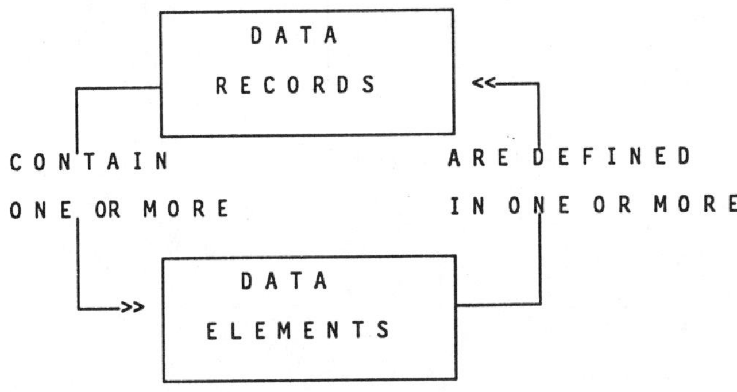

Figure 3.22a Many-to-Many Relationship (direct)

3.2.4.1.7 One-to-One Relationships

The one-to-one relationship is not employed often. It binds a single data record instance from one data record type to a single data record instance of another data record type. The most common use of this relationship type is to segment the data record elements from one data record type into two or more data record types. Suppose a data record type had four hundred data record elements, and that 90% of the time only 10% of the data record elements were accessed, and that the other 90% of the data record elements were accessed only 10% of the time. If a one-to-one relationship type were used to segment the data record type into two data record types, 360 data record elements could be in the little accessed data record type and the other, often accessed, 40 data record elements could be in the other data record type. Dramatic performance improvements would be achieved. While

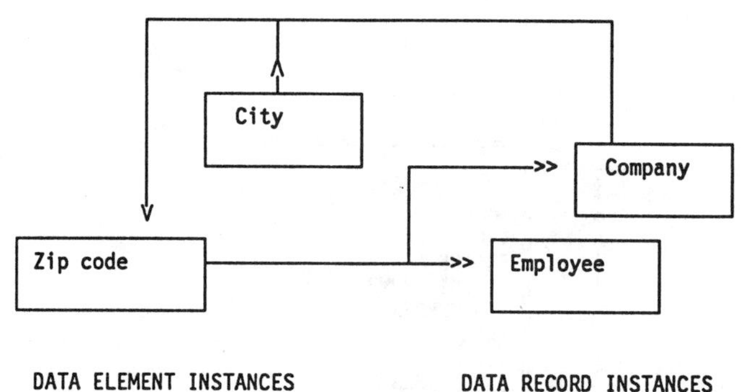

Figure 3.22b Many-to-Many Relationship (direct) --instances

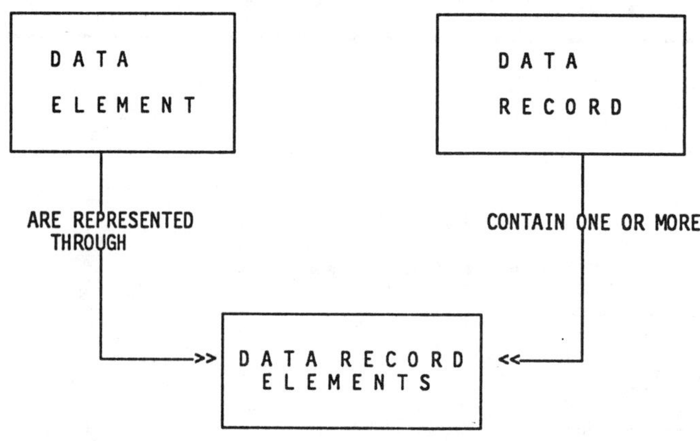

Figure 3.23a Many-to-Many Relationship (decomposed)

this is process analysis driving database design, such techniques are sometimes required to get a day's processing accomplished in just one day.

A one-to-one relationship specifies that there is one owner instance and one member instance without any program intervention for support. To say that the DBMS supports the relationship means that the DBMS, upon receiving a request to store a second member, would return an error message indicating that one member instance is already present. If the DBMS does not support one-to-one relationships, the application programmer is required to develop the logic to discover that there is already a member instance and to refuse to install an additional member instance.

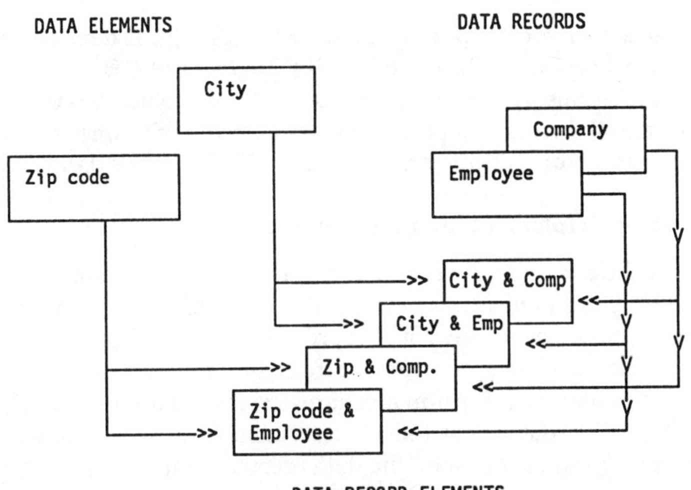

Figure 3.23b Many-to-Many Relationship (decomposed)--instances

3.2.4.1.8 Inferential Relationships

The inferential relationship relates data record instances from two data record types. This relationship, however, does not involve the primary key of either data record type. A typical example is PRODUCT-CONTAINER. The basis of the relationship is the dimensions of the product and the dimensions of the container. The relationship states that the product is able to fit in the container, but this does not mean that it is actually stored there.

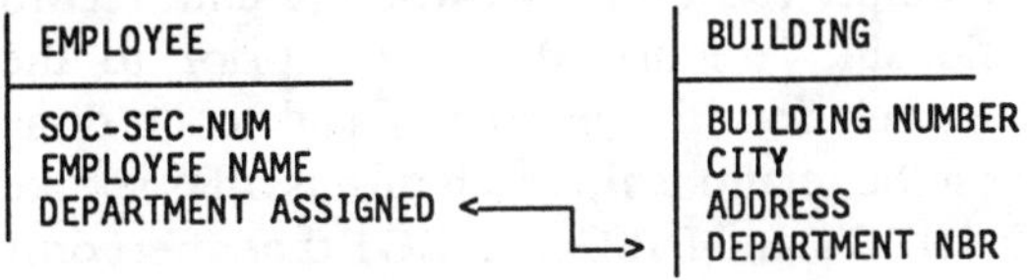

Figure 3.24 Inferential Relationship Illustration

Figure 3.24 illustrates another example of an inferential relationship. In this example, an employee is assigned to a department. In the other data record, a department is located in a building. The department may also be located in other buildings. The relationship between employee and building is thus inferential: it can be inferred that the employee is located in one of the buildings, but not specifically which building. If there are four buildings that house that department, then there is a 100% probability that the employee is in one of the four buildings, but only a 25% probability that the employee is in any randomly selected building.

3.2.4.1.9 Relationship Type Summary

Figure 3.12 illustrates a very important point. Even though it depicts only three different data record types, REGION, SALESPERSON, and CUSTOMER, there are five different relationships representing four different types. To presume that a valid and substantial database application can be served with one or a few types of relationships is to be operating database from Alice's Wonderland.

3.2.4.2 Relationship Implementation Mechanisms

Relationships are bound into data record instances through either a static or dynamic relationship mechanism. A static relationship mechanism is one controlled by the DBMS as the user performs data record instance additions or deletions. A dynamic relationship mechanism is one controlled by the end user.

In a DBMS with static relationship mechanisms, data manipulation operations both ADD and DELETE data record instances to and from the database and also modify relationship instances between the data record instances. For example, the DML ADD operation not only adds a data record instance to a database, but also triggers a DBMS action that creates a relationship instance that relates the just loaded data record instance to its owner(s), its member(s), or its sibling(s). Conversely, the DML DELETE operation not only deletes a data record instance from the database but also triggers a DBMS action that adjusts the relationship mechanisms among the data record instances that previously pointed to the just deleted data record instance. The data record instance relationship mechanisms affected would be the deleted data record's former owner(s), its former member(s), and its former sibling(s). Thus, in a DBMS with static relationship mechanisms, both the quantity of data record instances that participate in the relationship and the identities of the actual data record instances are known both before and after the ADD/DELETE operation. During a retrieval operation, these data records, already bound into relationships, are simply retrieved. Because the data record instances that participate in a relationship are already known prior to the execution of a retrieval statement, the relationship binding is said to be done statically. DBMS facilities that support static relationship mechanisms offer special relationship processing verbs like CONNECT and DISCONNECT that affect only the relationships that exist between data record instances. They do not affect the data record element values contained in the data record instances.

A dynamic relationship mechanism is always controlled by the end-user, as the relationship is manifest only through the value of a data record element within a data record instance. As a user ADDs or DELETEs a data record instance, not only is the data record instance added or deleted, the quantity of data record instances implicitly represented by the data record element's value (relationship) is also affected. If a CUSTOMER belongs to a specific TERRITORY, then both must be data record types, and the TERRITORY-IDENTIFIER must appear in the CUSTOMER's data record instance. The quantity of data record instances both before and after the ADD or DELETE can only be known by a SELECT clause (retrieval). Thus, the number of CUSTOMERs in a TERRITORY can only be known after the execution of a SELECT statement containing the condition . . . WHERE TERRITORY EQ <territory identifier>. Because the data record instances are known only upon the execution of a retrieval statement (SELECT), the relationship binding is said to be done dynamically. As a user performs a MODIFY that affects the value of the relationship bearing data record element, the relationship instance (materialized through a SELECT) in which the data record instance participates also changes. That means that a change to the TERRITORY-IDENTIFIER value changes the territory of the customer.

In both static and dynamic relationship environments, end user actions can affect relationship instances among data record instances. With static relationships, relationship membership changes take place because end user data record type actions--such as ADD and DELETE--trigger additional DBMS operations such as CONNECT and DISCONNECT. A MODIFY data record type operation cannot affect relationships among data record instances as data record element values do not directly participate in relationship operations. With dynamic relationships, the end user actions such as ADD, DELETE, and MODIFY directly affect the relationships.

Relationships that are required to be value-based are always dynamic. That is because the value that is the basis of a data record instance membership to a relationship instance is a contained data record element value.

Arbitrary relationships can be either static or dynamic. If there is a data record element in the SALESMEN data record instance called BEST SALESMEN and it contains the data value YES, then that arbitrary relationship is value-based (BEST=YES) and the relationship would be dynamic. If the arbitrary relationship is static, however, then the relationship identifier of the first *BEST SALESMAN* is stored in the regional manager's data record instance, and the relationship identifier of the second *BEST SALESMAN* is stored in the first salesman's data record instance, and so on. The most common form of the relationship identifier used in static relationships is the relative data record instance address. Figure 3.25 identifies the critical differences between static and dynamic relationships.

It is important to understand that a relationship instance that binds data records together may or may not also reflect the data record's physical order. For example, if EMPLOYEE data records are physically stored in the database in the order of birth, then a sequential access of the database also represents a chronological access. However, if EMPLOYEE record instances are stored in a physical sequence that is EMPLOYEE-ID, as illustrated in Figure 3.15, then it is very unlikely that a sequential access will produce data records in FULL-NAME alphabetical order. To accomplish the alphabetical order report, the data record instances must be copied from the database and sorted. Alternatively, there may be a separately maintained association among the data record instances that is used for data record instance access. Such an association (ANSI/NDL SET) is illustrated in Figure 3.26

This alphabetical association can be represented as relative data record instance address pointers stored in the data record instances. The association is easiest to create when the DBMS initially stores the data record instances. Upon

DBMS TYPE (Inter-record relationships)	
STATIC	DYNAMIC
Defined through DDL	Optionally defined
Created through DBMS	Created through user Defined field values
Bound at load/update	Bound at retrieval
Changed through delete and re-add	Changed through field update

Figure 3.25 Inter-record Relationships
Static and Dynamic Relationship DBMS Comparison

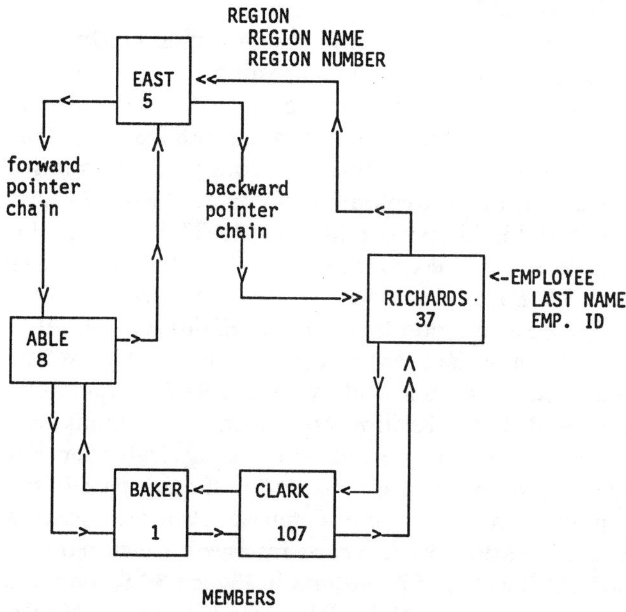

Figure 3.26 Chain Represents Forward and Backward Alphabetical Order
Logical Relationship Illustration

storage, the data record instance's address and the alphabetical value of FULL-NAME on which the sort is to be based are stored by the DBMS in a temporary work file. As the last data record instance is stored, the temporary work file is sorted by the DBMS by the FULL-NAME alphabetical key order. The stored data record instances can then be accessed by the DBMS in alphabetical order via the sorted set of data record instance addresses. The pointer space within the data record instance that is used for chaining to the *next* data record instance is filled with the address of the *next* data record instance and then the data record instance is written back to the database. This DBMS process of data record instance access and *next* data record instance address storage continues until the DBMS accesses and stores the alphabetical sequence of pointers in all the data record instances. The final data record instance, depending on the DBMS, usually contains a special flag to indicate *end-of-chain,* or points back to the owner data record instance.

After initial loading, the alphabetical order can be maintained by first storing the newly entered data record instance, then accessing the existing data record instances in alphabetical chain order until the data record instance is found that represents the immediately preceding alphabetical data record instance. Then, the address of the newly stored data record instance replaces the address of the existing *next* pointer in the alphabetically preceding data record instance. Finally, the *old* next pointer is stored in the new data record instance.

Traditionally, these pointers are stored in the data record instances. However, they might be stored in structures separated from the data records, commonly called pointer arrays. Regardless of how these pointers are stored, relationships are association mechanisms among data record instances that may have little or nothing to do with the actual storage addresses of the data record instances. This is certainly true if the *pointers* that point from one data record instance to another in the relationship chain are primary-key values such as EMPLOYEE-ID. If all the EMPLOYEE-IDs are stored in an array, having been first sorted by the alphabetical key, then when an EMPLOYEE-ID is accessed, it is used to locate and access the data record instance.

The advantage of having data values as relationship mechanisms instead of data record instance addresses is that data record instances can be relocated without having to modify relationship pointer addresses. The disadvantage is that, since the data value does not point directly to the location of the data record instance, extra database accesses are needed to locate and retrieve the data record instance. Figure 3.27 illustrates the use of primary keys as *next-pointers* in a relationship chain. The primary key value is the REGION-NUMBER data record element. The use of the EMPLOYEE-NUMBER as a next-pointer is represented in the data record instances as the value contained in angle brackets. The owner data record instance, REGION = East, contains the member-pointer value of <8>, which is the primary key value of the first member data record instance (EMPLOYEE = Able). The first member contains the next-pointer value of <1>, which is the primary key value of the next member data record instance (EMPLOYEE = Baker).

It is possible, however, for the mechanism of relationship to be a data value and the relationship still not be dynamic. In the case described above, the relationship is clearly static, for three reasons:

- The EMPLOYEE-ID value is intended solely to represent the alphabetical association of one data record instance to the next.

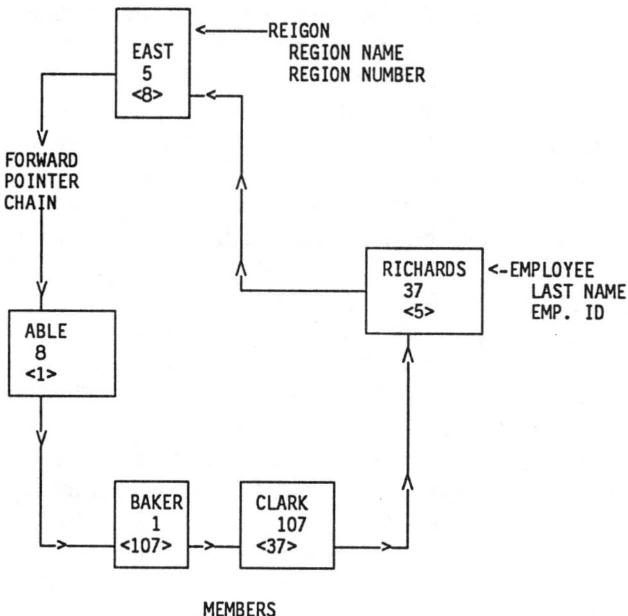

Figure 3.27 Chain Represents Forward Alphabetical Order Logical Relationship Illustration

- When a data record instance is removed, the alphabetical association among the data record instances breaks and an alphabetical scan is no longer possible: the data record instance whose *next* pointer was the primary key of the removed data record instance now points to nothing, and the data record instance whose *prior* pointer was the primary key of the removed data record instance also points to nothing.

- When a new data record instance is added, a dynamic relationship DBMS has no mechanism to add the data record instance in the proper location within the alphabetically sorted list of data record instances.

If the DBMS possesses the mechanisms to add, delete, and repair relationship links (whether pointer or data value), then the DBMS is static. Without these mechanisms, the DBMS is dynamic and must possess syntactic constructions within the interrogation languages to command the DBMS to discover which data record instances participate in relationships. A static relationship DBMS allows for the establishment of named relationships among two or more data record types. Additionally, a static relationship DBMS allows multiple data record type relationships to connect one owner data record type with one or more multiple-member data record types.

As stated many times above, there are two methods by which a DBMS knows of a relationship: static and dynamic. A static relationship is created by the DBMS and is normally stored in the *pointed-from* data record. A dynamic relationship is created by the user and is exercised by the DBMS through shared data value, one in the owner, and one in each of the *pointed-to* members.

3.2.4.2.1 Dynamic Relationships

The value-based relationship exists between two data record types when the element upon which the relationship is based contains values acceptable to the rules stated in the relationship.

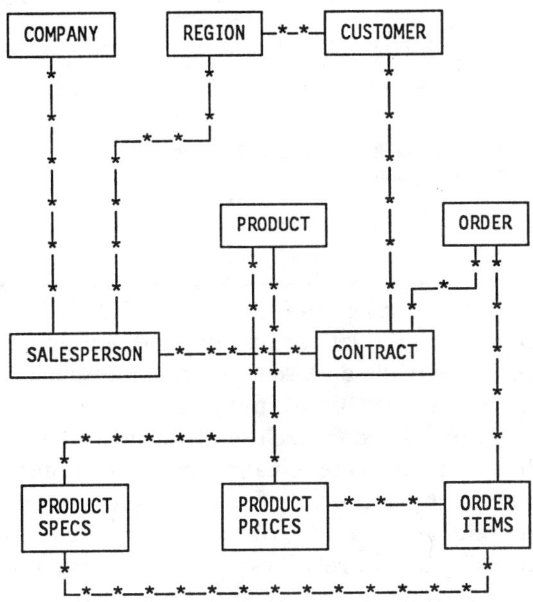

Figure 3.28 Relational Data Model
Ten Simple Record-type (Tables) Databases

For example, in Figure 3.28, the ORDER data record type with its element ORDER CONTRACT ID is related to the CONTRACT data record type with its element CONTRACT ID. A relationship exists between instances of these two data record types when a CONTRACT data record type data record instance's CONTRACT ID element contains the same value as the ORDER data record type data record instance's ORDER CONTRACT ID element. In this example, the relationship is one-to-many.

In a database system, if two data record instances are related to each other with two one-to-many relationships, one in either direction, and if the semantics of both relationships are the same, then the relationship between the two data record types has common semantics, and is termed a many-to-many relationship. Figure 3.29 shows a many-to-many relationship.

In a dynamic relationship DBMS, there are two ways to represent many-to-many relationships. Figure 3.30 illustrates the triple data record type representation. This technique is appropriate for ANSI/SQL and relational data model DBMSs. Figure 3.31 illustrates the double data record type representation,

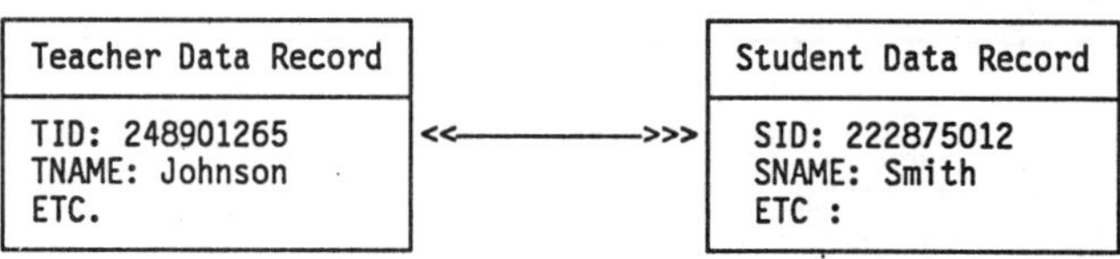

Figure 3.29 TEACHES Many-to-Many Relationship Between Student and Teacher

which is typically accomplished by independent logical file data model DBMSs. Of these two representations of a many-to-many relationship, only the double data record type representation is explicit. The triple data record type representation is, at best, a simulation of the many-to-many relationship type.

If the two data record instances are related to each other in two many-to-many relationships, one in either direction, and if the semantics of the relationship are the same, then the relationship between the two data record instances is really only one relationship, and only one relationship should be created and represented. If, however, the semantics of the two relationships are different, then the two relationships must be separately named, defined, created, and maintained. Figure 3.32 represents two many-to-many relationships between STUDENT and TEACHER, one for TAUGHT BY and the other for TUTORS.

Figure 3.27 shows a static, ordered relationship between REGION and EMPLOYEE. To accomplish that with dynamic relationships requires two steps. First there must be the REGION-NUMBER data record element in the EMPLOYEE data record type to store the value EAST. Second, the user must extract the appropriate data record instances (SELECT . . . WHERE REGION EQ EAST), and then sort the data record instance keys into the right order (BY LAST-NAME). In short, what is accomplished in a single step with static relationships requires two steps with dynamic relationships.

Most dynamic relationship DBMSs do not allow for the formal definition of relationships through DDL. Rather, the burden of knowing which relationships

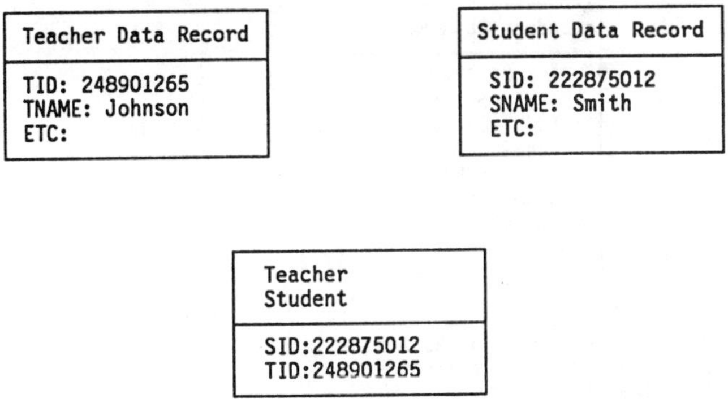

Teacher Data Record
TID: 248901265 TNAME: Johnson ETC:

Student Data Record
SID: 222875012 SNAME: Smith ETC:

Teacher Student
SID:222875012 TID:248901265

Figure 3.30 A Many to Many Relationship:
TAUGHT BY: Between Student and Teacher
Three Data Record Approach

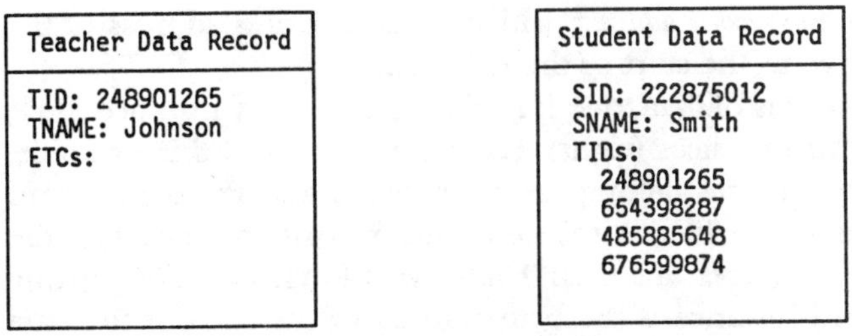

Teacher Data Record
TID: 248901265 TNAME: Johnson ETCs:

Student Data Record
SID: 222875012 SNAME: Smith TIDs: 248901265 654398287 485885648 676599874

Figure 3.31 A Many to Many Relationship:
TAUGHT BY: Between Student and Teacher
Two Data Record Approach

are defined and the burden of knowing how to select data record instances according to a relationship implied through commonly named data record elements is left to the user.

3.2.4.2.2 Static Relationships

Static relationships are sometimes called information-bearing relationships because the relationships themselves convey information that normally cannot be verified through data values. For example, when the first ORDER data record instance is retrieved for a given CONTRACT, it might be inferred that the first ORDER data record instance represents the first ORDER placed under the contract, the second data record instance represents the second ORDER, and so forth. The sequence of the data record instances corresponds to the date when the ORDER was placed.

Teacher Data Record
TID: 248901265 TNAME: Johnson TUTEE-ID: 222879815 223009876 872083567 123489748 265897654

Student Data Record
SID: 222879815 SNAME: Smith TAUGHT-BY-ID: 248901265 654398287 485885648 676599874

Figure 3.32 Two Many-to-Many Relationships:
TAUGHT BY: Student-to-Teacher
TUTORS: Teacher-to-Student

The static relationship mechanism is normally controlled by the software system that inserts and retrieves data record instances. The form of a relationship instance is normally a data record instance's relative data record instance's address within the O/S file. This address is stored in the data record instance's owner or prior member's data record instance. This location is commonly referred to as a data record instance's *relative record address*, which is the starting address of the data record instance relative to the start of the O/S file.

Figure 3.33, shows two sets of data, one for relationship array instances (left) and another for data record instances (right). For the purposes of this example, all the relationship array instances belong to one O/S file and the data record instances belong to another O/S file. Within the data record instance file, the EMPLOYEE data record instances are each 1000 bytes long, and the starting address of each data record instance is the byte address of the start of the data record. Thus, in the example, the relative data record instance address of the EMPLOYEE data record instance is 5000. The relationship arrays are similarly constructed, each being 10 bytes long. The second array is shown, starting at address 10. It ultimately points to its corresponding data record instance, EMPLOYEE, which has the data file relative data record instance address of 5000. The technique and benefits of separating relationships from the actual data record instances are presented in Chapter 4.

As another example of relative data record instance addresses, if a data record type's length is 100 bytes, and if each data record instance is stored in a DBMS physical data record instance that is 1000 bytes, there are 10 data record instances per physical data record. If the relative data record instance address of a data record instance is 37, the data record instance is the seventh data record instance of the fourth DBMS data record. The relative data record instance addresses of a data record instance are created and stored by the DBMS during data loading or data update.

If a mistake is made regarding the order of the database data record instances for ORDERs, the pointers that logically represent the order of the two data record instances must be physically reversed. For example, if the third ORDER is really

RELATIONSHIP POINTERS — DATA RECORDS

10 RTI	NEXT	MEMBER	OWNER	ADDRESS
Employe	???	20	????	5000

5000
EMPLOYEE

20 RTI	NEXT	MEMBER	OWNER	ADDRESS
Course	30	???	10	7500

7500
COURSE

30 RTI	NEXT	MEMBER	OWNER	ADDRESS
Course	40	????	10	8000

8000
COURSE

40 RTI	NEXT	MEMBER	OWNER	ADDRESS
Degree	????	????	10	9700

9700
DEGREE

RTI means record type identifier

Figure 3.33 Examples of Relative Record Addresses

the second, the second ORDER must be retrieved from the database into a computer program, its database representation deleted through a DBMS delete data record instance command, and then the computer program's representation of the data record instance stored back into the database *after* the next ORDER.

The control that must be exercised by the user over static relationship facilities through commands such as CONNECT, DISCONNECT, and sort orders is in marked contrast to the user's casual exercise of control over the dynamic relationship facilities through simple data record element value updates. To change the dynamic relationship merely requires a change to the data record element's value that is used as a basis of a relationship. For example, changing the current value of a CONTRACT ID in an ORDER data record instance to another value automatically changes the ORDER instance's CONTRACT.

Static relationship DBMS relationships are fast to traverse, but slow to update. There are three types of updates: add, delete, and modify. To add a relationship instance to a data record instance that is already stored, but not yet a member of a relationship, requires three steps:

- The user must obtain the data record instance that is to be a member.
- The user must invoke DML verbs to locate the proper position within the relationship chain, usually a GET NEXT command.
- The user must then invoke a DML verb like CONNECT that modifies the relationship references in the data record instance's prior and next data record instances to reflect the addition of the data record's relationship reference.

The relationship deletion operation is the inverse of the add operation. The modify operation is the combination of the delete operation and the add operation.

To review briefly, Figures 3.15 and 3.26 illustrate the collection of static relationships that bind data record instances. This collection forms a chain. The head of the chain--that is, the start of the linked relationship--is called the owner. In the owner data record instance there is a pointer that refers to the first member. In the first member there is a pointer that refers to the next member, and so forth. If the last member contains a pointer that refers back to the owner, the chain forms a ring. Some relationships also have prior and owner pointers.

The DBMS's relationship specification clauses state whether new data record instances are stored automatically at the front of the chain, at the end of the chain, or in sorted order. When the DBMS automatically sorts the relationships that represent the data record instances, the DDL sort clause contains one or more data record elements that serve as sort keys. The sort clauses clearly state how duplicate values for the combined sort keys are handled, that is, whether they are stored at the head or the tail of the chain, or rejected altogether.

Because a database built through a static relationship DBMS has a large collection of relationship and integrity clauses, the data is highly organized. All the data record instances are stored in a very specific order and can be retrieved only in that order. If there is to be any other order, the data record instances must be removed, placed in an external file, and sorted.

When the application's processing logic is the same as the organization of the data record instances in the database, the application runs very efficiently. When the application's processing logic is significantly different from the data record instance organizations in the database design, either the application cannot be carried out, or it performs very slowly, or the database has to be completely reorganized and reloaded before the application operates efficiently. When another new set of reports comes along, this database reorganization process must begin again.

3.2.4.3 Relationship Integrity

Relationship integrity, commonly called referential integrity, is a shorthand name for a defined set of rules and actions that apply to identified relationships. The rules relate to the type of relationships that must be maintained, and the actions are the identified activities that must take place to enforce a rule or respond to a change in the database in order to maintain the database's referential integrity.

Referential integrity rules govern relationships that involve both an owner and member data record type, for example, one-to-many or one-to-one. Referential integrity actions concern two basic data record instance operations ADD (insertion) and DELETE (retention). Referential integrity is affected by the type of relationship implementation mechanism that governs the ADD (insertion) and DELETE (retention) operations, in other words, by whether the DBMS uses static or dynamic facilities.

Specific actions, for example, reject, are taken when referential integrity conditions are not met. For example, there can be a referential integrity rule that rejects a DELETE data record instance command whenever that specific data record instance has other data record instances related to it as members. If this rule applied to CONTRACT and its corresponding ORDERs, the command DELETE CONTRACT WHERE CONTRACT ID EQ 1234 would be rejected if there were any orders related to that contract. If the action is the inverse, that is, to store a new ORDER data record instance, then there must be a corresponding parent CONTRACT data record instance or else the *child* data record instance is not allowed to be stored.

Another referential integrity action, NULL, means that when a *parent* data record instance deletion occurs all the member data record instances are specially modified to indicate a *no owner* condition. If a CONTRACT data record instance is deleted, all its corresponding ORDERs belong to the NULL contract set (static), or the CONTRACT ID data record element in ORDER is set to NULL (dynamic). If the action is the inverse, that is, to add a new ORDER data record instance, if the corresponding CONTRACT data record instance is not already present, then the ORDER data record instance belongs to the NULL owner set (static), or the CONTRACT ID data record element in ORDER is set to the NULL value (dynamic).

A final referential action is CASCADE DELETE. It is the same as DELETE except that all the data record instance members of a deleted member are also deleted. The CASCADE DELETE operation is most appropriate for hierarchies. For example, if the ORDER data record instance had ORDER-LINE-ITEMs member data record instances, it makes no sense to keep these when the ORDER itself is deleted.

3.2.4.3.1 Static Insertion Referential Integrity

Insertion referential integrity affects only the addition of new *member* data record instances. Generally, a member data record instance is allowed to be inserted (added) only if there is an appropriate *owner* data record instance already stored.

For static relationships, the *owner* data record instance is defined through the data definition language's relationship clause. Static referential integrity can be either value-based or arbitrary. In ANSI/NDL the insertion options are AUTOMATIC and MANUAL.

If the NDL relationship integrity is AUTOMATIC, then the data record instance can be inserted in the database only if it can also belong to at least one relationship instance. If the NDL relationship integrity is MANUAL, then the member data record instance is stored in the database without connecting it to a relationship instance.

As an example, if a company wants to pay only valid invoices, it would reject an invoice that did not relate to an already approved vendor and was not drawn against an approved open purchase order. APPROVED VENDOR and the PURCHASE ORDER are owners of the INVOICE, and the insertion options attached to the relationships between these two data record types and the INVOICE data record type are identified as AUTOMATIC. If both owner data record instances are not present, the insertion is rejected.

If the NDL insertion option is MANUAL, however, the INVOICE is accepted into the database without having to pass either of those two DBMS imposed tests. But, the INVOICE is not a part of any relationship instance between VENDOR and INVOICE, nor between PURCHASE ORDER and INVOICE.

3.2.4.3.2 Dynamic Insertion Referential Integrity

Dynamic insertion referential integrity also affects only the addition of new *member* data record instances. Again, a member data record instance is allowed to be inserted (added) only if there is an appropriate *owner* data record instance already stored.

For dynamic relationships, the DBMS attempts to select the appropriate owner data record instances (VENDOR and PURCHASE ORDER) and, if they are present, accepts the invoice for payment. The selection is through the use of the VENDOR ID and the PURCHASE ORDER ID that must be supplied with the invoice data record instance. If the owner instances are not present, then the test fails.

In this example, the basis of dynamic referential integrity is the VENDOR ID and the PURCHASE ORDER ID on the invoice. These are the primary keys of the VENDOR and PURCHASE ORDER data record types.

Dynamic insertion referential integrity has a capability analogous to the static manual insertion option. It is accomplished by the DBMS's referential integrity rule stating that either the PURCHASE ORDER ID or the VENDOR ID data record elements can contain the NULL value in the INVOICE data record instance. In such a case, the validity of the invoice can not be proven as there are no appropriate owner data record instances present.

3.2.4.3.3 Static Retention Referential Integrity

Data record instance retention referential integrity means that data record instances are retained in the database only under certain conditions, or until certain conditions are no longer fulfilled.

For an ANSI/NDL static relationship DBMS specification, there are three variations to retention: FIXED, MANDATORY, and OPTIONAL.

A data record instance that is governed by the FIXED retention option remains a member of the specific relationship instance to which it is initially connected until it is deleted from the database. For example, if a company has a database that stores invoices only until they are paid (open), then its retention is FIXED. Once an application program *cuts a check*, it would delete the invoice data record instance, which in turn, would cause the DBMS to delete the data record instance from the open invoice class.

If the company modified the system so that invoices remained in the database after they were paid, then one choice for the invoice data record's retention option would be MANDATORY. The invoice remains part of the database, so long as it belongs to some other relationship instance, for example, paid.

The company might further modify the bill paying system to allow the retention option of OPTIONAL. This allows the invoice to remain part of the database even though it belongs to neither of the two approved categories: open or paid.

The retention option dramatically affects delete statements. For example, if a deletion occurs to an owner data record instance in which there are members connected by a FIXED retention option, then all the members are also deleted. If the retention option is OPTIONAL, then the data record instances become disconnected, but still remain even if they do not belong to another relationship. Finally, if the retention option is MANDATORY, then the data record instances remain only if they are part of another relationship. For example, if the invoices are from an approved vendor, they are probably related to the vendor through a FIXED option. These same invoices probably belong to the INVOICE STATUS relationship with a MANDATORY option, or possibly an OPTIONAL option.

3.2.4.3.4 Dynamic Retention Referential Integrity

Dynamic retention referential integrity is analogous to the corresponding static facility. If the CASCADE option is specified, then the data record instance selected from the owner data record type and all the matching data record instances of the member are deleted. If the option is SET NULL, then the foreign key value in the member data record instance is set to NULL. If the option is SET DEFAULT, then the value is set to whatever value was established as the default.

3.2.4.3.5 Referential Integrity Surprises

Referential integrity initially is a simple concept. When fully specified in a production database, however, ambiguities and anomalies arise that produce surprising results. For the ANSI/SQL, referential integrity was not included in the first version of the standard (October, 1986). Since that time, X3H2 worked diligently to develop a special referential integrity addendum to the SQL standard, which combined with SQL/86, is now called SQL/89. During the development of the referential integrity addendum, X3H2 found that about one-third of nine different meetings (18 months) was spent reviewing members' papers dealing with referential integrity anomalies. At each instance of an anomaly, additional rules were placed in the addendum. One member remarked that the rules section on referential integrity was likely to be larger than the original standard itself!

One X3H2 member proposed that to determine inconsistent referential integrity, the vendor's SQL schema processor digest all the referential integrity statements and determine if there are ambiguous paths. A path is a candidate for ambiguity if, for example, there is more than one way to get from one data record instance to another. The path is ambiguous if different results are produced when the referential actions occur along the different paths. In this situation, the software that checks for referential integrity consistency must not accept definitions of referential integrity actions that result in ambiguity.

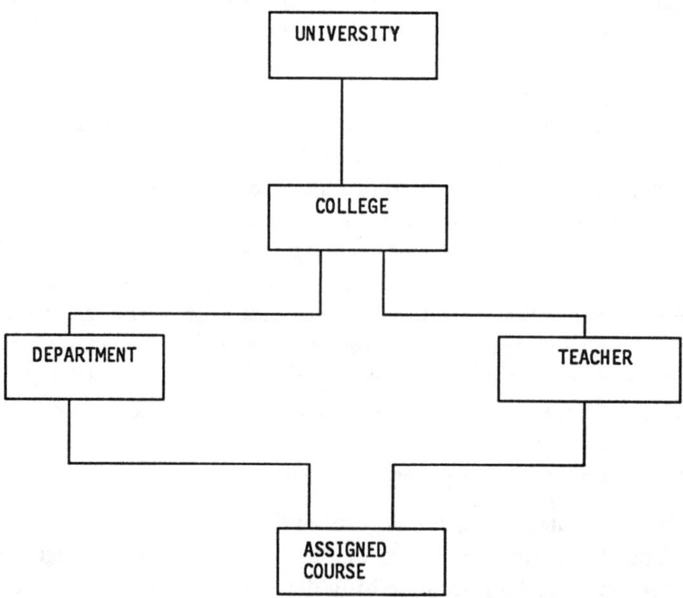

Figure 3.34a Ambiguous Referential Integrity Access Path Data Record Types

Figure 3.34a and 3.34b illustrates the types of problems that can arise with referential integrity. In these Figures, there are five data record types: UNIVERSITY, COLLEGE, DEPARTMENT, TEACHER, COURSE. There is also an appropriate set of data record instances for these data record types. Because the

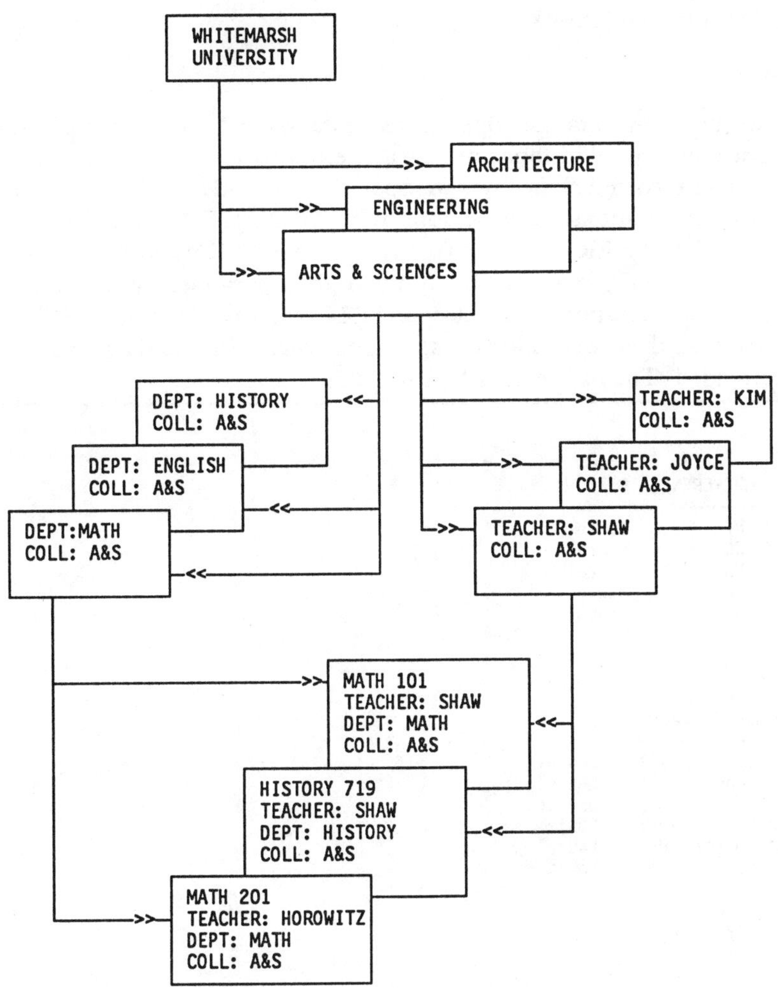

Figure 3.34b Ambiguous Referential Integrity Access Path Data Record Instances

data record types are all connected, it is possible to get different results when an update occurs on the COURSE data record type, based on data record element selection criteria in COLLEGE data record type. For example, DELETE COURSE WHERE COLLEGE EQ 'ARTS & SCIENCES'. If the DEPARTMENT side of the diagram is traversed, the COURSEs deleted are those connected to the DEPARTMENTs, which in turn are connected to the selected COLLEGEs. If however, the TEACHER side of the diagram is traversed, the COURSEs deleted are those taught by TEACHERs of the COLLEGEs selected. As Figure 3.34b illustrates, the data record instances deleted depend on which side of the diagram is traversed. Hence, the ambiguity.

3.2.5 Operations

There are three types of database operations: data record, relationship, and combination. The data record instance retrieval operations are: FIND, GET, and PROJECT. The data record instance update operations are ADD, DELETE, and MODIFY. The eleven relationship operations are: CONNECT, DISCONNECT, JOIN, DIVIDE, GET OWNER, GET MEMBER, GET NEXT, INTERSECTION, DIFFERENCE, PRODUCT, and UNION. Some of the operations are actually a combination of several operations, for example, FETCH, MODIFY, and INSERT.

To understand all these operations, a set of relational tables and data record instances are provided. They appear in Figure 3.35.

Relation : Team

T#	TNAME	CONFERENCE	CITY
T1	Black Birds	NE	Bowie
T2	Capitals	SE	Laurel
T3	Metros	NW	Laurel
T4	Bears	NE	Bowie
T5	Maulers	NW	Croom

Relation : Player

P#	PNAME	COLLEGE	WEIGHT	CITY
P1	Jackson	Colby	180	Bowie
P2	Beaner	Hamline	165	Laurel
P3	Tufts	St. Mikes	165	Savage
P4	Tufts	Colby	205	Bowie
P5	Larson	St. Mikes	180	Laurel
P6	Bowes	Colby	190	Bowie

Relation : Team-Player

T#	P#	GOALS
T1	P1	50
T1	P2	37
T1	P3	40
T1	P4	37
T1	P5	22
T1	P6	22
T2	P1	50
T2	P2	40
T3	P2	37
T4	P2	37
T4	P4	50
T4	P5	40

Figure 3.35 Three Relational Tables: Player, Team, and Team-Player

3.2.5.1 Data Record Instance Operations

Fundamentally, data record instance operations are independent of data model in that data record instances are either stored or deleted. The exact behavior of the operations, however, depends on whether there are static or dynamic relationships involved in the database structure. If there are no relationships involved, then the operation's behavior is the same for static and dynamic. If there are static relationships then it is necessary for the DBMS to connect the data record instance to one or more relationships, or to delete the data record instance from one or more relationships. In such a case, the insertion option would be AUTOMATIC.

Operation	STATIC	DYNAMIC
FIND	SELECT According to STORED order	SELECT AND Put into DML Specified Order
GET	Obtain Record from find	Ditto
ADD	Install a new data record into database	Ditto
DELETE	Remove an existing data record from database	Ditto
MODIFY	Change some data element values in existing data record	Ditto

Figure 3.36 Record Operations

If the DBMS that provides static relationship binding is sophisticated, then the DBMS optionally defers the immediate processing of relationship changes to a later time when it may be more cost effective. In such a case, the insertion option has to be MANUAL.

If the DBMS's relationships are dynamic, then no relationship processing occurs whenever a data record instance is stored or deleted, except an action that may be imposed by referential integrity.

Figure 3.36 contrasts the actions resulting from the different data record instance operations for both static and dynamic relationship bindings on data record instances. Figure 3.37 and 3.38 illustrate the PROJECT operation that has the DISTINCT operator in effect. Figures 3.39 and 3.40 show a simple SELECT operation.

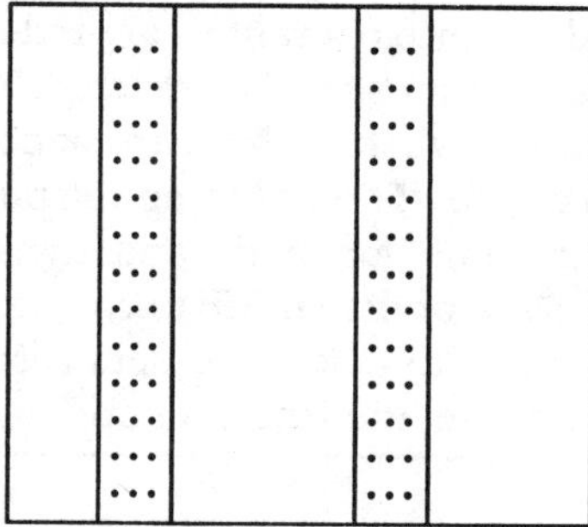

Figure 3.37 Relational Operation: Project

SQL Syntax:

```
Select Distinct COLLEGE, CITY
From   PLAYER
```

GIVEN: Relation = PLAYER

Relation : PLAYER

P#	PNAME	COLLEGE	WEIGHT	CITY
P1	Jackson	Colby	180	Bowie
P2	Beaner	Hamline	165	Laurel
P3	Tufts	St. Mikes	165	Savage
P4	Tufts	Colby	205	Bowie
P5	Larson	St. Mikes	180	Laurel
P6	Bowes	Colby	190	Bowie

RESULT:

COLLEGE	CITY
Colby	Bowie
Hamline	Laurel
St. Mikes	Savage
St. Mikes	Laurel

Figure 3.38 Relational Operation: Project Example

3.2.5.2 Relationship Operations

Relationship operations are quite different for static and dynamic relationship DBMSs. The CONNECT and DISCONNECT operations and the GET OWNER, GET NEXT, and GET MEMBER operations are included exclusively in the static data model DBMSs. The INTERSECTION, DIFFERENCE, JOIN, DIVIDE, PRODUCT, and UNION operations are exclusively in the dynamic data model DBMSs. Figure 3.41 enumerates all eleven relationship operations and briefly defines the results.

The static CONNECT operation *connects* an already stored data record instance to a relationship. The DISCONNECT operation *disconnects* an already connected data record instance from a relationship.

The dynamic operations are often shorthand references to actual programs that the user must create and execute. The INTERSECTION, DIFFERENCE, JOIN, DIVIDE, PRODUCT, and UNION relationship operations are graphically and programmatically presented in Figures 3.42 through 3.53.

3.2.5.3 Combination Operations

Combination operations are two or more data record instance and/or relationship operations. Figure 3.54 identifies the more common combination operations and their component operations.

3.2.6 Logical Database Components Summary

The logical database consists of components. These are domains, data record types, data record elements, relationships, and operations on the data record instances.

Domains, the first component, contain the specifications of the legal values for classes of data record elements. Domains also specify the legal combinations of various data record elements within DBMS operations such as select, join, and so on.

Data record elements, the second component, contain the specifications of the data to be represented through the data record instances. Each data record element has a name and a data type clause. If the data record element is single-valued or a dimensioned (single or multiple) array, then all the data record element instances are of the same data type, that is, character, fixed decimal, and the like. If the data record element is a group or a repeating group, then the data record element contains subordinate data record element definitions, each with its own data record element name and data type clause.

Data record types, the third component, contain their own naming clauses, any applicable integrity conditions, and an enumeration of the member data record elements. The data record type's definition also identifies the roles played by the various data record elements, namely: primary key, candidate key, secondary key, and foreign keys.

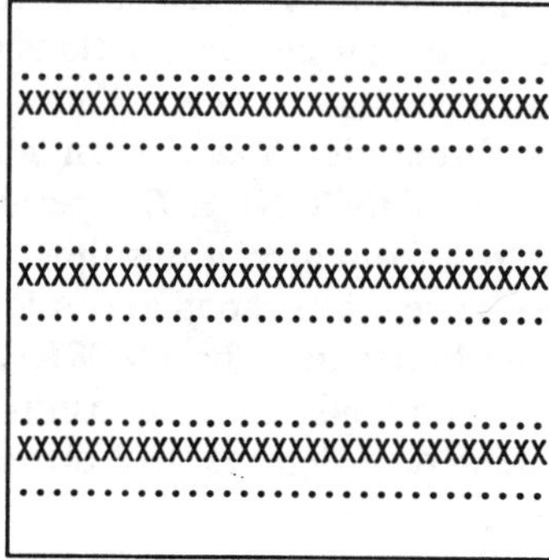

Figure 3.39 Relational Operation: Select

SQL Syntax:

```
Select * From TEAM
 Where CITY = "Bowie"
```

GIVEN: Relation = Team

T#	TNAME	CONFERENCE	CITY
T1	Black Birds	NE	Bowie
T2	Capitals	SE	Laurel
T3	Metros	NW	Laurel
T4	Bears	NE	Bowie
T5	Maulers	NW	Croom

RESULT

T#	TNAME	CONFERENCE	CITY
T1	Black Birds	NE	Bowie
T4	Bears	NE	Bowie

Figure 3.40 Relational Operation: Select Example

OPERATION	STATIC	DYNAMIC
CONNECT	Add to a named RELATIONSHIP in specific ORDER	N/A
DISCONNECT	Delete from RELATIONSHIP	N/A
GET OWNER	Obtains the parent of the data record that is current	N/A
GET MEMBER	Obtains the first child of the owner for the named relationship	N/A
GET NEXT	Obtains the next data record within the named relationship	N/A
INTERSECT	n/a	Find and keep only the common
DIFFERENCE	n/a	Find and keep only the not common
JOIN	n/a	"Append" relations to each other
DIVIDE	n/a	Subset
PRODUCT	n/a	Cross-product
UNION	n/a	merge and drop duplicates

Figure 3.41 Relationship Operations

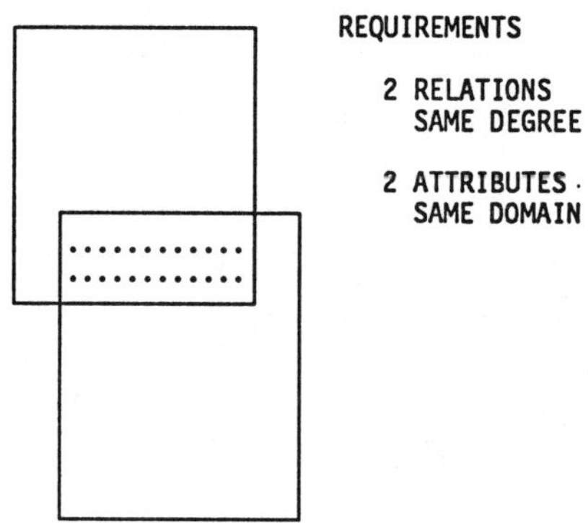

REQUIREMENTS

2 RELATIONS
SAME DEGREE

2 ATTRIBUTES
SAME DOMAIN

Figure 3.42 Relational operation: Intersection

SQL Syntax:

```
Select * From A
     Where Exists
     ( Select T# From B
          Where B.T# = A.T# )
```

GIVEN RELATION = A (Bowie Teams)

T1	Black Birds	NE	Bowie
T4	Bears	NE	Bowie

AND RELATION = B (Player 1's Teams)

T1	P1	50
T2	P1	50

THEN, THE RESULT IS:

T#	TNAME	CONFERENCE	CITY
T1	Black Birds	NE	Bowie

Figure 3.43 Relational Operation: Intersection Example

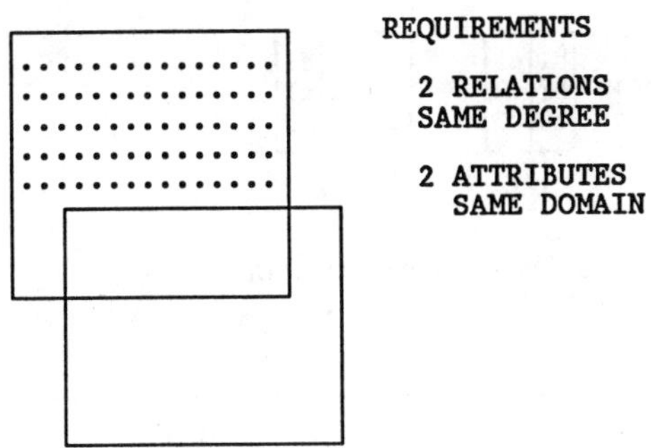

Figure 3.44 Relational Operation: Difference

SQL Syntax:

```
Select T# From A
Where Not Exists
    ( Select T# From B
    Where B.T# = A.T# )
```

GIVEN RELATION = A (Bowie Teams)

```
T1 Black Birds    NE         Bowie
T4 Bears          NE         Bowie
```

AND RELATION = B (Teams of Player P1)

```
T1 P1 50
T2 P1 50
```

THEN, THE RESULT IS:

T#	TNAME	CONFERENCE	CITY
T4	Bears	NE	Bowie

Figure 3.45 Relational Operation: Difference Example

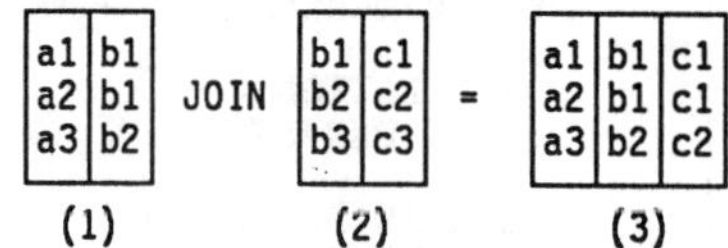

Figure 3.46 Relational Operation: Join
(1) joined with (2) produces (3)

SQL Syntax:

```
Select TEAM.*, PLAYER.*
From   TEAM, PLAYER
Where  TEAM.CITY= PLAYER.CITY
```

GIVEN Relation = Team

T#	TNAME	CONFERENCE	CITY
T1	Black Birds	NE	Bowie
T2	Capitals	SE	Laurel
T3	Metros	NW	Laurel
T4	Bears	NE	Bowie
T5	Maulers	NW	Croom

AND Relation = Player

P#	PNAME	COLLEGE	WEIGHT	CITY
P1	Jackson	Colby	180	Bowie
P2	Beaner	Hamline	165	Laurel
P3	Tufts	St. Mikes	165	Savage
P4	Tufts	Colby	205	Bowie
P5	Larson	St. Mikes	180	Laurel
P6	Bowes	Colby	190	Bowie

RESULTS IN:

T#	TNAME	CONFERENCE	P#	PNAME	COLLEGE	WEIGHT	CITY
T1	Black Birds	NE	p6	Bowes	Colby	190	Bowie
T1	Black Birds	NE	p1	Jackson	Colby	180	Bowie
T1	Black Birds	NE	p6	Tufts	Colby	205	Bowie
T2	Capitals	SE	p2	Beaner	Hamline	165	Laurel
T2	Capitals	SE	p5	Larson	St. Mikes	180	Laurel
T3	Metros	SE	p2	Beaner	Hamline	165	Laurel
T3	Metros	SE	p5	Larson	St. Mikes	180	Laurel
T4	Bears	NE	p1	Jackson	Colby	180	Bowie
T4	Bears	NE	p6	Bowes	Colby	190	Bowie
T4	Bears	NE	p6	Tufts	Colby	205	Bowie

Figure 3.47 Relational Operation: Join Example

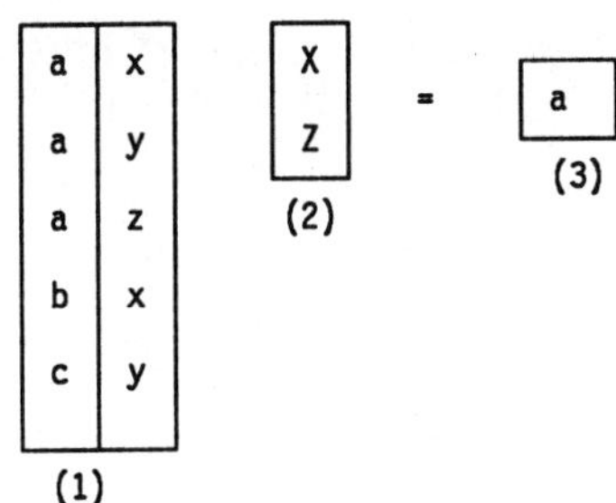

Figure 3.48 Relational Operation: Divide
(1) divided by (2) produces (3)

SQL Syntax:

```
Select Distinct P# From TEAM-PLAYER
  Where Not Exists
   ( Select P# From TEAM-PLAYER
   Where Not Exists
    ( Select T# P# From TEAM-PLAYER
     Where TEAM-PLAYER.T# = HOT-TEAM.T# ) )
```

GIVEN: Relation : Team-Player

```
T# P# GOALS      And Relation: HOT-TEAMS
-- -- ---
T1 P1 50      (SELECT T# FROM TEAM-PLAYER where GOALS > 37)
T1 P2 37
T1 P3 40                 +----+            +----+
T1 P4 37                 | T1 |            | P# |
T1 P5 22   DIVIDED       | T2 |   EQUALS   +----+
T1 P6 22     BY          | T4 |            | P2 |
T2 P1 50                 +----+            +----+
T2 P2 40
T3 P2 37
T4 P2 37
T4 P4 50
T4 P5 40
```

Figure 3.49 Relational Operation: Divide Example

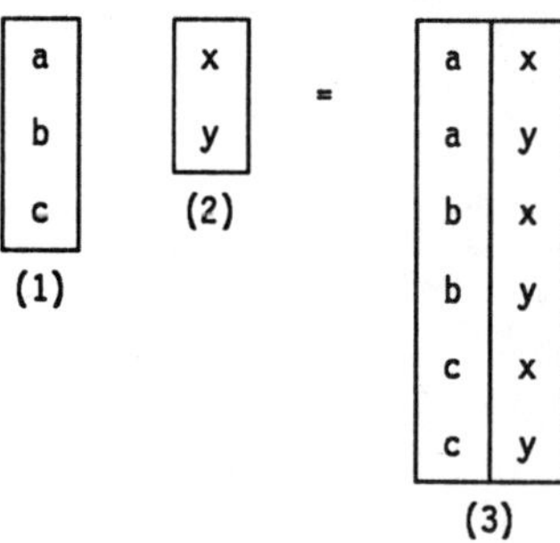

Figure 3.50 Relational Operation: Product
(1) on (2) produces (3)

SQL Syntax:

```
Select TEAM.*, TEAM-PLAYER
From   TEAM, TEAM-PLAYER
```

GIVEN:

Relation : Team

T#	TNAME	CONFERENCE	CITY
T1	Black Birds	NE	Bowie
T2	Capitals	SE	Laurel
T3	Metros	NW	Laurel
T4	Bears	NE	Bowie
T5	Maulers	NW	Croom

AND

Relation : Team-Player

T#	P#	GOALS
T1	P1	50
T1	P2	37
T1	P3	40
T1	P4	37
T1	P5	22
T1	P6	22
T2	P1	50
T2	P2	40
T3	P2	37
T4	P2	37
T4	P4	50
T4	P5	40

RESULT:

T#	TNAME	CONFERENCE	CITY	P#	GOALS
T1	Black Birds	NE	Bowie	P1	50
T1	Black Birds	NE	Bowie	P2	37
T1	Black Birds	NE	Bowie	P3	40
T1	Black Birds	NE	Bowie	P4	37
T1	Black Birds	NE	Bowie	P5	22
T1	Black Birds	NE	Bowie	P6	22
	ETC				
	ETC				

Figure 3.51 Relational Operation: Product Example

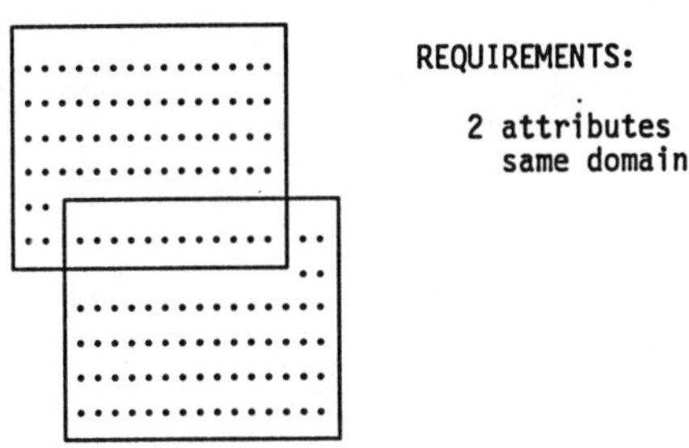

Figure 3.52 Relational Operation: Union

SQL Syntax:

```
Select P# From PLAYER
where WEIGHT > 180
Union
Select T# From TEAM-PLAYER
where T# = "T2"
```

Relation : Player

P#	PNAME	COLLEGE	WEIGHT	CITY
P1	Jackson	Colby	180	Bowie
P2	Beaner	Hamline	165	Laurel
P3	Tufts	St. Mikes	165	Savage
P4	Tufts	Colby	205	Bowie
P5	Larson	St. Mikes	180	Laurel
P6	Bowes	Colby	190	Bowie

And

Relation : Team-Player

T#	P#	GOALS
T1	P1	50
T1	P2	37
T1	P3	40
T1	P4	37
T1	P5	22
T1	P6	22
T2	P1	50
T2	P2	40
T3	P2	37
T4	P2	37
T4	P4	50
T4	P5	40

RESULT:

P#
p1
p2
p4
p6

Figure 3.53 Relational Operation: Union Example

Relationships are the fourth component of the logical database. There are eight types of relationships:

- One-to-many
- Owner-multiple member
- Singular-one member
- Singular-multiple-member
- Recursive
- any-to-many
- One-to-one
- Inferential

Operations are the final component of the logical database. Whether a particular operation is permitted or not depends on whether the relationship binding method is static or dynamic.

The next section brings together four popular combinations of these five logical database components in order to define the four data models common to most DBMSs.

3.3 DATA MODELS

Every DBMS's logical database is controlled by a set of rules. The combination of the rules that allow network or hierarchical relationships, that bind data records through either static or dynamic relationships, and that permit distinct operations is called the DBMS's data model.

Because data models have different data record instance structures and relationship binding methods, each data model also permits specific operations to manipulate these structures. A data model's definition is thus in three parts:

- The formal definition of the permitted data record type structure, *AND*
- The formal definition of the number, types and kind of relationships that can be defined between data record instances of the same and different types, *AND*
- The formal definition of the operations that can take place on the resultant data structure of data record and relationship instances

The study of data models is important, because a data model determines the data structure, operations, and relationships that are applied to the data record types. Any data structures and operations beyond those set by the DBMS must be created by the application's designers and programmers on the basis of shared data record element values. Programs are needed to navigate among the data record instances to effect the operations required by the application's designers. Finally, in most cases, the application designer is also responsible for the maintenance of the non-supported data structures and operations. In short, the data model of the DBMS determines the default set of allowed data structures and operations. Anything beyond these defaults has to be required by the application designer and then programmed by the application programmers.

For example, suppose one DBMS contains an operation that found the occurrences of one data record type that did not have a shared data record element's value in another data record type, while another DBMS supports that operation. The first DBMS explicitly supports answering the question: FIND STUDENTS NOT ASSIGNED TO ANY CLASS. The second DBMS requires a programmer to write a program to access a student data record instance and then search the class data record instances to see if the student is assigned to any classes; if not, then that student is reported. The program then has to pick up the next student data record instance and perform the search again, until all the student data records are exhausted.

The point of this example is not whether the first DBMS can perform the operation faster than the programmer-written program can, but that the first DBMS explicitly supports the operation, while the second requires that the user program it. Because the first DBMS explicitly supports this operation, there is no need for program design, development, or debugging, as these have already been accomplished by the DBMS developers.

While the five components of the logical database can be brought together in any number of combinations to create many different data models, there are four combinations that are most popular. These are:

- Network
- Hierarchical
- Independent logical file
- Relational

```
Fetch = FIND + GET

MODIFY = FIND + GET + STORE

INSERT = STORE + CONNECT
```

Figure 3.54 Combination Operations

Most of the popular DBMS literature acknowledges the existence of only the network, hierarchical, and relational data models. To ignore the existence, however, of the independent logical file data model is to refuse to acknowledge the existence of some of the most popular DBMSs, e.g., ADABAS, FOCUS, Inquire, Nomad, Model 204, and RAMIS. To be both complete and correct, this book describes the independent logical file data model and its capabilities.

The relationships built by the network and hierarchical data models are static, and the relationships used by the independent logical file and relational data models are are dynamic. A network data model database permits multiple complex data records and allows a member data record instance to be owned by multiple data record instances from different data record types (see Figure 3.9). A hierarchical data model database permits a single hierarchy of segments, each of which is simple. The entire collection of segments is actually one complex data record type. Each segment in the hierarchy is owned by only one owner segment (see Figure 3.8). The data record elements in the segments can only be single valued. An independent logical file (ILF) data model database permits multiple

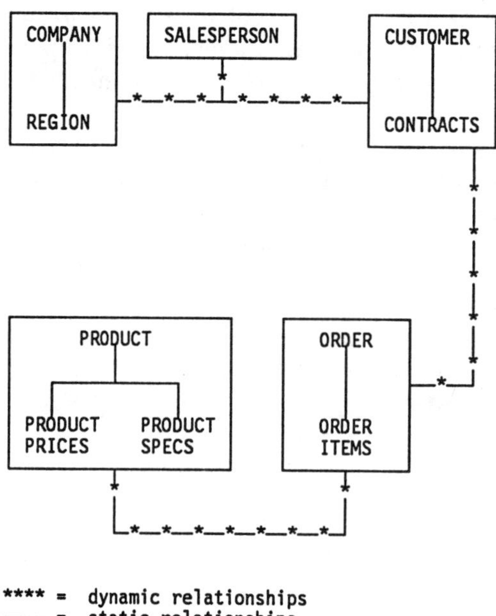

Figure 3.55 Independent Logical File Data Model
Five Databases with Complex and Simple Record Types

complex data record types (see Figure 3.55). A relational data model database permits multiple data records (see Figure 3.28). However, unlike the ILF data model, all relational data record types can only contain single-valued data record elements.

In general, the emphasis in the network data model is complex database and data record structures which then only require simple operations, while the emphasis in the relational data model is simple database and data record structures which then require complex operations. The network data model provides facilities for strong, central, schema-based control over data record type structures. Thus, the network data model has a complex data record type structure

Functions of Network	Functions of Relational
data structure (.8) & operations (.2)	data structure (.2) & operations (.8)

Figure 3.56 Location of Static and Dynamic Functionality

and many types of relationships. Because of this strong structure, network data model operations are defined in terms of navigating these structures. In short, the number and variety of explicit DDL-defined data structures is greatest in the network data model. Conversely, the relational data model provides only simple data record structures but complex operations. Figure 3.56 expresses the approximate proportions of components for these two data models.

The hierarchical data model has simpler data record type structures than the network data model and similar operations. The hierarchical data model is actually a subset of the network data model.

The ILF data model has complex data record type structures, thus it has some operations similar to the network data model. The ILF data model also has dynamic relationships between data record types, thus the ILF supports operations similar to relational. The ILF data model is a superset of the relational data model.

The manner in which relationships are created and maintained by the DBMS is also very important. It is generally true that the network data model DBMSs are built to utilize static relationships. There are a few network data model DBMSs, however, that have dynamic relationships.

The static relationship is declared explicitly by the database designer--through the DDL--and then its instances are automatically generated by the DBMS whenever an owner data record instance is created and one or more member data record instances of the relationship are inserted. The relationship is usually a relative data record instance address. Traditionally, this address is stored in the owner data record instance for its first member data record instance, and each member data record instance has the address of the next member data record instance. Some static relationship DBMSs additionally allow both the owner data record instance's address and the prior member data record instance's address to be stored in each member data record instance. These relationships are built as the data record instances are loaded into the database, and are maintained through updates.

An advantage of a static relationship is the speed with which it can be traversed. A disadvantage is that whenever the data record's relationship needs to be changed, the data record instance must first be *disconnected* from its owner and then *reconnected* to the new owner.

In most dynamic relationship DBMSs, the relationships between data record types are not declared in any way. As stated above, the basis of the relationship is a defined data record element in both the owner and member data record type. Since a dynamic relationship is represented through a data record element's value, the relationship that one data record instance has with another may be changed through a simple update. While changing a relationship is very simple, the amount of computer resources required to traverse a dynamic relationship (from owner to all members) is normally greater than it would have been in a static relationship.

The reason for the performance difference is as follows. In the vast majority of static relationship DBMSs, the relationship mechanism is a relative data record instance address of the data record instance. Thus, when there is a request to traverse from an owner data record instance to its first member, the member's relative data record instance address (the location of the data record instance) is already known and stored, usually in the owner. Once the address has been obtained, the only step left in the relationship traversal process is to get the data record instance from its location. Getting the *next* member data record instance requires only accessing the *next* relative data record instance address and going to that address to get the data record instance. In contrast, in the vast majority of dynamic relationship DBMSs, the relationship mechanism is a shared data record element value, which most often is the value of the owner's primary key, replicated in each of the member data record instances. To access the set of member data records, the typical dynamic relationship DBMS has to first use the owner data record's primary key in a secondary key search for the member data records. Such a search often results in a list of member data record instance primary keys. Then each of these keys must be used in a primary key search to locate and retrieve each member data record instance.

The data record structure is formally defined through the data definition language (DDL), and the operations occur through the expression of the various data manipulation languages (DML) that are supported by the DBMS. This division of function can also be used to distinguish static from dynamic. In a static relationship DBMS, the DDL contains both the definition of data record type structures and relationships, while the DML contains only the operations. In a dynamic relationship DBMS, the DDL contains only the data record type structures, while the DML contains the relationship definitions and operations. Figures 3.57 and 3.58 depict these differences. Figures 3.59a and 3.59b tabulate the combinations of facilities that are present in the four data models.

When the concept of data model is combined with the concept of static and dynamic, a 2 x 4 matrix results. The names of DBMSs along with their principal data model are identified in Figure 3.60. It should be noted that a number of DBMSs support more than one data model. Today's popular combinations are network and relational (IDMS/R and SUPRA), hierarchical and relational (FOCUS and RAMIS), and independent logical file and relational (ADABAS, Datacom/DB, FOCUS, Inquire, Model 204, and RAMIS).

Data Model Type	Data Definition. Language Components	Data Manipulation Language Components
Static	Record structures Relationships	Operations
Dynamic	Record structures	Relationships Operations

Figure 3.57 Comparing Static and Dynamic Components

$$\text{Data Model} = \left\{ \begin{array}{l} \text{Record} \\ \text{Organization} \end{array} \right\} + \left\{ \begin{array}{l} \text{Inter-record} \\ \text{Relationships} \end{array} \right\} + \left\{ \text{Operations} \right\}$$

$$\text{Data Model} = \left\{ \begin{array}{l} \text{Data Definition} \\ \text{Language} \end{array} \right\} + \left\{ \begin{array}{l} \text{Data Manipulation} \\ \text{Language} \end{array} \right\}$$

$$\text{Dynamic Data Model} = \left\{ \text{DDL} \left\{ \text{RO} \right\} + \left\{ \text{DML} \left\{ \text{REL + OPS} \right\} \right\} \right.$$

$$\text{Static Data Model} = \left\{ \text{DDL} \left\{ \text{RO + REL} \right\} + \left\{ \text{DML} \left\{ \text{OPS} \right\} \right\} \right.$$

WHERE:

DDL = Data Definition Language
DML = Data Manipulation Language
RO = Record Organization
REL = Relationships
OPS = Operations

Figure 3.58 Data Model Components

CHARACTERISTICS		DATA MODELS: STATIC — Network	STATIC — Hierarchic	DYNAMIC — Indep. Logical File	DYNAMIC — Relational
Record Organ.		SV, MV, MD G, RG	SV segments	SV,MV,RG	SV
Relationship (REL)		A B → C	A → B C	A B C / D E F	A B C D E F
OPERATIONS (OPS)	REK	A,D,F,M	A,D,F,M	A,D,F,M	A,D,F,M P
	REL	C,D,GO, GM,GN	GO, GM, GN	J, INT DIV, UN DIF	J,INT, DIV, UN PR, DIV
DDL		REL, RO	REL, RO	RO	RO
DML		OPS	OPS	REL & OPS	REL & OPS

Figure 3.59a The Four Data Models

RECORD ORGANIZATION		SV SINGLE VALUE MV MULTIPLE VALUE MD MULTIPLE DIMENSION G GROUP RG REPEATING GROUP
OPERATIONS	REK	A-ADD D-DELETE M-MODIFY P-PROJECT F-FIND
	REL	C-CONNECT DIS-DISCONNECT P-PROJECT J-JOIN DIV-DIVIDE GO-GET OWNER GM-GET MEMBER GN-GET NEXT INT-INTERSECTION PR-PRODUCT UN-UNION DIF-DIFFERENCE

Figure 3.59b The Four Data Models--legend

D B M S T Y P E			
STATIC		DYNAMIC	
NETWORK	HIERARCHICAL	ILF	RELATIONAL
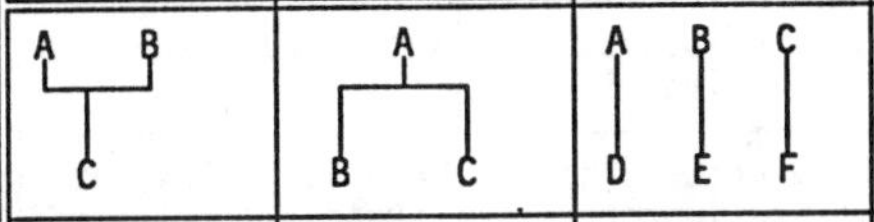 A B / C	A / B C	A B C / D E F	A B C / D E F
SUPRA IDMS/R * IDS * DMS-2 DMS 1100 * IMAGE VAX-DBMS * PRIME-DB *	IMS SYSTEM 2000 FOCUS RAMIS NOMAD	MANAGE Model 204 INQUIRE ADABAS NOMAD FOCUS RAMIS DMS 170 DATACOM DB	INGRES * ORACLE * IDMS/R * SQL/DS * SUPRA DB2 FOCUS RAMIS NOMAD
* ANSI-NDL			* ANSI-SQL

NOTE: By ANSI/NDL or ANSI/SQL, it is meant that the DBMSs at least generally conform to the data model and the process models specified by these two standards. The exact syntax and semantics may vary slightly, making each DBMS more or less compatible.

Figure 3.60 DBMS Data Models

Figure 3.61 tabulates the effects the four data models have on database applications. Independent of this comparison is the effort to create a quality database design, which, regardless of data model, is the same. That is because all the design work necessary for a quality database must be done before any transformation steps are begun.

3.3.1 Data Models and DBMSs

As stated above, a data model is a formalized approach to the organization of data. By permitting some data structures and forbidding others, a data model determines the types of operations that can be performed against the data structures. Within specific DBMSs, relationships are either explicitly declarable or they can be simulated through special data manipulation operators. When a relationship is explicitly declared and data is loaded according to these explicitly declared relationships, the pre-executed relationships exist for all to use without regeneration.

A relationship can be simulated through the use of a special data manipulation language operator. Then, if twenty different users need to select data record instances from two different data record types, the DBMS must determine

CHARACTERISTIC	DATA MODEL			
	NETWORK	HIERARCHY	ILF	RELATIONAL
Structure	Complex	Moderate	Complex	Simple
Record order control	Update	Update retrieval	Retrieval	Run-unit
Relationship binding	Load or update	Load or update	Only at retrieval	Only at retrieval
Mandatory design work	High	Moderate	Low	Lowest
DBMS control over programmer	High	Moderate	Low	Lowest
Ease of database design change	Poor	Less poor	Better	Best
Effort to design a quality data database	Great	Great	Great	Great

Figure 3.61 Data Model Effects On Application Development

the set of data record instances belonging to those relationships--twenty different times.

Relationships are explicitly declarable only in the network (NDL) and hierarchical data models. A relationship is a formalized expression of the nature of the allowed interaction between two data record types. In the network model, the relationship is defined through the use of the SET clause. In the hierarchical data model, for example, in SYSTEM 2000, the relationship is explicitly stated through the use of a RG IN <parent repeating group id> clause. In the independent logical file data model, the relationships are implicitly defined only within data record types through the use of multiple-valued data record elements, or through the use of repeating group data record elements. In the relational model, most notably ANSI/SQL, relationships cannot be explicitly or implicitly defined. The relational model can only simulate relationships through the use of specially defined operators such as JOIN and UNION that interrelate data record instances at execution time.

Figure 3.62 identifies the different types of relationships that can be explicitly defined in the four data models. A relationship can be implemented either statically (S) or dynamically (D), and can be accomplished directly (D) without having to define additional data record types, or can be accomplished indirectly

RELATIONSHIP TYPE	DATA MODEL			
	DDL DECLARATION		DML SIMULATION	
	ANSI NETWORK	HIERARCHY	ILF	ANSI-SQL RELATIONAL
OWNER- 1 MEMBER	D S	D S	D D	D D
> 1 MEMBER	D S	No	No	No
NO-OWNER 1 MEMBER	D S	No	No	No
>1 MEMBER	D S	No	No	No
RECURSIVE	D S	I D	D D	I D
MANY TO MANY	I S	I D	D D	I D
INFERENTIAL	I D	No	D D	D D
ONE TO ONE	D S	I D	D D	D D

D S means direct, static relationships
I S means indirect, static relationships

D D means direct, dynamic relationships
I D means indirect, dynamic relationships

No means no practical method

Figure 3.62 Method of Relationship Implementation by Data Model

(I) once additional data record types are defined. A data record type is considered to be *additional* whenever the DBMS cannot execute the relationship directly without the database's designer first defining another data record type. For example, the many-to-many relationship depicted in Figure 3.31 can be executed directly by ADABAS with only two data record types. To accomplish that relationship in DB2, however, first requires the definition of the three data record type structure represented in Figure 3.30. To accomplish an indirect (I) relationship type requires the definition of additional data record types. Thus, the relationship type is not really accomplished; rather it is transformed into a different relationship type, and then executed through custom programming in the various application programs. Finally, Figure 3.62 declares a relationship-data model intersection as a *no* whenever there is no practical method of accomplishing the relationship.

DBMSs implementing data models not standardized by ANSI are only generally equivalent even though they might be identified as having the same data model. An example of this general comparability is IBM's Information Management System (IMS) and SAS's SYSTEM 2000.

As stated above, there are four commonly employed data models; two are static--network and hierarchical, and two are dynamic--independent logical file and relational.

Because of the ANSI network data model standard, some static network DBMSs compare favorably to the ANSI/NDL. These are: Computer Associate's IDMS/R, Unisys' DMS-1100, Digital's VAX/DBMS, and Honeywell's IDS-2. While Unisys supports another network data model DBMS, DM-2, it does not compare favorably to the ANSI requirements. CINCOM's SUPRA network data model is the same as it was in the early 1960s, thus it does not conform to either the ANSI/NDL nor this book's more general specification of the network model.

There are two hierarchical DBMSs, SAS's SYSTEM 2000 and IBM's IMS. There is, however, no ANSI standard data model for hierarchies, and no standard is contemplated.

There are a number of independent logical file DBMSs. Since there is no ANSI standard for this data model, however, their similarities, while significant, cannot be depended upon for database and application portability.

A version of the relational data model has been standardized through the specification of ANSI/SQL. A number of DBMSs either already conform to the ANSI/SQL standard or are in the process of delivering SQL facilities. DBMSs in the former category include DB2, ORACLE, INFORMIX-SQL, and INGRESS. DBMSs in the latter category include IDMS/R, Model 204, ADABAS, and SUPRA.

IDMS/R and SUPRA are identified as both network and relational because they support both network and relational processing. IDMS/R is generally a superset of ANSI/NDL and provides support to the ANSI/SQL language for accessing IDMS/R's relationally defined tables. While SUPRA's network model is non-standard, SUPRA offers ANSI/SQL support against its *master* data record types.

Notwithstanding their differences, all DBMSs supporting the data models defined in this book are fundamentally the same--from the perspective of data models. Further, all static relationship DBMSs possess a common major characteristic--static relationships between data record instances of the same or different type. All dynamic relationship DBMSs possess a common major characteristic--dynamic relationships between data record instances of the same or different types. What this implies is that the most suitable of each DBMS type should be procured. Having several static, or several dynamic, relationship DBMSs, is of little value.

If an organization judges that a static-hierarchy DBMS is the most appropriate for its applications, then it would be appropriate to perform a detailed comparison of IMS and SYSTEM 2000 to determine which one contains the features most suitable for the organization.

Similarly, if a dynamic relationship DBMS is also desired, then an examination of Datacom/DB, DB2, ADABAS, Inquire, Model 204, and Oracle would be appropriate.

What would not be appropriate would be, for example, a comparison of IMS and ADABAS, or of SYSTEM 2000 and INQUIRE. The desire to make such comparisons indicates that the evaluators do not yet understand either DBMS or the needs of their applications, or both.

3.3.2 Static Data Models

The network and hierarchical data models are founded mainly on static relationships. Within a database the relationships are static. Relationships between databases are dynamic. Fewer dynamic relationships are needed in the network data model than in the hierarchical data model, simply because the network model supports more relationship-modelling capabilities than does the hierarchical model.

3.3.2.1 Network Data Models

The data structure characteristic unique to the network data model is the ability of a data record instance to be a member of two different relationships. This is

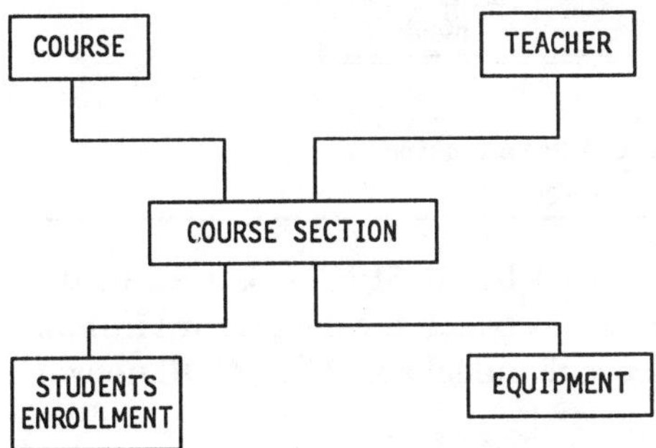

Figure 3.63 Network Data Structure

illustrated in Figure 3.63, where COURSE-SECTION is a common member to both COURSE and TEACHER. Figure 3.63 contains five data record types. The owners of the COURSE-SECTION data record type are COURSE and TEACHER. The dependents of the COURSE-SECTION data record type are the student's ENROLLMENT and the EQUIPMENT needed for the COURSE-SECTION.

As illustrated in Figure 3.62, the network model can accomplish all the relationship types. Six are accomplished directly. Two are accomplished indirectly, and only one requires dynamic relationships.

The network data model has several major versions. Notable among these is the COnference on DAta SYstem Languages (CODASYL) model that has been standardized by ANSI as NDL and implemented by Honeywell (IDS-2), Unisys (DMS-1100), VAX/DBMS, and Computer Associates (IDMS/R). Since the ANSI/NDL is a subset of the CODASYL network model, most subsets of all these DBMSs comply to ANSI/NDL.

Models		Structure	Element Example
CODASYL	ANSI		
Yes	Yes	Primary Key	SSN
Yes	Yes	Non-Repeated Fields	Name Address Sex
Yes	Yes	Vectors	Nicknames
Yes	Yes	Matrix	MONTHLY-DIVISION-SALE
Yes	No	Repeating Group	Job Title Start Date Stop Date
Yes	No	Nested Repeating Group	FAMILY KIDS HOBBIES

Figure 3.64 Network Record Organization

The data record instance structure allowed by ANSI/NDL is identified in Figure 3.64. In this same figure is a comparison between the data record instance structure allowed in both the CODASYL network model and ANSI/NDL network model.

In general, the ANSI network data model allows multiple relationships between an owner and its members, among members of the same and different types with and without an owner, and between owners and members of the same type. Relationships that do not have another data record type as an owner are called singular relationships. Relationships that have the same data record type as both owner and member are called recursive. Figures 3.10, 3.11, 3.13, 3.14, and 3.16 illustrate the different types of relationships explicitly definable by the NDL's data definition language. The many-to-many relationship can only be implemented indirectly within the NDL. Thus, to model the many-to-many relationship (Figure 3.20) involving two data record types (COURSE and STUDENT) a triple data record type structure (COURSE, STUDENT, and ENROLLMENT) has to be created. This three data record type structure is illustrated in Figure 3.65.

Figure 3.12 illustrates a composite of different relationships that can all be defined at the same time on the identified data record types within the ANSI/NDL.

Another type of network data model is SUPRA (formerly TIS (formerly TOTAL)). It is a very restricted subset of the capabilities of the ANSI/NDL model. SUPRA's network data model has remained essentially unchanged since the middle 1960s. It only permits single-value fields within the data record type. It

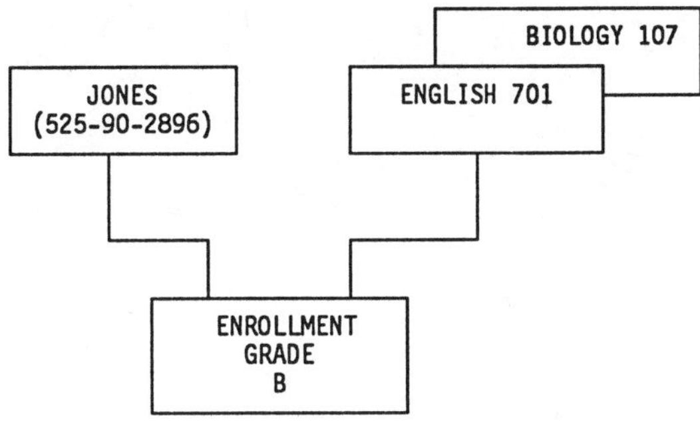

TWO SET TYPES

STUDENT WITH GRADE RECORDS

COURSE SECTION WITH GRADES

Figure 3.65 Indirect Network Relationships

does not contain singular, multi-member, or recursive sets. Further, the owner data record type of SUPRA's single member relationships cannot be defined to be the member data record type of another relationship. Because of this restriction, intermediate data record types have to be invented, which requires extra user written programs.

The operations allowed in the network model are identified in Figure 3.66. As stated above, relationships in NDL must not be required to be value based. That is, the relationship definition must not require that the primary key value of the owner data record instance nor any other owner element values be present in the member data record instance. This feature insulates member data record instance occurrences from having to be accessed and modified if the primary key of the owner is changed.

NDL DBMSs permit great sophistication in placing new data record instances within the context of a relationship, that is, always at the head, always at the end, or in sorted order. This way, if data records are stored in time sequence, and if the store order is always HEAD, then the oldest data records are always towards the end, and the newest data records are always at the front.

Storing data records in sorted order within the context of a relationship is certainly less expensive than storing an entire data record type in a sorted order. However, the DBMS's maintenance of the sorted order is more expensive than retrieving data records and then sorting afterwards. Sorting after retrieval also requires that all the natural languages contain sort verbs.

```
Record operations
     Retrieval
          Find
          Get
     Update
          Store
          Delete
Relationship operations
     Get owner
     Get Member
     Get Next
     Connect
     Disconnect
Combination operations
     Insert
     Fetch
```

Figure 3.66 Network Operations

3.3.2.2 Hierarchy

The hierarchical data model represented by IBM's IMS and SAS's SYSTEM 2000 is simpler than the network data model because each hierarchical database only allows one complex data record type. Each segment in the data record type can have only one owner, and there can be only one relationship between an owner segment and its member segments. The only relationship type allowed is owner-single-member. Whenever a connection between hierarchical databases is required, a dynamic relationship must be created (see Figure 3.8). For example, the relationship between PRODUCT and PRODUCT SPECIFICATION segments is static, but the relationship between the PRODUCT PRICE and ORDER ITEM segments is dynamic.

Each segment within a hierarchical data model data record instance has traditionally been restricted to single-valued data record elements (see Figure 3.67). Each member segment type can only have one owner.

As illustrated in Figure 3.62, the hierarchical model directly accomplishes only one relationship type. Two others are accomplished indirectly and dynamically. One is accomplished directly but dynamically. Four relationship types are identified as *no*.

Figure 3.68 illustrates a typical hierarchical structure. Normally there is no practical limit to the number of levels in the hierarchy, nor to the number of segments on each level. In SYSTEM 2000, for example, if each segment (called a

PRIMARY KEY	SSN
Single-valued-elements	BIRTH DATE SEX CURRENT JOB DEGREE MAJOR MARITAL STATUS

Figure 3.67 Hierarchical Data Element Examples

repeating group) contains about 9 data record elements, SYSTEM 2000 would then allow up to 100 segments to be configured. Each repeating group (segment) and data record element definition counts towards a maximum of 1000. A SYSTEM 2000 hierarchy can be 32 levels deep and can contain as many repeating groups and data record elements as may be necessary so long as the 1000 count is not exceeded. In IMS, the depth of the hierarchy is restricted to nine levels.

Most production applications that use hierarchical data model databases require that multiple hierarchies be related to avoid unnecessary data redundancy. For example, if a STUDENT is taught by multiple TEACHERs, it is redundant to represent each TEACHER's data under each student or each STUDENT's data under each TEACHER.

To avoid redundant data definition and storage, the multiple hierarchies are tied together through dynamic relationships. The two major hierarchical data model systems, SYSTEM 2000 and IMS, differ significantly in this regard. IMS allows the explicit definition of dynamic relationships (twins) between data record types within the same or different hierarchies. In SYSTEM 2000, intra- or inter-hierarchy relationships are specified linguistically by the application designer-programmer and executed by SYSTEM 2000. Notwithstanding its lack of explicit networking, SYSTEM 2000 is far simpler to use than IMS. Additionally, SYSTEM 2000's storage structure, although static, supports efficient ad hoc inquiry within the design constraints of the defined hierarchical structure, while IMS's does not.

The allowable operations for the hierarchical data model appear in Figure 3.69.

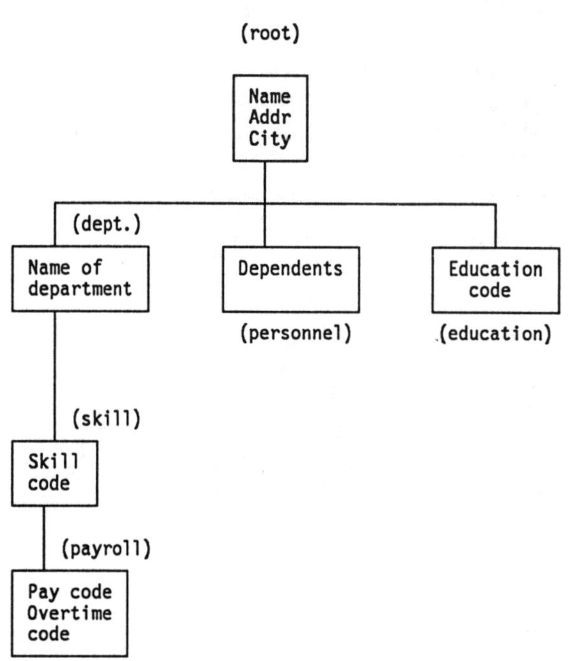

Figure 3.68 Hierarchical Relationships

```
RECORD OPERATIONS

     RETRIEVAL
          FIND
          GET

     UPDATE
          INSERT
          MODIFY
          DELETE

RELATIONSHIP OPERATIONS
     GET OWNER
     GET MEMBER
     GET NEXT

COMBINATION OPERATIONS
     MODIFY
     DELETE TREE
```

Figure 3.69 Hierarchical Operations

3.3.3 Dynamic Data Models

The independent logical file (ILF) and the relational data models, illustrated in Figures 3.55 and 3.28, are based on dynamic relationships. The ILF data model contains complex data record types. The relationships between data record types are represented through shared data values. Figure 3.60 lists some of the popular ILF systems. A relational data model has only simple data records and, like the ILF data model, represents relationships between data record instances through data values.

3.3.3.1 Independent Logical File Data Model

An independent logical file (ILF) database allows data record types to be complex. But the complexity is sometimes restricted to just two levels--a CUSTOMER and its CONTRACTs (see Figure 3.55). For some ILF DBMSs, the additional level of ORDERs for the CONTRACTS is represented by adding another data record type to the database and then connecting the first data record type to it through a dynamic relationship. For example, in Figure 3.55, the COMPANY data record type contains a repeating group, REGION. The relationship between the SALESPERSON and the REGION data record types is dynamic. That is, the REGION ID from the REGION data record instance is also present in the SALESPERSON data record. The types of data record elements allowed in an ILF data record type are represented in Figure 3.70.

FOCUS allows the definition of data record types as complex as SYSTEM 2000. FOCUS also permits the definition of simple data record types like relational DBMSs. Relationships between data record types in FOCUS can be across the *tops* of data record types, and also between lower level segments within the hierarchy.

As illustrated in Figure 3.62, the ILF data model requires all the relationships to be dynamic. Five of the relationships are direct, and three are *no*. A sophisticated ILF DBMS explicitly permits:

- One-to-many
- One-to-one
- Inferential
- Many-to-many
- Recursion

Figure 3.71 illustrates an ILF one-to-many relationship. A many-to-many relationship is depicted in Figure 3.21, an inferential relationship is depicted in Figure 3.24, and a recursive relationship is presented in Figures 3.16 through 3.18.

The operations allowed in the ILF data model are listed in Figure 3.72.

Structure	Element Example
Primary Key	SSN
Non-Repeated Fields	Name Address Sex
Vectors	Nicknames
Matrix	Monthly by Division by Sales
Repeating Group	Job Title Start Date Stop Date
Nested Repeating Group	Project Proj-id Hours Desc

Figure 3.70 Independent Logical File Data Element Types

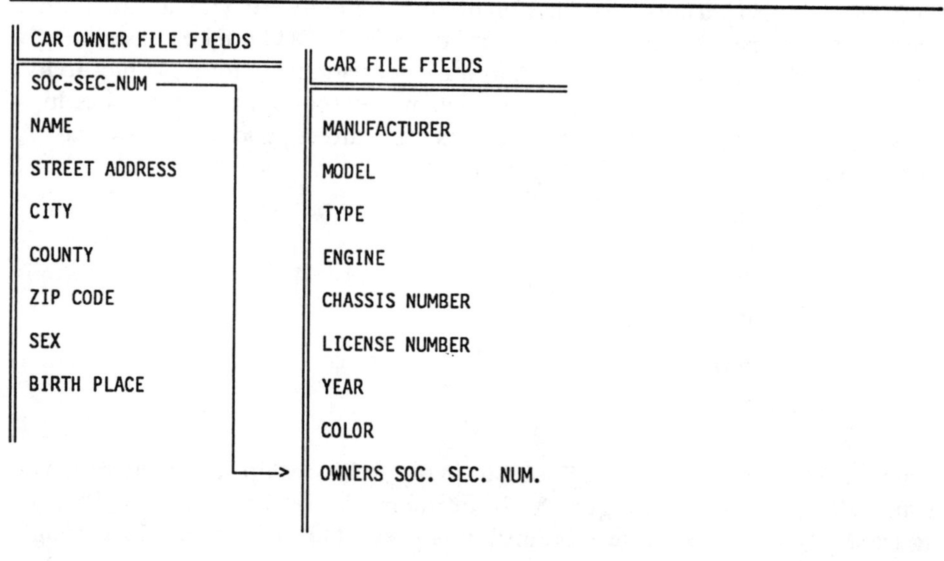

Figure 3.71 ILF Relationships--One-To-Many

3.3.3.2 Relational Data Model

The fourth data model, relational, is the simplest. A relational database is restricted to simple data record types called tables. All relationships between tables must be dynamic. For example, in Figure 3.28, the SALESPERSON table is related to the CONTRACT table by the SALESPERSON-ID stored in the CONTRACT data table.

```
RECORD
     RETRIEVAL
          FIND
          ADD
          DELETE
     RELATIONSHIP
          CONNECT <FILE-NAME> TO <FILE-NAME>
          VIA  <FILE-NAME-1-ELEMENT> EQUAL
          FILE-NAME-2-ELEMENT>

     COMBINATION OPERATIONS
          SELECT  <RECORD-NAME>
               ORDERED BY <FIELD-NAME>(S)
               WHERE <FIELD-NAME> RO....

          MODIFY
```

Figure 3.72 Independent Logical File Operations

Figure 3.62 shows that the relational model accomplishes all relationship types dynamically. Three relationship types are directly modelled. Two can only be modelled indirectly, and three cannot be modelled.

The terminology commonly utilized in relational databases is identified in Figure 3.73. Figure 3.74 provides an example that supports the use of these different terms.

The operations that are defined for the relational model are listed in Figure 3.75. Examples of each of these operations are provided in Figures 3.42 through 3.53.

3.3.3.3 Dynamic Data Model Summary

Of the two dynamic data models, the more sophisticated is the ILF model. It has the richest data record type structure and the largest number of explicit relationships to model real world problems.

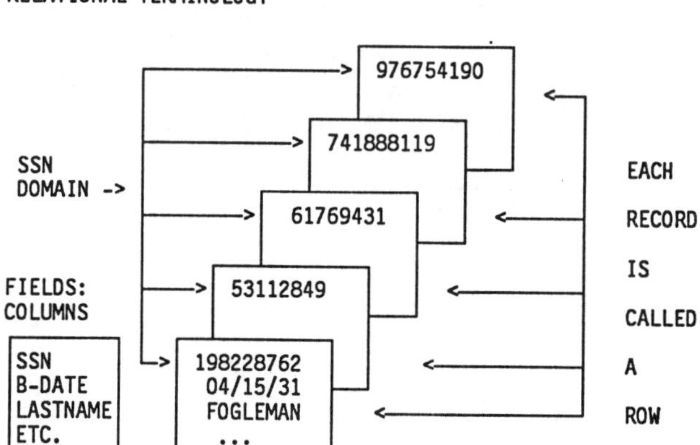

Figure 3.73 Relational Terminology

ROW ID	COLUMNS		
	SSN	BIRTHDATE	LASTNAME
1	123	04/15/31	FOGLEMAN
2	235	.....	...
3	643	....	...

Figure 3.74 Relational Columns and Rows

3.3.4 Data Model Summary

The network data model is far richer than the relational data model. Of the eight different types of relationships that can be defined among data record types and between data records, the SQL data model can simulate only three of these relationships, while the NDL data model can directly declare six. The network model can accomplish the other two relationship types by defining extra data record types and by programming. Similarly, the ANSI/SQL data model can accomplish the other five relationship types after first defining extra tables, executing views, and through end-user programming. Figures 3.8, 3.9, 3.28 and 3.55 depict the four data models and identify the static and dynamic relationships supported by each.

NDL describes quite sophisticated referential integrity. Because NDL referential integrity is not value-based like SQL, but is based on sets, it is actually more effective. There may be multiple sets between data records of different types, and thus there may be multiple types of NDL referential integrity. DBMSs

```
RELATIONAL OPERATIONS

Record

     Add
     Delete
     Modify
     Select
     Project

Relationship

     Product
     Union
     Intersection
     Difference
     Join
     Divide

CRITICAL REQUIREMENT FOR SOME OPERATIONS

     UNION COMPATIBLE

     SAME DEGREE (NUMBER OF COLUMNS)
     2 ATTRIBUTES FROM SAME DOMAIN
```

Figure 3.75 Relational Operations

supporting NDL can thus indicate whether integrity constraints are to be placed on the connection and disconnection of data records to or from relationships in the database. This type of capability prevents deletions posted by a run-unit from actually happening. For example, suppose that a view data record instance is constructed of data record elements from the CUSTOMER data record, the ORDER data record, and the ORDER-LINE-ITEM data record. If the command to delete occurs, then these DDL-based restrictions prevent the ORDER and CUSTOMER data record instance from being deleted if there are any other relationships between these data records and other database data records.

NDL, unlike SQL, can store data record instances and defer connecting them to relationships. For example, if there is an on-line order entry system, and if the orders are collected during the day, but the database's financial statistics have to remain unchanged during the whole day to permit consistent financial reporting, the deferral capability prevents the day's order data records from affecting these financial statistics. Not only is this capability useful for retaining consistency, it also lessens I/O and CPU resources consumed during the day, postponing them until a night batch run.

In keeping with NDL's version of referential integrity, NDL can indicate whether the DBMS has cascade delete authority. The default is no cascade delete, and if the option is turned on, then cascade delete is active.

3.4 DATA DEFINITION LANGUAGE

The language that communicates the logical database to the DBMS is called the data definition language (DDL). Once the DBMS successfully processes these language clauses, it produces the database's schema. The definition process itself and the specification of the data record types and the data record elements are the same for both static and dynamic relationship DBMSs. The DDL tends to be tailored to the DBMS's data model, regardless of whether its data record types are simple or complex, or whether its relationship mechanism is static or dynamic.

A static relationship DBMS's DDL typically contains more editing and validation clauses that affect multiple data record types than would a dynamic relationship DBMS's DDL. In a dynamic relationship DBMS these editing and validation clauses relate only to a single data record type. Some dynamic relationship DBMSs allow for a central schema of multiple, dynamically connected data record types. In such a case, the dynamic relationship DBMS DDL becomes more like its static relationship DBMS counterpart.

The data definition language has traditionally been syntax oriented. There is no reason, however, why it can not be represented through interactive screen displays that accomplish the correct syntax. Such a facility exists for FOCUS, and is called FILETALK. A DDL typically contains the syntactic specifications to support:

- Schemas
- Domains
- Data record instances
- Data record elements
- Relationships

Figure 3.76 illustrates the DDL for an ANSI NDL database. Figures 3.77 and 3.78 show DDLs for IMS and SYSTEM 2000. Figure 3.79 contains the DDL for a FOCUS schema. Figure 3.80 contains the DDL for an SQL database.

The data definition language interface enables those who define database structures to communicate those structures to the DBMS. The database structure consists of clauses for data record types, data record elements, and relationships (static only). The data record type clauses include the data record type's name,

```
SCHEMA NAME IS FACULTY-DATA

RECORD NAME IS FACULTY
     DUPLICATES ARE NOT ALLOWED
     NAME TYPE IS CHARACTER 25
     ADDRESS TYPE IS CHARACTER 40
     SSN TYPE IS CHARACTER 11

RECORD NAME IS JOBHIST
     JOBTITLE TYPE IS CHARACTER 25
     JOBCODE TYPE IS FIXED DECIMAL 2

SET NAME IS FAC-JOBHIST
     ORDER IS SORTED
     OWNER IS FACULTY
     MEMBER IS JOBHIST
          AUTOMATIC MANDATORY
          ASCENDING KEY IS JOBCODE
          DUPLICATES ARE ALLOWED
```

Figure 3.76 ANSI/NDL Data Model DDL

```
dbd      name=ecudpdbd
segm     name=course, bytes=256
   field name=(coursenbr,seq),bytes=3,start=1
   field name=title,bytes=33,state=4
   field name=descripn,bytes=220,start=37
segm name=prereq,parent=course,bytes=36
   field name=(coursenbr,seq),bytes=3,start=1
   field name=title,bytes=33,start=4
segm name=offering,Parent=course,bytes=20
   field name=(date,seq,m),bytes=6,start=1
   field name=location,bytes=12,start=7
   field name=format,bytes=2,start=19
segm name=teacher,parent=offering,bytes=24
   field name=(empnbr,seq),bytes=6,start=1
   field name=name,bytes=18,start=7
segm name=student,parent=offering,bytes=25
   field name=(empnbr,seq),bytes=6,start=1
   field name=name,bytes=18,start=7
   field name=grade,bytes=1,start=25
```

Figure 3.77 Hierarchical (IMS) Data Model DDL

primary keys, foreign keys, and data record element clauses. The data record element clauses indicate whether the data elements are single valued, multiple valued, groups, or repeating groups. The data record element clauses also state the data types, and any edit and validation rules. The final set of clauses define the relationships, that is, single or multiple member, one to one, many to many, recursive, inferential, etc. SQL referential integrity clauses are defined within the CREATE TABLE statements. In NDL, referential integrity is defined in the NDL SET clauses, which define NDL relationships.

```
STATIC HIERARCHY (SYSTEM 2000)

1*  COURSE TITLE (INT 9(6))
2*  COURSE DESCRIPTION (NAME X (25))

     3*  PREREQUISITES (RG)
          4*  PREREQ COURSE NBR (INT 9(6) IN 3)
          5*  PREREQ COURSE TITLE (INT 9(6) IN 3)

     5*  OFFERING (RG)
          6*  SECTION NBR (INT 99 IN 5)
          7*  DATE ( DAYS OF WEEK (NAME X (12) IN 5)

          8*  TEACHERS (RG IN 5)
               9*  TEACHER NBR (INT 9(9) IN 8)

          10*  STUDENTS (RG IN 5)
                11*  STUDENT ID (INT X (9) IN 10)
                12*  FINAL GRADE (NAME XX IN 10)
```

Figure 3.78 Hierarchical (SYSTEM 2000) Data Model DDL

```
FILENAME=TEACHER,SUFFIX=FOC
SEGNAME=TEACHER,SEGTYPE=S1
FIELDNAME=T-SSN,ALIAS=,FORMAT=I9,FIELDTYPE=I,$
FIELDNAME=T-NAME,ALIAS=,FORMAT=A30,$

FILENAME=COURSE,SUFFIX=FOC
SEGNAME=COURSE,SEGTYPE=S1
FIELDNAME=COURSE-NBR,ALIAS=,FORMAT=I5,FIELDTYPE=I,$
FIELDNAME=COURSE-NAME,ALIAS=,FORMAT=A30,$

FILENAME=COURSECT,SUFFIX=FOC
SEGNAME=COURSECT,SEGTYPE=S3
FIELDNAME=COURSE-NBR,ALIAS=,FORMAT=I5,FIELDTYPE=I,$
FIELDNAME=SECTION-NB,ALIAS=,FORMAT=I2,$
FIELDNAME=T-SSN,ALIAS=,FORMAT=I9,FIELDTYPE=I,$
```

Figure 3.79 Independent Logical File DDL (FOCUS)

The quantity and sophistication the data definition language clauses reflect are inverse to the amount of effort required to develop database applications. The fewer and less sophisticated the clauses, the larger the design and programming effort. The greater the quantity and sophistication of the clauses of the data definition language, the smaller the design and programming effort. Given that COBOL programs can have a life cycle cost of 100,000 to 300,000 dollars, it is easy to see that increased capabilities can save hundreds of thousands of dollars in a very short time.

Alongside definitions of data record types, data record elements, and relationships must be the data integrity clauses. Data integrity clauses are rules

```
Create Table Student
   ( Student_Id  Char(5) Not Null
     Sname  Char(20),
     Status Smallint,
     Major  Char(15) );

Create Table Teacher
   ( Teacher#  Char(6) Not Null
     TeacherName  Char(20),
     TeacherDegree  Char(5) );

Create Table CourseSection
   ( Course#  Smallint Not Null
     Section# Smallint Not Null
     Year Smallint Not Null
     Semester Smallint Not Null
     Teacher# Char (6) );

Create Table Enrollment
   ( Course#  Smallint Not Null,
     Section# Smallint Not Null,
     Student# Smallint Not Null,
     Year Smallint Not Null
     Semester Smallint Not Null
     GradeReceived Char (1) );
```

Figure 3.80 SQL Data Definition Language

and regulations just like other clauses in that they control operations on the database. Integrity clauses are of two types: procedure-oriented and value-oriented.

Procedure-oriented clauses enable the execution of preprogrammed logic that serves to accept or reject data record element values, data record instance adds/deletes/modifications, or invoke other programs that cause actions to happen such as reorders. Value-oriented clauses are used to verify that only allowable values are stored in the database.

It is very important for a DBMS to have integrity facilities. Integrity facilities increase programmer productivity by permitting the use of natural languages over COBOL for updating. Even if COBOL were as easy to use as a natural language, integrity facilities would still be important, because they permit all the clauses to be defined and maintained in the database's schema rather than in each update program. This makes it unnecessary to find, modify, recompile, and retest many COBOL programs every time a data integrity rule is changed.

3.5 LOGICAL DATABASE SUMMARY

The logical database is the expression of the database's data organization. The language that communicates this data organization to the DBMS is called the data definition language (DDL). The two different relationship binding mechanisms are static and dynamic. Within the static mechanism, the two data models are network and hierarchical. Within the dynamic mechanism, the two data models are independent logical file and relational.

Ideally, every DBMS should support the maximum number of relationships allowable within its data model. As stated above, these relationships are:

- One-to-many
- Owner-multiple member
- Singular-one member
- Singular-multiple-member
- Recursive
- Many-to-many
- One-to-one
- Inferential

There should be no restriction on the inherent properties of data record types. Any data record type should be capable of being both an owner of one data record type, and a member of another. If a data record type can be only an owner or a member, then additional data record types must be created to make up for the DBMS's inability to have a data record type serve both roles. In addition to the additional data record types, there will also be additional disk space, additional I/Os for reading and writing, and in the case of a DBMS or database failure, additional resources for recovery.

Integrity constraints are critical to quality database. These constraints can be defined for the single data record element, between data record elements within the same data record type, and between data record elements in different data record types. Even though an integrity constraint between data record elements from different data record types is an interrecord relationship, it must be noted that the value is not the basis of the relationship. It serves as an additional integrity constraint to make sure, for example, that districts are related to their regions.

Just as there must be integrity procedures for data record elements and data record types, there must be integrity procedures for relationships. These procedures or formulas are executed whenever a relationship operation is executed, and they determine the success or failure of the relationship operation. Further, they reduce the time spent on creating applications programs, and eliminate the need to make updates when users perform illegal operations.

All the integrity procedures should be written in either a compiler language or a natural language. Further, the invocation of a procedure should be for a specific purpose, so that the procedure matching the specific purpose can be changed as needed.

In summary, the network (ANSI/NDL) data model is a richer data model than is hierarchical, and the ILF data model is a richer model than is the relational (ANSI/SQL) model. *Proposals within ANSI's X3H2 have been presented to make the SQL language support ILF data model structures. When, and if these proposals pass, the ANSI/SQL language will no longer be restricted to relational data structures.*

If an organization wishes to procure DBMSs that enhance portability, it should procure DBMSs that have languages conforming to ANSI/NDL and ANSI/SQL. Most ILF DBMSs can be restricted to operate like relational DBMSs. Thus, procuring an ILF DBMS and restricting its databases to relational structures for portable applications, but allowing complex data record types for non-portable applications, is a way to have portability when it is needed and data model richness otherwise. In short, buying an ANSI/NDL data model DBMS, as well as an ILF data model DBMS that can optionally conform to ANSI/SQL, is clearly the best choice.

4

THE PHYSICAL DATABASE

4.1 PHYSICAL DATABASE COMPONENTS

The physical database, the second component of a DBMS, involves the creation and maintenance of the actual database. The preceding chapter, the Logical Database is about the database's logical structure, that is, its data record types, data record elements, and relationships. In essence, the *logical database* is the database's *blueprint* and the *physical database* is the database's *construction*.

This chapter addresses the DBMS's and the computer's view of these components, and the techniques the DBMS employs to minimize both access times and mass storage use. This chapter then is a study in architecture and techniques, none of which have been--nor should ever be--standardized by ANSI. While the ANSI data models identify DBMS commonality, that is, data model and data manipulation language interfaces, physical database is a DBMS discriminator that sets apart the DBMS vendor's investment in DBMS performance and mass storage efficiency.

Generally speaking, the physical database involves much more than just the layout of the operating system files that store data record instances. It also covers data record instance access strategy, data loading, data record instance update effects and capabilities, and database maintenance (backup).

The physical database coincides with many of the aspects of the ANSI/SPARC internal schema. The edited version of the ANSI/SPARC report describes it as

> specifications of the internal objects, indices, pointers, and other implementation mechanisms, other parameters affecting (optimizing) the economics of internal data storage, integrity, security, recovery, and administrative matters. (1)

Because this book was written 15 years after the ANSI/SPARC draft report, it has a more refined view of the technology of database. Thus certain aspects of the internal schema, e.g., integrity, security, and recovery are addressed in the system control chapter.

4.2 STORAGE STRUCTURE

The storage structure of a database consists of four parts: dictionary, indexes, relationships, and data. This architecture, like the logical database's architecture, is communicated to the DBMS through a language that is often called the data storage definition language (DSDL). The critical differences among static and dynamic storage structures are presented in Figure 4.1

	STATIC	DYNAMIC
Storage Structure	Often multiple component physical files Typically dictionary, indexes, relationships and data	Often single component physical files Typically dictionary, indexes, and data
Access Strategy	Primary key and relationship searching via data record processing	High number of indexes Dynamic matching/ merging of record extracts via data element values
Data Loading	Complete logical records Careful planning Exact placement Large volumes All or nothing	Record tape by record tape Load what you have Incremental building
Data Update	Very careful Far reaching effects HLI only Periodic database reorganization	Casual, add new records, data elements at will Seldom needs reorganization
Database Maintenance	Usually one or a few databases Global save/restore at high level	Many storage structures Careful planning Many commands at low levels

Figure 4.1 Physical Database: Static and Dynamic Relationship DBMS Comparison

The dictionary is the repository of the information represented by the compiled DDL. Dictionaries contain many types of information, such as validation rules and extra space lists. The DBMS creates the dictionary upon successful processing of the DDL. It is automatically maintained by the DBMS during various processes. Some DBMSs store the dictionary data for each database in a common *super* dictionary, that is, an IRDS.

Indexes are mechanisms for fast access. They exist either as primary indexes (unique value guaranteed) or secondary indexes (repeated values allowed). Indexes usually point either to the relationship instances that exist distinct and separate from the data record instances (static only), or to the actual record instances (both static and dynamic). In most DBMSs, defined indexes are automatically created during database loading, and are automatically maintained during update.

Relationships are the connections among data record instances. If a relationship is static, then it is usually a relative record address that is stored in the owner data record instance (pointing to the member) or the member data record instance (pointing back to the owner data record instance and/or to the next and/or prior data record instance). If the relationship is dynamic, then the data value that is uniquely contained in the owner data record instance is replicated in many member data record instances. In a static relationship DBMS, relationships are created automatically according to data record instance loading sequences and special data loading verbs. Subsequent to database loading, the static relationship DBMS relationships are maintained through special user language verbs. In a dynamic relationship DBMS, relationships among data record instances exist implicitly as shared data values, and are maintained through data record element value changes.

The last part of the storage structure is the data record instance. Its storage structure design can have several data record types for each operating system file, or only one data record type in each operating system file. This component is created and maintained as data record instances are stored during loads, updates, or deletes.

The sophistication of a DBMS's storage structure indicates the power of the DBMS for certain applications. Complex storage structures boost the efficiency of one particular kind of report processing over another. The simple storage structure, on the other hand, is ready for any interrogation that comes along; that is, it has no structural orientation toward any particular type of report. For applications in which no type of report predominates, simplicity is highly desirable. But if an application has a large number of data record types and a great volume of data, a simple storage structure will probably not be able to handle efficiently a report that involves complex relationships and report ordering. For an application in which certain reports are executed frequently, a storage structure favoring these reports is highly desirable.

4.2.1 Dictionary Component

The component that separates an ordinary data file from a database is the dictionary. In traditional applications, the knowledge of the organization of a file is stored in the application programs. If there are fifty such programs, then all fifty have to have the same information. A natural outgrowth of this was to push all this information into a single routine and to then have all the other routines invoke it. When this information was removed from the routine and stored in a stand alone file, database was born. Since this information addressed only one file, it was referred to as file management. When databases grew to be able to handle many such files, the dictionary became both more complex and more useful. Data files and the various data types and relationships that existed between data record elements could be reviewed at a glance.

Over time, the dictionary has grown to encompass much more than just data record element names. Included now are data record element editing and validation rules. Included also are triggers that call other programs to accomplish DBMS-controlled processing on a data record instance before it is stored, modified, deleted, or retrieved.

An organization that has a DBMS installed for several years is likely to have developed fifty or more databases, each with its own dictionary. And, just as the file information was redundant when stored in many programs, so too is the individual database dictionary information redundant when stored in many databases. A sophisticated DBMS allows this information to be *lifted* from each individual database and stored in another repository that functions as a super-dictionary. ANSI's X3H4 committee has standardized the super dictionary, calling it the Information Resource Dictionary System (IRDS).

When data dictionaries were first developed, distinct systems arose. Each had to be specially defined, loaded, reported, and updated. Because this work was redundant to DBMS data definition work, these separate data dictionary systems have faded. The scope of today's DBMS integrated data dictionary systems has enlarged from being merely a passive repository of data structures to being a *command and control* center for multiple databases. Because of this scope change, each DBMS vendor created its own version of a data dictionary and integrated it into the DBMS software. Because it is integrated, it is able to be active, automatically recording in the IRDS any changes to the individual databases.

The standardization of the data dictionary has been completed by the ANSI committee X3H4, and was confirmed as an ANSI standard in early 1989. The facility is not restricted in its contents. The X3H4 IRDS can store data about database's design, the DBMS, and database applications. Data about a database's design is called metadata.

There are really no clear distinctions between static relationship DBMS data dictionaries and dynamic relationship DBMS data dictionaries. Each type of dictionary and each DBMS vendor's dictionary seem to have the same common fundamental information, such as data record element and data record type names, expository definitions, and their usage in various programs, providing, of course, that the programs have been properly compiled. In addition to that basic set of common data, all data dictionaries contain other facilities required by the specific data model, or required for fully defining and controlling database (not DBMS) environments.

To have a complete and fully functional database environment requires both a passive IRDS that contains all the application's specification metadata, and one or more active DBMS-IRDS that contains all the applications' implementation, operational, and maintenance metadata.

4.2.2 Index Component

An index is a data value based access path to one or more data record instances. Some indexes are primary and others are secondary. A primary index is most often used to locate a single data record instance. A secondary index locates one or more data record instances.

It is commonly thought that primary indexes must have unique values and that secondary indexes must have non-unique values. A company might, however, have its own employee identification number that is used to identify employees and to store and find data record instances in a database. The fact that the employee also has a social security number (SSN) and that the SSN is used to access an employee whenever it is the only number known, does not make the SSN a primary key. In the terminology of the previous chapter, the SSN is called a candidate key. Since most DBMSs do not have a candidate key type, the only way to achieve its effects is to declare it an index with a unique value integrity constraint.

Primary indexes are also sometimes used along with secondary indexes to provide data record instance *addresses* whenever a secondary key search needs to locate data record instances for a data record element value that is not unique. For example, the query FIND EMPLOYEES WHERE JOB CODE EQ PROGRAMMER is likely to turn up several employees, and the list of data record instance addresses resulting from the query would usually consist of the primary key of each employee's data record type. Two typical ways of organizing primary key indexes are hierarchies and hashing (see Figures 4.2 and 4.3).

A problem arises whenever the DBMS actually uses a data record instance's primary key value to compute the storage address assigned to the data record instance by the database. The problem is that, whenever the data record instance's primary key value has to change, then the DBMS must perform the following actions:

- The old primary key value must be used to retrieve the data record instance from its old location.
- The data record instance must be deleted from its old storage location.
- The new primary key value must be used to discover the new physical location for the data record instance.
- The data record instance must be stored in the database at its new location.

Figure 4.3 illustrates this problem when the actual value of the primary key determines the storage location of the data record instances. If the value of the primary key changes, then the data record instance has to be located, retrieved, deleted, relocated, and then re-stored.

Furthermore, if that data record instance contains several data record elements that are indexed, and if the secondary key value entry in the index table is composed of a concatenation of the secondary key value and the primary key value, then whenever the primary key value is changed, the secondary key value entries in the index would also have to be adjusted. While the DBMS performs all these locate, delete, relocate, and re-store operations automatically, computer resources are still consumed, and since data record instances are *moving* around in the database, there is an increased window for database damage should some DBMS, system software (O/S), or hardware failure occur.

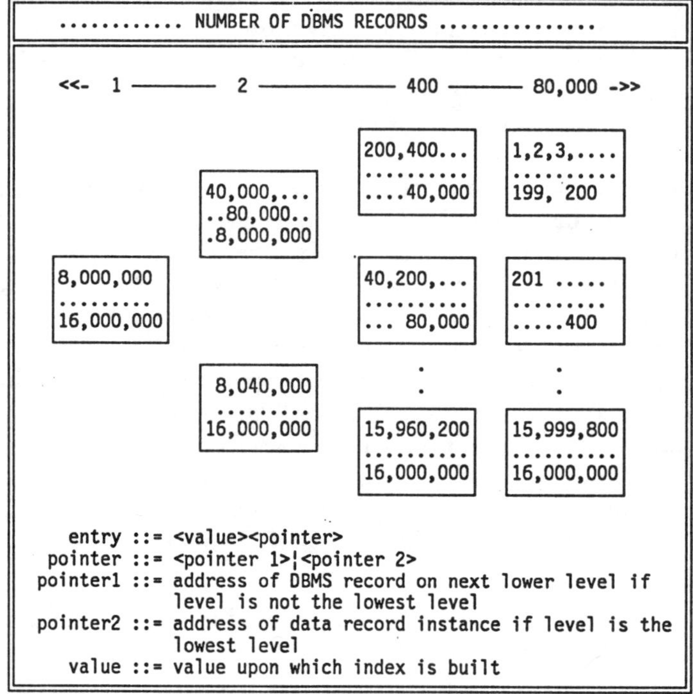

Hierarchical Index Organization
200 index component entries per DBMS record
16,000,000 Records Represented in Four Levels

Note: See appendix A for notation definition.

Figure 4.2 Hierarchical Index Organization

Figure 4.4 illustrates the construction of an index. The data record element column identifies the name of the indexed data record element. The unique value column identifies the unique values associated with each of the two data record elements. In the case of SKILL, the unique values are CODER, DBA, . . ., SYSTEMS ANALYST. The multiple occurrence column contains an array of primary key data record element values (e.g., PK1, . . ., PK109). In this example, the primary key values are EMPLOYEE-IDs. If the value of an EMPLOYEE-ID is changed, then not only must the primary key value of the actual EMPLOYEE data record instance change, but also the index entries for the data record instance's SEX and SKILL data record element values.

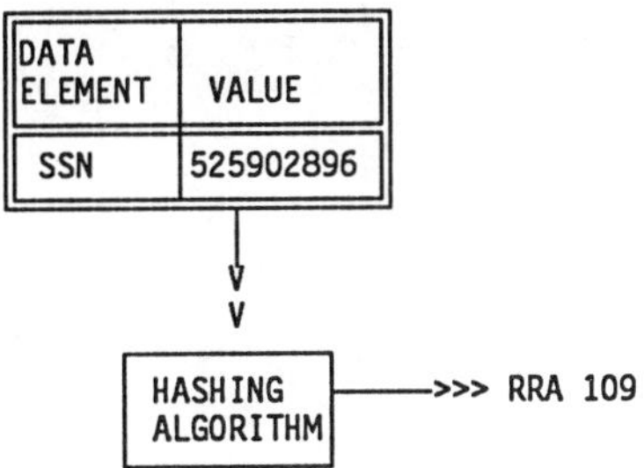

Note: RRA means relative record address

Figure 4.3 Hash-based Primary Key Index Organization

DATA ELEM	INDEX: UNIQUE VALUE	INDEX: MULTIPLE OCCURRENCES	DATA
SEX	M	PK1,...PK10,...,PK109	
			PK 107
	F	PK100, PK111,.,PK107	MARY LIBRARIAN F
SKILL	CODER	PK1,PK101,PK184	MORE DATA
	DBA	....	
	LIBRARIAN	PK2,PK107,PK384,PK410	PK 109
	MANAGER	....	
	PROGARMMER	PK248, PK109,..,218	JOHN PROGRAMMER M
	SYSTEMS ANALYST	PK1008, PK9982	

Note: PK means primary key, and PK1 means the first primary key.

Figure 4.4 Multiple Key Access (static or dynamic)

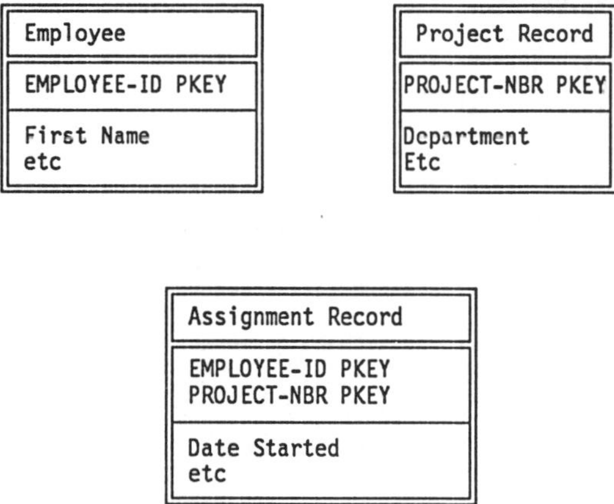

Figure 4.5 Project Assignment

As a further complication of this problem, suppose there is a data record type called PROJECT-ASSIGNMENT (see Figure 4.5) that is used to identify the employees assigned to specific projects. The primary key of this data record type is likely the combination of the EMPLOYEE-ID and the PROJECT-NUMBER. If, as in the example above, the data record element value for EMPLOYEE-ID is changed, then in addition to the changes cited above, every PROJECT-ASSIGNMENT data record instance involving the employee has to be selected, retrieved, deleted, updated, reselected, and then re-stored. Of course, if any of the data record elements in the PROJECT-ASSIGNMENT are indexed, then these index structures also have to be changed.

To avoid such a situation, some DBMSs use the user-defined primary key only as a logical identifier, and translating it through a table look-up into a permanent DBMS-generated physical identifier. This physical identifier is then independent of user value changes. Figure 4.6 illustrates the use of this indirect technique. The indexes on the SSN and GPA data record elements both point to the primary key value of <525902896>. In the translator part of the storage structure (lower left), the <525902896> value points to a DBMS record address of <1000>. This in turn points to the actual internal data record instance location <200> (within DBMS record 1000) of the actual data record instance. The other problem of having EMPLOYEE data record instances that have the wrong EMPLOYEE-ID value still has to be addressed, but at least none of the data record instances have to be deleted and re-stored. An additional benefit resulting from this logical-to-physical key lookup table is that none of the data record element index structures associated with any affected data record instances have to be updated just because the EMPLOYEE-ID primary key of the employee data record type is changed. Furthermore, DBMSs designed in this way do not require primary keys at all.

DICTIONARY	INDEX ORGANIZATION
SSN	>525902896
GPA	1.0 1.8 2.5—> PK, PK,...,525902896, PK 2.7 3.4

ASSOCIATOR: ORGANIZED BY PRIMARY KEY VALUE	
RECORD	
KEY	ADDRESS
149248819	123
219194187	512
325902896	250
423134781	183
525902890	1000

1000

DATA AREA

200

525902896 DATA

KEY AREA

<PK><RA>	<PK><RA>
<PK><RA>	<PK><RA>
<525902896><200>	

Figure 4.6 Indirect Index Organization for a Student Database

Clearly, indexes are far more complicated than they first appear. The quality of the design of a DBMS's indexes and the manner in which they are used by the DBMS, regardless of the DBMS's data model, dramatically affects the types of applications that can be handled satisfactorily.

4.2.2.1 Index Alternatives

This section presents the essential components of a case study from an organization that has a real need for sophisticated indexing. For the sake of simplicity, this case study assumes that each computer access consumes one I/O, and that each DBMS record is 6000 bytes long. Any improvements due to blocking, in-memory hits, and the like are not factored in, except where noted. Also, for the sake of simplicity, all calculations are approximate and serve only to illustrate differences in index constructions and strategies.

The company services both central office and field offices. The field offices obtain orders and enter them into a centralized system. Daily reports are produced for each field office, its sales staff, and for various headquarters sales support organizations. Additionally, the order entry data is allocated to the various types of product categories so that the product managers can keep track of their products. Comparisons are needed by different time periods, namely, by seasons, quarters, and days. For the sales management staff, comparisons are needed by different sales regions, by districts, by territories, and by sales staff members. For the marketing research staff, demographic comparisons such as the average sales by product to persons over 18 who are living in rural areas, or small towns, or large cities are needed so that product penetration can be determined and marketing dollars can be wisely spent. Clearly, the problem involves much more than generating invoices.

To handle such a complicated problem, DBMS vendors trumpet indexes to facilitate quick access of different sets of data record instances based on a data record element's value.

An index is a value-based relationship among a set of data record instances. When a WHERE clause is constructed for use in any of a DBMS's languages (for example, host language interface or query), the programmer must determine the relative benefits derived from including only one data record element indexed condition, several such conditions, or a mixture of indexed and non-indexed conditions.

Almost all DBMSs can improve processing speed by using indexes. However, some DBMSs can only use one index within a search clause to improve performance while other DBMSs can use multiple indexes and achieve even greater processing speeds. The first type of DBMS is termed a record processor, and the second type is termed a list processor.

In record processing DBMSs, if a WHERE clause contains two conditions, both involving indexed data record elements, the DBMS only employs one index to help find a set of data record instances. The DBMS then searches those data record instances to find the net set of data record instances possessing the value from the other condition. In the case study, there are indexes for REGION and another for PRODUCT, and a query is to determine the sales for a given product within a specific region. A record processing DBMS can only take advantage one of the indexed data record elements (for example, REGION) to retrieve all the invoice data record instances for orders within that REGION. The record processing DBMS then searches these data record instances for the specific PRODUCT. The record processing DBMS functions just as if PRODUCT is not indexed at all. A list of some of the popular record processing, *IBM* mainframe DBMSs by data model is provided in Figure 4.7.

Type of Processing	Static		Dynamic	
	Network	Hierarchical	ILF	Relational
Record	IDMS/R SUPRA	IMS	FOCUS	DB-2 IDMS/R SUPRA
List		System 2000	ADABAS M-204	

Figure 4.7 Popular List or Record Processing DBMSs

List processing DBMSs, in contrast, improve processing speed by employing more than one indexed data record element in the WHERE clause. Typically, when several indexed conditions are included, each is processed separately, resulting in a list of data record instance identifiers (or relative record addresses) for each selection condition. These lists are then combined appropriately (AND or OR), resulting in a final list of data record instance identifiers. In the example, the list processing DBMS determines one list of data record instances for REGION and another list of data record instances for PRODUCT. These two lists are then ANDed together to determine the list of data record instance identifiers that represent the set of invoices meeting both conditions. A list of some of the popular list processing, *IBM* DBMSs is presented in Figure 4.7.

Regardless of whether a DBMS is a list processor or a record processor, if one or more conditions included in the WHERE clause involve a non-indexed data record element, the data record instances acceptable to these non-indexed conditions are determined as follows. If the non-indexed condition is joined to the other conditions with an AND, then the selection is against only the index-selected data record instances. If the non-indexed condition is joined to the other conditions with an OR, then the data record instances not passing the index tests also have to be searched; but because this means searching all data record instances, all index benefits are lost.

The organization in the case study needs to perform interrogations on the order data from three different perspectives:

- Marketing research
- Headquarters sales
- Field sales

The marketing researcher needs to compare the sales of various items of different brands and their four different promotion variants, all of which were offered in different areas of the country for the past five Easters. Of special interest is whether various trade promotions and mass advertising campaigns affected the sales in three of the five areas. Further, since two of these promotions were price discount coupons for different products, did these coupons affect the sale of these products? Did all of these promotions affect the sales of similar items of the competitors? And did the promotion affect the sales of the organization's existing items?

In contrast, a headquarters sales staffer wants to identify the various regions, districts, and territories that are not performing as well as others. Additionally, the staffer performs intense research on the best and worst districts to determine differences in sales managers, salespersons, and in the demographics between these best and worst sales districts. Further, he wants an alert report each Monday of all districts that are performing at a rate significantly different from last month's, or last year's, or whenever..

As for the third perspective, the salesperson in the field wants to plan the next week's sales calls. Clearly, if there is a push from the home office to make sales on a particular item, the salesperson needs to know the ranked order of the customers for that item during this time period for the last few weeks, months, and years. Armed with that information, the salesperson can visit the high probability customers first. And, before visiting these clients, the salesperson has to know which orders were placed recently, which orders were being delivered next week, and which orders are back ordered to assess the client's disposition.

4.2.2.2 Problem Specification

Clearly, the data needs of the case study company are quite complex. The marketing researcher needs data for different items for different areas of the country during different calendar weeks (Easter is not on the same day every year). The researcher also needs competitive data for the same periods to determine whether any gain or loss of sales is different from the competition's gains or losses. Sales data is needed for the areas of the country that both did and did not offer promotions so that the results can be compared. Promotional cost data is needed to determine the real gains or losses. Finally, the sales data shows whether the destinations of the items are within the areas that are measured for gain or loss.

The second user, the headquarters sales manager, needs data by the various sales organizational units across time: Furthermore, norms need to be developed so that the sales units that deviate from the norms can be easily identified and reported to both headquarters.

The individual salesperson, finally, needs to be able to review the order data for distinct clients in order to plan sales trips. This data is needed at the order level, customer level, and item level (for special sales and promotions).

The amount of data available is enormous. The granularity of the data is at the order and line item level, and is organized by client, by the various types of selling organizations, by various product configurations, and so on. The data is longitudinal to accurately track various types of promotions, brands, and customers over a number of years. Of course, any other changes in the product have to be considered, such as price changes or weight changes. And lastly, it is necessary to consider outside factors such as fluctuations in the economy.

The problems cited above are just some of the many types of problems that need to be solved in this typical business application. Furthermore, the data resulting from solving any one of these problems is sure to lead to other new problems. Questions produce answers that uncover new questions. In any analysis, once the basic data is found, it should be easy to feed it to statistical processors, graphics packages, and the like for analysis and refinement.

If the company in the case study had only about 25 items, one or two hundred customers, several orders for each customer, and needed only to research the past several month's data, then the solution to a problem like this would fall within any DBMS's capabilities. There are DBMSs that can store and retrieve the data, and follow-on processors that can accomplish the statistical analysis. Finding solutions to these problems should take no longer than a few minutes to, at most, a few hours. The case study company, however, has about 278,000 line items from within 27,000 orders per month and the company has determined that it needs five years (60 months) of this data. Multiplied, that is about 16.7 million line item data record instances. The space required is 1.1 billion characters.

It is often said that 10% of the data is used 90% of the time and 90% of the data is used 10% of the time. In terms of report needs, this means that only a small amount of the data from the line items is needed for most interrogations. The set of often-used data is depicted in Figure 4.8. The first data record elements are part of the primary key (PK(1) to PK(3)). Appendix A contains a more detailed explanation of this key notation. Each data record element is also a foreign key (FK(n)) to another data record type. To help understand the data distribution, the quantity of unique values over the 16.7 million data record instances is provided. Finally, a picture clause indicates the type of data for each data record element.

To assist in appreciating the relative performance differences in the various indexing alternatives, a simple computer performance model was constructed. The computer used for the calculations is a mid-1980s, large IBM mainframe, with a throughput rate of about 81 data record instances per wall clock second for serial searches, and about 50 data record instances per second for random searches. These through put rates were determined over a number of months of actual observations during the times of day that the case study computer system was operating, and are therefore quite realistic given the computer's configuration and all the other applications competing for service.

```
LINE ITEM

LENGTH = 66
MAXIMUM COUNT = 16,700,000
COUNT PER MONTH = 278,000
TOTAL SPACE = 1.102 Billion characters

CUSTOMER-NUMBER (PK(1), FK(1), UNIQUE VALUES = 47,000, PIC 9(11))
ORDER-NUM (PK(2), FK(2), UNIQUE VALUES = 1,500,000, PIC YYYYMMDDNNNN)
LINE-NUM (PK(3), PICTURE 99)
MANUFACTURER-ID (FK(3), UNIQUE VALUES = 1, PIC X(5))
ITEM-NUM (FK(4), UNIQUE VALUES = 500, PIC X(5))
VERSION-NUM (FK(5), UNIQUE VALUES = 10, PIC 99)
MARKETING-PROGRAM-ID (FK(6), UNIQUE VALUES = 1000, PIC YYYYNNN)
ITEM-ORDER-QTY (PIC 9(7))
REGION (FK(7), UNIQUE VALUES = 24, PIC 99)
DISTRICT (FK(8), UNIQUE VALUES = 150, PIC 9999)
TERRITORY (FK(9), UNIQUE VALUES = 750, PIC 999999)
DIVISION (FK(10), UNIQUE VALUES = 10, PIC 99)
SELLING-ORGANIZATION (FK(11), UNIQUE VALUES = 99, PIC 99)

Note: See appendix A for notation definition.
```

Figure 4.8 Logical Database Design

4.2.2.3 Initial Solution

The company began its first attempt to solve the problem by calculating how long it would take to serially sweep all the order-item data record instances in order to select a specific subset (see Figure 4.8). The calculation was performed as follows: 16,700,000 logical data record instances / 81 logical data record instances per second = about 206,172 seconds, which comes to 57.27 hours. Since the blocking factor on the file was about 12, the rate for reading DBMS (physical) data record instances was determined to be about 7 per second. Not surprisingly, the organization decided that a 57-hour response time to an on-line interrogation was unacceptable. In response, they tried to develop a manageable number of statistical summarizations of the line item data record type, and to generate these summaries every month. This meant that the 16.7 million invoice line items did not have to be searched for every interrogation. Without this summarization approach, the organization determined the application would not be possible. An example of a summary is the total product sales for a particular division for a particular program for a particular sales organization for a particular company month (DIV-PROG-ORG-SLS-MON-AMT). Another example is a summary of the total product sales of an item-version for a particular sales region for a particular month (ITEMVER-REGN-MON-AMT).

All in all, there were about 100-200 such summaries. All the summaries were created and formatted as data record instances for summary level data record types, which were loaded into a sales and marketing database. These summary level data record types were used to meet the needs of the marketing, sales, and research departments. So, for any particular problem, if there was a summary that fit the data needs, then everything was fine. But if not, researchers had to solve the problem by getting reports, sifting and selecting data, and recompiling new statistics--all manually. As an alternative to manual work, the data processing department created an additional data extract, summarized the data into a new summary level data record type, modified the sales and marketing database by loading the data record instances from the new summary data record type, and then allowed the staff to access it. The creation of each new summary data record type required about one staff month. In short,

- If the summary data was used, queries could run much faster, but the improvement would apply only to problems that fit a particular summary.
- If the raw data was used, any kind of problem could be researched, but each query would take 57.27 hours.

The summary approach was implemented at the client site. After several years three problems emerged:

- The demand for new summaries kept growing making it increasingly difficult to keep current.
- As existing summaries became outmoded, it was necessary either to drop an old summary by reorganizing the database at great expense, or to keep paying for generating and updating unused data.
- The end user, that is, the researcher, was dependent on the data processing department to develop the necessary computer programs to select data record instances, combine them with others, and produce a report.

Two conclusions were drawn:

- The data processing department was unable to keep up with the development of summaries that were to feed the database.
- The data processing department was also unable to generate new reports in a timely manner.

In short, because of the method of solution implementation, the backlog in data processing kept costs increasing and progress slowing.

For these reasons, a search to replace the summary approach began. At the beginning of the search, specific criteria were established so that alternatives could be properly evaluated. To be acceptable, a solution had to:

- Store data efficiently

- Enable users to directly formulate interrogations of any kind
- Have computer response times that were reasonable

4.2.2.4 The Company's DBMS

An obvious way to begin the search for a new solution was to examine the client's DBMS to see if its indexing facility could assist. The DBMS's data model installed at the client site was network. The DBMS did have an indexing capability to speed searches, and this capability could be applied to one or more data record elements. However, if multiple indexed data record elements within a data record instance were employed, the DBMS used only one of them. This meant that to achieve the effect of a multiple-data-record-element index, the data record element values had to be concatenated, with the resultant value being stored as a single string in the index file. In short, the DBMS was a record processor, not a list processor.

For an illustration of how indexing is beneficial, assume that it is necessary to total all the sales for one of the 24 regions. The DBMS would, of course, suggest that the data record element REGION be indexed. Using this method, the access time is twenty-four times less, or about 2.39 hours. Obviously this is an improvement. The improvement for totaling all the sales for one month is even greater if month is indexed. The elapsed time using a MONTH index is 57.27 hours / 60, or about 1 hour.

The corporation's DBMS also allowed indexed data record elements to be combined to make compound indexes. For example, the MONTH and REGION data record elements can be combined into a single index. This has the effect of shortening the query time to about 2.39 minutes ((57.27 / 60 / 24) * 60).

To build indexes, the client's DBMS appends, for example, the primary key (25 characters) of the record to the unique value of the REGION, producing the

```
<region><customer number><order number><ln>
   8       249241142        198901221223  01
   8       249495200        198802017524  01
   8       262625949        198802017524  02
   8       566669405        198802017534  03
   8       548645913        198802017534  04
   8       657671952        198812150001  01
   8       733738170        198812150001  02
   8       939399791        198811130765  01
   8       939934155        198811130765  02
   8       939992240        198811130765  03
```

Figure 4.9 Secondary Index Organized as a Primary Key Index

index shown in Figure 4.9. The primary key is identified as the concatenation of the first three data record elements. The data record elements that comprised the key are identified in Figure 4.8. Summing the character space required by their combined picture clauses results in 27 characters. The size of such an index is the sum of the secondary key's length plus the primary key's length (see Figure 4.8) multiplied by the number of data record instances. For example, the size of a REGION index on the line-item file is: (2 bytes + 27 bytes) * 16.7 million data record instances, or 450.9 million bytes. If all the indexes are two bytes long, then for 13 such indexes, the total space required for the single-data record element indexes is 13 * 450.9 million characters, or about 5.861 billion characters.

Now, for the compound indexes, the space has to be expanded for the additional data record elements that are concatenated with the indexed data record element. For example, if an indexed data record element is created that consists of the primary key (27 characters) and the REGION (2 characters), SELLING-ORGANIZATION (2 characters), and DISTRICT data record elements (3 characters), then the index size is: (27 + 2 + 2 + 3) * 16.7 million, or about 534.4 million characters. To index the 20 most popular compound indexes, the total index space is 10.688 billion characters. Adding that to the index space required for the single indexed data record elements, the total index space comes to 16.54 billion characters.

To implement indexes, the company's DBMS creates large files of small index record instances. While index processing to find the list of line-item data record instances is faster than reading the entire set of data record instances in the line-item file, the indexing done by the organization's DBMS has drawbacks in two areas:

- It requires concatenated indexes to achieve multiple index processing
- It is large. In fact, the total required space for indexes is 15 times more than for the data

The reason the DBMS requires concatenated indexes is that the DBMS does not use list processing, that is, ANDing or ORing multiple lists of keys to arrive at the target set of record identifiers. If the DBMS used list processing, each list of keys could be created by processing an index to find all the keys for a specific index value. To simulate list processing, the company's DBMS offered compound indexes. These compound keys, however, only increased the problem, as each takes up an increasingly larger amount of space, and each has to be updated by the DBMS. The DBMS's indexing strategy thus seems to be nothing more than replacing threaded lists of pointers in the data record instances with large files of small data record instances of specially constructed primary keys.

At first blush, indexing seemed to be a solution to the sales and marketing problem. The indexing strategy employed by the company's DBMS, however, does not include list processing, and this results in the definition, creation and constant maintenance of compound indexes. Furthermore, the DBMS's indexes, singly or as compound indexes, consume large amounts of disk space. Having 16.54 billion characters of DBMS index space for only about 1.102 billion characters of data seriously reduces its value as a solution.

What is the solution, or is the problem impossible to solve?

4.2.2.5 Looking Beyond a Popular Myth

The key to finding the right solution is to look beyond the widespread myth that indexes are always an add-on feature to database management systems, and not a fundamental component of a DBMS's access strategy. This myth leads one to believe that index mechanisms necessarily consume large amounts of space and require considerable resources for updating. But, in fact, there are a number of DBMSs that have indexing facilities designed especially to handle problems similar to the one in the case study.

4.2.2.6 Index Effects on Access Strategies

While the data model of a DBMS is clearly an important way of distinguishing one DBMS from another, access strategy is the DBMS component that provides real speed. For example, there is nothing in the relational data model that prohibits a DBMS from relying completely upon magnetic tape for storage and serial access for processing and calling itself relational. In fact, a DBMS called SIRS, developed in the 1960s by the National Aeronautics and Space Administration (NASA), was completely based on tape files, one for each data record type. Thus, conforming to one data model or another has nothing to do with performance.

What primarily determines the DBMS's speed is the sophistication of its access strategy. The two most important components of a DBMS's access strategy are indexes and relationships. The third most important component of a DBMS's access strategy is data storage formats. Both relationships and data storage are covered later in this chapter.

Although many people know that the fastest mechanism for accessing data is an index, few know that there are several different types of index organizations, and that some of these organizations can be very efficient in storage and very fast in processing. Figure 4.10 identifies a number of the more popular index structures and indicates their relative size and performance rankings.

4.2.2.7 Index Structures

Indexes can be built on single data record elements or on groups of data record elements. The first is simply called an index, while the latter is called a compound index. An index may also be built on a data record element that represents multiple values within a data record. For example, an employee may have a multiple-valued data record element: TELEPHONE NUMBER. ILF and some network DBMSs allow this case, while hierarchical and relational DBMSs prohibit it outright (because the data model does not allow multiple-valued data record elements). Most ILF DBMSs handle the index values by pretending that a *subordinate* data record type exists to contain the indexed data record element. This

Index Type	Unique Value	Multiple Occurrence	Within Group Rank	Overall Speed Ranking
Primary	Hash/Calc	N/A	n/a	1
	Hierarchical	N/A	n/a	2

Times Slower From Fastest	Unique Part	Multiple Occurrence Part	Record Access	Multiple Occurrence Table Size	Logical Accesses to Obtain Data Record Insts.	Access Time
24	None	None	Serial	None	16.7 million	57 hrs
4	Hierarchical	Combined	Hier.	450.9 mil.	2,803,504	9.6 hrs
2	Hierarchical	Combined	Hash	450.9 mil.	1,403,504	4.8 hrs
4	Hierarchical	Prim. Key List	Hier.	17.4 mil.	2,802,901	9.6 hrs
2	Hierarchical	Prim. Key List	Hash	17.4 mil.	1,401,901	4.8 hrs
4	Hashed	Prim. Key List	Hier	17.4 mil.	2,802,900	9.6 hrs
2	Hashed	Prim. Key List	Hash	17.4 mil.	1,401,900	4.8 hrs
1	Hierarchical	DBKEY	Hier	2.1 mil.	700,354	2.4 hrs
1	Hashed	DBKEY	Hash	2.1 mil.	700,350	2.4 hrs
1	Hierarchical	Bit Map	Hier	600 k	700,018	2.4 hrs
1	Hashed	Bit Map	Hash	600 k	700,017	2.4 hrs

Figure 4.10 Primary and Secondary Index Structures Performance Comparisons for Single Data Element Select Statements

enables each value from a multiple-valued data record element to be distinctly addressable.

Every index entry contains two components: the unique value component and the location component. The location component can either be a single location component or a multiple location component. The unique value component represents the data record element values extracted from the data record instances. The location component contains, in some form, the address of the data record instance from which the data record element value was obtained.

The unique value component of a data record element's index portrays the set of data values from one or more data record elements across the entire set of data record instances for a specific data record type. This set of data values can be either all unique or can initially contain some duplicates. When the value set is unique, then the quantity of instances in the unique value set is the same as the number of data record instances. These index types are often called primary keys and are useful for invoice numbers. Thus, a primary key index instance has a unique value component and single location component instance.

When the unique value component's value set is not unique, that is, it contains some duplicate values, then more than one data record instance must have the same index value. In this case, the index is called a secondary key type index. As the duplicates are removed the quantity of unique values becomes less than the quantity of data record instances. Each removed duplicate leaves behind its location component. These *orphaned* location components are all collected around their common unique value and are contained in the index's multiple occurrence component.

For each unique value there exists a multiple occurrence component which contains one or more location components. Each location component instance contains, in some form, the address of the data record instance from which the data record element value was obtained. Normally, the quantity of all location component instances contained in all the multiple occurrence components for an index is the same as the quantity of data record instances. If the DBMS contains the NULL concept and includes that special value (NULL = *do not know*) in the index then the quantity is the same as the data record instance count. If NULL is not represented in the index then the quantity is equal or less depending upon the existence of NULLs in the set of data record element values. Secondary (key) indexes are useful for finding whole classes of data record instances such as REGION, TERRITORY, and the like.

As stated above, when an index represents only unique value references, it contains the unique value component and is called a primary (key) index. When an index is a secondary index, it contains both the unique value component and the multiple occurrence component (a set of location components). Figure 4.2 illustrates a hierarchically structured index organization that contains only the unique value portion. Figure 4.3 illustrates a hashed structured index organization that contains the unique value portion. Figure 4.11 illustrates a hash-organized unique value component combined with a multiple occurrence component making it a secondary key. Figure 4.12 illustrates a hierarchically organized unique value component combined with a multiple occurrence component making it a secondary key. From Figure 4.11, the select clause SELECT SSN, NAME FROM EMPLOYEE WHERE SKILL EQ PROGRAMMER would return the EMPLOYEEs whose RRAs are 93, 25, 108, and 175. From Figure 4.12, the select clause SELECT CUSTOMER NUMBER WHERE REGION EQ 8 would return CUSTOMERs meeting that condition including customer 249241142.

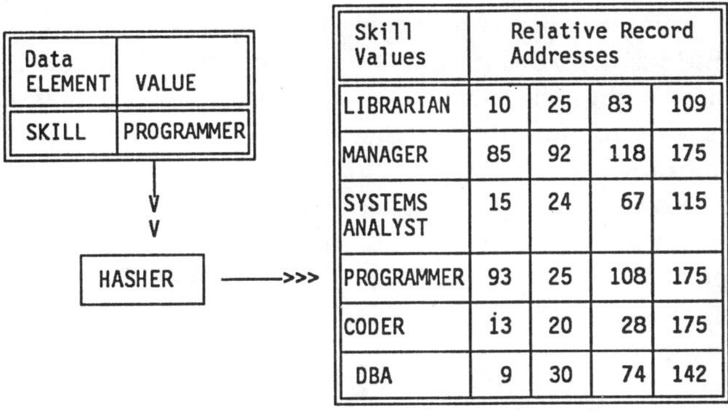

Skill Values	Relative Record Addresses			
LIBRARIAN	10	25	83	109
MANAGER	85	92	118	175
SYSTEMS ANALYST	15	24	67	115
PROGRAMMER	93	25	108	175
CODER	13	20	28	175
DBA	9	30	74	142

Figure 4.11 Hash-based Secondary Index Organization

DICTIONARY	INDEX ORGANIZATION	
DATA ELEMENT	Unique Values	Multiple Occurrences Arrays
REGION	1 ... 8 ... 24	8 ——> CN, CN,..,249241142,.. CN

Figure 4.12 Multiple Occurrences Component of an Index Structure for Customer Numbers

4.2.2.7.1 Unique Value Component of an Index

The unique value component of an index contains the set of all unique values. For the data record element REGION, the case study contains only twenty-four values, 1 through to 24. The unique value portions of these indexes are typically organized in one of two ways--hierarchical or hash/calc--each having its own advantages and disadvantages.

4.2.2.7.1.1 Hierarchically Organized Unique Value Component

A hierarchically organized unique value component of an index is typically constructed of a series of DBMS data record instances containing the collection of unique values in a hierarchically organized structure. The lowest level contains DBMS data record instances with unique values in increasing value order. When a DBMS record of these values is filled up, another DBMS record is constructed. Eventually all DBMS data record instances on the lowest level are filled. The DBMS then determines whether the index structure has two or more DBMS data record instances with unique values at the lowest level. If so, the DBMS builds a higher level DBMS record. It places in the first DBMS record of this second higher level the greatest value of the keys that were stored in the lower-level DBMS record. When the first higher level DBMS record fills, then a second DBMS record is built. When all these second level DBMS data record instances are built, the DBMS determines whether there are more than two DBMS data record instances of unique values within this second level of index. If so, then the DBMS begins to build a third level. The DBMS continues building these additional levels until there is only one DBMS record at the top.

Figure 4.2 illustrates the result of a hierarchical index. It can be seen that with about 80,000 DBMS index record instances, 16,000,000 data record instances can be represented. Representing 16.7 million data record instances (the case study requirement) requires slightly more space. The space required by such an index is the sum of the space required at each index level. In the example, the lowest level contains 80,000 pages. Each index entry consists of the primary key value and one of either of the two pointer types. Usually each pointer requires three bytes. This lowest level requires 467.6 million bytes (16.7 million * (25 +3)). The next higher level, assuming that 200 higher level pointers (about 6000 characters) are stored in each DBMS record, requires about 2.4 million characters (400 DBMS data record instances). The third level requires only 12,000 bytes (2 DBMS data record instances). The top level contains one DBMS record and requires 6000 characters. The total index space is about 470 million characters. To find the location component of any data record instance requires accessing no more than four DBMS record index instances in this hierarchically organized index.

To represent the unique value part of a secondary key, the hierarchical component only has to store the unique values that exist within the complete set of data record instances. In the case of CUSTOMER-NUMBER and LINE-ITEM, there are 47,000. This requires less than 240 DBMS data record instances of index space and about 1.45 million characters.

An advantage of a hierarchical index is that it enables range searching. So, if a query needs to find all invoices with INVOICE TOTAL between $20,000 and $25,000, the index processor finds the corresponding record identifiers for invoices where the indexed data record element INVOICE TOTAL has values between those two values.

A disadvantage of the hierarchical index is that in this example it can take up to four accesses to find the data record instance's location component. Further, updates can affect multiple levels of the index. Typically however, 95% of the unique values are found within the first 20% of the data record instances that are loaded. Thus, the real effect is to the lower level DBMS data record instances whenever a new value has to be included. Inclusions in the lowest level seldom affect the upper levels as values newly included in the lower levels are seldom outside the ranges of values in the upper levels.

4.2.2.7.1.2 Hash/Calc Organized Unique Value Component

A hash/calc unique value component is organized very differently from its hierarchical counterpart. Simply, a data value is entered, and through a formula, an address is produced that points to the DBMS/data/index record instance location. At the location of the address, what is found is either a data record instance or the address of the data record instance. In the first case, the addressing scheme is direct, and in the second, indirect. An illustration of a hash/calc unique value component of an index is contained in Figure 4.3.

If the addressing is direct, then the data record instances must, in turn, be stored in random order. The space required for hash/calc direct index is inconsequential as the formula produces the address of the DBMS record on which the data record instance is stored. Alternatively, if the addressing is indirect, then the data record instances can be stored in the order in which they are entered, in a sorted order by primary key, or in some other order.

The value of indirect addressing is that a change to the primary key value does not require that the data record instance be moved. Such a benefit is not free, however. The space consumed by the indirect addressing is the space required by the cross reference table. This is the space required by each unique value and the data record instance address. Not surprisingly, this is typically the same amount of space required by the lowest level of hierarchical index. As in the previous example, for a hierarchically organized primary key, this is about 467.6 million bytes. The address produced by the hash/calc/scheme is likely to be the DBMS record containing the primary key value. The space required for this cross reference table for just the customer number secondary key is about 240 DBMS data record instances, or 1.45 million characters.

In summary, if a hierarchical unique value component is used, its advantage is that it enables ranges searches, but in terms of the case study, it takes four accesses to find one record in 16.7 million. If a hash/calc unique value component organization is used, then while range searching cannot be performed, it takes only one or two accesses to find the one data record instance.

4.2.2.7.2 Multiple Occurrence Component of an Index

As stated earlier, an index consists of a unique value component and a multiple occurrence component. If the index is a primary key type index then the multiple occurrence component is not present. If, however, the index is to be used to find a class of data record instances, for example, all line-item data record instances within REGION 8, then the index consists of both the unique value component and a multiple occurrence component. Each instance of the multiple occurrence component contains some form of the data record instance's address. Again, when the index consists of both components it is often called a secondary index.

Fundamentally, there are four different ways to organize the components of a secondary key index:

- Combined secondary key and primary key
- Separated secondary key and primary key
- Separated secondary key and DBKEYs
- Separated secondary key and bit maps

4.2.2.7.2.1 Combined Secondary Key and Primary Key

The first type of multiple occurrence component is not really a separate structure, but a hybrid of the hierarchically organized unique value component. It is formed by concatenating the data record instance's secondary key value to the data record instance's primary key value. If, for example, there are 2000 customers in the San Francisco region (REGION 8), the value <8> is the prefix of each customer line item's data record instance's primary key (see Figure 4.9). This list is shown sorted and organized hierarchically. To add or delete from this type of secondary index, the proper value is located and either added or deleted. Higher levels of DBMS data record instances might have to be adjusted as well during updates. The size of this index type for REGION is 450.9 million characters ((25 + 2) * 16.7).

The number of accesses to acquire the REGION 8 customer's line items in a hierarchically organized primary key index is 2,803,504: four to work through the index to the lowest first value within the range, 3500 for obtaining the line item primary keys for the customers within the range, and then four for each of the 700,000 REGION 8 customer line items. If the primary key index is hash/calc then there are only two accesses for each of the 700,000 REGION 8 customer line items, giving a total number of access of 1,403,504.

4.2.2.7.2.2 Separated Secondary Key and Primary Key

The second type of multiple occurrence component, separated secondary key and primary key, separates the multiple occurrence component of the index from the unique value component of the index. The value of the primary key, the customer number, is stored in an array representing all customers in REGION 8. An array containing the customer numbers REGION 8 is illustrated in Figure 4.12. A significant disadvantage of having the actual value of the customer number stored in the multiple occurrence array is that it is not the address of the customer's data record instance. The DBMS has to take the customer number and use some primary key access strategy to find the locations of the data record instance(s) representing the customers within REGION 8. As a consequence of separating the unique value portion and the multiple occurrence portion of the index there are four subcases to consider:

1) Hierarchical unique and hierarchical record access

2) Hierarchical unique and hashed record access

3) Hashed unique and hierarchical record access

4) Hashed unique and hashed record access

If the unique part of the secondary key is a hierarchically organized index (1), and the data record instances are organized through a hierarchical primary key access, the space is the sum of the space required for the hierarchical unique portion and the hierarchical record access portion. The hierarchical unique portion is one DBMS record (6000 bytes) as all 24 regions' data record element values surely fit on one DBMS record. The multiple occurrence portion is the space required for all the lists (24) containing all the primary keys. That is, the sum of the space required for all the primary keys, or about 417.5 million characters (16.7 million * 25). Assuming the accounts are evenly distributed, each list is 2900 DBMS data record instances long (417.5 million / 24 / 6000 bytes per DBMS record). Once the primary key values are found, the DBMS proceeds to perform a hierarchical data record instance access. The total number is 2,802,901: one to work through the hierarchical index, 2900 to obtain the complete list of all 700,000 REGION 8 customer numbers, and 2.8 million to obtain the 700,000 REGION 8 customer line items.

If the unique part of the secondary key is a hierarchically organized index (2), and the data record instances are organized through hashing, the space is the sum of the space required for the hierarchical unique portion and the hashed record access portion as defined in subcase (1). The multiple occurrence portion too is defined as in subcase (1). The total number of accesses is 1,402,901: one to work through the hierarchical index, 2900 to obtain the complete list of all 700,000 REGION 8 customer numbers, and 1.4 million to obtain the 700,000 REGION 8 customer line items.

If the unique part of the secondary key is hash organized (3), and the data record instances are organized through a hierarchical primary key access, the space is what is required for all the lists as computed in subcase (1) above. The total number of accesses is 2,802,900: one to work through the hierarchical index, 2699 more to obtain the remaining REGION 8 customer numbers, and 2.8 million to obtain the 700,000 REGION 8 customer line items.

If the unique part of the secondary key is hash organized (4), and the data record instances are organized through a hash organized primary key access, then the index space is only the amount required for the lists as computed in subcase

(1). The total number of accesses is 1,402,900: one to work through the hierarchical index, 2699 to obtain the remaining REGION 8 customer numbers, and 1.4 million to obtain the 700,000 REGION 8 customer line-items.

It should be noted that the first two cases allow the secondary key selection clause to express a range clause while the last two cases do not.

4.2.2.7.2.3 Separated Secondary Key and DBKEYs

The third type of multiple occurrence component, separated secondary key and DBKEYs, relates the secondary key value to the actual address of the data record instance. A DBKEY is a DBMS generated data record instance address. A DBKEY is typically three bytes and thus 2000 DBKEYs can fit on each DBMS record. If the multiple occurrence part of the index contains, not customer numbers, but the actual addresses of the data record instances, then the number of accesses for hierarchically organized indexes drops to 700,351: one to work through the hierarchical index, 350 to obtain the complete list of all 700,000 DBKEYs, and 700,000 to obtain the REGION 8 customer line-item data record instances. The saving results from using DBKEYs, thus eliminating the additional index search operation to find the data record instance's address using the customer number. The space required by this index is considerably smaller than the prior cases. All 700,000 DBKEYS can fit on 350 DBMS data record instances and take up only 2.1 million characters. Since every data record instance has one of the 24 region values, then the total space for all the REGION secondary index is 50.1 million characters (16.7 * 3 bytes).

For hash/calc index organizations, the number of accesses is 700,350: 350 to access the array of DBKEYs for the REGION 8 customers, and 700,000 to obtain the customers.

Again, if the secondary key value part of the index is hierarchically organized then range searching is allowed. If the secondary key value part is hash/calc organized, range searching is not possible.

4.2.2.7.2.4 Separated Secondary Key and Bit Maps

The fourth type of multiple occurrence component, separated secondary key and bit maps, relates the secondary key value to a bit map representation of DBKEYs. Traditionally, the notion of a DBKEY means relative record address. The *record* in relative record access often refers to the DBMS record number, and then the logical record's position within the DBMS record. Thus, if there is a blocking factor of 10, a DBKEY value of 85 means the fifth logical record within the ninth DBMS record. If, however, the DBKEY value itself is not stored in the multiple occurrence array, but a bit string of 85 bits is stored, then a bit map can be used to determine whether a data record instance has the value of the secondary key value as follows: if the n-th bit is on (value = 1) then the n-th data record instance contains the indexed data record element's value. If the n-th bit is off (value = 0) then the n-th data record instance does not contain the indexed data record element's value.

Bit maps save considerable storage space. A traditional DBKEY, for example, is three bytes long. Thus, to store 2000 DBKEYs, 6000 bytes are needed. With bit maps, the same number of bytes could store references to 48,000 data record instances, a twenty-four-fold density increase. If 20% of the 16,700,000 data record instances are for sales to the West Division, then the length of the traditional DBKEY array will be .2 * 16,700,000 * 3 bytes, about 10,020,000 bytes. If bit maps are used, the total number of bits is 16,700,000 (one for each data record instance), or about 2.087 million bytes, about five times less than with the traditional approach.

If the blocking factor of secondary key multiple occurrence arrays is 6000 bytes per DBMS record, then about 1670 DBMS data record instances (10,020,000 / 6000) are needed to store the traditional DBKEYs. If the same blocking factor is utilized for the bit map, then the storage requirement is (16,700,000/(8 * 6,000), or about 348 DBMS data record instances, again about five times less. For our REGION 8 example, only about 4% of the data record instances are valued with an *8*. Using DBKEYs, the space requirement for the multiple occurrence list is 2.087 million characters ((16.7 million/24) * 3 bytes), or about 350 DBMS data record instances. The bit map approach for that multiple occurrence list requires 2.087 million characters (16.7 million / 8 bits per byte). The total space for all the regions for the bit map approach is 24 times larger, or 50.1 million characters. For this sparse valuation example, the index space requirement for the multiple occurrence list for DBKEYs and bit maps is coincidentally the same.

As illustrated, the same unique value is not in every data record instance. If that were the case, all the data record instances would belong to REGION 8 and all the bits for that index's multiple occurrence array would be set to *on*. The other 23 multiple occurrence lists would be set to *off*. If the DBMS can determine that whole DBMS data record instances of index bits for that unique value are set to *off*, then there is no need to read that DBMS record of bits for either an AND or an OR operation. In the case study, that situation is likely as only 4% of the data record instances have a value of *8*. In such a case, a higher level array of bits, analogous to the higher level in a hierarchical index, can serve to indicate which DBMS data record instances of bits possess data record instances with the data value that is being looked for. As there are 16,700,000 data record instances, the array at this higher level is 348 bits. This higher level bit array is used to accomplish a preliminary screening of multiple condition WHERE clauses before actually searching through the lower level DBMS data record instances of bits. This technique also reduces space since the lower level DBMS data record instances that do not contain *on* bits do not have to exist. In the case study, the space is thus reduced by at least 66% to about 700,000 bytes. Thus, for this sparse example, the bit map requirement is not the same as DBKEYs, but one-third that of DBKEYs. The number of DBMS pages that have to be scanned for one list is thus reduced to about 117. The total space for all 24 of the bit map organized multiple occurrence arrays is 24 times larger, or 16.8 million. That is 66% smaller than the space required for DBKEYs.

DBMS record counts provide a direct link to performance. For the Western Division example, it takes 238 seconds (1670 / 7 I/Os per second) to obtain all the DBKEYs of the customers. Since there are only 348 DBMS data record instances for the bit maps, the time is about 49 seconds (348 / 7) to find the data record instances. That is about 5 times faster than the traditional three-byte index addressing scheme (238 / 49). It is even faster if any DBMS data record instances of bits could be screened out at the higher level bit map. In practice, at least one-half of the DBMS data record instances are screened in this way, and thus the time is 24 seconds. That means that the bit map index search performs about 10 times faster than the DBKEY index. For the REGION 8 case study example, the DBKEY list contains 350 DBMS data record instances and takes 50 (350/7) seconds to acquire. The bit map approach only requires about 17 (117/7) seconds. Thus, the bit map approach is three times faster.

Now, to actually obtain the data record instances takes additional time. This data record instance access time is independent of whether the DBKEY is a traditional three-byte address or a bit map address. While the theoretical maximum number of I/Os is 1 per data record instance access, the experienced rate on the case study's computer, considering blocking factors and in-memory hit rate, is about 50 data record instances per second. That means that the time to access the index selected (bit map or DBKEY) data record instances is (16,700,000 * 20%) / 50 data record instances per second), or about 18 hours. Utilizing the non-indexed method, the time was calculated above to be about 57 hours. The indexing produces a savings in excess of 66%.

Some sets of single-index select criteria result in selected data record instance populations closer to 0.1% than 20%. For example, to pick the sales data for only one of the 47,000 customers produces only 356 data record instances (16,700,000/47,000), which is only 0.00215%. The space required by the DBKEYS is 1020 bytes, or less than one DBMS page. For the bit map approach the space is about 700,000 bytes (already reduced because of all *0* index DBMS data record instances) or about 117 DBMS data record instances. In this very sparse example, the bit map approach takes more space and takes longer to process than the DBKEY approach. This clearly shows that the physical database designer has to know the characteristics of the data before choosing the type of index construction.

The top part of Figure 4.10 ranks the speed of the unique value component of an index. From the calculations in previous sections, the hash/calc alternative is faster, but it cannot accommodate range searching.

The second part of Figure 4.10 presents a summary of secondary index structure analyses. The first row, no indexes, clearly takes the longest to process a single data record element select statement. The next two rows, combined secondary and primary keys, consume a large amount of space, but do produce an 800 percent improvement. The next four rows provide a distinct improvement in index space size, but provide no improvement. The last four rows cut the access time in half and also significantly reduce index space size. The clear choice then is DBKEYS for bit maps, with either hierarchical or hashed data record instance access. If hashed is chosen, however, range searching is not possible. The access time column is determined by dividing the number of accesses by 81 to give seconds. That result is divided by 60 minutes, and that result divided by 60 for hours.

The *times slower* column indicates the ratio of the fastest index type to the slowest. Four index structures perform the same (1.0), three others perform two times slower, three more perform four times slower, and one (no indexes) performs 24 times slower.

Because the four fastest index types (last four rows) are available in popular DBMSs, only these index types are further pursued in the next section. DBMSs that only support index types from the first six rows should be avoided if at all possible.

4.2.2.8 Multiple Condition WHERE Clauses

The presentation of different index structures and the estimates of the access resources consumed are all based on having only one condition in the WHERE clause. For the case study, and also in almost all real world applications, WHERE clauses contain multiple conditions. If the DBMS can only increase the performance of operations through the inclusion of at most one indexed data record element, then it is termed a record-processing DBMS. It retrieves the data record instances selected and then searches the selected data record instances--one at a time--for the other conditions in the WHERE clause.

If the record-processing DBMS is able to automatically optimize WHERE clauses, then the amount of resources consumed in a query depends on whether the DBMS stores information about its own indexes, and whether the conditions in the WHERE clause are connected by ANDs or ORs. For example, if the DBMS stores the number of data record instances for each unique value at the head of each of the multiple occurrence lists, the DBMS knows the counts that are present in column 2 of Figure 4.13. If the eight conditions are all connected through ANDs, then the DBMS picks the shortest list (number 1), retrieves the data record instances, and searches for the data record element values represented by the other conditions. The total accesses takes about 1000 seconds (50,000/50) or about 17 minutes. While not fast enough to be interactive, it is much faster than performing a serial sweep of 16.7 million data record instances (about 57 hours).

If, however, the select conditions are connected with ORs, and conditions 1 and 5 are in the select list, then both sets of data record instances have to be retrieved and the lists joined, dropping duplicates. The time this takes is determined by adding the time required to access the 50,000 data record instances and the 2,000,000 data record instances. That is about 17 minutes for the 50,000 data record instances, and about 11 hours for the 2 million data record instances. The total time probably approaches 12 hours considering the effort required to drop the duplicates. If all the eight conditions are included, then the time to find the data record instances approaches 57 hours. When the number of data record instances searched approaches 40%, whole file sweeps are often a more cost effective choice.

Select Condition	Number of Records Selected	Traditional DBKEY Reads	HI Lvl Bit Map Ands	Lo Level Bit Map Reads
1	50,000	25	333	3
2	100,000	50	167	3
3	500,000	250	83	3
4	1,500,000	750	42	3
5	2,000,000	1000	21	3
6	500,000	250	11	3
7	100,000	50	6	3
8	2,000,000	1000	3	3
xxx	xxx	3375	xxx	24

Figure 4.13 Multiple Occurrence DBMS Record Reads

The DBMSs in Figure 4.7 optimize the multiple condition WHERE clause through a technique called list processing. List processing involves taking the DBKEYs, or primary keys found from each of the select conditions, and ANDing or ORing these keys together to produce the final set of identifiers of the data record instances.

In Figure 4.13, there are eight lists of selected data record instances. The length of each list is provided in the second column. If the operation between two lists is an AND, the two lists are merged and the DBKEYs retained are only those that are in both lists. If the operation is an OR, then after the two lists are merged all the DBKEYs are retained except for duplicates.

A common technique for merging sorted lists of DBKEYs is based on a numbering sequence invented by the 13th century mathematician, Fibonacci. The technique for ANDing and ORing bit maps is based on Boolean algebra.

As the number of search criteria within a WHERE clause increases, the performance advantage of bit maps over traditional DBKEYS increases even more. Figure 4.13 illustrates the number of DBMS record reads necessary to read lists of multiple occurrence pointers and bit maps. Each item in the third column is derived by dividing the number of data record instances selected (50,000) by the blocking factor of DBKEYS to the DBMS record (2000). Column four of the first row is the number of bits (333) in the higher level bit map. The number in each succeeding row is halved since the probability of finding a desired DBMS record is halved with each higher level bit map AND.

The bit map processing is accomplished in three steps. The first is the identification of the desired higher level bit map arrays. This is done with a hash/calc index. The required value for the indexed data record element is combined with the data record element's name code to form a unique data-element-name unique-value pair that is used in a hash/calc index to determine if the value is present in any data record types. If not, the search is terminated. If present, the particular high level bit map array is identified.

Next, the identified high level bit map array is examined to determine if there are any desired lower level bit map DBMS data record instances. This is accomplished through an examination of the higher level bit map array cells. If a cell is on, then the corresponding lower level DBMS record of bits contains at least one *on* bit. When the lower level DBMS record is examined, if a bit is *on*, then the corresponding data record instance contains a data record element with the key value.

When individual conditions in the WHERE clause are all connected with ANDs, the processing of the conditions can proceed in parallel. That is, all the higher level arrays are determined first, then they are ANDed together, probably dropping a good number of arrays with each AND. If 50% are dropped with each AND, then only three DBMS data record instances of each of the 50,000 bit arrays are finally reviewed. That means that a total of 24 accesses are performed, and merging the bit maps takes about 1/2 second. Added to this time is the time to actually retrieve the data record instances, which is about 100 seconds (5000 data record instances / 50 data record instances per second), or a total time of about 1.68 minutes. The ratio of bit map index processing to data record instance retrieval is 1:50, or fifty times faster to identify a data record instance through the indexes than to retrieve it from the database.

With the traditional DBKEY solution, not only do the data record instances have to be read, they must be merged. The overhead of the Fibonacci merging technique doubles the I/Os (sorting, writing, and so forth) with each four select conditions. Thus, since there are eight select conditions, the I/Os for the traditional DBKEYs are not 3375, but 6750 for the first four and then 13,500 for the second four, for a total of about 20,250 accesses. That means that merging the lists takes about 7 minutes. Added to this time is the time to actually retrieve the data record instances, which is about 100 seconds (5000 data record instances / 50 data record instances per second), for a total time of about 8.67 minutes, about 5 times slower than the bit map solution. The ratio of DBKEY index processing to data record instance is 4.2:1, or four times slower to identify the data record instance through the indexes than to retrieve it from the database.

The overall ratio of bit map indexes to DBKEYs in the case study is about 200:1. That is, the bit map indexes are 200 times faster than the DBKEY indexes. But when data record instance time is incorporated, the overall performance ratio between bit maps and DBKEY is 5:1 in favor of bit maps.

4.2.2.9 Case Study Summary

To successfully solve the problem posed in the case study, three considerations have to be addressed:

- Queries have to use line-item detail data stored for five years to answer the needs of headquarters sales and marketing, and to respond to the needs of field sales. Such queries, however, were estimated to take 57 hours to perform a serial search.

- While summarized data was initially used to achieve acceptable response times, the only problems that were easily solved were those fitting within the scope of the summaries. It was not long after the initial set of summaries were built that dissatisfaction with the choice of summaries started to build. Creating additional summaries was seen to be a never ending project.
- If indexes are to be used to achieve acceptable response times, the indexes have to solve more problems than they create. First, the underlying DBMS has to perform list processing with the conditions present in the WHERE clause, rather than record processing. Second, the actual space required for indexes has to be small. And third, the amount of time necessary to update the indexes has to be short enough to be practical.

DBMSs that offer choices among sophisticated index structures can truly perform interactive queries with 8 or more conditions that select about 5,000 data record instances from databases with 16.7 million or more data record instances in a single data record type. Certainly, that solves the problem of query response

Number of Records:	16,700,000
Number of Records Retrieved:	5,000
Number of Conditions:	8
Time to select and retrieve:	
No Indexes (serial sweep)	57 hours
Traditional Index structure	8.67 minutes
Bit Map Index structure	1.68 minutes

Figure 4.14 Summary of Index Strategy Times

time (see Figure 4.14). DBMSs that support bit map list processing index strategies operate five times faster than DBMSs that support the best list processing traditional index access strategy.

With respect to having the correct set of summaries, if the raw data is stored, then there is never a summary that can not be derived, unless, of course, the data required by the summary has not been collected at all!

With respect to index sizes, if a DBMS offers an indexing strategy that is built into its access strategy, and further, if these indexes are very sophisticated in design, then not only can the required processing speeds be achieved (eliminating the need for summary level data), but also the size of the indexes need not be excessive. Figure 4.10 clearly shows that fast indexes do not have to consume a large amount of disk space.

As for solving the needs of the three user groups, marketing's needs are met because their data needs are founded upon weekly level, line-item data. Headquarter's needs are met because they can access data by sales unit across specific times. If the line-item data is loaded daily, then the reports are almost in real time. Finally, the field's needs are met because salespersons can find the delivered orders, near term deliveries, and those that are back ordered. They can use past performance data to plan the next week's sales strategy.

4.2.2.10 Index Summary

From the presentation of the case study, it is obvious that sophisticated indexes are quite different from ordinary indexes. An index serves not only as a fast access to a set of data record instances, but also as a way to completely avoid the writing of complicated program logic to narrow a set of data record instances initially selected on the basis of one indexed data record element. Because indexes save so much time and effort, sophisticated ones make possible entire applications that are not practical by any other means.

This section on indexes has focused on the selection of data record instances of the same type. For the vast majority of real business applications, selection of data record instances from just one type is too simplistic. For example, while it is certainly important to find all the orders that have a TOTAL-ORDER-AMOUNT over a certain value, it is probably more important to know the name of the CUSTOMERs placing the order. Another very reasonable query is to find all the CUSTOMERs located in the WESTERN REGION with TOTAL-ORDER-AMOUNT over a certain value. This query not only involves relationship processing (ORDER and CUSTOMER), but also index processing from two different data record types.

The next section deals with relationships, which are not only important in their own right, but also contribute to the cost-effective solution of the above-mentioned query types.

4.2.3 Relationship Component

Relationships are the third component in the storage structure of any database. If the DBMS supports building static relationships, then the form of the relationship is normally a relative record address established during loading. If the DBMS has dynamic facilities, then the form of the relationship is always a shared value stored in the source and target record of the relationship. Notwithstanding these differences, both static and dynamic relationship DBMS facilities must support referential integrity. Finally, relationships dramatically affect the ability of the DBMS to handle interrogations involving multiple data record types and the indexed data record elements within them.

4.2.3.1 Relationship Basics

The manner in which relationships are bound into data record instances constitutes a fundamental difference between static and dynamic relationship DBMSs. In a static relationship DBMS, the relationship stated in the DDL is bound into the data record instances by the DBMS during data loading or update. In a dynamic relationship DBMS, relationships exist in the data record instances as shared values. Dynamic relationships between data record types are presumed by the user and then uncovered by the DBMS when it actually finds the data record instances during an interrogation.

4.2.3.1.1 Static Relationship Basics

A static relationship is most often a relative record address. The address of the *next* data record instance is stored in the *prior* data record instance. The address of the *prior* data record instance is stored in the *next* data record instance, and the address of the *owner* data record instance is stored in all the member data record

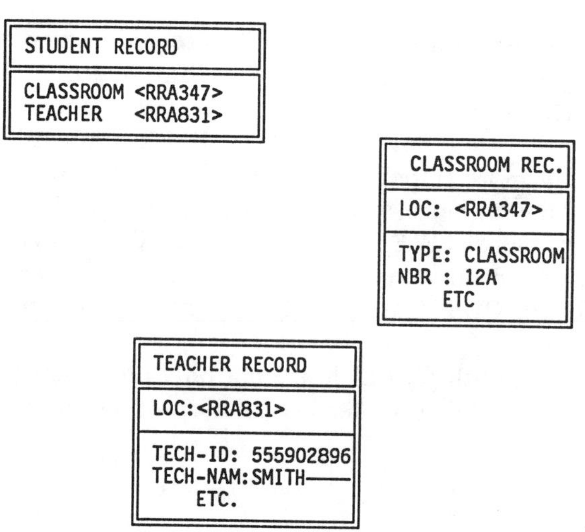

Figure 4.15 Embedded Static Relationships

instances. Figure 4.15 illustrates the use of embedded relative record addresses. In the STUDENT data record instance, the relative record address <RRA347> points to the actual CLASSROOM data record instance stored at relative location <RRA347>. The STUDENT record also contains the relative record address, <RRA831>, which points to the actual TEACHER data record instance stored at <RRA831>. Figure 4.16 illustrates the embedded pointers linking one owner ADMINISTRATION data record instance to the four EMPLOYEE data record

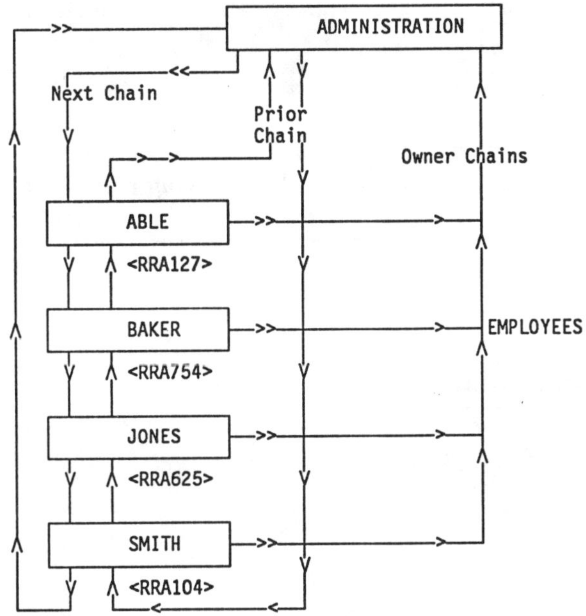

SET: DEPT-EMPL
OWNER: DEPARTMENT
MEMBER: EMPLOYEES
ORDER: SORTED ON LAST NAME

Figure 4.16 Traditional Next, Prior, and Owner Chains

instances, ABLE, BAKER, JONES, and SMITH. The EMPLOYEE data record instances are shown sorted, while the actual physical storage order (relative record addresses) is quite different from the illustrated sorted order. These sets of pointers linking owner to member, member to member, and member to owner are commonly referred to as chains.

The three types of chains are next, prior, and owner. The next chain connects an owner to the first member, then connects the first member through the members to the last member and back to the owner. The prior chain connects the owner to the last member, then connects the last member through the prior members to the first member and back to the owner. The owner chain directly connects each member to its owner. These three chain techniques are illustrated in Figure 4.16.

There are a number of variations to this basic static relationship scenario. Three are: pointer arrays, primary key as owner relationship values, and separated relationship arrays.

4.2.3.1.1.1 Pointer Arrays

Some DBMSs place an array of member relative record addresses in the owner record. This makes it possible to select *n-th* member without having first to access

RING STRUCTURES

POINTER ARRAY: PRIOR, NEXT AND OWNER POINTERS

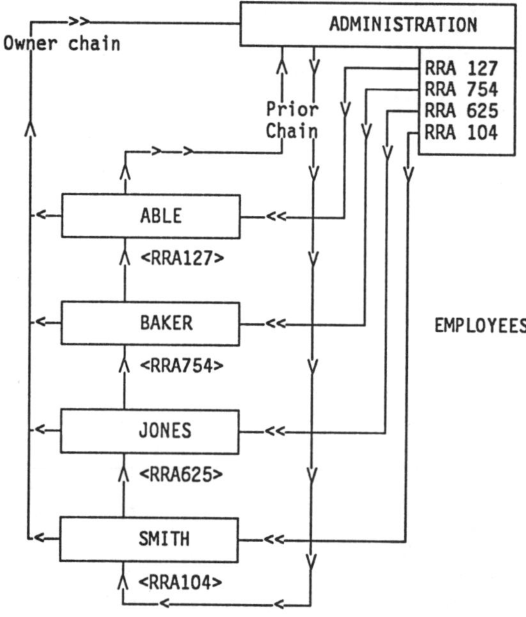

SET: DEPT-EMPL
OWNER: DEPARTMENT
MEMBER: EMPLOYEES
ORDER: SORTED ON LAST NAME

Figure 4.17 Pointer Array: Next, Prior, and Owner Pointers

all the preceding members in the chain (see Figure 4.17). Another advantage is that, if a query is constructed to determine the number of employees in the ADMINISTRATION department, the DBMS only has to count the links in the list that is stored in the owner. It does not have to access all the individual data record instances for ABLE, BAKER, JONES, and SMITH and then count them.

If, however, the query must count the data record instances at a level below employees, for example the number of courses taken by all the employees, then all the employee data record instances have to be accessed to get access to the array of RRAs for employee courses.

A real drawback of this scheme is that the data record instance has to be variable length. For each data record instance, its length not only consists of the actual data, which also may be variable length, but also must consist of the total number of RRA lists of each set of descendent data record types.

4.2.3.1.1.2 Primary Key as Owner Relationship Value

Some DBMSs place the primary key value in the member data record instance as the owner address. This has both an advantage and a drawback. The advantage is that if the owner is moved, then its address, which also changes, does not have to be changed in each of its members. The drawbacks are two:

- Access to the owner can only be through a primary key search.
- To efficiently access the owner, the owner's primary key must be indexed.

4.2.3.1.1.3 Separated Relationship Arrays

SYSTEM 2000, for example, extracts all the relationship mechanisms from the data record instances and places them in a separate component of the storage structure. Figure 4.18 illustrates this technique. The ??? marks in Figure 4.18 are this book's convention to show that the illustration is partial. Because SYSTEM 2000 is hierarchical, each database contains only one complex data record type consisting of multiple repeating group data elements that are also called segments. The data structure illustrating the relationship among the EMPLOYEE, COURSE, and DEGREE segment instances is illustrated in Figure 4.19. Each relationship array from Figure 4.18 represents the hierarchical relationships that a specific segment instance has with its related segment instances. In this particular example, taken from SYSTEM 2000, there are four relationship arrays, one for each of the four segment instances. The segment instances are <RRA5000> (EMPLOYEE), <RRA7500> (COURSE), <RRA8000> (COURSE), and <RRA9700> (DEGREE).

Each relationship array instance contains five parts: segment type, next, member, owner, and address. The segment type component indicates the type of segment type represented by the array (COURSE or DEGREE or EMPLOYEE). For example, in <RRA10> the segment type indicator states that the relationship array represents an EMPLOYEE segment instance.

The next component contains the RRA of the next relationship array instance along a next chain. For example, in the <RRA20>, the next component contains

RELATIONSHIP POINTERS — DATA RECORDS

10

RTI	NEXT	MEMBER	OWNER	ADDRESS
Employe	???	20	????	5000

5000
EMPLOYEE

20

RTI	NEXT	MEMBER	OWNER	ADDRESS
Course	30	???	10	7500

7500
COURSE

30

RTI	NEXT	MEMBER	OWNER	ADDRESS
Course	40	????	10	8000

8000
COURSE

40

RTI	NEXT	MEMBER	OWNER	ADDRESS
Degree	????	????	10	9700

9700
DEGREE

RTI means record type identifier

Figure 4.18 Separated Relationship Pointers

the value <RRA30> indicating that the relationship array at <RRA30> represents the next segment instance along a courses chain.

The member component contains the RRA of the first member in a child (member) chain. For example, <RRA10> contains an entry <RRA20> that is the address of the first *child* for the employee.

The owner component contains the RRA of the relationship array that represents the segment instance of the owner. For example, <RRA30> contains the address <RRA10>, which points to the EMPLOYEE relationship array.

Take note of the fact that in SYSTEM 2000 there is only one member component in each relationship array. That would seem to imply that any data record type could only have one descendent data record type. SYSTEM 2000, to accommodate multiple descendent data record types, links all member data record

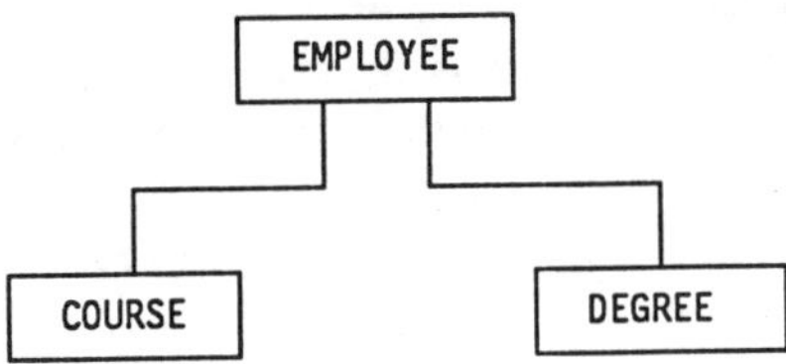


```
Counts:  Employees:     50,000
           Courses: 3,000,000 or 60 per employee
            Degree:     75,000 or 1.5 per employee
```

Figure 4.19 Employee Data Structure
Data Record Instance Counts
and Population Ratios

instances, regardless of data record type (COURSE or DEGREE). The segment type indicator (STI) component of the relationship array indicates which data record type is represented. That is, whether it is an EDUCATION, COURSE, DEGREE, or EMPLOYEE relationship array. That is the reason why DEGREE <RRA40> is a NEXT relationship instance to COURSE.

When a particular segment instance is actually required, for example an EMPLOYEE segment instance, access is accomplished by determining the actual segment instance address, <5000>.

This technique of separating relationships from the actual segment instances has its advantages and disadvantages. The principal advantages are three:

- To count member segment instances without having to access them
- To obtain a member segment instance on the fourth level without first having to pass through three levels of data record instances
- To AND and OR index created lists that belong to different segment types

The principal disadvantage is:

- If the segment instances themselves are required for the interrogation, then accessing relationships separately from the segment instances consumes slightly more resources than accessing segment instances alone with the relationships buried in them.
- Maintenance is slightly more expensive as two different storage structure components have to be updated during data record instance adds or deletes.

4.2.3.1.2 Dynamic Relationships

If a DBMS's relationships are pointers, its relationship mechanism is static. If there are no separate relationship structures, and if the only relationship mechanism between two data record instances is a shared data value, then the DBMS's relationship mechanism is dynamic. It is false to state that static relationship DBMSs have relationship mechanisms and dynamic relationship DBMSs do not. If that were true, then the dynamic relationship DBMS that performed relational operations such as JOIN is doing so on the basis of magic. The relationship is based on values present in both of the related data record instances. For example,

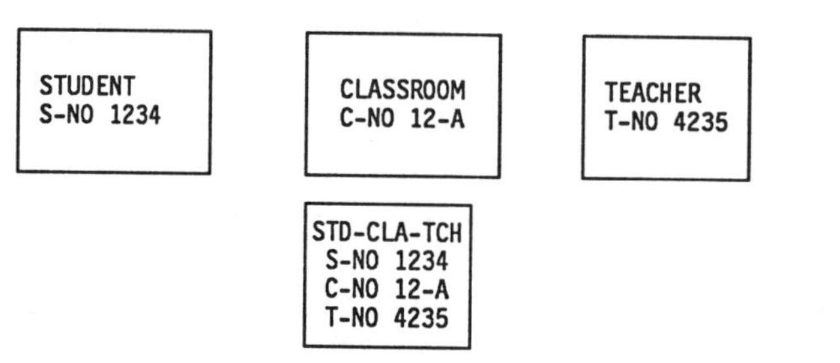

Figure 4.20 Value-based Relationships

in Figure 4.20, the STUDENT can be JOINed with the TEACHER because TEACHER-NUMBER and the STUDENT-NUMBER are both data record elements that are defined as part of the data record type STUDENT-TEACHER-CLASSROOM. And the STUDENT data record instance can be JOINed with the CLASSROOM data record instance because the data record elements STUDENT-NUMBER and CLASSROOM-NUMBER are defined in the STUDENT-TEACHER-CLASSROOM data record type.

An owner-member relationship is accomplished in a dynamic relationship DBMS by defining the primary key (or candidate key) data record element from the owner data record type as a data record element in the member data record type. For example, in Figure 4.21 the primary key EMPLOYEE-ID from EMPLOYEE is defined as part of a compound data record element COURSE-ID and EMPLOYEE-ID in COURSE. An owner-member relationship between two or more owner data record instances is defined similarly except that their common member data record type might contain only the concatenation of the primary keys of the owners. Figure 3.30 represents such an example.

```
Schema is Personnel

     Record is Employee
          Primary key is Employee-Id
          Secondary key is Employee-class
          Elements are
               Employee-Id
               Employee-Class
               Employee-Name

     Record is Course
          Primary key is Employee-Id, Course-Id
          Secondary key is Course-Name
          Foreign key is Employee-Id references Employee
                     On update set null.
          Elements are
               Employee-Id
               Course-Id
               Course-Name
               Course-Grade

     Record is Degree
          Primary key is Employee-Id, Degree-Name
          Secondary key is State-of-School
          Foreign key is Employee-Id references Employee
                     On update set null
          Elements are
               Employee-Id
               Degree-Name
               State-of-School
```

Figure 4.21 Data Definition Language for Personnel

4.2.3.2 Sophisticated Relationships

In the section on indexes, the case study contrasts the different types of index structures and compares list processing with record processing. The key difference is that sophisticated indexes and list processing indexes make certain applications possible that are otherwise impractical.

The index case study centers on selecting data record instances from the same type. If the WHERE clause involves conditions from different but connected data record types, the DBMS not only must find the data record instances from each data record type, but also must figure how to intersect the data record instances from the different data record types. The methods of resolution differ if the DBMS processes relationships in a static or dynamic manner.

Figure 4.21 presents the data definition language for three personnel data record types. The data definition language is constructed along value-based relationship guidelines so that the relationships are obvious. If the DBMS is NDL then the foreign keys would be replaced by SET clauses after the definition of all the data record types. The population of data record instances for each data record type is shown along with its graphic structure in Figure 4.19. An EMPLOYEE may be taking COURSES and may have also received one or more DEGREEs. Take the interrogation requirement such as

PRINT EMPLOYEE-ID, EMPLOYEE-NAME WHERE
EMPLOYEE-CLASS EQ *FULL-TIME* AND
EMPLOYEE HAS (COURSE-NAME EQ *ENGLISH* AND
COURSE-GRADE EQ *A* AND
STATE-OF-SCHOOL EQ *PENNSYLVANIA*)

When this is executed against the database, the method of DBMS processing differs with the form of relationship (static or dynamic) and the type of indexing (list processing or record processing). The six cases, two dynamic and four static, are:

- Dynamic, record processing
- Dynamic, list processing
- Static, embedded pointers, record processing
- Static, embedded pointers, list processing
- Static, separated pointers, record processing
- Static, separated pointers, list processing

To help quantify the relative performance differences among these six cases, assume that 50% of the employees are full-time (25,000); 10% of all courses are English (300,000); 10% of all course grades are *A* (300,000); and 15% of all degrees (11,250) are from schools in PENNSYLVANIA. These percentages are uniformly distributed through the structure. Thus, of the 25,000 full-time employees, 150,000 of the courses taken by the employees are English (six per employee); 10% of the employees in these English courses receive an A (15,000). Assume further that 5000 of the full-time employees receive at least one A in an English course; and 5625 of the employee's graduation schools are from PENNSYLVANIA. Finally, assume that a total of 750 of the full-time employees pass all the selection criteria.

Also assume all indexes have hierarchically organized unique value portions, with a separated secondary multiple occurrence DBKEYs. It takes 4 accesses to find one employee, degree, or course. For secondary key accesses, it takes one additional access to obtain each 2000 data record instance identifiers. For actual data record instance accessing, it takes one access for each data record instance. For embedded relationship processing, it takes only six accesses to obtain all COURSE data record instances, as there are 10 COURSE data record instances per DBMS record. Figure 4.19 indicates 60 courses per employee. For the same type of processing against the DEGREE member data record instances, it only takes one access (Figure 4.19 indicates 1 or 2 per employee). For separated relationship array processing it takes .25 accesses to obtain the relationship array instance implied by an index. The .25 access is due to the high density of arrays per DBMS record. For separated relationship arrays, it takes one access to process the entire set of relationships for each employee.

```
10  SELECT SALESPERSON, ON ERROR GOTO 100, AT END GOTO 110
20  GET MEMBER CONTRACT, ON ERROR GOTO 100, AT END GOTO 10
30  GET MEMBER ORDER, ON ERROR GOTO 100, AT END GOTO 20
40  GET MEMBER ORDER-ITEMS, ON ERROR GOTO 100, AT END GOTO 30
    GET OWNER PRODUCT-SPECIFICATIONS, OR ERROR GOTO 100
    GET OWNER PRODUCT, ON ERROR GOTO 100
    IF PRODUCT-MFG-CITY EQ SALESPERSON-BIRTH-CITY AND
       PRODUCT-MFG-STATE EQ SALESPERSON-BIRTH-STATE
       THEN PRINT SALESPERSON-NAME, PRODUCT-NAME,
       SALESPERSON BIRTH-CITY, SALESPERSON-BIRTH-STATE
    ELSE GOTO 40
100 PRINT "ERROR"
110 END
```

Figure 4.22 Network (static) Program Illustration

The steps in each of the six cases illustrate the type of processing performed. The actual program syntax to accomplish these steps varies from that depicted in the requirement. This interrogation requirement syntax was adapted from the SYSTEM 2000 DBMS. While not the same interrogation requirement, a network record processing DBMS syntax is constructed to conform to that depicted in Figure 4.22. Also, while not the same interrogation requirement, a dynamic list processing DBMS utilizes a syntax similar to that depicted in Figure 4.23. It is presumed that the programmer constructing the interrogation is supported by a language that permits optimum processing of the database's storage structure. For all these reasons, the steps in each case must differ. Finally, since every DBMS has a different access strategy and storage structure, the exact steps are likely to differ in some respects from those listed here. The point to this case study is not to compare the quantity of the steps, but to compare the efficiencies of the relationship processing alternatives.

```
CONNECT PRODUCT TO ORDER-ITEM
   VIA PRODUCT-NBR EQ ORDER-ITEM-PRODUCT-NBR
FIND MATCH AND KEEP PRODUCT-NAME, ORDER-ID,
   PRODUCT-MFG-CITY,PRODUCT-MFG-STATE IN LIST-1
CONNECT SALESPERSON TO CONTRACT
   VIA SALESPERSON-NBR EQ CONTRACT-SALESPERSON-ID
FIND MATCH AND KEEP SALESPERSON-NAME, CONTRACT-ID,
   SALESPERSON-BIRTH-CITY, SALESPERSON-BIRTH-STATE
   IN LIST-2
CONNECT LIST-2 TO ORDER VIA CONTRACT-ID OF LIST-2
   EQ ORDER-CONTRACT-ID
FIND MATCH AND KEEP ORDER-ID, SALES-PERSON-NAME,
   SALESPERSON-BIRTH-CITY, SALESPERSON-BIRTH-STATE
   IN LIST-3
CONNECT LIST-1 TO LIST-3
   VIA ORDER-ID OF LIST-1 EQ ORDER-ID OF LIST-3 AND
   SALESPERSON-BIRTH-CITY EQ PRODUCT-MFG-CITY AND
   SALESPERSON-BIRTH-STATE EQ PRODUCT-MFG-STATE
FIND MATCH AND PRINT SALESPERSON-NAME, PRODUCT-NAME,
   SALESPERSON-BIRTH-CITY, SALESPERSON-BIRTH-STATE
```

Figure 4.23 ILF or Relational (dynamic) Program Illustration

If the interrogation is presented to a dynamic relationship DBMS and if the DBMS' index strategy is record processing (first case), the steps:

- 17 accesses to obtain the DBKEYs of all full-time employees.
- 25,000 accesses to obtain the full-time employee data record instances for their primary key values.
- 300,000 accesses to obtain the course data record instances for the ENGLISH courses.
- Some amount of processing to check each course data record instance to see if the grade received is an A, and then more processing to see if the EMPLOYEE-ID for that course matches one of the employees already selected. If so, then the employee is kept. All employees not matched are dropped.
- 10 accesses to obtain the primary keys of all degree data record instances (STATE-OF-SCHOOL EQ PENNSYLVANIA).
- 11,250 accesses to obtain the degree data record instances.
- Some amount of processing to check each degree to see if the EMPLOYEE-ID on each selected data record instance the employees that remain; if so, then the employee is kept. All employees not matched are dropped.

The total accesses for this case are 336,277.

If the interrogation is presented to a dynamic relationship DBMS (second case), and if the DBMS' index strategy is list processing, the steps are:

- 335 accesses to build four lists, one for full-time EMPLOYEEs (17 accesses), one for DEGREEs from PENNSYLVANIA schools (10 accesses), one for ENGLISH COURSEs (154 accesses), and one for courses receiving an A (154 accesses).
- Some amount of processing to AND the two course data record type identifier lists to produce just one list of DBKEYs for the two course select conditions.
- 25,000 accesses to obtain the employee data record types to obtain their primary key values.
- 150,000 accesses to select the employee's COURSE data record instances and to determine whether the primary keys of the selected COURSE data record instances match the primary keys of the data record instances on the COURSE list. Employees not having an A grade are dropped from the EMPLOYEE list.

- 7,500 accesses to obtain the employee's DEGREE data record instances and to determine whether the primary keys of the selected DEGREE data record instances match the primary keys of the data record instances on the DEGREE list. Any employee not having a PENNSYLVANIA degree is dropped, leaving a list of only those employees meeting all four criteria.

The total accesses is 182,835.

If the interrogation is presented to a static relationship DBMS, the relationship mechanism is embedded pointers, and the DBMS' index strategy is record processing (third case), then the steps:

- 17 accesses to obtain the DBKEYs of all full-time employees.
- 25,000 accesses to obtain the full-time employee data record instances.
- 75,000 accesses to process each employee's COURSE chains to determine if the course is ENGLISH and the grade is A. If yes, then the employee is initially identified as satisfying the second criterion. Employees not tagged after processing all selected employees are dropped from further processing. It should be noted that if all the course data record instances were checked then 150,000 accesses are needed. 75,000 is estimated on the assumption that on average only half the data record instances need to be accessed to satisfy the select condition that an employee has an A on one or more of the ENGLISH courses.
- 5000 accesses to process each employee's degree chain to determine if it is from a PENNSYLVANIA school. If yes, then the employee also satisfies the last condition. Employees not tagged after processing all selected employees are dropped from further processing.

The total accesses are 105,017.

If the interrogation is presented to a static relationship DBMS, the relationship mechanism is embedded pointers, and the DBMS' index strategy is list processing (fourth case), then the steps are:

- 308 accesses to build two lists, one for ENGLISH COURSEs (154 accesses), and one for courses receiving an A (154 accesses). Only two lists are built as the strategy starts at the COURSE data record type, moves up to the EMPLOYEE data record type and then accesses the DEGREE data record types.
- Some amount of processing to AND the two course data record type identifier lists to produce just one list of DBKEYs for the two course select conditions.
- 15,000 accesses to obtain the A grade ENGLISH courses.

- 15,000 accesses to obtain the set of all employees that are the parents of the selected courses. Upon retrieval the 5000 full-time employees are found.
- 5,000 accesses to process the employees' degree chains to determine if the degree is from a PENNSYLVANIA school. If yes, then the employee is identified as satisfying the last criterion. Employees not tagged after processing all selected employees are dropped from further processing.

The total accesses are 35,308.

If the interrogation is presented to a static relationship DBMS, the relationship mechanisms are separated, and the DBMS' index strategy is record processing (fifth case), then the steps are:

- 17 accesses to perform an index search that obtains the addresses of the relationship arrays for all the full-time employees.
- 6250 accesses to obtain the relationship arrays from the addresses in step 1 for the full-time employees.
- No accesses to find the course relationship arrays for the employee.
- 75,000 accesses to process the employee's COURSE chains to determine if the course is ENGLISH and the grade is 'A'. If yes, then the employee is initially identified as satisfying the first AND. Employees not tagged after processing all selected employees are dropped from further processing. It should be noted that if all the course data record instances are checked, then 150,000 accesses are needed. 75,000 is estimated on the assumption that only half the data record instances are accessed to satisfy the select condition that an employee has an A on one or more of the ENGLISH courses.
- 5,000 accesses to process the employee's degree chains to determine if it is from a PENNSYLVANIA school. If yes, then the employee also satisfies the last condition. Employees not tagged after processing all selected employees are dropped from further processing.

The total accesses are 86,267.

If the interrogation is presented to a static relationship DBMS, the relationship mechanisms are separated, and the DBMS' index strategy is list processing (sixth case), then the steps are:

- 335 accesses to build four lists of relationship array addresses, one for full-time EMPLOYEEs (17 accesses), one for DEGREEs from PENNSYLVANIA schools (10 accesses), one for ENGLISH COURSEs (154 accesses), and one for courses receiving an 'A' (154 accesses).

- Some amount of processing to AND the two course data record type identifier lists of relationship array addresses to produce just one list for the two course select conditions.
- 6250 accesses to obtain the relationship arrays for the full-time employees.
- 3,750 accesses to obtain the relationship arrays for the A ENGLISH courses.
- 2813 accesses to obtain the relationship arrays for the PENNSYLVANIA schools.
- Each course relationship array instance is processed by finding its employee owner relationship array instance. If the owner's relationship array address is the address of an already selected employee, the employee relationship array is tagged as satisfying both the full-time and course conditions. After all the course relationship array instances are processed, all the untagged employee arrays are dropped.
- Each PENNSYLVANIA school array instance is processed by finding its employee owner relationship array instance. If the owner's relationship array address is the address of an already selected employee, the employee relationship array is tagged as satisfying the last criterion. After all the PENNSYLVANIA relationship array instances are processed, all the untagged employee arrays are dropped.

The total accesses are 13,148.

As can be seen from the different cases, the effect of the storage structure's indexes, list processing, and types of relationships is quite significant.

4.2.3.3 Relationship Summary

All databases having multiple data record types have relationships between the data record instances. If the relationships are dynamic, the DBMS will always incur the extra processing overhead associated with primary and secondary key access as the method of processing relationships. If the relationships are static, the DBMS will always know exactly where the target of the relationship is located, thus avoiding the extra processing incurred by the dynamic relationship DBMS.

The major value of having static relationships separated from the data record instances is achieved when indexes point to these separated relationships rather than to the data record instances. When this in turn is coupled with sophisticated indexes, applications such as the one described in the case study become practical.

The order of sophistication of relationship constructions and their relative performance degradations from best to worst are presented in Figure 4.24

Case	Times Slower than Best	Relationship Type	Number of Accesses	Access Time
1	25	Dynamic, record processing	336,277	69.00 min
2	14	Dynamic, list processing	182,835	37.62 min
3	8	Static, embedded pointers, record processing	105,017	21.61 min
5	6	Static, separated pointers, record processing	85,267	17.54 min
4	3	Static, embedded pointers, list processing	35,038	7.27 min
6	1	Static, separated pointers, list processing	13,148	2.71 min

Figure 4.24 Summary Comparison of the Relative Performance of Relationship Mechanisms

4.2.4 Data Component

DBMSs vary greatly in the storage of data record instances. The variations range from storing all the data record instances from each data record type in separate O/S files to storing all the data record instances for all the data record types in one O/S file. Broadly, the three major sets of distinctions relate to O/S file storage formats, data record instance storage formats, and data record element storage formats. For O/S file storage formats the most common alternatives are:

- One data record type per file
- One file for all data record types
- Multiple data record types per file
- Multiple files per data record type
- Data record instances and key formatted files

For the data record type storage formats, the alternatives are:

- Fixed format, fixed length data record types
- Fixed format, variable length data record types
- Variable format data record types

For data record element storage formats, the alternatives are:

- Simple data record element formats
- Complex data record element formats

TYPE OF FILE FORMAT	RELATIONSHIP BINDING CLASSIFICATION			
	STATIC		DYNAMIC	
	NETWORK	HIERARCHICAL	ILF	RELATIONAL
1 data record type per file	IDMS/R SUPRA		M-204 Inquire	DB-2 SUPRA
All data record types in 1 file	IDMS/R	System 2000	ADABAS M-204	IDMS/R
>1 data record type per file	IDMS/R	IMS	M-204 Focus	
>1 file per data record type	IDMS/R		M-204	

Figure 4.25 Data File Storage Formats by Relationship Type, Data Model, and DBMS for Various Popular IBM Mainframe DBMSs

As indicated in Figures 4.25, 4.26, and 4.27 the data model of the DBMS provides no definite preset pattern among file, data record instance, and data record element formats. The DBMSs that are cited more than once offer multiple format choices. In general, Figures 4.29 through 4.37 contain a definition part (e.g., Figure 4.29a), and an example part (e.g., Figure 4.29b). References in this section are only to the general figure number (i.e., 4.29) rather than to the individual part (i.e., Figure 4.29a). Each figure contains a BNF (Backus Naur Form) format, which is defined in Appendix A.

4.2.4.1 File Storage Formats

Figures 4.28 through 4.32 illustrate and provide examples of the different file storage formats. A file is an operating system file. These storage formats are used in DBMSs as indicated in Figure 4.25. In general, the more options a DBMS offers, the more it can be optimized. More options, however, increase a DBMS's complexity and training requirements.

TYPE OF DATA RECORD FORMAT	RELATIONSHIP BINDING CLASSIFICATION			
	Static		Dynamic	
	Network	Hierarchical	ILF	Relational
Data record & key format files	IDMS/R		M-204	
Fixed format fixed length data records	IDMS/R SUPRA		M-204 Inquire	DB-2 SUPRA
Fixed format variable length data records	IDMS/R	SYSTEM 2000	ADABAS M-204	IDMS/R
Variable format data records			M-204	

Figure 4.26 Data Record Instance Storage Formats by Relationship Type, Data Model, and DBMS for Various Popular IBM Mainframe DBMSs

TYPE OF DATA ELEMENT FORMAT	RELATIONSHIP BINDING CLASSIFICATION			
	Static		Dynamic	
	Network	Hierarchical	ILF	Relational
Simple data element formats	IDMS/R	IMS SYSTEM 2000	M-204 ADABAS FOCUS	IDMS/R SUPRA
Complex data element formats	IDMS/R		M-204 ADABAS FOCUS	

Figure 4.27 Data Element Storage Formats by Relationship Type, Data Model, and DBMS for Various Popular IBM Mainframe DBMSs

4.2.4.1.1 One Data Record Type per File

The simplest storage structure of all is one data record type per file. Each file contains all the data record instances from only one data record type. Figure 4.28 illustrates this file storage format. The BNF indicates that the database has one or more files. Each file is defined to have one or more data record instances for the same data record type. These data record instances can be sorted or loaded in some primary key order. These data record types are easy to reorganize; all that is required is to modify the data record type's format by adding or deleting a data record element.

BNF

```
Database ::=  <file X> [ <file Y> ... ]

<file> ::=  <data record T> [ <data record T> ...]
```

DDL

```
    DATABASE IS personnel
    RECORD is department
    RECORD is employee
    RELATIONSHIP IS deptempl
    OWNER IS department
    MEMBER is employee
```

DSDL

```
FILE department CONTAINS department

FILE employee CONTAINS employee
```

Figure 4.28a One Data Record Type Per File Organization

For simple databases performing simple functions, the single file per data record type design is appropriate. If, however, the application requires sophisticated performance and other types of flexibility, the design is just too simple. For example, if a report is desired that pulls together many data record instances from different data record types, the number of accesses can be prohibitive.

4.2.4.1.2 One File for All Data Record Types

The one file for all data record instances format is the inverse of the first format. Each file is structured to contain all the data record instances from all data record types. In the BNF from Figure 4.29, the data portion of the database consists of one file. That file contains one or more data record instances of one or more different data record types.

Since the file is to contain data record instances of different data record types, the DBMS must have a way to locate a specific data record instance within each DBMS record. This is sometimes accomplished by storing the actual address of the start of the data record instance in whatever data record instance access mechanisms exist, for example, primary or secondary indexes. The actual length

BNF

```
Database ::= <file X>

<file X> ::=  <data record S> [ <data record S> ...]
             [ <data record T> [ <data record T>...] ...]
```

DDL

```
DATABASE IS personnel
RECORD is departments
RECORD is employee
RELATIONSHIP IS deptempl
OWNER IS department
MEMBER is employee
MODE IS via
```

DSDL

```
FILE db CONTAINS department, employee
```

Figure 4.29a One File for All Data Record Types

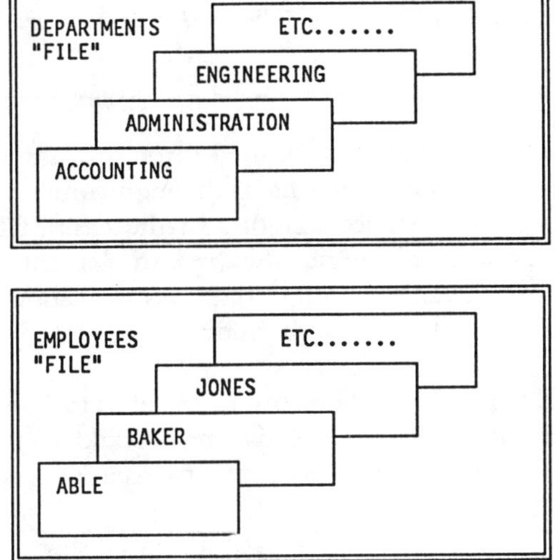

Figure 4.28b One Data Record Type Per File Organization

PHYSICAL RECORD 1

ACCOUNTING	ABLE	BAKER
GRODMAN	KERR	PERKINSON
ADMINISTRATION	EDMONDS	CRITENDEN

PHYSICAL RECORD 2

FRANCIS	GIMBLE	HARRISON
JONES	ENGINEERING	APPLETON
QUINCY	RICHARDSON	ZIEGFIELD

Figure 4.29b Example of One File for All Data Record Types

of a data record instance is either determined through computations of the data record type's data record element lengths or through computations of the actual data record element value instance lengths. In the case of fixed format fixed length data record instances, the defined data record element lengths are defined in the DDL. In the case of variable length data record instances, the data record element lengths are computed through information stored in the actual data record instance.

Another method of locating data record instances is to store the address of the DBMS record (sometimes called the relative record address) in the data record instance access mechanism. When a DBMS record instance is accessed, the DBMS determines the actual starting address of the data record instance by finding the data record instance's primary key value (and its paired start address) in a special section of the DBMS record instance.

In general, the second method of data record instance location is better than the first as the DBMS is free to *shuffle* data record instances around within the DBMS record to accommodate data record instance expansions, deletions, or additions without first having to modify any part of the data record instance access mechanism. Under either of these formats, load engineering is possible (see Section 4.4).

4.2.4.1.3 Multiple Data Record Types per File

Another way of organizing data record instances is to allow data record instances of different types to be stored in the same file. The BNF from Figure 4.30 indicates that the data portion of a database consists of one or more data files. A file contains one or more data record instances of one or more data record types. Note from the BNF that all the data record instances from one data record type are restricted to just one file. This capability should be in addition to the ability to store all the data record instances from all the data record types in a single file. That is, a database designer should be able to define the data record types separately, and then decide, on the basis of performance and the like, which files are assigned which data record types.

If multiple data record types are able to have their data record instances stored in the same file, then efficiency can be improved in some situations. For example, Figure 4.30 illustrates the storage of two data record types, DEPARTMENT and EMPLOYEE. A data record instance for the ACCOUNTING data record type is stored in DBMS record 1. Next to it are the employees in that department, ABLE, BAKER, GRODMAN, KERR, and PERKINSON. The next department, ADMINISTRATION, is stored along with its employees EDMONDS and CRITENDEN. The main benefit of this type of structuring is that member data record instances can be as physically close to their owners as possible. Reports of DEPARTMENTs and their EMPLOYEEs only require one access to obtain all the related data record instances. Of course, the disadvantage of such a scheme is that reorganization becomes more complicated, as more than one type of data record instance has to be accommodated during the reorganization process. Additionally, once data record instances of one type are spread over a large area, concentrated reporting of data from just one data record type consumes more resources.

4.2.4.1.4 Multiple Files per Data Record Type

If an application has millions of data record instances in a single data record type, it is often useful to spread the set of data record instances over multiple files. The BNF in Figure 4.31 illustrates this file storage format. In this BNF, the data portion of the database is contained in one or more files. Each file contains data record instances from one or more data record types. The BNF for both file definitions is exactly the same, indicating that the data record instances from the same data record type can be stored in one or more data files. The DBMS knows which set of data record instances are in which file through the data storage definition language (DSDL) intermediate allocation table. In this example, the database administrator must state, for example, that the department data record instances AA . . . DZ are stored in file 1 while the remaining data record instances are stored in file 2. This capability permits some sets of the data record instances to be moved off-line until needed. For example, if the EMPLOYEE data record type stored full-time, part-time, and former employees, it might be wise to remove

BNF

```
Database ::= <file X> [<file Y>...]

<file X> ::= <data record S> [<data record S>...]
             [{ { <data record T> [<data record T>...] }...}

<file Y> ::= <data record U> [<data record U>...]
             [{ { <data record V> [<data record V>...] }...} ]
```

DDL

```
DATABASE IS personnel
RECORD is department
RECORD is employee
RELATIONSHIP IS deptempl
OWNER IS department
MEMBER is employee
MODE IS via
```

DSDL

```
FILE db CONTAINS department, employee
```

Figure 4.30a Multiple Data Record Types Per File

FILE 1, DBMS RECORD 1

ACCOUNTING	ABLE	BAKER
ADMINISTRATION	EDMONDS	CRITENDEN

FILE 1, DBMS RECORD 2

JONES	ENGINEERING	APPLETON
QUINCY	RICHARDSON	ZIEGFIELD

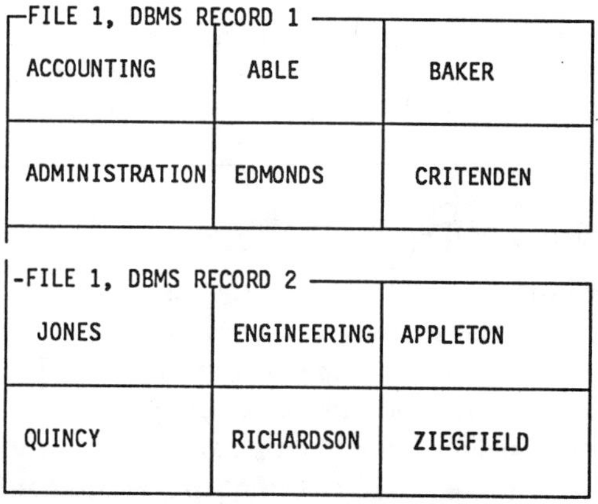

Figure 4.30b Example of Multiple Data Record Types Per File

BNF

```
database ::=  <file X> [<file Y>...]

<file X> ::= <data record S> [<data record S>...]
             [{ { <data record T> [<data record T>...] }...} ]

<file Y> ::= <data record S> [<data record S>...]
             [{ { <data record T> [<data·record T>...] }...} ]
```

DDL

```
     DATABASE IS personnel
     RECORD is departments
     RECORD is employee
     RELATIONSHIP IS deptempl
     OWNER IS department
     MEMBER is employee
     MODE IS via
```

DSDL

```
FILE one CONTAINS department WITH department-id FROM aa TO dz
FILE two CONTAINS department WITH department-id FROM ea TO zz
```

Figure 4.31a Multiple Files Per Data Record Type

FILE 1, DBMS RECORD 1

ACCOUNTING	ABLE	BAKER
ADMINISTRATION	EDMONDS	CRITENDEN

FILE 2, DBMS RECORD 1

JONES	ENGINEERING	APPLETON
QUINCY	RICHARDSON	ZIEGFIELD

Figure 4.31b Example of Multiple Files Per Data Record Type

the former employees from on-line status, as they are not likely to be used often. Another reason for splitting up the data record instances might be to spread all the ORDERs for a 24 hour order-entry system into different files so that maintenance, backup, and consolidated reporting could be performed on the *closed* (i.e., off-line) sections of the ORDER data record type. Without the ability to split a data record type into multiple files, this is impossible.

4.2.4.1.5 Data Record Instances and Key Formatted Files

Some DBMSs have DBMS data record instances that contain *intelligence* about the contents of the DBMS record itself. The BNF in Figure 4.32 illustrates the format of DBMS data record instances in any database file. A DBMS record is either a simple format or a key formatted record. In the former case, the DBMS record consists of a series of data record instances, from *top to bottom*. The exact starting address of the data record instance must be stored elsewhere in the database's storage structure.

In the later case, the exact starting address of the data record instance is determined only after the DBMS record is obtained. After the DBMS scans the set of data record instance keys to find the correct key, it then knows the exact starting address of the data record instance.

As shown in Figure 4.32, the actual DBMS record format typically has a DBMS record broken into two parts. The first part is for the storage of the actual data record instances. The second part is for the storage of primary key values and addresses of the start of the data record instance. This permits the contraction and expansion of data record instances within the DBMS record. It also permits the expansion of the file size resulting from increasing DBMS record size without the data record instances leaving their home DBMS record. This type of DBMS record construction is most often used with the multiple data record type file storage format and with the following data record type storage formats:

- Fixed format, fixed length data record instances
- Fixed format, variable length data record instances
- Complex data record instance formats
- Variable format data record instance formats

4.2.4.2 Data Record Type Storage Formats

Figures 4.33 through 4.35 illustrate the different data record instance storage formats. These data record instance storage formats are used in DBMSs as indicated in Figure 4.26. In general, the more options a DBMS offers, the better its performance. Again, more options, however, increase a DBMS's complexity and training requirements.

The data record type format depends upon whether the data record type is fixed or variable length, and fixed or variable format.

BNF

```
<file>::= { <simple DBMS record>...} ¦ { <key formatted DBMS record>...}

<simple DBMS record> ::= { <data record A> [<data record B>...] }

<key formatted DBMS record> ::= { <data record A> [<data record B>...] }
                                { <data record address key A>
                                [<data record address key B>...] }

<data record address key>::= {<data record start address>
                             <data record key value>}
```

DDL

```
DATABASE IS personnel
RECORD is departments
RECORD is employee
RELATIONSHIP IS deptempl
OWNER IS department
MEMBER is employee
MODE IS via
```

DSDL

Any DSDLs from Figures 4.28 through 4.31

Figure 4.32a Data Record Instances and Key Formatted Files

PHYSICAL RECORD 1		
RA=100 PK=ACCOUNTING ETC	RA=200 PK=ABLE ETC	RA=210 PK= BAKER ETC
RA=220 PK=GRODMAN ETC	RA=230 PK=KERR ETC	RA=240 PK=PERKINSON ETC
RA=250 PK=ADMIN ETC	RA=350 PK=EDMONDS ETC	RA=360 PK=CRITENDEN ETC
KEY—	—RELATIVE ADDRESS MATCH	
100ACCOUNTING 220GRODMAN 250ADMIN	200ABLE 230KERR 350EDMONDS	210BAKER 240PERKINSON 360=CRITENDEN

Figure 4.32b Example of Data Record Instances and Key Formatted Files

4.2.4.2.1 Fixed Format, Fixed Length Data Record Types

The most traditional format for a data record instance is fixed format and fixed length. In Figure 4.33, the BNF illustrates that the data record instance consists of a series of simple data record element value instances. The length of each data record element's value is defined in the DDL, and space is allocated by the DBMS for all the data record element value instances within the data record instance whether the data record element's value exists or not. The space for a value representation for every data record element defined is contained in every data record instance. The value representation takes on one of two states: a fixed number of NULLs or a fixed length value. In the example contained in Figure 4.33, the LAST NAME data record element has a fixed length of 11 characters. If a last name of more than 11 characters is stored, all characters to the right of the 11th are chopped off. The total length of every fixed format, fixed length data record instance is the sum of the defined data record element lengths. In this example, the data record instance length is 39 characters. Some DBMSs allow numeric data to be stored in compressed formats such as packed decimal or binary integers. In such cases the actual space consumed is less than the sum of the defined lengths.

A benefit of fixed length and fixed format data record instances is that the DBMS does not need to spend any time decoding lengths and formats. A drawback is that a very detailed understanding of the application's use of the data is needed so that these fixed length parameters can be set up in a way that results in no data loss.

4.2.4.2.2 Fixed Format, Variable Length Data Record Types

Many database applications today require variable length data record types. In the BNF notation from Figure 4.34, a data record instance is composed of zero or more simple data record element values and zero or more complex data record element values. The length of each data record element value is defined in the DDL for the simple data record elements (e.g., SSN) and is stored (in some way) with the data record element's value for complex data record elements (e.g., EVALUATION SUMMARY).

As with the fixed format, fixed length data record instances, every data record element in the data record type is contained in every data record instance and takes on either of two states: a variable/fixed number of NULLs or a variable/fixed length value. This capability is most useful for storing textual data and repeated instances of values. For example, if the data record type illustrated in Figure 4.34 represents the evaluations of EMPLOYEEs, there should be room for comments of varying lengths. If variable length data record instances were not available, either the comments have to be truncated, or room for the largest possible comment has to be allocated. Neither is acceptable. The evaluation comment from Figure 4.34 is 47 characters long. The length indicator is the first part of the data record element's instance. Other data record instances could contain evaluation comments of any length.

BNF

```
<data record> ::= <fixed format data record>
                | <variable format data record>

<fixed format data record>::= <simple data record>

<simple data record> ::= <simple data element A>

                         [<simple data element B>...]
```

DDL

```
LAST-NAME, TYPE IS CHARACTER 11

FIRST-NAME, TYPE IS CHARACTER 12

BIRTHDATE, TYPE IS DATE, FORMAT IS YYYYMMDD

SX, TYPE IS CHARACTER 1
```

Figure 4.33a Fixed Format and Fixed Length Records (Simple)

SSN	LAST	FIRST	B-DATE	SEX
525902896	GORMAN	MICHAEL	19410322	M

Figure 4.33b Example of Fixed Format and Fixed Length Records

BNF

```
<data record> ::= {<fixed format data record>
                  |<variable format data record>}

<fixed format data record>::= [<simple data record>]

                              | [<complex data record>]

<complex data record> ::= [<simple data element>...]

                          [<complex data element>...]
```

DDL

```
SSN, TYPE IS INTEGER 9(9)

LAST-NAME, TYPE IS VARCHAR

FIRST-NAME, TYPE IS VARCHAR

SX, TYPE IS CHAR 1

BIRTHDATE, TYPE IS DATE FORMAT IS YYYYMMDD

EVALDATE, TYPE IS DATE, FORMAT IS YYYYMMDD

EVALUATION SUMMARY, TYPE IS VARCHAR
```

Figure 4.34a Fixed Format and Variable Length Records (Complex)

SSN	LAST	FIRST	B-DATE	SEX	...
525902896	5SIBLO	3BOB	19350822	M	...

...	EVALDATE	EVALUATION SUMMARY
...	19871027	47VERY TALENTED HOCKEY COACH, AND FINE INDIVIDUAL

Figure 4.34b Fixed Format and Variable Length Records

Variable length data record elements, however, have drawbacks. The DBMS must read the DBMS data record instances, and must decode the actual format of the data record type, which almost always requires building a fixed-length record for use by compiler languages such as COBOL or FORTRAN.

BNF

```
<variable format data record>::= {{<data element indicator><data element>}
                                  [{<data element indicator><data element>}...] }

<data element>::= { <simple data element> ¦ <complex data element> }
```

DDL

Data Elemt CODE	DDL Data Element's NAME AND TYPE
FA	SSN, SVI, NUM 9
FB	LAST NAME, SVI, VARCHAR
FC	FIRST NAME, SVI, VARCHAR
FD	B-DATE, SVI, DATE
FE	SEX, SVI, CHAR 1
FF	SKILL, MVI, VARCHAR
FG	NICKNAME, MVI, VARCHAR

Figure 4.35a Variable Format Data Record

4.2.4.2.3 Variable Format Data Record Types

Variable format data record instances permit storage of data in different formats. The BNF in Figure 4.35 gives an example of the content of a variable format data record instance. It consists of a series of data record element value instances just like the fixed format data record instance illustrated in Figure 4.33. In the fixed format data record instance, every data record element is contained in each data record instance either as a value or as a NULL. In the variable format data record instance, the appearance of any data record element value is entirely optional. A variable format record's data record element value can appear in any order within the stored data record instance and can occur any number of times. Unless the DBMS had clauses to enforce single values and uniqueness on its data record elements, a particular employee could end up with two or more Social Security Numbers of different values within the same data record instance!

As illustrated in Figure 4.35, each data record element is assigned a specific code. Data record element FC is the code for FIRST NAME, and FG is for NICKNAME. Data record element values can be either fixed length or variable length. In the first line of the example, the SKILL data record element values

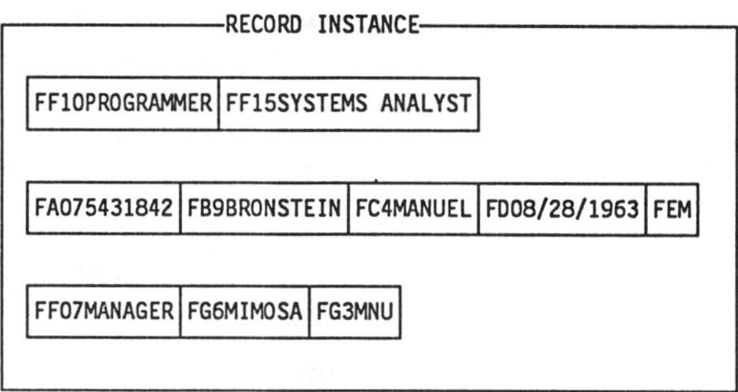

Figure 4.35b Example of Variable Format Data Record

appear twice. In the second line there is a fixed length data record element for SSN; two variable length data record elements, LAST NAME and FIRST NAME; a date type data record element; and a single-digit SEX data record element. In the third line, another SKILL data record element value appears, and then two NICKNAMEs.

The variable format data record type has both advantages and drawbacks. The only real drawback is the amount of decoding the DBMS has to perform to translate the DBMS's data back into a *regular* form, which is required by all programming languages. The big advantage is reorganization. The addition of a data record element type to a data record instance has no effect on the database until its data record element values are added. When added, the data record element value is merely appended to the end of the data record instance.

When a data record element type is removed from the database, the DBMS would simply not map the discarded data record element value from the existing data record instances to any program requesting it. Furthermore, each time a data record instance is updated, the discarded data record element value is dropped from the existing data record instance when the data record instance is returned to the database.

4.2.4.3 Data Record Element Storage Formats

Figures 4.36 and 4.37 illustrate the different data record element storage formats. These storage formats are used in DBMSs as indicated in Figure 4.27. Again, the more options a DBMS offers, the better its potential performance at the cost of increased complexity and training requirements.

In addition to the data record element instances within a data record instance being either fixed or variable length, the data record elements may represent either a single data record element value instance or multiple data record element value instances. In the former case, the data record element is termed simple, and in the later case the data record element is termed complex.

When a data record instance is defined through a DDL to contain only simple data record elements, the data record instance is known as a simple data record instance. When a data record instance is defined through the DDL to contain at least one complex data record element, the data record instance is known as a complex data record instance.

4.2.4.3.1 Simple Data Record Element Formats

Simple data record elements represent the storage of single value instances of a data record element. The BNF from Figure 4.36 illustrates that a simple data record element can be either fixed or variable length. For fixed length data record elements, the space defined in the DDL for the data record element value contains either values, blanks, or NULLs. As the BNF illustrates, no subordinate data record element structures are allowed, and a data record element is not allowed to represent repeated values.

BNF

```
<simple data element> ::= <fixed length data element value>
                        | <variable length data element value>

<fixed length data element value> ::= [<value> [<blank>...] | <null>...]

<variable length data element> ::= {  [ {  <length><value> } | <null>...]...}
```

Figure 4.36a Simple Data Element Formats

In the examples thus far presented, all the data record element types have been simple, for example, SSN, FULL NAME, and EMPLOYEE EVALUATION.

4.2.4.3.2 Complex Data Record Element Formats

Some DBMSs permit complex data record instances. The BNF from Figure 4.37 illustrates complex data record elements, which are required for a complex data record instance. There are three different types of complex data record elements: vectors, groups, and repeating groups. A vector is a data record element that would otherwise be simple except that it represents multiple value occurrences. An example of a vector is TELEPHONE NUMBER, where an organization or person is allowed to have several telephone numbers.

A group data record element is a data record element that is defined to have subordinate data record elements, each of which, in turn, may be a simple or vector data record element. A very common example of a group data record

```
SOCIAL-SECURITY-NUMBER, TYPE IS INTEGER 9(9)

FULLNAME, TYPE IS VARCHAR
```

SSN	FULLNAME
648711400	9BOB SIBLO

Figure 4.36b Example of Simple Data Element Formats

element is ADDRESS. The subordinate data record elements are DWELLING STREET NUMBER, STREET NAME, CITY, STATE, and ZIP. While this example only contains simple data record elements, some DBMSs allow a group to contain vector data record elements as well, for example DWELLING TELEPHONE NUMBERS.

A repeating group data record element is a data record element that is defined to have subordinate data record elements. A repeating group is different from a group data record element in that a group data record element can only have one set of values for its defined set of subordinate data record elements, while a repeating group can have multiple sets of values. Figure 4.37 illustrates the difference between a group and a repeating group. Some DBMSs, for example FOCUS and SYSTEM 2000, allow repeating groups to be nested. The DDL in Figure 4.37 illustrates the situation in which an EMPLOYEE has DEPENDENTS, which in turn have the repeating group data record element HOBBIES and the repeating group data record element MEDICAL CLAIMS, as well as the two data record elements FIRST NAME and BIRTHDATE. The nested repeating group data record element HOBBIES is defined to contain two data record elements, HOBBY NAME and HOBBY ANNUAL COST.

In addition to having one or more nested repeating group data record elements and one or more simple data record elements, a repeating group may also contain vector data record elements.

The flexibility added to a data record type by allowing complex structures far outweighs the disadvantages. For example, if an EMPLOYEE needed to store multiple TELEPHONE NUMBERs, DEGREEs, or the like, the only way a DBMS adhering to the relational data model can accommodate that requirement is to add an additional data record type, which would require defining, loading, and maintaining the additional data record type for just one data record element, DEGREEs.

In the ILF or network data models, the complex data record elements might be stored as illustrated in Figure 4.37. The first example in this figure shows variable-length multiple-valued data record elements with an indicator of the number of values at the head of the array. The second example shows fixed length

```
BNF

<complex data element>::= <vector data element>
                         |<group>
                         |<repeating group>


<vector data element> ::=  { <qty> <simple data element value>...}


<quantity> ::= the number of occurrences for <simple data element value>


<group data element> ::= { <simple data element A>
                         [ <simple data element B>...]
                         [ <vector data element>...] }


<repeating group> ::= { <complex data element A>
                      [<complex data element B> ...] }
```

Figure 4.37a Complex Data Element Storage Formats: BNF

values with an indicator of the number of values at the head. The third example shows a repeating group. Of course, within each occurrence of the group there is either a fixed format or a variable format for the data record elements contained in the group.

The main reason for allowing storage of complex data record types is to reflect the way data exists in real business organizations. To require subordinate repeating group instances and/or multiple valued element instances to be data record types (tables) in their own right is to distort reality. A drawback, however, is that the DBMS will have to digest, decode, and then present these to the users. However, the effort pays off, given the main reasons for allowing storage of complex data record types.

4.2.4.4 Data Summary

As can be seen from Figures 4.25, 4.26, and 4.27 and from the presentation of the different types of storage formats for files, data record types, and data record elements, knowledge of the DBMS's data model is not complete knowledge of a database's internal structure and design.

A sophisticated DBMS can store data record instances from different data record types in the same O/S file. If data record instances of several data record types can be stored on the same O/S file, I/O efficiency will be better than if all instances from each data record type must be stored in one O/S file. This optimization is due to the fact that applications often require collections of related data record instances of different types, for example, a DEPARTMENT, its EMPLOYEEs, and the PROJECTs that are assigned to EMPLOYEEs. If these data

DDL

```
TELEPHONE, TYPE IS INTEGER 9(9), OCCURS UP TO 10 TIMES


ADDRESS TYPE IS GROUP
     HOUSE NUMBER, TYPE IS CHARACTER 5
     STREET-NAME, TYPE IS CHARACTER 25
     CITY, TYPE IS CHARACTER 10
     STATE, TYPE IS CHARACTER 2
     ZIP, TYPE IS INTEGER 9(9)


RECORD NAME IS EMPLOYEE
     PRIMARY KEY IS EMPLOYEE-ID
     ELEMENTS ARE
     EMPLOYEE-ID, TYPE IS INTEGER 9(9)
     EMPLOYEE-FULL-NAME, TYPE IS CHARACTER 15

     ....

     DEPENDENTS, TYPE IS REPEATING GROUP, OWNER IS EMPLOYEE
          FIRST-NAME, TYPE IS CHARACTER 10
          BIRTH-DATE, TYPE IS DATE, FORMAT IS YYYYMMDD

          HOBBIES, TYPE IS REPEATING GROUP, OWNER IS DEPENDENTS
               HOBBY-NAME, TYPE IS CHARACTER 15
               HOBBY-ANNUAL-COST, TYPE IS MONEY, FORMAT IS 99,999.99

          MEDICAL-CLAIMS, TYPE IS REPEATING GROUP, OWNER IS DEPENDENTS
               etc.
```

Figure 4.37b Complex Data Element Storage Formats: DDL

record instances are contained on three different O/S files, then there must be I/Os to each of those files to obtain the necessary data for the interrogation. If these data record instances are all located in the same O/S file, and stored in the same or in nearby DBMS data record instances, then the interrogation will be much faster.

A DBMS should also have the ability to store different sets of data record instances from the same data record type on different O/S files. For example, if all the invoices sent to customers are stored on O/S files by month, that is, if there is one O/S file for January's data record instances, one for February's data record instances, and so on, then when a new year begins, the prior January's O/S file containing its data record instances could be moved off-line, clearing disk space for the new January's data record instances, without having first to unload the *old* data record instances. These off-line O/S files must be able to be brought back on-line through a RESTORE operation.

In addition to being able to store data record instances of different types in the same O/S file, a DBMS should be able to store these data record instances in the same DBMS record. This makes possible an even more sophisticated type of

Vector:

Telephone numbers, up to 10 occurrences			
3012229876	2019981284	....	

Group:

House number	Street	City	State	Zip
1234	Maple St.	Sadlebrook	NJ	029879999

Repeating Group:

Dependents

First-name	Birth-date
Bobby	19780817

Hobbies

Hobby-name	Hobby-annual-cost
Ice hockey	2000.00
Model boats	500.00
Soccer	250.00

Figure 4.37c Examples of Complex Data Element Storage Formats

optimization. The specification of this capability is usually contained in the relationships section of the DBMS's data storage definition language (DSDL), whereby member data record instances are targeted to be stored *close* to their owner. Such clauses may affect the access strategy that is chosen for the member data record type. For example, if an owner data record instance's location is determined by hash/calc, that is, randomly, and if a member's data record instances are all targeted to be stored within the DBMS record that contains the owner data record instance, then the member's access strategy typically cannot be hash/calc.

To aid in the optimization of these complex file structures, the DBMS should be able to change the blocking factor of an O/S file. In some DBMSs, the size of the DBMS record instance can be either the same size as the O/S record instance that is actually read by the O/S's software routines, or it can be smaller so that, for example, five DBMS data record instances fit in one O/S record. In such a case, the blocking factor is five. The DBMS must be able to spread data record instances across DBMS record boundaries. If this is possible, then all the space contained in the O/S record will be used. If not, then either the O/S record size must be an exact multiple of the DBMS record size, or there will be unused space.

Sophisticated DBMSs should be able to store data record instances of varying length to accommodate either complex data record types or variable length data record elements. How the DBMS handles variable length data record instances is important. For example, as data record instances shrink, the space should be made available for new or adjacent expanded data record instances. In the event the DBMS moves a data record instance from one location to another, then a sophisticated DBMS will not have to reorganize indexes, relationship addressing schemes, and the like. If these have to change as well, the update operations will certainly take longer. An additional benefit of complex data record instance storage schemes is fast reporting. When a report request is executed, a single DBMS instigated file I/O is likely to obtain most of the requested DBMS data record instances, and therefore most of the data record instances from one or more types that is needed for a single logical sequence of owner and members.

In addition to the different formats described above, some DBMSs allow free space in the DBMS record for expansion of individual data record instances. Once the space is used up, the DBMS usually divides the contents of the DBMS record in half, with one half of the data record instances and their associated key values staying in the original DBMS record, and a pointer to the new DBMS record storing the remainder of the data record instances and their keys.

DBMSs that allow the many different data formatting options described above permit great flexibility in database construction and maintenance.

4.2.5 Data Storage Definition Language

A sophisticated, high performance DBMS separates the definition of logical data structures (elements, data record instances, and relationships) from the definition of the mapping of the data record instances onto O/S files. The components of a data storage definition language (DSDL), which accomplishes the mapping of logical definitions to physical structures, must include clauses to define at least these six components:

- Files
- Areas
- Data record types & instance allocations

- Data record element physical characteristics
- NDL sets (relationship definitions)
- Indexes

There is generally a sequence to the definition of these DSDL components.

- Files are defined, including declaring the blocking factor for O/S data record instances.
- Areas are defined, including the allocation of areas to files.
- Data record types are then defined and their instances are allocated to areas.
- Data record element physical characteristics are defined, that is, fixed or variable length, etc.
- Indexes are defined. The type of index is specified and, if appropriate, so is the allocation of index structures to specific areas (and in turn, files).
- If ANSI/NDL, then sets are defined, specifying principally whether the member data record instances are to be collocated with the owner instance of the set in a specific DBMS record.

4.2.5.1 File Clauses

A file is a commonly understood operating system component. DBMS data record instances are added to, modified in, and deleted from files. File specifications typically include the type of access method used by the operating system to access the file's data record instances, and the name, type, and location of the actual physical device (disk drive spindle) on which the file is to reside. For an IBM VSAM file, the various access methods that could be defined are key sequence data sets, entry sequence data sets, or relative record data sets. A most important subclause in the file's specification is the O/S record clause. It typically specifies the file's size and other information, such as the blocking factor. The blocking factor defines the number of DBMS data record instances present in each O/S record.

Some DBMSs clauses indicate what happens when a DBMS record becomes full of component instances from indexes, relationships, or data record types. A common practice is that the DBMS retains half the contents in the current DBMS record and then creates new DBMS record.

4.2.5.2 Area Clauses

An area is a DBMS *creation* used to identify a specific collection of data record instances from one or more data record types. Because the operating system, rather than the DBMS, actually places data record instances on the disk, an area is only a logical specification of the space, and not a physical specification of space. The area clause would thus contain specifications for its initial size and allowable expansion sizes, and the mapping between it and O/S files.

The size subclause of an area is typically in the form of how many DBMS data record instances can be stored in the area, e.g., 100,000.

The mapping subclause typically specifies the relationship between the AREA and one or more O/S files. Some DBMSs only allow an AREA to be contained in one file; other DBMSs allow AREAs to be contained in multiple O/S files; and still other DBMSs allow multiple AREAs to be contained in one or more O/S files. If more than one AREA is assigned to a file, then the portion of the file that the AREA is to occupy is also identified.

4.2.5.3 Data Record Instances

Data record instance clauses specify the type of access strategy to be used for data record instance storage and selection, and also the mapping of the instances of data record types and areas.

Storage specification subclauses typically indicate whether the data record instances are to be randomly scattered over the entire space identified for data record instance storage, sequenced by entry or by one or more data record elements, or whether the data record instances are to be placed in the same DBMS record as their owner.

In some DBMSs, all the instances of a data record instance must belong to only one area. In such a case, the area mapping clause only requires the identification of the area name. In DBMSs that allow the instances from one data record type to belong to multiple areas, the mapping clause must include both the area name and the identification of the DBMS record instance range for the data record instances.

4.2.5.4 Data Record Elements Clauses

If a DBMS has only a general specification of the type of data represented, for example, character or numeric, then the DSDL must complete the specification. In the case of CHARACTER data, it specifies whether the length is fixed or variable. If variable, then the specification states whether the data record element has a maximum length or an indeterminate length. For numeric data record elements, the specification indicates whether the data record element is integer or decimal. If integer, then the length is specified. If decimal, then the length and number of decimal places is specified.

4.2.5.5 NDL Set Clauses

NDL set specifications specify both the owner and the member data record type(s) that participate in the relationship and also the access strategy for the member data record instances of the set. Set organizations are typically random, chained, or sorted. For a random set, the DBMS uses the values of one or more data record elements to calculate the location of the data record instance within the space identified for the storage of data record instances belonging to the set. For chained set organizations, data record instances are stored and accessed in loaded order. In sorted sets, the data record instances are ordered according to the value(s) of the data record element(s) defined as the set's sort key(s).

When there are multiple data record types as members, then the set clause indicates whether the data record instances are to be accessed by data record type, or by the order of a commonly existing sort key (one or more defined data record elements) across all the data record types. An organization might have, for example, four data record types: FULL-TIME-EMPLOYEES, PART-TIME-EMPLOYEES, RETIRED-EMPLOYEES, and FORMER-EMPLOYEES. To create a list of all employees, regardless of type in an NDL (or CODASYL) DBMS requires the definition of a set that has COMPANY as the owner and all four data record type as members. The set additionally indicates that the members are sorted by EMPLOYEE-NAME. The set could additionally indicate that in the case of a duplicate name, the FULL-TIME employees appear before the PART-TIME, who appear before the RETIRED, who appear before the FORMER.

In a non-NDL or non-CODASYL system, this effect could certainly be achieved by having all employees in one data record type with an employment indicator data record element which states that *A* means full-time, *B* means part-time, *C* means retired, and *D* means former. A retrieval sort clause could then be generated that retrieves all employees and then sorts them by name and then by employment indicator. While such a scheme is possible, it requires that all employees be on-line all the time. Since many companies have a significant employee turn-over every 36 to 48 months, a company of 7000 current employees might have a file of about 21,000 employees. That is a waste of space if the combined sorted list is needed only quarterly. In the case of an NDL or CODASYL DBMS, the three other data record types could be placed in a separate area and then moved off-line until needed, making for a much more cost-effective solution. Additionally, all programs accessing only the full-time employees would not then have to include a select condition that stated . . . AND NOT (PART-TIME OR RETIRED OR FORMER). The reader merely has to review the cost and complexity of the indexing section to know the cost savings of NOT having to use indexes when they are otherwise unnecessary.

4.2.5.6 Index Clauses

Index specifications indicate the type of index organization that is operative for a particular data record type's data record elements. Since every index type consists of a unique value component and a multiple occurrence component, the selection is from among alternatives within each component.

As to the unique value component, the two common alternatives in the selection clauses are either hash/calc or hierarchical. Hash/Calc is more appropriate for primary or candidate keys, and hierarchical is more appropriate for secondary keys in which range searching is a common requirement.

As to the multiple occurrence component, the alternatives are listed in Figure 4.10. Most DBMSs do not offer a choice. The design of the multiple occurrence component that exists, however, typically indicates whether indexes are an integral component of a DBMS's design or an afterthought. From Figure 4.10, the secondary index types that are the four fastest are generally an indication of the fact that indexes are an integral component of the DBMS's design.

4.2.5.7 DSDL Summary

There are six types of clauses in any data storage definition language: files, areas, data record types and instance allocations, data record element physical characteristics, NDL sets (relationship definitions), and indexes. Of the six types of clauses within a physical database's specification, the only one that depends on the data model is the one specifying NDL sets. All the other types of clauses are independent of data model. A sophisticated DBMS preserves this separation of physical from logical. A DBMS that does not maintain this separation will probably be too simplistic to be employed on high volume, production applications--regardless of data model.

A very sophisticated DBMS offers the maximum number of alternatives in each of these clause types. Because of the great variety, it is certainly impossible for the novice user to instantly understand them all and put them to use effectively. To overcome this, most DBMS vendors allow these clauses to be defaulted to some practical or common use. Then, as the application and/or database grows in size and complexity, the purpose of these clause alternatives becomes obvious. At that time their value will be appreciated. If all these alternatives are not available, frustrated users and poorly performing applications are the result.

4.2.6 Storage Structure Summary

As stated above, the minimum required capabilities for the dictionary storage structure component are the same for both static and dynamic relationship DBMSs. A good data dictionary must have fundamental information such as data record and data record element instance names, expository definitions, and specifications for their use in various programs that have been properly compiled according to DBMS conventions. Beyond the minimum set of information, the capabilities differ widely. To obtain a DBMS that only supports the minimum capabilities is not a good idea, as a fully functional IRDS can be a tremendous assist in the development of fully specified database applications.

The second component, indexes, serves a number of different uses. First, it permits fast access to a set of data record instances. Second, it also can be a way to avoid writing complicated program logic that narrows a set of data record instances from the set produced through a WHERE clause that only had one index to the set of data record instances that would result when the WHERE clause had multiple conditions, each involving different indexed data record elements. And, in the situation described through the case study, sophisticated indexes enable whole applications to exist that otherwise are impractical.

All databases have relationships of two types: among data record instances of the same type and among data record instances from different types. If the relationship mechanisms of the DBMS are dynamic, the DBMS will always incur the extra processing overhead associated with primary and secondary key access as that is the method of dynamic relationship DBMS relationship processing. If the relationships, however, are static, then the DBMS will always know exactly where the data record instances are and will avoid this extra processing.

While relationships are important in their own right, separate relationship pointers are critically important for the cost-effective solution of multiple data record type, index-selected, list processing queries. Indexes are able to point to these separated relationships rather than to the data record instances. Multiple data record type queries can then be processed up to the time of determining the final set of data record instances that comprise the answer set without having to access data record instances.

There are many different types of data storage structures, but the DBMS's data model alone does not determine whether the DBMS is suited to ad hoc questions, high volume performance applications, both, or neither. A DBMS that only allows a single data record type per O/S file is certainly the least sophisticated. DBMSs that allow many data formatting options provide for sophisticated database construction and maintenance.

Selecting a DBMS on the basis of its storage structure is probably more important than selecting a DBMS on the basis of its data model. Any DBMS vendor who asserts that selecting a data model is more important than selecting the appropriate storage structure is either presuming extreme naivety on the part of the evaluators, or has never built a large, high volume, production-oriented database application.

4.3 ACCESS STRATEGY

A DBMS' access strategy is the method by which the DBMS accesses data record instances in the database. In some DBMSs, the access strategy can be controlled by user language verbs, for example, GET-MEMBER or GET-OWNER. In other DBMSs, the access strategy is controlled by the DBMS, for example, FIND SALESPERSON WHERE REGION EQ *EAST*. As might be expected, static and dynamic relationship DBMSs access data record instances in very different ways.

4.3.1 Static Access Strategy

The access strategy of a static relationship DBMS employs data manipulation language (DML) verbs to navigate among the data record instances of the data definition language related data record types. The programmer must specify the sequence for examining the data record types and then follow the inter-record relationship instances that have been created during the data loading or update process.

The user has a lot of power because most of the database processing is through a host language. Initial access is usually through a primary key; then, through a series of GET MEMBER, GET NEXT, and GET OWNER commands, the database is traversed until all the data is accumulated for the report, or until all the updates are completed.

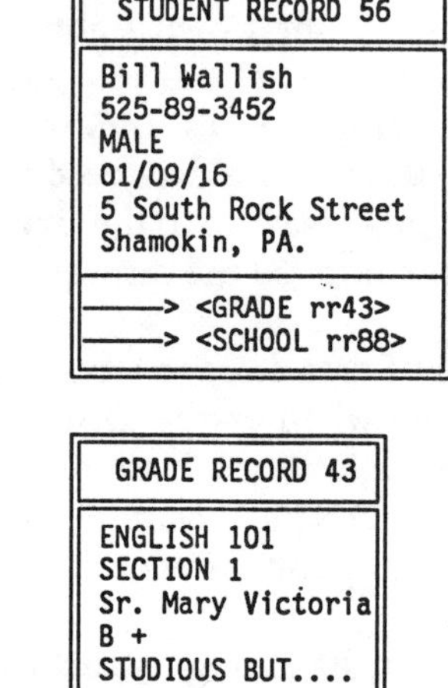

Figure 4.38 DBMS Based Pointers, Embedded Static

In Figure 4.38, for example, a user FETCHes (FIND + GET) the STUDENT data record instance on the basis of the SSN = 525-89-3452, and then utilizes a GET NEXT command to get the first data record instance on the SCHOOL set. Since the DBMS has stored the relative record address of the first school in the student's data record instance, the DBMS knows exactly where to find the school data record instance. A command often used is:

FIND <record-type> <selection-expression>

After execution of the <selection expression> a subset of the data record instance identifiers is returned to the run-unit for processing.

For example,

FIND STUDENT WHERE COURSE EQ ENGLISH 101.

returns the COURSE data record instance identifiers that are ENGLISH 101. A command sequence to get the student for the course is:

- The COURSE record instance is brought into memory by the GET COURSE command.
- Then, the GET OWNER COURSE command is issued.
- Then the specific STUDENT record instance is brought into memory.

As can be seen, the programmer navigates the DBMS's traversal of the database.

The programmer must initially determine the data record type navigation sequence for each application from a diagram of the database's structure. Figure 3.9 is a database structure diagram. The navigation sequence requirements must be explained by the programmer to the database administrator so that a judgment can be made on the appropriateness of the access strategy for other user interrogation and update requirements.

Using the database structure contained in Figure 3.9, the access strategy might be as follows: all data record types are directly accessed except for ORDER, PRODUCT-SPECIFICATION, PRODUCT-PRICE, and ORDER-ITEM. Direct access means that the data record instance is retrieved directly on the basis of its key. Generally, no record instances are scanned to find the target record instance; it is found directly.

The PRODUCT-SPECIFICATION, PRODUCT-PRICE, and ORDER-ITEM data record instances are stored *VIA*. The term *VIA* means that the data record instances are stored within the same DBMS record as their owner data record instance or as near to that DBMS record as is possible. If a data record type is VIA to one data record type, it typically cannot be VIA to a different data record type. That means, for example, that the ORDER-ITEM data record type cannot be VIA within the relationship that goes from the PRODUCT-PRICE data record type to ORDER-ITEM data record type. If there is a relationship between two or more direct access data record types, then the owner data record instance contains the address of the member data record instance. That address, of course, is a direct address, and most often is a DBMS record address value different from the owner's DBMS record address value.

Hierarchical DBMSs access strategies are much more straightforward. In Figure 3.8, the owners and the members are already set out. Generally, in a hierarchical DBMS, a specific data record instance can be accessed by a primary key such as CUSTOMER-ID. A selection of data record instances can be found through a secondary key like STATE for a CUSTOMER. This access strategy is used by both IMS and SYSTEM 2000. Beyond this general similarity, these DBMSs differ significantly. For example, in IMS, the pointers among data record instances are all embedded as in Figure 4.16. In SYSTEM 2000, the pointers are all separated from the data record instances as illustrated in Figure 4.18. Because of this difference, SYSTEM 2000 supports a list processing access strategy, which is essential to efficient ad hoc query processing. IMS, because it is a record processing DBMS, cannot perform efficient ad hoc queries.

There is a growing need in database environments for on-line access for both ad hoc questions and standard reports. Since a static database is primarily designed to answer the needs of interrogations that mirror the database's organization, many ad hoc questions can cause extensive processing. This is unfortunate as database is supposed to bring diverse data together and make it available to many users with different needs.

The reason this problem arises is because some static relationship DBMSs require data record instances to be searched whenever:

- The search criteria involve non-primary key data record elements, and/or
- The search criteria involve more than one indexed data record element, and/or
- The search criteria involve data record elements from different data record types.

For example, in the query, whose data record type structure is represented in Figure 4.39,

FIND ALL EMPLOYEES WHERE

CURRENT-JOB-TITLE EQ SYSTEMS ANALYST, AND

SALARY GT $30,000, AND

FORMER-JOB-TITLE EQ PROGRAMMER,

there is no primary key expression, and the FORMER-JOB-TITLE assignment is within a data record type that is a descendent of EMPLOYEE.

Three components are required to make such interrogations practical in a static environment:

- Indexes
- List processing

- Efficient relationship normalization

These are detailed in earlier sections.

The first component, indexes, speeds access to the data record instances on the basis of data record element values that are not primary keys. In the query described above, CURRENT-JOB-TITLE, SALARY, AND FORMER-JOB-TITLE have to be indexed to avoid data record instance searching.

The second component, list processing, indicates that the DBMS builds data record instance address arrays (lists), one for each indexed condition in the selection clause. It also indicates that the DBMS processes the lists together through AND and OR operations to determine the final set of data record instance addresses that meet the conditions set out in the query. Each of the conditions that come from the same data record type (SALARY and CURRENT-JOB-TITLE) can have its lists ANDed. Conditions that come from different data record types cannot be ANDed together without first having their data record instance addresses (relationships) normalized.

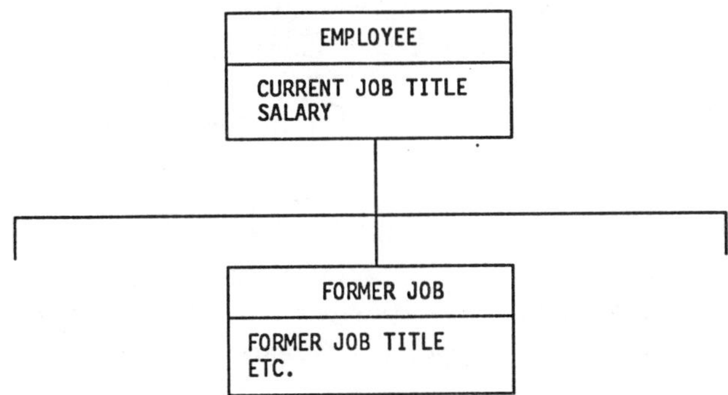

Figure 4.39 Relationships Case Study Record Type Digaram

The third component, relationship normalization, requires that all the data record instances pointed to by the addresses in the lists that are the consequence of processed selection criteria must point to the same data record type. In the case of the data structure represented in Figure 4.39, two of the select conditions (CURRENT-JOB-TITLE EQ SYSTEMS ANALYST, AND SALARY GT $30,000) result in lists of data record instance identifiers from the same data record type, while the third condition, FORMER-JOB-TITLE EQ PROGRAMMER, produces a list of data record instance identifiers of a data record type from a descendent level. To resolve this disparate level situation, all the addresses of the data record instances must be brought to a common level. To accomplish that, addresses of data record instances resulting from the query condition FORMER-JOB-TITLE

EQ PROGRAMMER need to be *raised* to the level of the addresses from the EMPLOYEE data record type. *Raising* is accomplished by traversing the owner relationships contained in the JOB data record instances to the EMPLOYEE data record instances. When this is done, there will again be two lists: one for the EMPLOYEES whose FORMER-JOB-TITLE EQ PROGRAMMER, and another for the EMPLOYEES whose CURRENT-JOB-TITLE EQ SYSTEMS ANALYST. Because these two lists are both on the EMPLOYEE data record type level, they can be ANDed to find the intersection list of data record instance identifiers. Normalization can also be achieved by *lowering*. This is accomplished by traversing the *member* relationships from the *owner* to the *members*.

Data record instance address normalization, while achievable when the relationships are embedded in the data record instances, is only practical when the relationships (see Figure 4.18) have been removed from the actual data record instances and placed in a separate storage structure component. If a data record instance is about 1500 characters long, and a relationship array is only 15 characters long, then the relationship normalization part of a query has been made 100 times more efficient. That is because under the former case there is one relationship instance every 1500 characters in contrast to the later case where there are 100 relationship instances for each 1500 characters. That is 100 times more dense.

When all three of these facilities (or their functional equivalents) exist in a static relationship DBMS, the static relationship DBMS can handle ad hoc interrogations. SYSTEM 2000 has all three implemented.

Notwithstanding the inclusion of these facilities, a static database is still a static database. That means that regardless of any improvement in the access strategy for servicing ad hoc inquiries, the ad hoc inquiry's data requirements must closely conform to the database's structure. For example, suppose there was a query:

PRINT STUDENT NAMES

WHERE STUDENT-BIRTH-STATE-CODE EQ TEACHERS-DEGREE-CODE.

While such a query borders on the ridiculous, it serves to illustrate the point that queries may arise that have not been designed into the database. If the relationships defined in the database's DDL did not explicitly support this specific query, then no enhanced access processing is going to eliminate the extensive programming and data record instance processing required to answer the interrogation. The only way to efficiently handle such a query is to state the relationship in the query, and then have the DBMS discover whether there were any students who were born in MA (Massachusetts) and who had teachers with an MA (Master of Arts) degree. Such a capability properly exists only in dynamic relationship DBMSs

4.3.2 Dynamic Access Strategy

In contrast to following the static relationships defined in the DDL that are actually created during the data loading or update process, the dynamic relationship DBMS automatically performs most of the navigation and sorting whenever interrogations are made by users. The user constructs an interrogation against a view of data that has the following three components:

SELECT <element-list-1>

SORTED BY <element-list-2>

WHERE <conditions list>

The <element-list-1> may include data record elements from one or more data record types. The sort clause (<element-list-2>) may include multiple sort keys, in ascending and descending sequences. The WHERE expression (<conditions list>) may include elements from different data record types, with conditions involving Boolean operators, relational operators, ranges, and so on.

If the conditions list involves searching different data record types, the syntax must also contain sufficient constructs so the DBMS *knows* how to process the relationship among the different data record types. The syntax for processing multiple data record type relationships is either specified from within the conditions list of the interrogation, as in the case of the SQL WHERE clause, or through separately issued relationship binding syntax that establishes the relationship prior to the actual conditions list execution. In the ANSI/SQL language, the following is the essential syntax for selecting the course identifiers and names for full time employees:

```
SELECT COURSES-ID, COURSE-NAME FROM EMPLOYEE, COURSE
WHERE EMPLOYEE.EMPLOYEE-ID EQ COURSE.EMPLOYEE-ID
AND EMPLOYEE-CLASS IS FULL-TIME
```

The following is the syntax required by the DBMS FOCUS that is sufficient for it to know how to process the relationship:

```
LINK EMPLOYEE VIA EMPLOYEE-ID TO COURSE VIA EMPLOYEE-ID
PRINT COURSE-ID, COURSE-NAME WHERE EMPLOYEE-CLASS IS
FULL-TIME
```

The actual mechanisms that determine how the DBMS performs multiple data record type processing vary widely. Some DBMSs determine the lowest node in the selection network and build a completely normalized data record type at that level, with the resultant data record instances passing through the various selection criteria to determine which data record instances fit.

If the query additionally contains one or more SORT clauses, then these selected data record instances are examined to see if all the data is identified to carry out the sort operation. If not, additional data record element values are collected so that the data record instances can be sorted. Once sorted, report formatting is started.

The view under which the interrogation was issued is then examined for any default report formats that may have been specified. If there were none, the interrogation is responsible for supplying all the necessary information. Finally, with all the selecting, sorting, and formatting tasks accomplished, the report is produced. The steps just described all take place automatically without user involvement subsequent to submitting the interrogation.

4.3.3 Comparing Access Strategies

The main difference between static and dynamic relationship DBMS access strategies is that in static access strategies, the user has complete navigational control across predefined structures, while in the dynamic access strategy, the user can specify only relationships across completely unconnected data record types that have data record elements sharing common values. In the static relationship DBMS environment, most of the structure definition decisions are made by the database designer on behalf of all users. The languages provide commands for the step-by-step navigation of the database's predefined structures. In the dynamic environment the language contains relationship specification commands in lieu of navigation commands.

For example, in Figure 3.9, if a user wants to know if any salespersons are born in the same town that manufactures a product that the salesperson sells, the static relationship DBMS assists by providing the various links from the SALESPERSON instance to the related PRODUCT instance. The program first has to retrieve a SALESPERSON instance and then traverse the structure by passing through the data record instances from CONTRACT to ORDER to ORDER-ITEM to PRODUCT-SPECIFICATION and finally to PRODUCT to determine whether the product is manufactured in the same town in which the salesperson was born. If the search is successful, elements from the product and salesperson data record instances are placed on a list in preparation for the report. Then the next ORDER-ITEM is checked. When the ORDER-ITEMs are exhausted for an ORDER, the next ORDER is checked, which in turn causes the ORDER-ITEM check to begin again. When the ORDERs are exhausted, the next CONTRACT is retrieved and the ORDER check cycle is begun. When all CONTRACTs are exhausted, the next SALESPERSON is retrieved, and the CONTRACT check cycle begins again. Figure 4.22 illustrates an abbreviated and rough pseudo-code program that accomplishes the task.

In contrast, in the dynamic access strategy, the expression of relationships that create inter-record structures during the query's execution is the responsibility of the user. Once these relationships are expressed by the user, the DBMS translates the relationship expressions into search strategies to accomplish navigation, record selection, and automatic sorting, and presents the user with the results. For example, using the dynamically organized database diagrammed in Figure 3.28, the problem described above might be recorded in a pseudo-code like that in Figure 4.23.

It is important to note that even though the number of statements is roughly the same, the process and the mechanism of the search is quite different. In the static example, every record between SALESPERSON and PRODUCT is scanned in search of a match. In the dynamic example, LIST-1 is derived directly, without retrieving data record instances in PRODUCT-SPECIFICATIONS. LIST-2 and LIST-3 are the result of pre-established connections. The match between LIST-1 and LIST-3 immediately produces the set of matches at one time, rather than iteratively as in the static example.

In the dynamic interrogation example, the generation of interim work files is unique. Once these files are created, some DBMSs allow them to be used completely outside the environment of the database. The DBMS is then free to service other requests such as updates.

4.3.4 Buffer Management

A very critical component of any access strategy, static or dynamic, is buffer management. A buffer is a set of memory-based DBMS data record instances or high speed disk-based DBMS data record instances that temporarily hold DBMS data record instances from the various databases, including sort files, derived AND/OR lists, and DBMS data record instances from the various storage structure components such as the dictionary, indexes, relationships and data.

Probably the most frequently used storage structure component is the dictionary. It is also usually the smallest, often comprising less than 1/2 million characters. This storage structure component is not changed often as changes are really logical database reorganization. Consequently, the entire dictionary is often brought into memory when a database is attached and there it stays. The next components that often stay resident in memory are all the edit and validation rules, referential integrity rules and table look-ups.

A *smart* buffer manager *learns* which DBMS data record instances from the other storage structure components (indexes, relationships, and data) are most often accessed and keeps them in memory in preference to other DBMS data record instances that are used less often and have the oldest last-accessed time.

An often used capability of the DBMS is the delayed-write feature. With it, the effects of an run-unit update transaction are either written immediately to disk or wait until the DBMS record is regularly written to disk. Waiting usually means waiting until a buffer becomes full of updates, or until the DBMS record has aged as required by the buffer management algorithms.

Buffers can often be different sizes, both in terms of the quantity of DBMS record instances the buffer can hold and in the size of each DBMS record. Frequently, the size of the DBMS record for each of the storage structure components can be determined at DBMS installation time. Sophisticated DBMSs permit DBMS data record instances from different databases and from different storage structure components to common or specific buffers.

Buffers are a major source of DBMS performance tuning. To effectively take advantage of buffers requires knowledge of their optimum quantities, sizes, and allocations. To acquire this knowledge a great deal must be known about the running database environment. That means that the database administrator must be acutely aware of the various applications. The application characteristics include assessing the update cycles, frequencies, volumes, on- and off-line tendencies, whether it is faster to rerun jobs or to perform database rollbacks and the like. A great deal of this knowledge comes from the statistics generated from each transaction. These statistics can be stored on the journal files, and can undergo analysis to properly determine the appropriate configurations for the buffer sizes, quantities and allocations. Because each write to the journal slows database operations, installations often have these statistics journals recorded only during the first weeks of a new application and only for several days a month to monitor any usage changes.

4.3.5 Access Strategy Summary

The main difference between the static and dynamic relationship DBMS access strategies is that the static relationship DBMS imposes predefined relationships that are navigated by DML commands. To navigate outside these relationships either is not possible, or requires extensive processing. In short, in the static relationship DBMS environment, most of the structure decisions are already made on behalf of the user. The languages provide commands for step-by-step navigation of the predefined structure.

In the dynamic access strategy, the expression of the relationship is the responsibility of the user. Once it is expressed, the DBMS takes over and performs the navigation, record selection, and sorting on behalf of the user.

4.4 DATA LOADING

Data loading is the process of inserting large quantities of data into the database at one time. DBMSs usually have special utilities to accomplish this task.

Some DBMSs allow data to be loaded in special ways to achieve efficiencies during subsequent updating and reporting. This is called load engineering.

4.4.1 Static Data Loading

Static relationship DBMSs require that the database be loaded according to the dictates of the structure. The owner is loaded first, then its members, and then their members. All the other owners to which a member is to be connected are then loaded. An already-connected member is then accessed and connected into relationships with its other owners. An alternative loading strategy is to load all the owners, then load a member and connect it to all its owners.

The process of loading a network database can be complex. The complexity is directly related to the number of relationships (sets) between and among data record types. Once loaded, however, the static database is ready for high-velocity reporting and updating, and the complexity and effort required for loading pay off. Data record instance connection to sets can be controlled by an INSERTION option on the DDL relationship (SET) syntax.

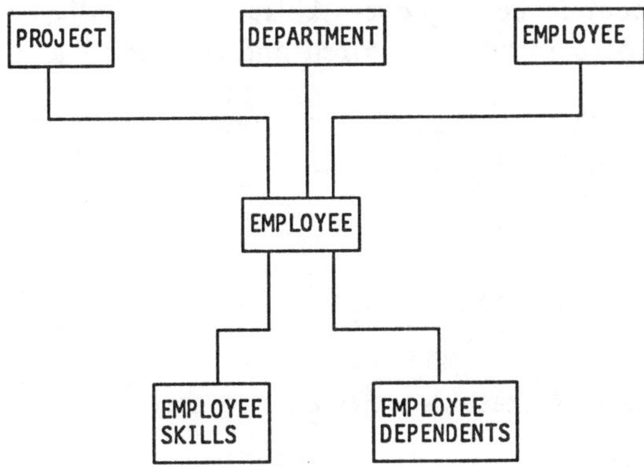

Figure 4.40a Data Record Types for Static Relationship DBMS Loading Strategy

```
STORE <project-1> STORE <employee-1>
CONNECT <employee-1> TO <project-employee> SET
STORE <department-1>
CONNECT <employee-1> TO <department-employee> SET
STORE <employee-1>
CONNECT <employee-1 TO <employee-class-employee> SET
STORE <employee-skills-1>
CONNECT <employee-skills-1> TO <employee-employee-skills> SET
STORE <employee-dependents-1>
CONNECT <employee-dependents-1> TO <employee-employee-dependents> SET
```

Figure 4.40b Manual Strategy for Static Relationship DBMS Loading

An example of a data loading strategy is presented in Figure 4.40a through 4.40c. In this example, there are six data record types: PROJECT, DEPARTMENT, EMPLOYEE CLASS, EMPLOYEE, EMPLOYEE SKILLS, EMPLOYEE DEPENDENTS. The loading strategy presented in Figure 4.40b is based on having their INSERTION options defined as MANUAL. That means that connecting a member to an owner must be done explicitly. The first two commands are to store data record instances <project-1> and <employee-1>.

The third command is to connect the <employee-1> data record instance into the <project-employee> set. The <department-1> data record instance is stored, and the <employee-1> data record instance is connected to the <department-employee> set. The <employee-class-1> data record instance is stored, and the <employee-1> data record instance is connected to the <employee-class-employee> set. The hierarchical process is started again by storing the <employee-skills-1> data record instance and connecting the <employee-skills-1> data record instance into the <employee-employee-skills> set. Finally, the <employee-dependent-1> data record instance is stored and connected to the <employee-employee-1> set.

```
STORE <project-1> STORE <department-1> STORE <employee-class-1>

STORE <employee-1>

STORE <employee-skills-1>

STORE <employee-dependents-1>
```

Figure 4.40c Automatic Strategy for Static Relationship DBMS Loading

When the INSERTION option is AUTOMATIC, then all the CONNECT commands are automatically performed by the DBMS. As can be seen in Figure 4.40c, only the STORE commands need to be issued. In Figure 4.40c, the actions are to automatically connect <employee-1> into the <project-employee>, <department-employee>, and <employee-class-employee> sets. Then, after <employee-skills-1> is stored, it is automatically connected into the <employee-employee-skills> set. Finally, after the <employee-dependents-1> data record instance is stored, it is automatically connected into the <employee-employee-dependents> set.

Consider Figure 3.9 for another example of data loading. There are three natural trees:

- COMPANY, REGION, CUSTOMERS, and SALESPERSON
- PRODUCT, PRODUCT-SPECIFICATIONS, and PRODUCT-PRICES
- CONTRACTS, ORDERS, and ORDER ITEM

This example assumes that data record instances from all data record types are available and have been properly loaded into O/S files that are accessible to the data loading program, and that all data record instances are automatically inserted into their proper relationships when sufficient information is available.

The data record instance loading sequence for the first natural hierarchy is the first COMPANY instance, the first REGION instance, then one or more

CUSTOMER instances, followed by one or more SALESPERSON instances. The second tree loads below COMPANY (assumes multiple companies and different products for each) a PRODUCT instance, one or more PRODUCT-SPECIFICATION instances, and one or more PRODUCT PRICE instances. The third tree locates a CUSTOMER instance and then below the located CUSTOMER, loads one CONTRACT instance, one ORDER instance, and finally one or more ORDER-ITEM instances.

So far, the data record instances have been loaded in a hierarchical fashion. To create the network connections, for example for CONTRACT and SALESPERSON, there must be a way to determine which salesperson is connected to which contract. If the SALESPERSON-ID is also present in the CONTRACT data record type, the specific SALESPERSON is identified and retrieved. Upon retrieval, the mechanism that binds the SALESPERSON instance and CONTRACT instances together is also made available for processing. Assuming that the contract is to be stored either as the NEXT, FIRST, or LAST instance within the set, this same process is performed to connect ORDER-ITEMs to PRODUCT-SPECIFICATIONs and PRODUCT-PRICES.

Hierarchical data loading is the same as network loading except that there is no step for network connections, as networks are not supported.

4.4.2 Dynamic Data Loading

Loading a dynamic relationship DBMS database is very quick and simple. The data record instances from each type are gathered together and then loaded into the appropriate data record types. If the data record instances are supposed to be related to other data record instances in a different data record type, then the data loading program must check--on its own--to determine that matching values exist. If the DBMS allows for the expression of referential integrity clauses, then the DBMS will access the referenced data record instances to validate the data record element value and store the data record instance if a match occurs. If there is no match, the load operation is rejected, or else the foreign key data record element value is set to null.

4.4.3 Load Engineering

Loading data in special ways to achieve high performance on certain interrogations is called load engineering. Traditionally, load engineering has been a characteristic of static relationship DBMSs. However, due to the efforts by dynamic relationship DBMS vendors to perform at the rate of their static relationship DBMS counterparts, load engineering techniques have been undertaken by all DBMS vendors.

The benefits of load engineering are illustrated by the following example. An organization desires to rapidly retrieve all purchase orders and receive invoices associated with contracts. If over the years the organization is able to determine that there is an average of 15 purchase orders and 2 invoices against each purchase order, then the highest level of retrieval performance is achieved if the disk space for all the data record instances of these three data record types is preallocated (reserved) within the same DBMS record rather than having the space allocated for them as they occurred--that is, scattered over the entire disk space. To achieve this, the total space for the contract, its 15 purchase orders, and the 30 invoices is computed. The load programs create all the necessary blank space for the 15 purchase orders and 30 invoices whenever a new contract is entered in the system. Thereafter, these preloaded blank data record instances--already stored--are retrieved and updated. The I/Os are kept to a minimum since all the data record instances are stored in the same DBMS record.

Without these and other physical performance tuning techniques, DBMS, static or dynamic, cannot be used effectively in high performance database applications. None of the four data models have a special claim on any physical performance optimization techniques. Rather than being a characteristic of one particular data model, these techniques are a characteristic of a sophisticated DBMS. Any DBMS not offering these techniques should not be procured whenever alternatives are available.

4.5 DATA UPDATE

Every database requires updating, which in the context of this book means adding, deleting, and modifying the data within a database that already contains a substantial amount of data. An understanding of how storage structure components react to certain types of updates (adds, deletes, or modifies) is essential to the effective selection, design, and implementation of applications for a particular DBMS.

Critical to application performance is how well the DBMS handles additions of new data record instances, deletions of existing data record instances, modification of relationship occurrences (not types: that is reorganization), and modification of data record element values. It is important to know how the DBMS access strategy accomplishes each update type, so that the database application can be designed in the most efficient manner. It is also important to note the efficiency with which auxiliary structures, such as indexes and relationships, are changed as data values are changed.

4.5.1 Data Record Type Changes

Figure 4.41 lists the types of effects on data record instances when ADDs or DELETEs are made to static and dynamic databases. In either environment data record instance additions are accomplished either according to a specific plan, or arbitrarily. If a plan is established through the DSDL, then as new data record instances become available they are stored according to the plan.

One plan developed in the early 1970s for CODASYL (static) network DBMSs is to store the member data record instances physically close to their owners through a technique called STORED VIA. Today, this technique is called data clustering. Data clustering can only be done for one of a data record type's

Context	OPERATION	
	STATIC	DYNAMIC
Adds	Store record, then adjust the next and prior pointers Adjust all indexes	Check the referen-tial integrity clauses, then store. Adjust all indexes.
Deletes	Find record then delete. DBMS adjusts prior and next records appropriately Adjust all indexes appropriately	Delete record if allowed by refer-ential integrity constraints, then Adjust all indexes appropriately

Figure 4.41 Static and Dynamic Effects on Record Adds and Deletes

owners. Data clustering is naturally practical with hierarchal DBMSs and can sometimes be accomplished with independent logical file DBMSs through the use of multi-valued data record elements and repeating groups. In relational DBMSs, this technique is only now being rediscovered in order to achieve performances commonly present with static DBMSs. The basis in dynamic DBMSs for clustering is the primary-to-foreign key relationship.

The drawbacks to both static and dynamic DBMSs are the same. As the data organization is optimized to serve the needs of one application, it is deoptimized with respect to other applications.

Whenever space is no longer available for the inclusion of a data record instance in a DBMS record, the DBMS record is either split according to a DSDL plan, or a new DBMS record is started with the new data record instance being stored there.

When data record instances are deleted, their former space may be available for re-use. With sophisticated DBMSs, space available lists are maintained so that as new data record instances are entered, the available space is consumed.

In static environment, additions and deletions of data record instances also affect relationship structures. These changes are presented in Section 4.5.3.

Common to both static and dynamic DBMS is the automatic adjustment of indexes when data record instances are added or when they are deleted.

4.5.2 Data Record Element Changes

In most respects, changing data record element values is generally the same for static and dynamic relationship DBMSs. The data record instance is located, the data record element value retrieved and changed, and the data record instance

CONTEXT	OPERATION		
	ADD	DELETE	CHANGE
Fixed length records	Change null to blank or value	Change value to null or blank	Change one value to another
Variable length records	Expand record size	Shrink record size	Expand or shrink record size
Indexed data elements	Add new links	Delete links	Delete link add link
Primary keys	Add new record	Remove record	Delete record add record

Figure 4.42 Data Element Change Effects

replaced in the database. Figure 4.42 tabulates the types of effects of data record element value changes depending on the operation and on the context of the change.

With fixed length data record instances, ADDs, DELETEs, or MODIFYs only change the value already stored in the space. If no value is stored, then the change is NULL to a value or vice versa. With variable length data record instances, the space occupied by the data record instance expands or contracts. If there is no room on the current DBMS record for an expanded data record instance, the DBMS's DSDL plan:

- Moves the data record instance to another DBMS record,
- Leaves (if very sophisticated) one of the expanded data record instances in the space and then with a forward referencing pointer,
- Moves half of all the remaining data record instances to a new DBMS record.

In any case, all the appropriate entries for indexes and relationships (static only) are adjusted.

If a data record element is also indexed, then whenever its value changes the appropriate index structures are changed.

If the data record element is also a primary key, value change effects range from dramatic to minimal. For some DBMSs the effects are so dramatic that changing the primary key value is prohibited altogether. Some other DBMSs allow the primary key value to change despite the effects. The effects arise whenever a

DBMS uses the primary key value to physically locate the data record instance. For those DBMSs, a change in a primary key value is the same as a data record instance delete and a re-add. Further complicating such an operation are the changes required to all the other data record instances containing the primary key value as a foreign key, and all the data record instances that are clustered around the existing data record instance.

If the primary key value is part of the secondary index storage structure component then a change to the primary key value automatically invokes changes to these secondary index storage structure components.

If the DBMS supports a logical-to-physical primary key strategy described earlier in this chapter, then none of the data record element index structures associated with any affected data record instances have to be updated just because the primary key value of the data record instance is updated. The only restriction is that its value can not be changed to an existing value.

4.5.3 Relationship Changes

A significant difference between static and dynamic DBMS approaches pertains to the relationship changes. Inter-record relationship changes for a static-based relationship are very different from the maintenance to a dynamic-based relationship. In a static relationship DBMS, the relationship change process consists of issuing a series of DML commands that:

- Locates the record,
- Disconnects it from its relationship,
- Finds the new and proper position, and finally
- Inserts it into the new relationship.

To accomplish this task, host language programs are usually written, because the process of correctly maintaining database relationships is complex. The complexity of the process is directly related to the number of data record types and the number of relationships among the data record types.

For example, in Figure 3.9 and in conjunction with the data loading example above, if a CUSTOMER is to be related to a different SALESPERSON due to a change in territory, then a SALESPERSON is located, and the relationship instances that thread through the CUSTOMER instances are processed until the proper CUSTOMER instance is found and disconnected from the relationship. Since it has to be assumed that the new SALESPERSON-ID is known, the disconnected CUSTOMER data record instance is connected to the new SALESPERSON using the verbs cited earlier. Figure 4.43 identifies the key actions that must take place to ADD, DELETE, and MODIFY relationships in this static network data model environment.

In the ANSI/NDL static DBMS environment, data record instance ADDs and DELETEs always affect relationships. If the relationship (SET) is defined to be

CHANGE TYPE	DBMS	
	STATIC	DYNAMIC
Add	Store record, then navigate to proper location and INSERT into set	Change null or blank to value
Delete	Find record then delete. DBMS adjusts prior and next records appropriately	Change value to blank or null
Change	Navigate to existing location, then Disconnect. Then navigate to new location and connect.	Change one value to another

Figure 4.43 Static and Dynamic Effects of Relationship Change

AUTOMATIC then the relationship instance to which the data record instance belongs is always affected. If the INSERTION option for a SET is MANUAL then the relationship change is deferred. The data record instance, while belonging to the database, does not belong to any SET. If a data record instance is deleted and the RETENTION option of the involved SET is OPTIONAL, then the data record instance can be deleted. If the RETENTION option is REQUIRED, then the delete request can be rejected.

The hierarchical data model's relationships are always affected when a segment in the hierarchy is added or deleted. When the top (root) segment is deleted there is almost always a cascade delete of all dependent segments. When a dependent segment is deleted then all lower level segments are deleted, the relationships between peer segments are changed, and the relationship to the parent's segment is changed.

When segments are added or deleted within a complex record structure of the independent logical file data model, the effects are the same as those for the hierarchical data model. For relationships across data record type instances, the effects are the same as for the relational data model.

Relationship modification in a relational data model DBMS is the simplest. The data record element that represents the relationship is located, and its value is changed. That's all (see Figure 4.43). If there are referential integrity rules defined, then a data record element change may be prohibited because it violates a referential action rule.

4.6 DATABASE MAINTENANCE

Database maintenance refers to the creation of a backup copy of a database. While creating a backup is certainly the first step in backup and recovery, the impact of the backup process needs to be understood from the perspective of physical database so that sufficient resources can be allocated for its accomplishment.

The number of storage structure units that constitute an individual database varies widely from DBMS to DBMS. In general, when a DBMS is static, the number is small; when a DBMS is dynamic, the number is large.

Because there is this disparity, and because one application may in fact require multiple physical databases to contain all the logical database data, the techniques employed for multiple database backup can be critical to the application.

For DBMSs like SYSTEM 2000, the process of database backup involves a special utility that locates and combines all the storage structure components of a database into a single file. The amount of time to accomplish this is not much more than the cumulative amount of time to copy each of the components onto individual backup files. While the amount of backup time may be insignificant for a small database, backing up a database of 8 billion characters to tape can take up to 10 hours (60 tapes of 6250 BPI, 135 million characters per tape, 10 minutes per tape to backup).

To accomplish such a backup, the database would certainly have to be segmented and backed up segment by segment. A segment might be a certain collection of O/S files that store specific data record type instances, as well as their associated inter-record relationships (if static) and indexes.

4.7 PHYSICAL DATABASE SUMMARY

The physical database, from the DBMS point of view, consists of a database's storage structure, access strategy, data loading, data update, and database maintenance. The four storage structure components are: dictionary, indexes, relationships, and data. The interactions of these four components to store and retrieve DBMS data record instances are the DBMS's access strategy. Data loading is the process of initial data storage. And data update is the process of adding, changing, or deleting data once a substantial amount of data has been stored. Database maintenance is the process of saving an on-line database onto some off-line media.

From the user's point of view, the database consists of data record instances. The DBMS sees the database from the same point of view, except that *data record instance* is understood differently. The user OBTAINs and PUTs data record instances from and to the DBMS. The DBMS accepts these data record instances and combines them into DBMS data record instances, which the O/S combines into O/S data record instances, which are then read from or written to mass storage devices. While a data record type instance may be coincident with a DBMS record instance, normally it is not. In most DBMSs, a DBMS record instance contains multiple data record type instances, and a data record type instance may span multiple DBMS record instances.

As the user reads and writes data record instances, the DBMS, in support of the user's requests, invokes read and write services from O/S utilities that place DBMS data record instances onto whatever storage structure components are necessary to support the user's data record type instances. The DBMS reads and writes DBMS record instances from all of its storage structure components--that is, from its dictionary, its indexes, its relationships (static only), and its data. If a user writes a single data record type instance to a database, the DBMS may place that data record instance in the appropriate DBMS record buffer and not write it to disk because the DBMS record buffer is not full.

Furthermore, the DBMS (static only), in support of the user's data record instance write, may have to create and store in the database multiple DBMS record instances in support of the data record type instance's relationships to other data record instances. The DBMS may also have to update the addresses for indexes that are changed, because the user's data record instance contains indexed elements. In short, a single user's data record instance WRITE might generate no DBMS record I/Os, one DBMS record I/O, or many DBMS record I/Os.

For the static relationship DBMS, once the database is created, it is bound together through the relationships that bind data record instances to each other. In contrast, once the dynamic database is loaded, the data record instances are not related until retrieval. Certainly, because so much less work is accomplished during the dynamic loading process, the dynamic database load is going to be significantly faster than the static load.

A critical difference between static and dynamic relationship DBMSs is in the area of data update. The dynamic relationship DBMS update is oriented towards the single data record type, while the static relationship DBMS handles complex multi-data record type updates through its comprehensive locking schemes.

Figure 4.1 contains a review of these critical differences in physical database between static and dynamic relationship DBMSs.

References

1. The ANSI/X3/SPARC DBMS Framework, Report of the Study Group on Database Management Systems, Tsichritzis and Klug, University of Toronto, Toronto, Canada, AFIPS Press 210 Summit Ave, Montvale, New Jersey 07645, page 9.

5

INTERROGATION

5.1 INTERROGATION EVOLUTION

The logical database establishes the fundamental structure of the data in terms of ANSI standard or nonstandard data models. The physical database defines the physical structures and defines the basic factors governing performance and space efficiency. The interrogation component provides the linguistic mechanisms to add, delete, and/or modify database data and to conform the data into reports. This chapter identifies the basic language access alternatives and illustrates each within the context of statically and dynamically oriented DBMS.

From the time when DBMSs were first developed in the early 1960s until the early 1970s, access to data was either through primitive natural languages or through host language interfaces (HLIs). A natural language is a special language invented by the DBMS vendor. A host language interface is a specially constructed interface between a compiler language, such as COBOL, and the database.

Today most DBMSs have a variety of access languages. Selection of the right language is important. A database programmer might choose a natural language because writing a program takes only a fraction of the human effort required to write the same program in COBOL. Conversely, one might choose the COBOL interface language for its sophisticated processing and reporting capabilities. Or COBOL might be chosen because the natural language is DBMS-dependent, and any programs written in that natural language have to be recoded if they are to be moved from one DBMS environment to another.

Determining the proper use of each DBMS language is important. A critical factor in the determination is portability. In general, natural languages should be used for tasks not intended to be ported from one DBMS to another. ANSI standard languages such as COBOL should be used for tasks that require portability.

The static or dynamic nature of a database has a profound effect on language for two reasons: navigation and relationship expression. Navigation is the expression of verbs to traverse already existing relationships. Relationship expression is the statement of new relationships between record types. In any type of DBMS, either navigation or relationships must be included in the end-user program.

In DBMSs with static facilities, navigation must be expressed with verbs such as GET OWNER, GET MEMBER, and so forth. Relationships do not have to be expressed as the relationships are already bound into the data record instances. In dynamic facilities, the relationships must be expressed with verbs such as:

```
CONNECT STUDENT TO GRADES VIA STUDENT.STUDENT-ID

EQ GRADE.STUDENT-ID,
```

Or the relationships must be expressed within WHERE clauses such as:

```
. . . WHERE EXISTS (SELECT GRADE.STUDENT-ID FROM

GRADES WHERE GRADE.STUDENT-ID = STUDENT.STUDENT-ID)
```

The DBMS takes in that relationship expression, and uses it with other components of the language to process selected data for either reporting or updating.

Both static and dynamic facilities require the programmer to know the database's structure. In a static relationship database the structure is predefined in the DDL and the data record instances are loaded according to the structure's dictates. In the dynamic relationship database the structure exists as shared values between data record types which await discovery during database retrievals.

The development of the skills needed to manipulate database structures is not a simple task. In general, small databases with simple structures usually imply a small user community. As databases become larger, the structures become more complicated and the user community grows. A natural consequence of a wider audience is a wider range of skill levels. There is likely to be a small community of very skilled persons who can easily grasp database structures and comprehend how to develop the appropriate navigation or relationship expression statements. There is always a larger audience for the data contained in the database. The corporation cannot always afford the time and resources to develop the needed skills, even if the ability and temperament are present.

In response to this problem, the DBMS vendor community has, starting in the late 1970s, developed an intermediary facility that removes the need for DBMS users to express syntax for database structure navigation or relationship expression. This intermediary facility, the view, was initially a part of the relational data model, but is now an integral interrogation component of all data models. The benefits derived from views are:

- Perceiving related data record types as a simple data record type called a view record
- Shielding users from having to express relationships or navigation
- Enabling the same end-user language to acquire data from multiple data model DBMSs
- Enabling the same end-user language to acquire data from multiple DBMSs

- Making the end-user program significantly less complicated
- Permitting greater database structure changes without automatically requiring end-user program changes

Notwithstanding the existence of a view mechanism, which may prevent the end-user from seeing what is really going on, static relationship DBMS facilities can only report and process data according to the dictates of the already executed database's structure. Dynamic systems allow users or views to express structure relationships and then report and process from the DBMS-discovered data.

A complete DBMS interrogation program includes:

- Its view, which contains either a set of data manipulation language (DML) verbs to perform database structure navigation, or dynamic relationship specifications which *instruct* the DBMS on the relationships to be executed.
- Reporting and update (add, delete, and modify) facilities appropriate for producing a database add, delete, modify, or report.

Access to the database can be through either compiler languages such as C, COBOL, and FORTRAN, or through natural languages. Compiler languages like C, COBOL and FORTRAN normally do not have DBMS verbs built into them. Thus, an interface is required.

The DML interface to either C, COBOL, or FORTRAN is through a specially built interface constructed by the DBMS vendor. The C, COBOL, or FORTRAN acts as the host for the DBMS verbs that the programmer uses. Hence the name, host language interface (HLI).

The ANSI database committee, X3H2, has developed generic specifications for HLI operations for both NDL and SQL data models. These may be used by DBMS vendors in any way they wish to interface their DBMS to COBOL, FORTRAN, or any other computer language such as query-update, report writers, and other natural languages. All of the HLI methods described below are compatible with the ANSI X3H2 specification.

A natural language is a specially created language tailored specifically to suit the needs of the DBMS and to provide a way of accessing a database. Natural languages come in many varieties. For example, a procedure oriented language is typically a many-statement program able to accomplish complex data selection and processing. A query-update language program, on the other hand, is a single sentence oriented language that accomplishes simple reports and updates. Finally, a report writer program can be used to produce sophisticated reports with sorting, break totals, and the like.

Natural language facilities vary from menu-driven, scroll and pick interfaces to complete languages. In the first case the natural language program may never be materialized, while in the second case the program may be hundreds of lines of source language.

This chapter presents an overview of the method of interfacing DBMS access languages to databases, and of the various types of DBMS access languages, both host and natural.

5.2 DBMSs AND LANGUAGE ORIENTATION

The static relationship DBMSs for the most part cater to the complex program and data environment. Their main programmer is normally a data processing professional and who uses COBOL to communicate with the database.

The dynamic relationship DBMSs for the most part cater to the simple program and a more simple data structure environment with dynamic relationships. Its main programmer is someone with good analytic skills who does not need to be connected to the data processing department at all. The skills required for a natural language programmer are similar to those required for the language BASIC. In addition to needing only analytical skills, the natural language programmer is often the dynamic database designer and user. Thus the predominate language of the dynamic DBMS environment is to be understood and used by this analytical, non-data processing person.

5.2.1 Static Relationship DBMSs and HLIs

Over the years, static relationship DBMSs have developed HLIs to a far greater degree than natural languages. This is for three reasons: interrogation requirements, fundamental inflexibility of the DBMS, and interrogation audience.

First, the interrogation requirements of many HLI reports often demand data from many different data record types, and the involvement of many totals, subtotals, and other types of calculations.

Second, the static relationship DBMS is not very well adapted to ad hoc interrogations. Thus, to develop a very comprehensive and flexible natural language for an on-line environment of ad hoc users is to promise both a capability and a level of performance that can not be delivered.

Third, the audience of most static database applications is generally considered to be *end-users* rather than database designers or programmers. To give these end-users powerful programming tools to create their own reports can cause a significant degradation in overall database performance, and can even lead to significant misinterpretation of database semantics.

5.2.2 Dynamic Relationship DBMSs and Natural Languages

Over the years, dynamic relationship DBMSs have developed natural languages to a far greater degree than HLIs. This is for three similar reasons: interrogation requirements, fundamental flexibility of the DBMS, and interrogation audience.

First, the interrogation requirements of many natural language reports require data from normally only a few data record types, and while there are totals, subtotals, and other types of calculations, reports are simple enough to be configured in the natural language.

Second, the dynamic relationship DBMS is very well adapted to ad hoc interrogations since it has no preconceived report production orientation. Thus, the development and on-going refinement of a comprehensive and flexible natural language for on-line, ad hoc users in no way compromises the performance capabilities of the DBMS.

Third, the audience of most dynamic database applications is generally considered to be the more analytical user, who also might be the database designer and programmer. Since most use of the dynamic relationship DBMS is through the natural language, almost all of the database design, loading, update, reporting and database reorganization tools are also in a natural language format.

5.2.3 Types of Interrogation Languages

There are four general classes of interrogation languages. These are:

- Host language interface (to C, COBOL, FORTRAN, etc.),
- Procedure oriented language,
- Report writer, and
- Query-update

Since the last three languages are all vendor proprietary natural languages, any given vendor's languages fit these categories only in a general way. For example, one vendor's language may have both query and report writing capabilities, but is more oriented to query. Another vendor's language may be procedure oriented but have sophisticated report writing capabilities. Because there are no ANSI standards for the natural languages, both a general description and vendor specific examples are given here.

The host language interface (HLI) is characterized by database utilization through ANSI standard compiler languages such as C, COBOL, and FORTRAN. The principal purposes of the HLI include:

- Data processing intensive applications
- Data migration and transfer to, from, and between databases and DBMSs
- Providing maximum control over user to database interaction

The procedure oriented language (POL) is for utilizing database data record instances and values through a commonly available, but vendor proprietary, language. The capabilities of this language are like COBOL and FORTRAN, but only at one-tenth of the coding. The principal purpose of the POL, similar to HLI, includes:

- Data selection and processing

- Data migration and transformation to, from, and between databases of the same DBMS
- Reasonable control over the user to database interaction

The report writer language is another DBMS vendor proprietary language. This language is usually specially designed to create complex reports. The report writer is often used for prototyping HLI programs. Building report writer programs typically requires only one tenth the resources necessary to build the same program in HLI. Capabilities typically included are:

- Row and column titles, totals, counts, etc.
- Sorting
- Special computation verbs
- Various levels of break totals and titles
- Table look-ups
- Complete control over the user to database interaction as the user cannot update and may only supply argument values

The final language type, query-update, is also vendor proprietary language. Its main role and purpose is to develop simple reports, lists of data record instances, and to perform various type of simple updates. The SQL language is often mistaken to mean Structured Query Language as if it were a query language, when in fact, it is a standardized interface language that other languages can employ to access data from an ANSI standard database. The typical amount of time to build a query language instance is likely to be about one-hundredth the amount of time required to build the same run-unit in HLI.

It is important to pick the right language for the job. That language should offer the least programmer resistance to producing the final result. That generally means trying a higher level language first (query), then using report writer or POL, and then finally resorting to HLI. Figure 5.1 provides a comparison of these four language types, their relative work efforts required to accomplish a task, the language's level of user control over the user-to-database interaction, and then the ability to port the resulting language from one DBMS to another.

5.3 SUBSCHEMA FACILITY

A DBMS subschema facility enables the organization's database administrator to define a user-to-database interface. Within the subschema interface there are four major components: language-independent clauses, language-dependent clauses, the data interface specification, and the select clause. The data interface component usually involves a subset of the data record elements from one or more data record types.

LANGUAGE SELECTION CRITERIA	INTERROGATION LANGUAGE TYPE			
	HLI	POL	RW	QUL
Task Development Effort	High	Med.	Med.	Low
Relative Work units	100	10	10	1
Level of user control over Data-base Interaction	LOW	Med.	Med.	High
Range of Portability from one DBMS to Another of the same data model	Med. to High	Low	Low	Low

HLI = Host Language Interface
POL = Procedure Oriented Language
RW = Report Writer
QUL = Query-Update Language

Figure 5.1 Comparative Development Effort by Language Type

Each of the four interface components is included their own special sections of an HLI user program. Because of this inclusion, and because the programmer must directly create program language statements that manipulate the variables contained in these four interface components, the program's database processing logic is tightly bound to the database's data model. This is a critical drawback of the subschema facility.

5.3.1 Language-Independent Specifications

The language-independent specifications include the subschema name, an enumeration of the data record names from the schema that belong in the subschema, and an enumeration of the data record elements from the schema to be used within the subschema data record instance, and some statement of how the data record instances from the different data record types are to be interrelated.

5.3.2 Language-Dependent Specifications

The language-dependent specifications are styled after the language used for database access. Included are syntax clauses dealing with data types, data conversion rules, data names, and natural languages.

5.3.2.1 Data Types

Each interrogation language may support data types different from those supported by the DBMS. Rules must be created for the proper translation of the database data types to the language data type. For example, data might be stored in the database in packed decimal format or variable length character strings to save space, but FORTRAN, for example, can understand only integer, floating point, and fixed length strings. Thus, the DBMS has to transform the data from packed decimal to integer or floating point, or from a variable length string to a fixed length string.

5.3.2.2 Conversion Rules

A DBMS might be able to store double precision floating-point numbers or numbers in scientific notation. In COBOL, these data types do not exist and so the data has to be converted from its DBMS stored format to the COBOL format. While the rules for conversion are certainly not within the province of the subschema, statements about the precision of the conversion need to be made.

5.3.2.3 Names

Each language requires different conventions for names. For example, if COBOL is the language, and if the schema names are multiple words without hyphens, then COBOL does not understand them. On the other hand, if FORTRAN is the language, and the names have hyphens, FORTRAN interprets the hyphens as minus signs. Consequently, the rules for natural language names vary from no blanks allowed in names to blanks allowed, to hyphens interpreted as minus signs, and so on. To overcome these anomalies, subschemas have a well-defined set of alias clauses.

5.3.2.4 Natural Language Editing and Default Formats

Natural languages also use subschema defined default formats for titles, spacing, edit masks, and so on, and default values for blanks, null values, etc. Figure 5.2 illustrates a subschema with these facilities. In this example, all the data record elements have default column titles, and some, in the event of no data, have default values whenever the DBMS representation of a NULL value has to be printed.

```
TITLE 'FALL SEMESTER GRADES'/DATE
COLUMN SPACING IS 5
DEVICE IS TERMINAL
PAGE IS 132 WIDE BY 55 LONG
DOUBLE SPACE
SUPPRESS BLANKS
PAGE EJECTS ON VALUE CHANGE
SKIP AFTER RECORD PRINT
SKIP BEFORE RECORD PRINT
SKIP AFTER CONTROL BREAK ON <DATA ELEMENT>
SKIP BEFORE CONTROL BREAK ON <DATA ELEMENT>
```

Figure 5.2 Report formatting

5.3.3 Data Interface Specifications

The data interface specifications contain the references to the data record types and the data record elements included in the interrogation. In general, these references are provided automatically whenever a DBMS's natural language is employed. In an HLI environment, these data record type and data record element references are contained in either Labelled Common (FORTRAN) or Working Storage (COBOL).

5.3.4 WHERE Clause Facilities

A critical component of any database subschema access is the WHERE clause. End-user programs, regardless of their language, need to select specific data record instances from within the set that may be made eligible to a subschema FIND.

There are seven different types of operators that can be contained within a WHERE clause:

- Unary
- Binary
- Ternary
- Arithmetic
- Statistical
- Boolean

- Parentheses

Unary operators are used to determine whether data exists or does not exist (FAILS) for a particular data record element. The operator is called unary because it involves only the operator. For example:

. . . WHERE SHIP-DATE EXISTS

. . . WHERE SHIP-DATE FAILS

In this example, the interrogation may merely want to access all orders that have either been shipped or have not been shipped. The EXISTS or FAILS operators determine whether there is any data at all in the data record element.

Binary operators are used to determine specific values, or classes of values. The operator is called binary because it involves the operator and a value. These operators include:

- Less than (LT)
- Less than or equal to (LE)
- Equal to (EQ)
- Not equal to (NE)
- Greater than or equal to (GE)
- Greater than (GT)

These operators are specifically used to select a class of data record instances that meets the specific condition. For example:

. . . WHERE ORDER-DATE GE 01/01/87

. . . WHERE ORDER-DATE LE 01/01/81

. . . WHERE ORDER-DATE EQ 11/15/86

Ternary operators also deal with classes of data record instances, but specifically define a range of values to be researched. The operator typically use keywords like SPANS. . . THRU. The operator is called ternary as it involves the operator and two values. An example of a ternary operator is:

. . . WHERE ORDER-DATE SPANS 01/01/81 THRU 01/01/87

Arithmetic operators deal with classes of data record instances that pass specific types of arithmetic tests. An example is to select all the orders that have a SHIP-DATE greater than 15 days after the ORDER-DATE. Such a calculation requires the use of date arithmetic to subtract the ORDER-DATE from the SHIP-DATE, and the comparison of the resultant number of days to the constant, 15. For example:

. . . WHERE ((SHIP-DATE - ORDER-DATE) GE 15)

Statistical operators are a special class of arithmetic operators. These include:

- Minimum (min)
- Maximum (max)
- Average (avg)
- Sum (sum)
- Count (count)
- Standard deviation

An example is to select all orders whose TOTAL-ORDER-AMOUNT is greater than the average of all orders. This example is constructed as follows:

. . . WHERE TOTAL-ORDER-AMOUNT GT AVG TOTAL-ORDER-AMOUNT.

Boolean operators enable multiple WHERE clause conditions to be connected. The operators are:

AND

OR (inclusive)

XOR (exclusive)

NOT

An example of Boolean operations is to find all the orders that have a SHIP-DATE more than 15 days after the ORDER-DATE with a TOTAL-ORDER-AMOUNT greater than the average TOTAL-ORDER-AMOUNT. Such a class of data record instances is important to find as they relate to significant amounts of noninvoiced products. For example:

. . . WHERE ((SHIP-DATE - ORDER-DATE) GE 15) AND

TOTAL-ORDER-AMOUNT GT AVG TOTAL-ORDER-AMOUNT

A variation on the theme is to find the data record instances related to either of the two conditions. For example:

. . . WHERE ((SHIP-DATE - ORDER-DATE) GE 15) OR

TOTAL-ORDER-AMOUNT GT AVG TOTAL-ORDER-AMOUNT.

The Boolean operator, NOT, accepts only those data record instances that fail the WHERE criteria. An example is to find all orders shipped earlier than five days of an ORDER-DATE and also later than 15 days of the ORDER-DATE. This involves ternary operators, date arithmetic, and the NOT operator. For example:

. . . WHERE NOT((SHIP-DATE - ORDER-DATE) SPANS 5 THRU 15)

The final operator is parentheses. These have already been illustrated within the previous examples. These are especially needed when arithmetic operators and Boolean operators are used. Parentheses are also used in combination with boolean operators. An example is to find all the orders in the West Coast sales region that have a SHIP-DATE more than 15 days after the ORDER-DATE or with a TOTAL-ORDER-AMOUNT greater than the average TOTAL-ORDER-AMOUNT. This example can be constructed as follows:

. . . WHERE ((SHIP-DATE - ORDER-DATE) GE 15 OR

TOTAL-ORDER-AMOUNT GT AVG TOTAL-ORDER-AMOUNT) AND

SALES-REGION EQ *WEST COAST*.

The two sets of parentheses are needed for the following reasons. The first set is needed to bracket the arithmetic operation that subtracts the dates. The second set is needed to bracket the two conditions connected by the boolean operator OR so that the result of that condition set is ANDed with the last condition.

As can be seen, WHERE conditions can be stylized to the individual need. The need to specify a WHERE clause is most acute in a query environment. While the view might be the same, the WHERE clauses need to be varied from one query statement to the next.

As database applications are developed, a standard set of views can also be developed that all the application programmers use. Depending upon complexity, some of these programs can be written in a compiler language (e.g., COBOL), some in report writer, and others in query-update. If a fully functional WHERE clause cannot be expressed in each and every one of these language types, then the DBA will need to be involved in virtually every HLI, POL, query-update, and report writer program.

To safeguard against inappropriate or inefficient WHERE clauses, DBMS activity audit trails can be used to capture the expressed WHERE clause and the resources consumed. In sophisticated DBMSs, these audit trails are themselves kept in a special database, and they can be browsed by the DBA, using a query language with a fully functional WHERE clause, to find the queries (and thus the users) whose consumed query resources exceed certain boundaries.

If the DBMS has a fully functional WHERE clause, programmers can specify the exact conditions that must be met before view record instances are issued by the DBMS to the program's working storage. If the DBMS does not have a fully functional WHERE clause, or if the programmer cannot express the WHERE clause within the program, program development time and complexity are increased. The programmer still has to construct program-based logic to perform the selection operations otherwise performed by the DBMS. The resultant logic still has to be tested, documented, and then maintained. If such logic requires an extra 100 lines in a COBOL program, then the life cycle cost of the program rises by $5000 ($50 per line).

Not having a fully functional WHERE clause is especially damaging to any natural language environment. Programs that would otherwise have been encoded in a report writer, POL, or a query language have to be encoded in COBOL. Simple reports that might have been constructed with 2 hours of programmer analyst time ($50/per hour) have to be replaced with 500 line COBOL programs that cost $25,000 each. The reason for this high cost is that such programs have to be designed, coded, tested, documented, and then maintained. Almost all of this activity is avoided with the use of a natural language.

It is also unsatisfactory to have a fully functional WHERE clause that can only be expressed as part of the view. This requires the DBA to be involved in the development of every query, report writer program, POL program, and HLI program. Clearly, such a requirement is wasteful of scarce company resources.

```
ORDERNUM
ORDERDATE
TOTALORDAMT
QUANTITY
EXTTENDEDPRICE
PRODUCTNAME
WEIGHT
UNITPRICE
```

Figure 5.3 Program View of Orders

5.4 View Facility

A view facility is an alternate form of the subschema facility. The view obviates the requirement for DBMS users to know the underlying DBMS data model. That means that the database user can think of data as a simple data record, as depicted in Figure 5.3, and use verbs such as GET, INSERT, DELETE, or MODIFY. In addition to eliminating the need for programmers to know about the database's data model, the view facility eliminates the program's database processing logic.

Thus, the program is not bound to either the DBMS or the database's data model. This is a significant benefit to the view facility.

Behind the view's definition are the same four components: language-independent clauses, language-dependent clauses, the data interface specification, and the WHERE clause. These components are stored in a special work area controlled by the DBMS.

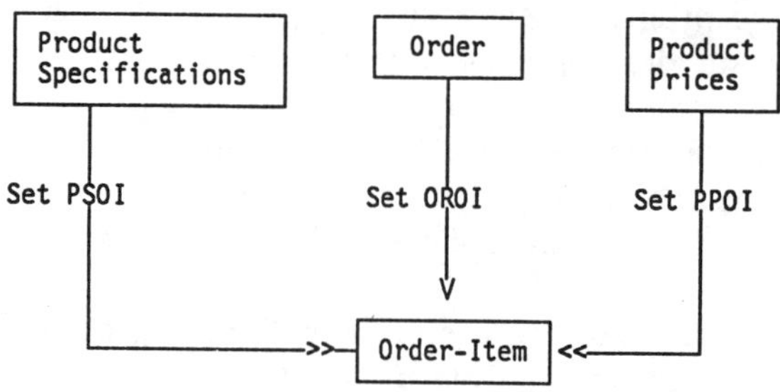

Figure 5.4 Bachman Diagram for Order Information

Figure 5.4 presents the structure of an NDL database. In a traditional subschema environment, if a report of stored orders involves data from the data record types in Figure 5.4, then a data structure interface must be created and made available to the program. Figure 5.5 illustrates the ORDERS schema. In addition to specifying the data record types, the sets that must be traversed must also be identified, that is, product price to order item (PPOI), order to order item (OROI), and product specification to order item (PSOI).

When a program is written to access data record instances from a database structured similarly to that represented in Figure 5.4, the program has to include a subschema specification similar to the one contained in Figure 5.6. Additionally, in order to produce the order information part of an invoice, the program has to contain logic similar to that contained in Figure 5.7. It should be noted that the illustrations in Figures 5.4 through 5.7 are not intended to be syntactically correct NDL. Rather, they are provided to illustrate a program utilizing NDL without a view facility.

Figure 5.7 clearly shows that the *programmer* has to know about data record types, set names, and a navigation oriented data manipulation language.

In an analogous way, users of an SQL database also have to know about data record types (tables), sets (columns from multiple tables with shared values), and a navigation-oriented data manipulation language. Figure 3.28 illustrates the set of tables appropriate to this example. The starred lines indicate the type of relationships that must be present through shared column values. Figure 5.8 provides an SQL version of the DDL for four tables from this relational database structure.

```
SCHEMA ORDERS

     RECORD ORDER
          ORDER NUMBER
          ORDER DATE
          TOTAL ORDER AMOUNT

     RECORD ORDER ITEM
          EXTENDED PRICE
          ITEM QUANTITY

     RECORD PRODUCT PRICE
          PRODUCT NUMBER
          PRODUCT PRICE
          EFFECTIVE DATE

     RECORD PRODUCT SPECIFICATION
          PRODUCT NUMBER
          PRODUCT NAME
          PRODUCT WEIGHT

     SET PPOI
          OWNER PRODUCT PRICE
          MEMBER ORDER ITEM
          INSERTION IS AUTOMATIC
          RETENTION IS OPTIONAL

     SET OROI
          OWNER IS ORDER
          MEMBER IS ORDER ITEM
          INSERTION IS  AUTOMATIC
          RETENTION IS OPTIONAL

     SET PSOI
          OWNER IS PRODUCT SPECIFICATION
          MEMBER IS ORDER ITEM
          INSERTION IS AUTOMATIC
          RETENTION IS OPTIONAL
```

Figure 5.5 Abbreviated ANSI NDL Order Database Schema

The database represented in Figures 5.5 and 5.8 illustrate two major differences between NDL and SQL. First, the NDL version of the database contains 11 data record elements, and the SQL version of the database contains 13 data record elements. Second, the NDL version contains three relationship specifications (sets) and the SQL contains none. These two differences, however, as far as this example is concerned, are merely different semantic forms of the same component: relationships. In the NDL version, relationships are expressed through sets, while in the SQL version, the relationships are expressed through shared column values (same names in this example).

The SQL subschema facility is called a view. It has been more refined than the NDL subschema. Every SQL view can contain both column references (like the NDL) and a WHERE clause that can select data record instances from WHERE-clause-referenced tables into the program materialized view table. Because of this WHERE clause capability, the SQL view depicted in Figure 5.9 corresponds to the combined NDL facilities from Figures 5.6 and 5.7. The SQL

```
SUBSCHEMA ORDERLIST OF ORDERS

     RECORD ORDER RENAMED ORDER

          ORDER NUMBER RENAMED ORDERNUM
          ORDER DATE RENAMED ORDERDATE
          TOTAL ORDER AMOUNT RENAMED TOTALORDAMT

     RECORD ORDER ITEM RENAMED ORDITEM

          ITEM QUANTITY RENAMED QUANTITY
          EXTENDED PRICE RENAMED EXTENDEDPRICE

     RECORD PRODUCT SPECIFICATION RENAMED PRODSPEC
          PRODUCT NAME RENAMED PRODUCTNAME
          PRODUCT WEIGHT RENAMED WEIGHT

     RECORD PRODUCT PRICE RENAMED PRODPRICE
          PRODUCT PRICE RENAMED UNITPRICE

     SET OROI
     SET PSOI
     SET PPOI
```

Figure 5.6 Order List NDL Subschema Specification

```
START

SUBSCHEMA ORDERLIST FROM ORDERS

NEXTORDER

     INPUT ORDNUM
     IF ORDNUM EQ "O" GOTO END

NEXTITEM

     FIND ORDER WHERE ORDERNUM EQ "1234"
     IF ORDER NOT FOUND, DISPLAY "NOT FOUND" GOTO END
     GET ORDER
     PRINT ORDERNUM, ORDERDATE, TOTALORDAMT
     FIND MEMBER OROI
     AT END GOTO NEXTORDER, ELSE
     IF ORDITEM NOT FOUND, DISPLAY "ORDER ITEM NOT FOUND" GOTO END
     GET ORDITEM
     FIND OWNER PPOI
     GET PRODPRICE
     FIND OWNER PSOI
     GET PRODSPEC
     PRINT PRODUCTNAME, QUANTITY, WEIGHT, UNITPRICE, EXTENDEDPRICE
     GOTO NEXTITEM
     END
```

Figure 5.7 NDL Pseudo Code to Obtain Complete Order

```
SCHEMA ORDERS

     RECORD ORDER
          ORDER NUMBER
          ORDER DATE
          TOTAL ORDER AMOUNT

     RECORD ORDER ITEM
          PRODUCT NUMBER
          ORDER NUMBER
          EXTENDED PRICE
          ITEM QUANTITY

     RECORD PRODUCT PRICE
          PRODUCT NUMBER
          PRODUCT PRICE
          EFFECTIVE DATE

     RECORD PRODUCT SPECIFICATION
          PRODUCT NUMBER
          PRODUCT NAME
          PRODUCT WEIGHT
```

Figure 5.8 Abbreviated ANSI/NDL Order Database Schema

```
CREATE VIEW ORDERLIST AS

     SELECT ORDER_NUMBER,
          ORDER_DATE,
          TOTAL_ORDER_AMOUNT,
          QUANTITY,
          ENTENDED PRICE,
          PRODUCT_NAME,
          WEIGHT,
          PRODUCT_PRICE
FROM ORDER, ORDITEM, PRODPRICE, PRODSPEC
WHERE ORDER.ORDER_NUMBER = ORDER_ITEM.ORDER_NUMBER AND
      ORDER_ITEM.PRODUCT_NUMBER = PRICE.PRODUCT_NUMBER AND
      ORDER_ITEM.PRODUCT_NUMBER = PRODSPEC.PRODUCT_NUMBER
```

Figure 5.9 SQL-like Subschema Definition

```
SELECT PRODUCT_NAME, QUANTITY, WEIGHT, UNIT_PRICE, EXTENDED_PRICE
FROM ORDERLIST
```

Figure 5.10 SQL Pseudo Code to Obtain Complete Order

view contained in Figure 5.9 contains the WHERE clauses necessary to determine the joins (shared column values) among the four SQL tables. Figure 5.10 contains an example of an SQL query that acts directly against the view definition in Figure 5.9. Another major difference is that an SQL view can be nested while the NDL subschema cannot.

```
VIEW ORDER FROM SUBSCHEMA ORDERLIST

START

     FIND ORDER
     IF ORD NOT FOUND, RETURN "NOT FOUND", GOTO END
     GET ORD

NEXTITEM

     FIND MEMBER OROI
     AT END, RETURN "NO MORE ORDER ITEMS", GOTO END
     IF ORDITEM NOT FOUND,
          DISPLAY "ORDER ITEM NOT FOUND", GOTO END
     GET ORDITEM
     FIND OWNER PPOI
     GET PRICE
     FIND OWNER PSOI
     GET PRODSPEC
     GOTO NEXTITEM

END
```

Figure 5.11 NDL View Specification ORDER

From the foregoing example, it is clear that although the problem to be solved is the same, when the underlying database design is different, the program itself is also different. The view serves as an important intermediary between the program and the database, obviating the need for the programmer having to know the data model under which the database was constructed. For the NDL, the view is derived from a subschema. The view contains the data interface as well as the navigation logic for the database producing view record instances. To support the NDL, the view references the subschema represented in Figure 5.6, and the navigation logic portion of Figure 5.7. The data interface for the view is depicted in Figure 5.3. The view generation logic is similar to that contained in Figure 5.11.

For the SQL, a view record instance can be from base tables or can be derived from an existing view. The initial view (Figure 5.9) contains all the joins necessary to materialize a complete order. A view defined on the initial view materializes a subset of the columns in the order view and a subset of the rows (data record instances), for example, those with a total order amount over $350.00. An illustration of such a derived SQL view is contained in Figure 5.12. Figure 5.3 depicts the program's data interface for the view.

A host language interface program can now be designed to deal with the view as a simple data record instance using four DML verbs, FIND, OBTAIN, MODIFY, and DELETE. Figure 5.13 illustrates the program logic used for both

```
CREATE VIEW BIGORDERS
SELECT * FROM ORDERLIST WHERE TOTAL_ORDER_AMOUNT GT 350.
```

Figure 5.12 SQL View Specification ORDER

```
OBTAIN ORDER WHERE TOTALORDAMT GT 350.00
```

Figure 5.13 Pseudo Code for View Based Program

the NDL and the SQL. The user program containing these four verbs is not legal COBOL or FORTRAN. Thus, the program must pass through a precompiler that maps the view back to the database and translates the appropriate NDL or SQL data manipulation logic to the appropriate legal COBOL or FORTRAN calls. The program then proceeds through a normal FORTRAN or COBOL compiler resulting in an executable program.

For natural languages, all the translation and binding between the natural language program and the DBMS is automatically handled by the DBMS.

This view mechanism is the typical method by which a DBMS vendor offers services from multiple data model DBMSs to application programs without requiring the application programs to be rewritten.

It is important, though, not to carry a good idea too far. For example, if the view mechanism only allows a restricted set of WHERE logic in the view, then there have to be many more views than necessary. For example, suppose there is a requirement to produce the same report but with the following three different sets of data:

WHERE TOTAL ORDER AMOUNT GT $350.00

WHERE PRODUCT NUMBER EQUAL 745A2

WHERE ORDER DATE WAS *over two weeks old.*

DBMSs requiring the view to incorporate the complete WHERE clause need three different views. If, on the other hand, the DBMS allows the programmer to base the WHERE clause on any set of data record elements identified in the view, then the number of views is restricted to one. Eliminating unnecessary views reduces view design, programming, and maintenance by the DBA. It does no good to relieve the programmer from the distributed work of defining views if the only result is a large, centralized pile of unfulfilled view requests on the DBA's desk.

In summary, the view facility provides the following benefits:

- Related data record types can be seen through one simple data record, called the view record.

- Users do not have to express relationships or navigation.
- End-user languages can use data from multiple data model DBMSs.
- The same end-user language can use data from multiple DBMSs.
- End-user programs can be simplified.
- Database structure changes can be accomplished without automatically requiring end-user program changes.

The view facility, once defined, is likely to be available in a view library so that different users can use the views through different languages. This allows an application dealing with customers to have a single set of appropriate views. These views can be used by the host language interface programs for complicated retrievals and updates, and by query languages and report writers for producing different types of reports.

If a DBMS offers a view facility, then the specific details related to navigation, whether static or dynamic, can be hidden from the programmer. The programmer must first know the data needed, however, and must communicate the data needs to a DBA. The DBA, in turn, researches the database structures finding the locations of the various data record elements, and then constructs the complete view, that is, the set of data record elements representing the program's needs and the navigation logic required to traverse the database's structures to access the data.

5.5 SCREEN DEVELOPMENT

Screens are appropriate for HLI, POL, report writer, and possibly query-update access to the database. Once a screen display format is determined, its programming and database access should be attemped in the highest language possible. That means query-update, then POL, or report writer, and finally HLI. If at each language attempt the screen has to be reprogrammed, the run-unit's development costs rise considerably. In addition, the utility of the screen generator is very questionable.

Most database applications use screens for data entry and update, whether the DBMS that controls the screens resides on a microcomputer, a minicomputer, or a mainframe. Every modern DBMS therefore has facilities for the development, use, and maintenance of screens. It is critical that these screen facilities be available for use by all the appropriate access languages, rather than having to develop screens for host language interface and then a duplicate set for each of the DBMS's natural languages.

Screens are needed for either data display or for data entry. Screens can be developed to provide menu access to types of update transactions, and then, for each update transaction, to redisplay the changed view record, seeking confirmation prior to writing the data back to the database. Since most applications are self-evident only to their creators, HELP screens should be available that can be called upon from any other screen, returning control to the calling screen.

```
Data Transformation Model Component:  Business Event

Business Event Name:  ADD CUSTOMER

PSEUDO CODE:

START TRANSACTION
 DO WHILE CUSTOMER EXISTS
 |  INSERT CUSTOMER, IF FAILURE THEN ROLLBACK
 |     DO WHILE CONTRACT EXISTS
 |     |  INSERT CONTRACT, IF FAILURE THEN ROLLBACK
 |     |      DO WHILE ORDER EXISTS
 |     |      |  INSERT ORDER, IF FAILURE THEN ROLLBACK
 |     |      |       TO WHILE ORDER-ITEM EXISTS
 |     |      |       |  INSERT ORDER-ITEM, IF FAILURE THEN ROLLBACK
 |     |      |       END ORDER-ITEM
 |     |      END ORDER
 |     END CONTRACT
 END CUSTOMER
END TRANSACTION
```

Figure 5.14 Add Customer Business Event

Most complicated applications need to have multiple screens since a given transaction can easily extend beyond one screen. For example, the business event, ADD CUSTOMER, defined in Figure 5.14, certainly contains more than one screen. In fact, each INSERT <record type name> probably contains one or more screens. Thus, there is a natural progression from the CUSTOMER screen, to the CONTRACT screen, to the ORDER screen, then a cycling of the ORDER-ITEM screens until the order is finished. Then there can be a screen to ask if there is another order. If there is, then the ORDER screen appears again. In short, there is not only a need for screen development, but also dialogue development for branching, looping, and the like.

For each screen, a number of characteristics need to be defined. The identifying characteristics include a screen's name, versions, authors, date of creation and update, and restrictions for updating and use. A good screen facility provides the ability to clone a different screen and make trivial changes to make the screen unique. Once a screen is defined, any error messages are flagged so that flawed clauses can be corrected.

As to actual screen definition and maintenance capabilities, the following list identifies capabilities of a sophisticated screen facility:

- Posiktioning literal fields
- Positioning data fields
- Varying the color of literal fields
- Varying the intensity of literal fields

- Changing the color of data fields
- Varying the intensity of data fields
- Specifying the position of data fields
- Changing the color of borders
- Performing automatic data editing and validation from IRDS stored tables
- Performing automatic table look-up from IRDS stored tables
- Enforcing required fields
- Automatic redisplaying of screens whenever errors are entered
- Automatic highlighting of errors through color or intensity change
- Automatic mapping of screen data fields to schema record elements
- Automatic invoking of database-defined data editing and validation facilities for screen data fields
- Automatic invoking of database-defined table look-up facilities for screen data fields
- Automatic building of menu screens once menu alternatives are defined
- Automatic building of help screens once help alternatives are defined

Once a screen has been developed, it should be usable in either a data entry or reporting mode. Screens should be usable for both the HLI and POL languages.

A screen becomes a useful component in any information system as there are only two sources for determining any statistics about the quantity of data stored in the database: screen data entry and batch data loading. A screen facility should therefore be able to generate use statistics and store them in a form for later reporting.

Once data is entered through a screen, the screen facility typically performs data editing, validation, and table look-up from IRDS stored tables, as well as enforcing data entry to required fields. This is all accomplished prior to the transmission of the data record instance to the database. When an error occurs, the screen facility highlights the error and provides a method for explaining the presented error message.

A final capability often present in screen facilities is the generation of statistics written by the facility to the IRDS so that the DBA or application manager can review the number of transactions attempted and the number that succeeded.

A necessary component of any screen driven program is the development of dialogues. This facility is needed to advance screens, transfer to other screens, and the like. The key capabilities that must be available in any screen navigation component are:

- Use PF keys (or mouse controls) to transfer control to next, prior, and top screens.
- Invoke screens from other screens by entering the target screen's name or identity.
- Invoke subroutines encoded in a compiled language, automatically when the screen's data is transmitted, to accomplish complicated processing.
- Present dialogue management messages so that flawed clauses can be modified.
- Store the *compiled* dialogue.

It is clear that screen and dialogue development and management are actually a whole programming environment in themselves. The results of this activity are a critical component of any database project. A sophisticated facility saves hundreds of thousands of dollars of design, development, and maintenance efforts.

5.6 RELATIONSHIP BETWEEN SCREENS AND VIEWS

There is a definite relationship between views and screen. A view is a set of view (data) elements presented to the program, and a screen is the format for the presentation of the view elements in the view. If all the view elements can fit on one screen, then the relationship is 1 to 1. If, however, there are more data record elements in a view than can fit on one screen, then there has to be more screens. Additionally, some of the view elements from an ORDER view might map to the CUSTOMER screen, some to the ORDER HEADER screen, and others still to the ORDER-ITEM screen. The point is that the screens and views must be defined separately, and then related.

5.7 SYSTEM CONTROL CAPABILITIES

The facilities of system control normally available through interrogation language programs include:

- Audit trails
- Message processing

- Backup and recovery
- Concurrent operations
- Multiple database processing
- Security and privacy
- Reorganization

5.7.1 Audit Trails

Audit trails, or journals, are logs of DBMS/database activity that organizations wish to track. Depending on the DBMS, audit trails can be kept for particular data record types, databases, applications, and entire central version environments. For very sophisticated DBMSs, a DBA might determine that the tracking is to be for updates only, for certain types of reports, for interactive but not batch updates, etc.

Audit trails oriented towards static relationship databases are normally well-developed and centralized to contain a single trail for all updates to all the data record types in the entire database. Some static relationship DBMSs also allow audit trails to be started, stopped, kept for times of the day, certain applications, and even for certain access languages but not others.

Audit trails oriented towards dynamic relationship databases are usually not so well developed, and often there is one audit trail for each data record type. Thus, the only way to have a multiple data record type audit trail is to have the DBMS' central version operate the audit trail on behalf of all data record types. This is further reason to keep updating strictly isolated to a single data record type when using a dynamic relationship DBMS.

DBMS central version audit trail transactions are kept principally to enable central version rollback and/or recovery in event of a hardware/software failure. Thus, this type of audit trail environment is independent of the static or dynamic orientation of the database. Audit trails are normally automatically available when the run-unit is operating, and are not optional. They are initiated and controlled by a centralized DBA group.

As expected, the sophistication of the audit trail is directly related to the cost of its accomplishment. For example, if the DBA decides that all updates are to be retained in a reprocessable and reportable manner and that along with the update transaction, the source of the update, the identification of the run-unit, the source language of the run-unit (HLI, POL, etc.), time of day, etc., along with the before and after image of the schema record instance that was changed, then a lot of extra processing and storage has to occur to accomplish that work.

For example, if there are 1000 on-line, update users to a database and they store one update every three minutes for a six hour day, and the update only affects one schema record instance, and if the schema record instance affected is 100 characters long, then the database grows by at least 24,000,000 characters each day (1000 users * 20 transactions per hour * 6 hours per day * 100 characters per schema record instance * 2 copies for before and after image), just to contain the before and after images of the audit trail. Added to that is the actual audit trail data record instance. If that is only 50 characters long, then the audit trail grows additionally by 6,000,000 characters (1000 * 20 * 6 * 50). The total daily audit trail size is then 30 million characters. At the logical transaction rate computed in Chapter 4 of 80 transactions per wall clock second, that takes an additional 4 hours of daily processing ((1 audit trail data record instance * 1000 users * 20 per minute * 6 hours per day) / (80 transactions per second * 3600 seconds per hour)).

In a multiple database environment, audit trails must be controlled by the DBMS across all active databases. The DBA must then determine whether there is to be a single combined audit trail, one for each database, and the like. Critical questions like the following must be answered:

- Can audit trail records stored on a single instance of a journal file be restricted to store updates to one or more databases?
- Can audit trail records stored on a single instance of a journal file be restricted to store updates to one or more database areas?
- Can audit trail records stored on a single instance of a journal file be restricted to store updates to one or more defined view record type instances?

If answers to these questions are positive then the audit trail resources can be reduced to an acceptable quantity.

5.7.2 Message Processing

A good message processing facility within any interrogation language automatically intercepts and processes DBMS or operating system messages, making them available to the user.

5.7.3 Backup and Recovery

In either the static or the dynamic database environments, well-designed backup and recovery are essential. A backup is the process of making a complete copy of the database onto another medium. Since backup is a proper activity for the database administrator rather than an application program, it is covered in Chapter 6.

There are three types of recovery: user instigated transaction roll-back, DBMS restart, and full recovery. The only type of recovery that is applicable to the run-unit is user instigated transaction roll-back. The other types of recovery are treated in Chapter 6.

The transaction roll-back activity consists of executing the transaction ROLLBACK. The roll-back operation reverses the effect of one set of transactions. A transaction set is bounded by the two commands START TRANSACTION and END TRANSACTION. For some DBMSs, a COMMIT operation signals an END TRANSACTION and an immediate START TRANSACTION. The command FINISH indicates a commit with an END DBMS command. In HLI languages, and in some POLs, the use of the two commands START TRANSACTION and END TRANSACTION can be explicit. In many query-update languages, these commands are implicit, and are automatically included by the DBMS in every command that performs an update.

Generally the roll-back operation is limited to just one transaction. Figure 5.14 illustrates roll-back levels programmed into an order-entry application. The logic states that if a failure occurs on any of the INSERT operations, then a roll-back is to occur. And in the case of ADD CUSTOMER transaction, the roll-back is at the highest level. That means if the very last INSERT ORDER-ITEM fails, all the prior INSERTs for that entire customer are rolled back.

5.7.4 Concurrent Operations

The very reason for creating the database discipline is to allow multiple users access to the same store of data--in a controlled manner. Even the most primitive DBMS allows concurrent access. The cornerstone of concurrent access is locking. Locking levels are:

- View record instance
- Schema record instance
- DBMS record instance
- All data record instance instances of the same type
- All DBMS record instances in a file
- All instances contained in an area
- The entire contents of a database

In general, the levels of locking cited above go from fine to coarse. A view record instance however can cross multiple schema record instances, and a schema record instance can cross multiple DBMS record instances.

When a database is opened by a run-unit, or an AREA is readied, or a view record instance is selected, the interrogation language usually provides some mechanism for locking. The locking level is specified by the DBA rather than the programmer. In SYSTEM 2000, for example, a user can access a database through either a DATABASE IS <database name> command or a SHARED DATABASE IS <database name> command. The former mode is exclusive and the latter is shared. If the site's DBA does not want any access other than shared, the DATABASE IS <database name> command can be disabled by the DBA.

Most DBMSs have a method of releasing locks that have been held *too long*. Since this varies both by data model and by DBMS, and is not covered by any ANSI standard, the levels of locking, their length, methods of release, etc. all have to be determined and understood before they can be properly used in any language run-unit.

In addition to locking at various levels against one database, the locking concept must also deal with multiple databases. An organization might determine that databases are to be defined along application boundaries rather than subject boundaries. Such a decision necessarily requires synchronization of the redundant data. To accomplish synchronization some run-unit updates must execute against multiple databases. That means that locks must be imposable on multiple databases at the same time and if an update fails on one database, the updates on the other database must automatically reverse.

The issue of deadly embrace surfaces often in database. If a run-unit needs to lock multiple resources, it is possible that after locking the first resource the DBMS finds the second resource locked by another run-unit. In such a case, the first run-unit is usually programmed to retry a lock on the second resource. During the reattempt the run unit may hold the lock on the first resource. If there is no finite elapsed time or limit to the number of reattempt failures that can occur, the first run-unit can be reattempting forever. Eventually, another run-unit which has locked other resources will attempt to lock a resource that is already locked by the first run-unit. Upon finding it locked, it too will fall into a cycle of reattempts. If enough of these forever-in-failure run-units are in execution, all real DBMS work stops. To overcome this situation, DBMS vendors have designed and implemented various schemes for deadly embrace resolution. Again, because this varies both by data model and by DBMS, and because deadly embrace is not covered by any ANSI standard, the methods of resolution have to be determined and understood before complicated run-units can be created with any level of confidence. Key questions that must be addressed are:

- Is the DBMS designed such that deadly embrace is automatically prevented and/or resolved?
- Is a deadly embrace resolved by stopping one of the run-units?
- Is a deadly embrace resolved by rolling back all the run-unit's transactions?
- Is a deadly embrace resolved by rolling back only the run-unit's committed transactions?
- Is a deadly embrace resolved by requiring the user to reinstigate the run-unit?
- Is a deadly embrace resolved by attempting a run-unit restart a predetermined number of times before permanent abort?

- Is a deadly embrace resolved by attempting a run-unit restart periodically for a predetermined wall-clock time before permanent abort?

Answers and explanations to these questions are critical before multiple-user, multiple database applications can be created. For example, if deadly embrace is resolved by terminating execution of the run-unit that effects deadlock, then these run-units have to be programmed so they are invoked by a higher level program that offers an opportunity to restart. Conversely, if run-units can establish a maximum number of reattempts, then does this number vary depending on whether the run-units operate in prime or nonprime time, or possibly batch, or on-line?

5.7.5 Multiple Database Processing

Because a static database is potentially very large, complex, and comprehensive, there is little need for multiple database processing. But when the need exists, the host language often provides the only method to accomplish it. The need for multiple database processing usually arises when someone needs a report that combines, for example, sales and marketing data from multiple divisions that have each implemented the same type of database. Ironically, the relationships that exist between multiple static databases are dynamic. The dashed lines in Figure 3.8 illustrate the fact that almost all hierarchical data model databases need to accomplish multiple database processing. In the dynamic database environment, multiple database processing is its normal mode in either the host language or the POL. Figure 3.28 depicts dynamic relationships, and Figure 4.23 illustrates how they are processed.

Neither the ANSI/NDL or ANSI/SQL standards address multiple database processing in any acceptable manner. This means that each DBMS, ANSI standard or not, has to be examined in this very important area. It must be determined what procedure is required for a run-unit to obtain raw data from multiple databases and combine it into a single integrated report. The technique may range from having a run-unit execute multiple times, one time for each database, to having a run-unit execute against multiple databases in a serial fashion, to having a run-unit being able to have multiple databases opened concurrently and run-unit commands executing against these multiple database, in a coordinated fashion.

5.7.6 Security and Privacy

A carefully constructed view facility restricts access to specific data record types and to specific data record element values for specific data record instances. Beyond that, the DBMS may abort run-units for illegal use of a DBMS operation or the attempted attachment of a data record type or data record element. The ANSI/SQL standard provides a reasonably good security facility. Security is not at all specified in NDL because the ANSI X3H2 committee (different membership at an earlier time) felt that security and privacy specification was the proper purview of an operating system's committee. Equal in importance to the specification of security is knowing how a DBMS reacts to security breaches. Some key questions that must be answered of any DBMS vendor for the proper assessment of a security facility are:

- Is a run-unit immediately terminated when it commits a security violation?
- After a security violation, can a run-unit attempt restart immediately?
- After a security violation, can a run-unit be prohibited from restart for a period of time?
- After a security violation, can a run-unit be prohibited from restart until the run-unit is *manually* revalidated?

5.7.7 Reorganization

Normally a language's run-unit is not involved in database reorganization. Some DBMSs, however, provide commands to the language that can cause the creation of an entirely new data record type including data record elements, index indicators, etc. This kind of capability is quite useful in the multiple database example described above. An application program can serially operate against multiple databases, creating and populating a new database and associated data record types so that a report writer or query-update language can operate against the combined data.

5.8 HOST LANGUAGE INTERFACE

Any host language interface (HLI) provided by DBMS vendors consists of the following components:

- HLI-DBMS interaction protocol
- Access language form
- View access
- Schema record access
- Screen development and utilization
- HLI cursors
- Updating
- DBMS and database attachment
- System control capabilities
- Error control

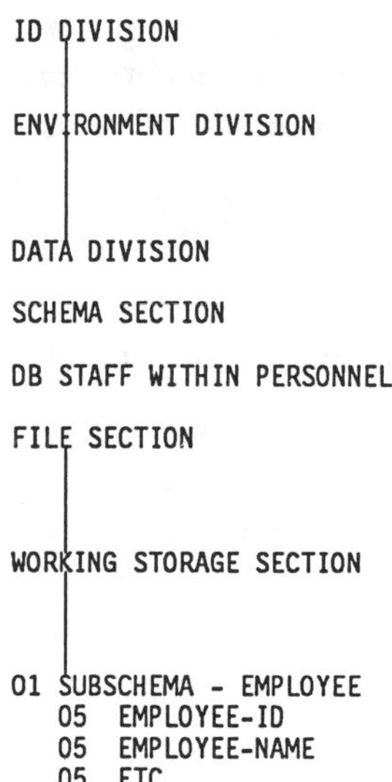

```
ID DIVISION

ENVIRONMENT DIVISION

DATA DIVISION
SCHEMA SECTION
DB STAFF WITHIN PERSONNEL
FILE SECTION

WORKING STORAGE SECTION

01 SUBSCHEMA - EMPLOYEE
   05  EMPLOYEE-ID
   05  EMPLOYEE-NAME
   05  ETC
```

Figure 5.15 Data interface Area Schema/Subschema systems

5.8.1 HLI-DBMS Interaction Protocol

The interface between a host language program and a database often requires a specially named data storage area within the program to act as a staging area for passage of data to and from the database. Figure 5.15 illustrates how a COBOL program interacts with IDMS/R. Within a program's data division, a subschema section identifies the name of the database and within the working storage section there are definitions of the data record types that act as the data staging area.

Additionally, each program has a specially configured set of DBMS commands to start and stop the DBMS; to find, select, add, delete, and modify data record instances; and to traverse data record instance relationships. Each non ANSI standard DBMS creates these interface components differently. If there is an intent to create programs that are DBMS independent, subroutines should be built to hold these DBMS interfaces. Programs call these interface subroutines to GET or PUT data regardless of the DBMS employed.

Analogous to data interfaces, application programs have an area for the passage of messages and status indicators to the DBMS regarding the database. Figure 5.16 illustrates the various types of variable names that appear in the messages area for one DBMS. Since there are variables for area and set, it can be assumed that the messages deal with a CODASYL type network DBMS. There is an especially large difference among DBMSs with respect to cursors. In static

```
              PROGRAM-NAME
              ERROR-STATUS
              DBKEY VALUE
              RECORD-NAME
                SET-NAME
Working        AREA-NAME
Storage        ERROR-SET
              ERROR-RECORD
              ERROR-AREA
              DIRECT-DBKEY
              DATABASE-STATUS
```

Figure 5.16 Message Interface

network relationship DBMSs, there are a large number of cursors (sometimes called currency idicators) that identify which database, area, relationship (set), view record, and view record instance is currently active. Because the network data model is very complex, network cursors are very complex. As the DBMS's data model becomes less complex, that is, from network to hierarchical to independent logical file to relational, the complexity of the cursors lessens.

The HLI program also includes commands specially designed to manipulate the data represented by the DBMS's data model. Both static data models use relationship hypothesis expressions to navigate owners and members and among members. The network data model also supports finding multiple owners for a member and performing recursive set operations, while the hierarchical data model cannot.

Both dynamic data models have relationship (e.g., JOIN) commands that relate data record instances together through common data values. The independent logical file data model also has commands to find dependent segments for complex data record instances. The relational data model can only select data from simple data record instances. The SELECT command in ANSI SQL can contain nested subqueries, each of which can contain a JOIN.

Some DBMSs have only simple commands such as FIND and GET, where others contain complex commands to represent the combined functionality of more than one command. For example, FETCH combines FIND and GET. Notwithstanding these variations, the following functions are normally supported by a host language interface capability:

- Data record instance selection
- Data record instance insertion
- Data record instance modification
- Data record instance deletion
- Structure navigation

Once a program has been precompiled, compiled, and link-edited, an execution version of the program (load module) is created. In some environments this execution version consists of all the routines necessary to complete the program's execution, while in other environments the execution version is able to invoke other load modules dynamically during the program's execution. In the first case, the execution time of the program is faster because no time is spent acquiring memory, I/Os, etc. for the dynamically loaded routines for DBMS, operating system, and telecommunications services. The second case, however, has an advantage because changes in the dynamically loaded modules does not force the program to go back through the precompiler, compiler, and link phases. This difference can be very practical. During the time an application is in development, aspects of a DBMS interface, such as a view, might change. Any such changes must be reflected in the programs using the view. If the programs have to pass back through the precompiler and compiler phases, the time to get affected programs back into production status can be longer. Clearly, the best environment is to have the option of including all components of the application program in the execution module or having them dynamically loadable during execution. When this option is available, quick changes can be made without reperforming all the compile steps, but once an application is finished and stable (changes only once each six months or so), the benefits of faster execution can be realized.

5.8.2 Access Language Form

There are three methods popularly used by DBMS vendors to interface compiler level languages (e.g., C, COBOL, FORTRAN, etc.) to database. Two are CALLs and the other is a specialized language. The CALLs formats are either function specialized or generalized. The function specialized CALL mechanism employs specially named CALLs like CALL GETROW USING <variable>, <variable>,

```
CALL 'GETROW" USING ERR WORKAREA EDIT-1
```

Figure 5.17a Specialized CALLS Interface

. . . , <variable>. Figure 5.17a illustrates this specialized CALL type of interface.

The second CALLs incorporates a generalized CALL facility like CALL 'ADABAS' USING <variable, variable, . . . >. In this case, each of the variables carries information to the DBMS, such as what operation is desired, the name of

```
CALL 'ADABAS' USING
     CONTROL-BLOCK
     FORMAT-BUFFER
     RECORD-BUFFER
     SEARCH-BUFFER
     VALUE-BUFFER
     ISN-BUFFER
```

Figure 5.17b Generalized CALLS Interface

the view record accessed, selection criteria, and so on. The value of this type of mechanism over the previous one is that all CALLs are through a single paragraph in the user's program, albeit not very structured. Even though there is only one place for calling the DBMS there still must be the various instruction sets in the program to set the proper values for the different variables. Figure 5.17b illustrates this technique.

The third technique is through a vendor tailored language. This language is a series of data manipulation language (DML) verbs such as START DBMS, OPEN <database name>, and FIND <record type name>. This technique is the one traditionally used in the various CODASYL DBMSs (network), SYSTEM 2000 (hierarchical), and in all ANSI/SQL DBMSs. Clearly, this technique is the most popular. The English-like statements are included in the source program. The combined-set-of-languages-run-unit is then submitted to a vendor provided precompiler. The output of the precompiler is a series of statements that are all C, or all COBOL, or all FORTRAN, etc. Figure 5.17c illustrates the translation through the precompiler of the three English-like lines to the five lines of COBOL.

In all three methods, the ultimate result is the same: data is accessed for a specific purpose. HLI mechanisms usually have automatic error procedure invocation, automatic data type translation, and automatic movement of data from the database to the user work area in the program. The HLI interfaces seem to be better developed in the static relationship DBMSs than dynamic relationship DBMSs. Most DBMSs seem to have either the generalized CALLs or the vendor tailored method of host language interface.

5.8.3 View Access

View facilities impact the requirements for data interface. With view facilities an application program must contain a set of view cursors, data areas for messages, and a simple set of database access commands.

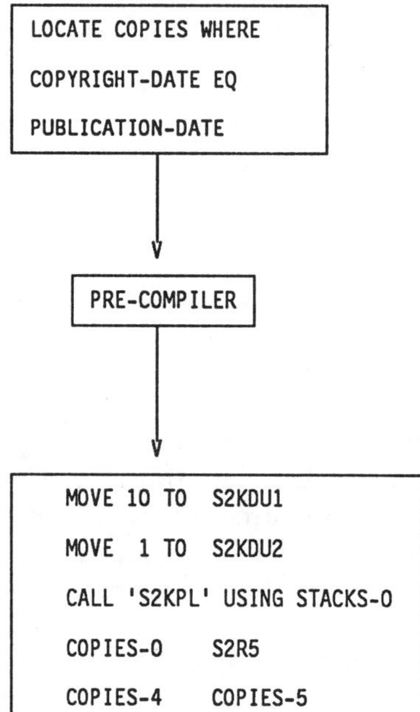

Figure 5.17c Precompiler Interface

5.8.3.1 View Operations

The basic view operations are:

- FIND, a command that determines the identifiers for a set of view instances. These instances are then available for record-at-a-time processing.
- GET, a command that obtains a specific view record instance from the queue of view instances found.
- DELETE, a command that removes a view record instance from the database. Some DBMSs will only allow database changes (insert, modify, or delete) to be performed on schema record type instances (base table instances).
- INSERT, a command that stores a new view record instance in the database.
- MODIFY, a command that changes existing view element value instances from one value (null, blank, or valued) to another value.

- START TRANSACTION, a command that indicates the start of an identified set of run-unit database change commands having their actions reversed--in unison--by the rollback command, or whose effects are automatically reversed by the DBMS after a DBMS or O/S failure.
- END TRANSACTION, that indicates the end of a set commands that are subject to a rollback.
- ROLLBACK, a command that can be invoked by the run-unit to cause the removal of a set of commands that have been demarcated by a start and end transaction.
- COMMIT, a command that causes the permanent storage of the run-units database changes.
- FINISH, a command that indicates that the uncommitted transactions are to be committed and that is the last command to be executed by the run-unit.

5.8.3.2 View WHERE Clauses

WHERE clause facilities impact program design and implementation. If the WHERE clause is not fully functional, then extra logic has to be built into the program to refine a gross set of view instances to just those view instances needed by the program. If the WHERE clause cannot be placed in the program, then the DBA has to create a view for every program. Both these additional requirements expand the analysis, coding, debugging, testing, and documentation time for each program.

The WHERE clause is appropriate for the FIND, DELETE, INSERT and MODIFY commands. A sophisticated WHERE clause contains:

- Unary operators (Exists and Fails)
- Binary operators (GT, GE, EQ, NE, LE, LT)
- Boolean operators (AND, OR, NOT)
- Ternary operators (SPANS, RANGES (i.e., GE <value> AND LE <value>))
- Arithmetic operators (+,-,*,/)
- Statistical operators (min, max, avg, sum, standard deviation)
- Parentheses (nesting)
- Partial schema record element value searches
- Exact mask searches
- Prefix searches

- Suffix searches
- *Contains* searches

While it is certainly possible to include indexed and non-indexed data record elements, it is important to know whether the WHERE expression can contain:

- All non-indexed data record elements from different data record types, or must contain at least one indexed data record element
- Multiple indexed data record elements from the same schema record type
- Multiple indexed schema record elements from different schema record types

Key to understanding the performance of a DBMS is knowing its access strategy, and knowing how that access strategy is applied to the different indexed and non-indexed view elements, different WHERE clause operations, and the effects of having different view elements from different schema record types, and finally the difference between static and dynamic relationship DBMS. The minimum set of cases that must be examined to determine if WHERE clauses are optimized are:

- Multiple non-indexed schema record elements from the same schema record type, rather than just one non-indexed schema record element.
- Multiple non-indexed schema record elements from different schema record types, instead of just one non-indexed schema record element.
- A single indexed schema record element in place of just one non-indexed schema record element.
- Multiple indexed schema record elements from the same schema record type, other than just one indexed schema record element and other non-indexed schema record elements from that schema record type.
- Multiple indexed schema record elements from different schema record types, rather than just one indexed schema record element from one schema record type, along with non-indexed schema record elements from other schema record types.

Some DBMSs publish exactly how their WHERE clauses are evaluated and processed. This gives the knowledgeable user the ability to construct WHERE clauses that take advantage of the DBMS's processing logic. For example, in SYSTEM 2000, WHERE clause processing logic is from right to left. Thus, when processing a WHERE clause that includes view elements from different schema record types, the WHERE clause processes faster if ordered right to left to contain view elements highest in the hierarchy as well as the most restrictive in value hits.

A more sophisticated DBMS will upon submittal of a WHERE clause analyze it to ascertain the most efficient method of processing, that is, indexed, sequential, and serial searches.

Since each DBMS vendor has complete freedom to construct the DBMS's storage structure and access strategy, only a careful examination and very carefully crafted benchmark tests determine the DBMS that is best for a given application.

A static relationship DBMS requires that relationship mechanisms exist between related record types. Thus, a select clause cannot contain view element WHERE criteria from unrelated schema data record types. In contrast, a dynamic relationship DBMS select clause can express relationships across different data record types within the WHERE clause. Some DBMSs require the joined data record elements from the different data record types be named the same whenever a relationship operation is to be performed. Other DBMSs expressly prohibit data record elements to be named the same. Some DBMSs required the joined schema record elements from the different schema record types to have exactly the same data types and picture clauses, while other DBMSs only require the data types to be generally the same.

5.8.3.3 Run-Unit Sort Clauses

The FIND command typically locates a set of view record instances as a consequence of the WHERE clause. Since different run-units often want the view record instances in different orders, sophisticated DBMSs provide sorting operations. Traditionally, most static relationship DBMSs provide sorting through a sort clause option on the DDL SET clause (see Chapter 3). If a user wants the view record instances in the order maintained by a SET clause, everything is fine. However, if the desired order is to be different from the SET maintained order, the user has to FIND the view record instances, retrieve them, place them in a separate O/S controlled file, invoke an O/S sort utility, sort the view record instances, and then re-retrieve them into the run-unit. While this procedure is practical for a COBOL run-unit, it is not practical for POL, report writer, or query-update run-units. As a consequence, DBMS vendors include their own sort clause capabilities in these languages. All dynamic and some static relationship DBMS vendors include sort clause capabilities in their HLI. Dynamic vendors always include sorting because maintaining multiple ordered relationships among the schema record instances is contrary to the very nature of the dynamic data model (ILF and relational data model DBMSs).

Sophisticated sorting supports:

- Single view element low to high sorting
- Multiple view element low to high sorting
- Single view element high to low sorting
- Multiple view element high to low sorting

- Combinations of view element high to low and low to high sorting

Sorting efficiency is critical. Some DBMSs speed up sorting whenever the sort element is indexed.

5.8.4 Subschema Access

If a view facility is not present within the DBMS or if the view facility is not sophisticated enough for the type of processing that is required, then it is necessary to process directly against the schema record types, mapped through a subschema facility. In this case, the data model of the DBMS cannot be shielded, and the commands that perform schema record type operations and relationship operations must be present. The application program must set aside a working storage area for each schema data record type (or subset of elements). In addition, the individual program must include a full set of navigation commands to traverse the database's structures. Each of these additional requirements expands the analysis, coding, debugging, testing, and documentation time for each program. The record type operations generally common to both static and dynamic relationship DBMSs are:

- Find
- Insert
- Delete
- Modify

Similarly, the operations that perform transaction control operations, also independent of data model, are:

- Start transaction
- End transaction
- Rollback
- Commit
- Finish

Relationship operations are dependent upon the data model of the DBMS. In general, the network and hierarchical data model DBMSs support the following relationship operations:

- Get first
- Get last
- Get next
- Get prior

- Get member
- Get owner
- Connect
- Disconnect

In general, the independent logical file and relational data model DBMSs support the following relationship operations:

- Join
- Outer join
- Division
- Union
- Outer union
- Intersection
- Difference

When there is direct manipulation of the schema record instances rather than view record instances, the sophistication of the WHERE clause is usually governed by underlying sophistication of the DBMS and whether the DBMS is static or dynamic. In static relationship DBMSs, the presence of DDL based relationship clauses usually permits the WHERE clauses to have schema record elements from different schema record types. In dynamic relationship DBMSs, there are two main subcases: SQL and all others. In SQL, the WHERE clause has a series of hierarchically nested relationship clauses within the WHERE clause. In *all others*, the typical dynamic relationship DBMS's WHERE clause determines a set of primary keys based on the conditions present in only one schema record type. These primary key values are retrieved and stored in a program defined array. A programming loop iterates through the array of primary key values and appends any other WHERE clause conditions relevant to each. Figure 5.18 illustrates this technique against the data structure depicted in Figure 5.8.

Sort clauses in the direct schema record type access environment are directed only to one schema record type at a time. These sort clauses should contain the same capabilities as described above.

5.8.5 Screen Development and Utilization

If an organization makes full use of an IRDS then the appropriate screen characteristics about data definitions are available from the IRDS component to define an interrogation screen. A critical characteristic of an IRDS is that once it contains the appropriate set of semantics and rules, the screen facility must then enforce them. A screen facility must not contain contradictory definitions. Further,

```
10 TABLE ORDERS (ORDER_NUMBER, TOTAL_ORDER_AMOUNT)

15 TABLE ORDITEM (ORDER_NUMBER, LINE_ITEM_NUMBER, EXTENDED_PRICE)

20 ARRAY ORDNUM (1000)

30 FIND ORDERS WHERE TOTAL_ORDER_AMOUNT GT 3500.00

40 FOR I = 1 TO COUNT.ORDERS

45 GET NEXT ORDERS

50 ORDNUM (I) = ORDER_NUMBER

60 NEXT I

65 FOR I = 1 TO COUNT.ORDERS

70 FIND ORDITEM WHERE ORDER_NUMBER = ORDNUM (I) AND
       EXTENDED_PRICE GT 1000.00

75 ..........

80 NEXT I
```

Figure 5.18 Basic-Language-Like Example of Schema Record Type Access

in the event these centralized semantics change, the specific screen affected by these changes must be automatically disabled from working. Such automatic semantic enforcement and/or automatic disabling of screen executions demarche active IRDS from passive IRDS.

Screens are almost always a critical requirement of an HLI based report or update program. If screens can only be defined with COBOL facilities rather than be copied from a library of screens, then the analysis, coding, debugging, testing, and documentation time for each program is expanded. The facilities of a good screen generator are described in Section 5.5 of this chapter.

5.8.6 HLI Cursors

Cursors are indicators of position. For example, if a WHERE clause has identified 500 view record instances and 75 have been retrieved, then the cursor position is 76. In the various data models, the number and types of cursors vary. The more complex the data model, the greater the number of cursors. This is illustrated in Figure 5.19.

Figure 5.20 illustrates the complexity and number of different cursors that exist in IDMS/R network. It shows that there is an indicator of the current RECORD NAME, AREA NAME, and SET NAME.

Figure 5.21 illustrates the SYSTEM 2000 cursor model. In SYSTEM 2000, a hierarchy can be 32 levels (0 to 31), and there can be up to 16 (0-15) different open WHERE clauses. Once a WHERE clause is executed, the identifiers of the

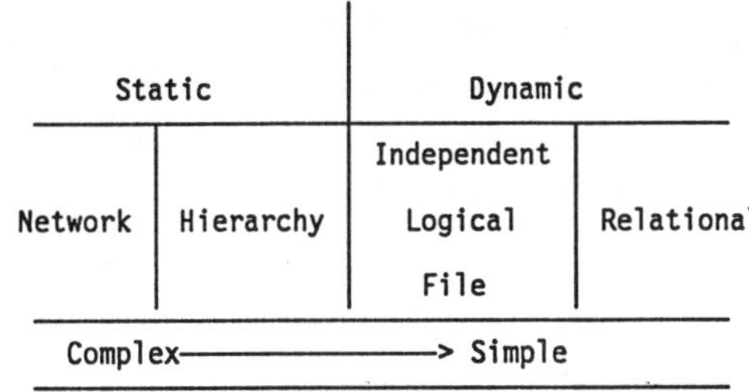

Figure 5.19 Cursor Complexity

```
01 SUBSCHEMA-CTRL
   03 PROGRAM-NAME        PIC X (8) VALUE SPACES
   04  ERROR STATUS       PIC X (4) VALUE"1400"
            88 DB-STATUS-OK VALUE"0000"
            88 ANY-STATUS
               VALUE"0000"-"9999"
            88 ANY-ERROR-STATUS
               VALUE"0001"-"9999"
            88 DB-END-OF-SET VALUE "0307"
            88 DB-REC-NOT-FOUND VALUE "0326"
   03 DBKEY               PIC S9(8)
                          USAGE COMP
                          SYNC
   03 RECORD-NAME         PIC X(16) VALUE SPACES
   03 RECORD-DEF          REDEFINES RECORD-NAME
      05 SSC-NODN         PIC X(8)
      05 SSC-DBN          PIC X(8)
   03 AREA-NAME           PIC X(16) VALUE SPACES
   03 SET-NAME            PIC X(16) VALUE SPACES
   03 ERROR-SET           PIC X(16) VALUE SPACES
   03 ERROR-RECORD        PIC X(16) VALUE SPACES
   03 ERROR-AREA          PIC X(16) VALUE SPACES
   03 DBMSSCOM-AREA       PIC X(100) VALUE LOW-VALUE
   03 DBMSSCOM            REDEFINES IDBMSCOM-AREA
                          PIC X
   01 SUBSCHEMA-SSNAME    PIC X(8) VALUE "DEMOSS01"
   01 SUBSCHEMA-RENAMES
```

Figure 5.20 IDMS/R Network Cursor Variables

relationship pointers (SYSTEM 2000 has separated relationship pointers shown in Figure 4.18) are placed into a programmer identified queue that in SYSTEM 2000 is called a stack.

Not only can there be a greater quantity of different cursors, but a DBMS may have multiple cursors of the same type. If there are 100 different run-units executing concurrently against a database then there must be at least 100 different cursors. If each run-unit is dealing with 10 different WHERE clauses then there are 1000 open cursors.

Level	Stack Number			
	0	1	2	3 15
0	a,1			
1	b,1		e,1	
2	c,1	d,1	f,1	
3				
4 5 . . . 31				

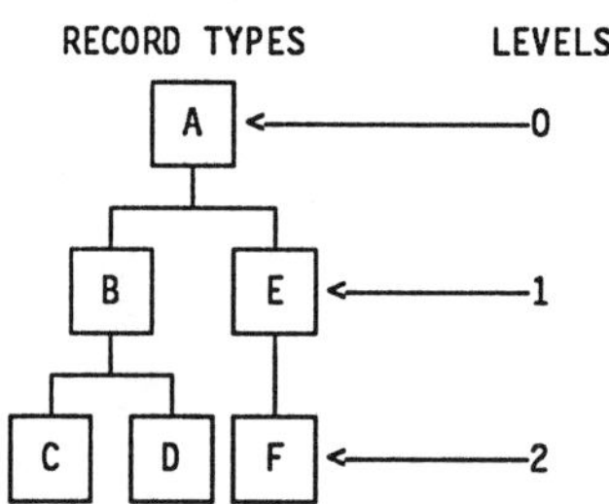

Figure 5.21 SYSTEM 2000 Hierarchy Cursor Model

In ANSI/SQL and the ILF data model, there is basically only one cursor type: that which results from a SELECT statement. This is illustrated in Figure 5.22. The SELECT statement is contained within a DECLARE CURSOR <cursor name> statement that identifies the name under which the view record instances are to be obtained.

There are more cursors in the NDL data model because its underlying network data model is far richer in explicitly definable relationships than is possible in SQL's underlying relational data model. The cursors that NDL supports are

- Schema record type
- schema record instance
- Set type
- Set position

Domain: single record type (relation/table/view)

Position: within record type (relation/table/view)

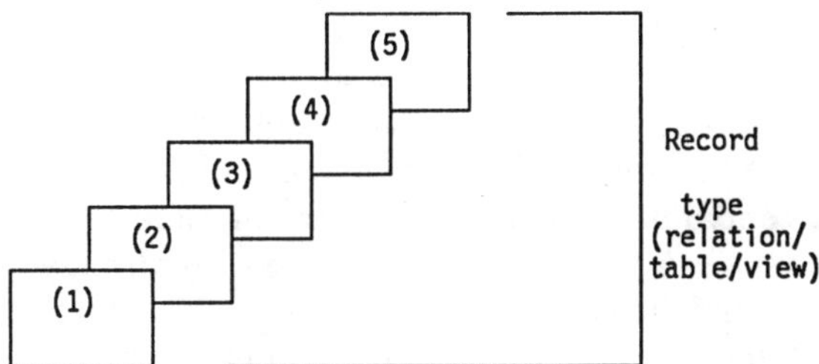

Figure 5.22 ILF/Relational Cursor Model

Cursor manipulated on behalf of	DBMS TYPE			
	Static		Dynamic	
	Network	Hier.	ILF	Rel.
Database	Yes	Yes	Yes	Yes
Area	Yes	No	No	No
Set type	Yes	No	No	No
Set instance	Yes	Yes	No	No
Record type	Yes	Yes	Yes	Yes
Record instance	Yes	Yes	Yes	Yes

Figure 5.23 Cursor Types by Data Model

In the CODASYL version of the network data model the AREA cursor is also present. Figure 5.23 summarizes the types of cursors present in each data model. Since ANSI standards only cover the NDL and the SQL, the cursor models of the various hierarchical and independent logical file data model DBMSs are different in detail, although fundamentally similar. The cursor models of the CODASYL network model DBMSs differ for two reasons: CODASYL was never an enforced standard, and the different CODASYL DBMSs were implemented from different versions of the CODASYL Journals of Development.

5.8.7 Updating

There are three types of updating: data record instance, data record element value, and relationships. Data record instance updating consists of adding, inserting, or deleting. If a data record instance is added or deleted from a static relationship DBMS, then not only is the data record instance affected, but so are any relationships that may be defined and any static referential integrity. In the case of a dynamic relationship DBMS, while there are no formally defined relationships, there may be referential integrity constraints defined. Thus, deletion of a data record may be disallowed. Additionally, if a data record instance is added, and is subject to an *owner* referential integrity action constraint, then the addition may be disallowed unless the proper *owner* data record instance is already stored.

Data record element value updating consists of changing a NULL to a blank or other value, changing a value to another value, and changing a value to blank or to NULL. Data record element value changes can be governed by clauses that prohibit the storage of NULL values, or when a value is removed replacing it with a default value. In ANSI/NDL, if a referential integrity clause is defined by a SET statement that is constrained by a data record element's value, then the update may be disallowed without first having removed all the data record instances associated with that value. In ANSI/SQL, if a foreign key data record element value is changed then the basis of the relationship is changed.

In static relationship DBMSs, relationships are changed by connecting or disconnecting a data record instance from the maintained relationship. In dynamic relationship DBMSs, data record element value updates can change relationships. In the ANSI/NDL the special verbs that perform relationship updating are CONNECT and DISCONNECT. These verbs are needed when the insertion option on SET membership is MANUAL rather than AUTOMATIC, or when the retention option on set membership is OPTIONAL.

If the HLI interface is flexible then the programmer can direct which view elements are updated by providing specific names rather than letting the DBMS update all the view elements contained in the view. Some DBMSs disallow updates whenever the view contains view elements from multiple data record types. In such a case there is usually one set of views for updates and another set (multiple data record type views) for retrievals. The critical update questions relate to whether a single run-unit command can add, modify, or delete a single view record instance that maps to

- A single instance from a single schema record type
- Multiple instances from a single schema record type
- A single instance from multiple schema record types

- Multiple instances from multiple schema record types

Clearly every DBMS can accomplish the first type of updating. Simply this means that the view maps to one schema record type and affects one schema data record type instance. An example is to add a new schema data record type instance for PRODUCT-SPECIFICATION, or to select and then modify a PRODUCT-SPECIFICATION schema data record type instance, or to select and delete a PRODUCT-SPECIFICATION schema data record type instance. In the delete case, such a deletion can cause a real problem for all the other ORDER-LINE-ITEM schema data record type instances that reference the same PRODUCT-SPECIFICATION schema data record type instance. In such a case, the defined referential integrity (static or dynamic) should prohibit the actual deletion of the PRODUCT-SPECIFICATION schema record type instance until all other ORDER-LINE-ITEMs using that PRODUCT-SPECIFICATION are deleted. If the referential action is CASCADE DELETE, then the ORDER-LINE-ITEM schema data record type instances are also be deleted. That is unacceptable. If the ORDER-LINE-ITEM schema data record instances are related to other schema record type instances, such as ORDER, its referential integrity clause prohibits the deletion of the ORDER-LINE-ITEM schema data record instances.

The second type of updating is more difficult as it requires the DBMS to select and affect multiple schema data record type instances from the same schema data record type. For example, there may be a need to increase the prices for all products by 10%. If the DBMS cannot affect multiple schema record instances from the same type through a single command, then the programmer will be required to develop looping logic. In the example above, a deletion action that affects multiple schema data record instances would wreak havoc throughout the database if all the referential integrity clauses and actions are not properly thought out.

The third type of update affects multiple schema record types, but only one instance from each. This type of update can create effects difficult to predict because of the relationships existing among the schema record types.

Beyond obvious relationships, there can be referential actions and data integrity rules that can affect a data record type and its instances beyond the scope of the view. For example, if a new employee is added to the database, the addition could produce new instances to many different schema record types. The addition can also set off a triggered procedure (data integrity rule) that adds the value of the EMPLOYEE SALARY schema record element to the existing value from the TOTAL EMPLOYEE SALARY schema record element in the DEPARTMENT schema record. If however, there was a constraint clause that limited the maximum value of TOTAL EMPLOYEE SALARY, (e.g., FROM 1 to 999,999.99), then the message EXCEEDED VALUE RANGE produced by an update to a schema record type far outside the scope of the programmer's view is impossible to deal with. The only course of action for the run-unit is to backout the new employee and report that the rollback is due to an unacceptable update to a schema record type beyond the scope of the view. To report a more detailed message violates the implied scope of the view.

Because of the inherent complications of updating through views that embrace multiple schema record types and multiple schema record type instances, many DBMS vendors, both static and dynamic, and many DBMS installations prohibit any type of updating except through views that map onto one and only one schema record type. While such prohibitions may initially appear onerous to the programmer, they are actually helpful as a programmer is likely to be far more capable of dealing with record instance violation messages dealing with a few schema record types and only a few schema record type instances than having attempted an action that affects many schema record types and instances that produces hundreds of error messages.

The fourth type of update is even more complicated than the third. Until all the problems of the third type of updating are solved, it is well beyond this book's scope to delve into its complications.

5.8.8 DBMS and Database Invocation

The DBMS invocation command is functionally similar in both static and dynamic relationship DBMSs. In a static environment, a database OPEN statement has many options. They deal with logging, locking, shared retrieval and update controls, and exclusive retrieval and update controls. If a view is not used in a dynamic environment, the database OPEN statement is usually restricted to a single data record type, and when it is opened for update, it may automatically be locked to all other use.

Most organizations have multiple databases, each serving different subject areas. In addition to vertical segmentation of an organization's data, there may also be a horizontal segmentation, that is, a database for operational data in one subject area, and another database for MIS level data in the same subject area. Reasons to have multiple databases include segmentation processing for more cost effective backup and recovery and for distributed processing.

In response to the need for consolidated reporting from multiple databases, the HLI facilities must allow for multiple database OPEN commands, select, retrieval, and update commands.

5.8.9 System Control Capabilities

Specific details about system control capabilities available through interrogation facilities are presented in Section 5.7 of this chapter. The facilities normally available through an HLI run-unit include the following:

- Audit trails
- Message processing
- Backup and recovery
- Concurrent operations

- Multiple database processing
- Security and privacy
- Reorganization

	DBMS Type	
Capability	Static	Dynamic
Sorting	Low	High
Selection	Med to low	High
Navigation	High	Low
Retrieval	Ok	Ok
Updating	Ok	Ok
System control	Varied to low	Varied to high

Figure 5.24 Static versus Dynamic HLI Differences

5.8.10 Static and Dynamic Differences

The principal difference in the HLI between a static and dynamic relationship DBMS environment is the method by which database structure navigation is accomplished. For example, in the static environment there are specific navigation commands to traverse an owner to a member. In the dynamic environment the programmer is often required to acquire an owner data record instance through a DML call statement, extract the connecting data value, and then use the value as a secondary key selection criterion in another DML call statement to find the members of the relationship. Figure 5.24 summarizes these differences.

5.9 NATURAL LANGUAGES

Natural languages are languages that provide access to the database for either reporting or updating. Common to all these languages is that they are proprietary to the DBMS vendor. Thus, the source code of one vendor's language is normally not able to be ported to another DBMS vendor's product. Some vendors of these languages, in an attempt to increase market share, are developing interfaces between these languages and other DBMSs. For example, Information Builder, Inc.'s FOCUS operates against many different DBMSs, hardware environments, and operating systems.

5.9.1 Natural Language Types

DBMSs generally employ three different types of natural languages. The first is a procedure-oriented language (POL), which is often used by ILF data model DBMSs as an alternative to HLI. The second natural language is report writer, which seems to be implemented regardless of the static or dynamic nature of the DBMS. The third language is query-update. In the static relationship DBMSs the query-update language serves mainly as a quick report writer against a well-structured database. In a dynamic relationship DBMS, the query-update language serves mainly as a heuristic research and reporting mechanism.

A very important distinction in the types of natural languages is whether each query command accesses the database directly or whether it accesses a subset of the database. Some DBMSs' query facilities cause the initially selected data to be extracted and placed in a work file that is used for the subsequent queries during that session. Others have each query statement in the query session execute directly against the database. Each alternative has its advantages and disadvantages. For the subset execution type, the entire subset of data is consistent and unchanging during the entire query session, but reports may not reflect the most current data. For the direct execution type, the advantages and disadvantages are reversed. For example, if there is a summary data record element that represents the number of employees in a department, NBR-EMPLOYEES, the data record element may not be the same as the count of employees in the chain if an ADD or DELETE executes completely between the start and the finish times of the query. An advantage to direct execution is that if the data record element is AMOUNT-UNENCUMBERED-DOLLARS, then the most current value can be retrieved directly so that funds are not over committed.

One type of natural language is not superior to the other. Instead, what must be decided is which type is more appropriate for the application.

5.9.2 Natural Language Execution Alternatives

There are often four different types of natural language run-unit execution strategies. These are

- Host language interface
- Interpretive
- Direct
- Compiler

An HLI execution natural language is actually a large sophisticated application of the DBMS written through an interface to a host language. Thus, the natural language command streams are actually strings of data that the HLI program reads, interprets, and then formulates into HLI calls to the database. An advantage of this form is that the natural language can be created merely by defining the mapping between its syntax units and the functions of the HLI. However, the translation of natural language to its actual executing functions cannot involve functionality not already present in the DBMS's HLI. This type of language is typically transaction oriented. That is, submit a unit of work, have it translated and executed, and then have a complete answer passed back.

An interpretative language form is one in which the DBMS determines what must be accomplished only after it has *seen* the command. If a loop is involved, the DBMS must interpret each command for every iteration of the loop, resulting in longer interpretation times, continuous reinterpretations for each cycle of the loop. Another disadvantage is that a natural language run-unit is often desired to be transaction oriented and the interpretive mode of run-unit construction and processing rarely supports transactions. The advantage of the interpretive language form is that its user is often able to interrupt and provide immediate alternatives to a failed syntax unit, and to interrogate the current values of variables, making corrections and simple debugging.

A direct mode execution natural language reads the entire command stream, determines what must be accomplished, and then performs all the needed operations by CALLing and then executing specifically created DBMS programs. An advantage of this mode is that the translation and execution are faster. Another advantage is that this language form is often able to have additional functions that are not available from HLIs, for example, automatic formatting.

The final type of natural language execution is a compiler variety. This type reads the source language and then creates a directly executing module that executes every time it is invoked. An advantage of this form is that once created, the resultant run-unit often executes much faster. That is always a strong benefit in production applications. Its one big disadvantage is the length of time initially taken to see run-unit execution results because the run-unit has to go through several levels of translation and intermediate product creation and storage.

Independent of all the modes of execution, the run-unit's languages must be able to direct its output to print files or disk files through commands within the natural language program. Any sophisticated natural language allows the invocation of user-written programs such as COBOL or FORTRAN. Finally, the natural language permits command redefinition for the establishment of a language designed for a specific audience.

5.9.3 Run-Unit Development

Since a natural language run-unit is actually an instance of a set of programming language commands, the development environment is typically interactive. In the interactive mode, syntax errors are flagged immediately after a line is entered. Once an error is presented, it should be easily correctable, allowing run-unit development to continue.

Run-units are also able to be created through a text editor. Once the syntax stream is submitted, the syntax errors surface. Because some POL run-units can be several hundred statements long, some POLs allow syntax only processing. Sophisticated POLs attempt to find all the errors they can during any syntax check. This is sometimes difficult. For example, if a literal is supplied but the closing quote mark is not included, the POL might assume that the next line is a continuation of the literal rather than a new command.

In large database environments, there is likely hundreds, maybe thousands, of natural language run-unit instances. Sometimes a database's schema definition changes affect the view used by many natural language run-units. When this happens a fully functional IRDS produces a report identifying the names of the affected POL programs and also automatically invalidates the POL run-units' views.

A critical aspect of a POL is the ability to restrict computer resources required for execution. Resources includes the quantity of view record instances selected, the CPU seconds, I/Os, etc.

The next three sections (5.10, 5.11, and 5.12) describe each of the three major types of natural languages: procedure oriented, report writer, and query.

5.10 PROCEDURE-ORIENTED LANGUAGE

While the procedure-oriented language (POL) was originated during the late 1960s as the primary natural language of dynamic relationship DBMSs, and in particular the ILF data model DBMSs, this language type is present today in almost every modern DBMS. Today, however, the POL languages are known by their catchy name: fourth generation languages (4GLs). From a historical perspective, it is important to note that these languages were implemented by DBMS vendors (e.g., Infodata (Inquire), Computer Corporation of America (Model 204), and Mathematica (RAMIS)) in the middle sixties, which is about the same time COBOL (a third generation language) was becoming popular. Thus, to call them *fourth* generation languages is somewhat inaccurate.

Because POL programs are not portable from one DBMS vendor to another, it becomes risky to create whole systems in POL if there is even an intention of changing DBMSs. This risk can be greatly alleviated if an ANSI standard language was created for POL. There is the beginning of such a move by some DBASE (Ashton-Tate) users and vendors who are attempting standardization of a general form of the DBASE-III language through the IEEE society, which is an accredited ANSI standards organization. Notwithstanding the DBMS variations of this language, there are enough uniformities to discuss the language as if it is commonly defined.

Most POL vendors have recognized the value of their language designs and have invented interfaces between the language and other DBMSs. The de facto standard fourth generation language is FOCUS from Information Builders, Inc., in New York City. FOCUS is both a DBMS and a language that can access data stored by almost every major DBMS, for example, IDMS/R, DB-2, and ADABAS. The most valuable of these extensions is the one to DB-2. That is because FOCUS is then able to interface with any SQL based DBMS. Since ANSI/SQL is the standard language of interface, FOCUS can interact with any DBMS that can *read* SQL. FOCUS as a DBMS operates on IBM mainframes, DECs, Wangs, IBM/PCs

(XTs, ATs and close compatibles). FOCUS has over 50% of installed fourth generation language sites. It is the most popular 4GL.

```
Problem: print salespersons who sell products
    manufactured where they were born


10 SELECT SALESPERSON, ON ERROR GOTO 100, AT END GOTO 110
20  GET MEMBER CONTRACT, ON ERROR GOTO 100, AT END GOTO 10
30  GET MEMBER ORDER, ON ERROR GOTO 100, AT END GOTO 20
40  GET MEMBER ORDER-ITEMS, ON ERROR GOTO 100, AT END GOTO 30
50   GET OWNER PRODUCT-SPECIFICATIONS, ON ERROR GOTO 100
60   GET OWNER PRODUCT, ON ERROR GOTO 100
70   IF PRODUCT-MFG-CITY EQ SALESPERSON-BIRTH-CITY AND
     PRODUCT-MFG-STATE EQ SALESPERSON-BIRTH-STATE
     THEN PRINT SALESPERSON-NAME, PRODUCT-NAME,
     SALESPERSON BIRTH-CITY, SALESPERSON-BIRTH-STATE
     ELSE GOTO 40
100  PRINT "ERROR"
110  END
```

Figure 5.25 Static POL Example

In general, every POL contains clauses for data record instance selection, sorting, terminal prompting, formatting, and logic branching. Originally, if a DBMS had a POL type of language, its HLI was seldom used, resulting in underdeveloped HLIs. When static relationship DBMSs have POLs, the approach to data access and navigation is similar to that illustrated in Figure 5.25. When dynamic relationship DBMSs have POLs, their approach to data access and navigation is similar to that illustrated in Figure 5.26. The minimum capabilities of POL, as illustrated through examples in FOCUS, that should be included in a POL, static or dynamic are:

- Basic capabilities
- View access
- Schema record access
- Screen development and utilization

- Dialogue management
- Updating
- Reporting
- Batch job execution
- System control
- Error control

```
Problem: print salespersons who sell products
         manufactured where they were born

CONNECT PRODUCT TO ORDER-ITEM
      VIA PRODUCT-NBR EQ ORDER-ITEM-PRODUCT-NBR
FIND MATCH AND KEEP PRODUCT-NAME, ORDER-ID,
      PRODUCT-MFG-CITY, PRODUCT-MFG-STATE IN LIST-1
CONNECT SALESPERSON TO CONTRACT
      VIA SALESPERSON-NBR EQ CONTRACT-SALESPERSON-ID
FIND MATCH AND KEEP SALESPERSON-NAME, CONTRACT-ID,
      SALESPERSON-BIRTH-CITY, SALESPERSON-BIRTH-STATE
      IN LIST-2
CONNECT LIST-2 TO ORDER VIA CONTRACT-ID OF LIST-2
      EQ ORDER-CONTRACT-ID
FIND MATCH AND KEEP ORDER-ID, SALES-PERSON-NAME,
      SALESPERSON-BIRTH-CITY, SALESPERSON-BIRTH-STATE
      IN LIST-3
CONNECT LIST-1 TO LIST-3
      VIA ORDER-ID OF LIST-1 EQ ORDER-ID OF LIST-3 AND
      SALESPERSON-BIRTH-CITY EQ PRODUCT-MFG-CITY AND
      SALESPERSON-BIRTH-STATE EQ PRODUCT-MFG-STATE
FIND MATCH AND PRINT SALESPERSON-NAME, PRODUCT-NAME,
 SALESPERSON-BIRTH-CITY, SALESPERSON-BIRTH-STATE
```

Figure 5.26 Dynamic POL Example

5.10.1 Basic Capabilities

A POL is a procedure oriented language. That means that whole programming procedures can be encoded. Such support requires capabilities for logic branching, screen generation, dialogue management, and reading and updating of data from nondatabase files. POLs permit command echoes, to keep the user aware of a program's progress. Sophisticated POLs allow for both element value and element name arguments. POLs permit graphic output, as well as tabular output. Supported are bar histograms, connected point plots, and scatter diagrams. Definable are labels, scales, headers and footers, and point annotation. Finally, natural language programs can be created, stored, and edited by their users.

5.10.2 View Access

View facilities have a definite impact on POL programs even though POL programs typically assume the responsibility for allocating their own working storage space, mapping to DBMS field names, data typing, and the like. If the DBMS does not offer a view facility, the individual POL program must include a full set of navigation commands to traverse the database's structures. Subschema and view access is explained in Section 5.3 and 5.4, respectively.

5.10.2.2 Run-Unit WHERE Clauses

WHERE clause facilities impact the utility of a POL. If the WHERE clause is not fully functional, then extra logic must be built into the program for these winnowing operations, and if the POL does not have sufficient selection logic capabilities, the POL cannot be used. That means writing the program in a third generation language, with the consequence of transforming three days of analysis and programming into a one to three month effort. Obviously, a fully functional WHERE clause is a critical component of any POL. The WHERE clause capabilities of the HLI should be equally present in the POL. WHERE clauses are more fully explained in Section 5.8.3.2

5.10.2.3 Run-Unit Sort Clauses

Since the POL is often used as the only programming language of end users, sorting capabilities like those described in the HLI section on sorting (see Section 5.8.3.3) are a very important characteristic of any sophisticated POL, regardless of whether the DBMS's orientation is static, dynamic, or both.

5.10.3 Schema Record Access

If the DBMS does not contain a view facility then there must be navigation facilities present in the POL language. The requirements of such facilities are described in the corresponding HLI sections (see Section 5.8.4) and must be present whether the DBMS is static, dynamic, or both.

5.10.4 Screen Development and Utilization

Screens are almost always a critical requirement of a POL based report or update program. If screens cannot be defined then the POL is not a really useful language. As stated in the earlier section on screens, there is not always a 1:1 mapping between screens and views. Some applications will require multiple screens to process all the data within one view.

Screens should not be tied to just one language type, for example, HLI or POL. The characteristics of a quality screen development facility are provided in Sections 5.5 and 5.8.5.

5.10.5 Updating

Updating capabilities of a POL must support single-value changes, multiple-value changes, view record instance additions and deletions, etc. The updating capabilities in a POL are the same as those described in the HLI section (see Section 5.8.7). A significant difference is that some POLs are designed to accomplish set-at-a-time processing without having to declare and manipulate cursors, while other POLs, e.g., FOCUS' MODIFY language are record-at-a-time processing language, but still without cursors.

5.10.6 Reporting

Because the POL is a natural, vendor proprietary language, its capabilities for reporting vary widely, and are all nonstandard. This book illustrates the most widely accepted POL, FOCUS, as a model for report writing capabilities. The examples provided are taken from the PC/FOCUS Users Manual, Release 5.5. Since Information Builders FOCUS procedures can translate into ANSI/SQL compliant access clauses, most every organization can use FOCUS as their de facto standard for POL and remain ANSI/SQL compliant with respect to the interface between FOCUS and any SQL DBMS engine that is used by FOCUS. It is important to emphasize that:

> *No report writer facility or any POL of any SQL compliant DBMS is ANSI standard. That is because the ANSI X3H2 committee only standardizes those aspects of SQL that define, protect, and modify the characteristics of tables and views, and that select and update view instances.*

Any SQL compliant DBMS vendor claiming that their POL is ANSI/SQL compliant:

- Misunderstands the process of standardization
- Does not understand the content of the ANSI standards that have been issued to date
- Presumes the reader is easily fooled

The only POL component that can be compliant is the select clauses.

In general, high quality POLs permit column and row totals, sums, counts, sorting by high to low and reverse, headers and subheaders, footers and subfooters, underlining, column headers, line folding, column spacing, control breaks, page breaks, and centering. The output from view element values allows for editing, such as zero suppression, floating dollar signs, and variable date formats. The output allows for multiple element value concatenation and encoded value table look-up.

When operations are performed on multiple dynamic databases, the relational operations of matching and merging should be allowed, as well as navigation between databases.

Reporting capabilities fall into eight categories:

- User prompting
- Statistical operators
- Titles and report headers
- Control break formatting
- Page formatting
- Sorting
- Graphical output
- Derived data

5.10.6.1 User Prompting

A critical component of any POL program is user supplied values to program defined arguments that allow prompted, user supplied argument values to be

```
-TOP

-PROMPT &WHICHCITY.ENTER NAME OF CITY OR DONE.

-IF &WHICHCITY EQ DONE GOTO QUIT;
     TABLE FILE SALES
     WRITE SUM.UNIT_SOLD
     BY PROD_CODE
     IF CITY IS &WHICHCITY
     END

-RUN

-GOTO TOP

-QUIT
```

Figure 5.27 Example of User-supplied Values from FOCUS

passed to the report clauses. In the FOCUS example contained in Figure 5.27, the user supplied arguments are indicated by the *&* character preceding the variable name, for example, &WHICHCITY. The - character which precedes some of the commands identifies those commands as part of the FOCUS dialogue manager facility. Briefly, the program's execution is as follows:

- Execution is started at the command just after the label TOP.
- A prompt is provided the user to solicite the value for the city or the value *DONE*.
- If the value *DONE* is provided, control is transferred to the label QUIT, otherwise the next command is executed.
- The TABLE command identifies the file name from which the data is to be acquired. A file in FOCUS's terminology can be synonymous with an SQL view.
- The first operator is WRITE, which with the *SUM* operator indicates that the values of UNIT-SOLD are to be totaled for each unique value of PROD-CODE.
- The WHERE clause is *IF CITY IS &WHICHCITY* and selects only those view record instances that pass the WHERE clause select operation.
- The END statement is the last statement in the report request.
- The -RUN command starts the execution of the report request. Once the view record instances are selected and the report is printed, control is transferred back to the *TOP* label.

FOCUS allows any syntactic unit's value to be provided through a variable. Thus, the relational operator *IS* can be supplied with an argument *&OPERATOR* and become *IS* or *IS NOT*.

5.10.6.2 Statistical Operators

Sophisticated POL provided statistical operators include:

- Count
- Sum
- Distinct
- Average
- Median
- Mode
- Minimum

- Maximum
- Percent
- Standard deviation

Some of these operations are already defined in the ANSI/SQL standard and apply to the data that has been selected for presentation through the view. For example, if an employee has had several salaries throughout the years, the AVERAGE SALARY for employees who are managers is presented through the following:

SELECT AVG(SALARY) FROM EMPLOYEE WHERE JOB = *MANAGER*

As another example, the first names of all employees named SMITH are acquired through the use of the query:

SELECT DISTINCT(FIRST_NAME) FROM EMPLOYEE WHERE LAST_NAME = *SMITH*

But what of the statistical operations not provided by SQL, for example, MODE, MEDIAN, and STANDARD DEVIATION? The FOCUS strategy is to use the statistical operations included in the ANSI/SQL standard as well as those not included. For those included in ANSI/SQL, the FOCUS-to-SQL translation program passes the operation through to the SQL-compliant DBMS. For the statistical operations not performed by the SQL-compliant DBMS, the FOCUS translator executes a select clause that returns the view instances to the FOCUS interface module, which then performs the statistical operation. For example, an operation that computes the percent of employees that each group represents within the data processing department can be expressed as follows:

WRITE PCT.CNT.EMP_ID BY GROUP IF DEPARTMENT IS *DATA PROCESSING*

The PCT.CNT.EMP_ID function initially causes a count of employees by group within the data processing department, and then the PCT function recasts the counts into percentages.

5.10.6.3 Titles and Subtitles

Every POL must support sophisticated titling to make the output suitable for managerial use. The minimum set includes:

- Column spacing
- Column totals
- Computer date access for headers or footers

- Computer time access for headers or footers
- Floating dollar signs
- IRDS-provided column headers
- Left and right data justification
- Line folding
- Multiple line column headers
- Multiple line footers
- Multiple line headers
- Multiple view element value concatenation
- Row titles
- Row totals
- Single line column headers
- Single line footers
- Title centering
- Underlining
- Variable date formats
- Zero suppression

5.10.6.4 Control Break Formatting

A control break provides the opportunity to perform certain actions whenever a particular event occurs. Typically the event is a change in value of one of the view elements presented to the report writing feature. If the control break view element is the data record instance's primary key, then when the primary key value changes (every data record instance change), the action occurs. Control breaks can be based on view elements other than the view instance primary key. For example, the EMPLOYEE view record instances can be sorted by three different view elements, such as DEPARTMENT, then GROUP, and then JOB TITLE. In such a case, the action occurs as if there are three nested loops: JOB TITLES within GROUP within DEPARTMENT.

The action taken can occur just after the value changes but before the new view instances are presented. In such a case, the action can be to present sums, counts, and the like. If the action is to occur before the new set of view instances is presented, sum and count variables can be reset, page ejects can occur, and new titles can appear.

Regardless of the type of action, it is important that the following minimum set of actions be available:

- Break titles
- Special formatting
- Break totals
- Page totals
- Final column totals

5.10.6.5 Page Formatting

Sophisticated page formatting prevents output reports from being placed first into output files and then loaded into some type of word processor or desk top publishing facility. Page formatting controls

- Page length
- Page width
- Logical pages within physical pages
- Page numbering
- Page titles
- Page footers

5.10.6.6 Sorting

While the database's data record instances may already be sorted (logically, of course) through clauses in the schema definition language, it is complete folly to assume that the schema's specification for data record instance sorting will be sufficient for all users. Consequently, upon selection, the view record instances must be able to be sorted by one or more view elements in either a low to high or a high to low fashion. Without sorting the whole concept of control breaks is lost.

5.10.6.7 Graphical Output

Clearly some reports are best presented graphically rather than through columns of numbers. The most popular types of graphical outputs produced are:

- Pie charts
- Bar histograms
- Connected point plots
- Graphs, and
- Scatter plots

```
GRAPH FILE CAR
ON GRAPH SET PIE ON
SUM AVE.RETAIL_COST
ACROSS CAR
ON GRAPH SET HIST OFF
END
```

Figure 5.28 FOCUS Graphics Command Language for a CAR Pie Chart

```
FILENAME=CAR,SUFFIX=FOC
SEGNAME=ORIGIN,SEGTYPE=S1
 FIELDNAME=COUNTRY,COUNTRY,A10,$
SEGNAME=COMP,SEGTYPE=S1,PARENT=ORIGIN
 FIELDNAME=CAR,CARS,A16,$
SEGNAME=CARREC,SEGTYPE=S1,PARENT=COMP
 FIELDNAME=MODEL,MODEL,A24,$
SEGNAME=BODY,SEGTYPE=S1,PARENT=CARREC
 FIELDNAME=BODYTYPE,TYPE,A12,$
 FIELDNAME=SEATS,SEAT,I3,$
 FIELDNAME=DEALER_COST,DCOST,D7,$
 FIELDNAME=RETAIL_COST,RCOST,D7,$
 FIELDNAME=SALES,UNITS,I6,$
SEGNAME=SPECS,SEGTYPE=U,PARENT=BODY
 FIELDNAME=LENGTH,LEN,D5,$
 FIELDNAME=WIDTH,WIDTH,D5,$
 FIELDNAME=HEIGHT,HEIGHT,D5,$
 FIELDNAME=WEIGHT,WEIGHT,D6,$
 FIELDNAME=WHEELBASE,BASE,D6.1,$
 FIELDNAME=FUEL_CAP,FUEL,D6.1,$
 FIELDNAME=BHP,POWER,D6,$
 FIELDNAME=RPM,RPM,I5,$
 FIELDNAME=MPG,MILES,D6,$
 FIELDNAME=ACCEL,SECONDS,D6,$
SEGNAME=WARANT,SEGTYPE=S1,PARENT=COMP
 FIELDNAME=WARRANTY,WARR,A40,$
SEGNAME=EQUIP,SEGTYPE=S1,PARENT=COMP
 FIELDNAME=STANDARD,EQUIP,A40,$
```

Figure 5.29 CAR Database Master-File Description (DDL)

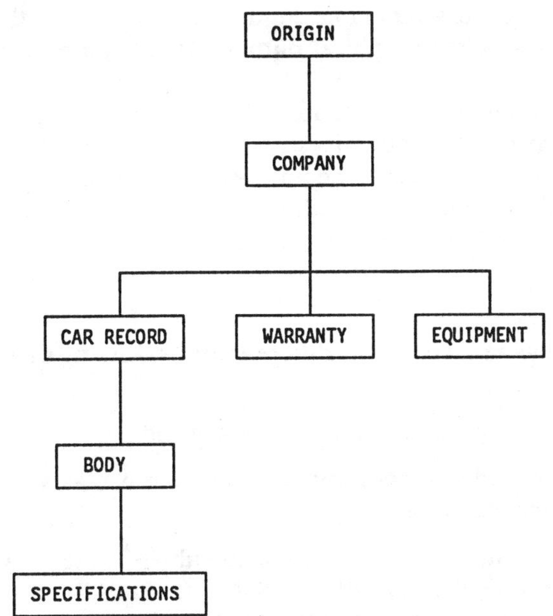

Figure 5.30 CAR Database Logical Bachman Diagram

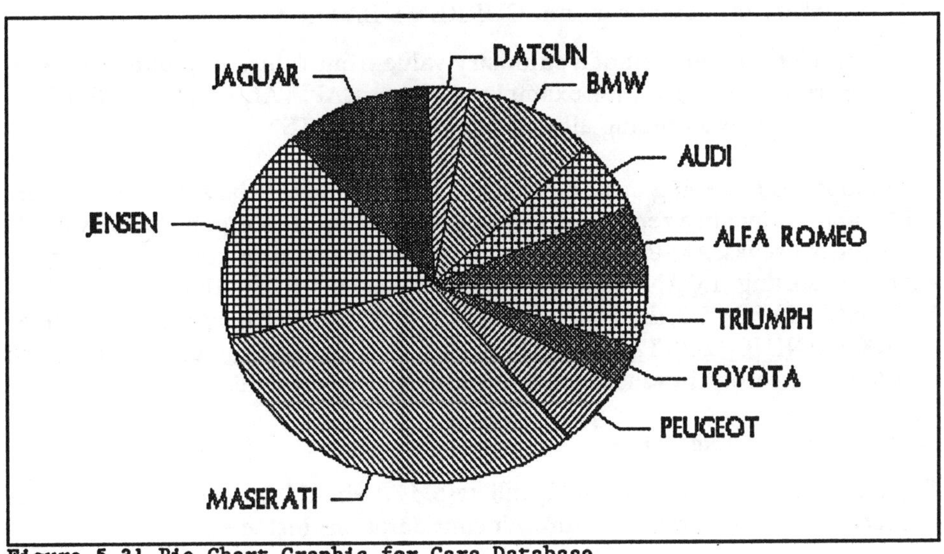

Figure 5.31 Pie Chart Graphic for Cars Database

Supporting these graphical outputs must be facilities for headers, footers, column headers, graph labels, scales, and point annotation. Figure 5.28 illustrates the command language necessary to produce graphical output FOCUS on a CAR database.

The data definition language for the CAR database is contained in Figure 5.29, and a logical Bachman diagram illustrating its structure is in Figure 5.30. The pie chart produces a number of *slices* equal to the number of CAR companies, and the size of each slice is equal to the average retail cost. The actual pie chart obtained through a screen capture utility appears in Figure 5.31.

5.10.6.8 Derived Data

Derived data is critical. Derived data takes on many different forms. Among these are:

- The use of table look-ups, for example, MD for Maryland
- The use of a DBMS provided sequence number, for example, as a LINE-NUMBER in a financial report
- The computation of new values from view element values in the view record instance, for example, deriving REMAINING-CAPITAL-BALANCE by subtracting CAPITAL-PAYMENTS-TO-DATE from ORIGINAL-AMOUNT
- The computation of the new value from a view element and a constant, for example, deriving AGE by subtracting BIRTH-DATE from the system constant CURRENT-DATE
- The computation of a summary value from values in multiple view record instances, for example, deriving CAPITAL-PAYMENTS-TO-DATE by summing all CAPITAL-PAYMENTS

In addition to generating these new values, it is important to be able to place them where appropriate in a report, for example, as an output column with its own title and control breaks. Another critical issue in the use of derived data is sorting, for example, sorting LOAN view record instances by REMAINING-CAPITAL-BALANCE. In FOCUS, the POL (the TABLE and MODIFY languages) must have the REMAINING-CAPITAL-BALANCE data field defined <u>and</u> computed on the selected view record instances prior to using it as a sort field.

5.10.7 Batch Job Execution

Once a POL run unit is created and tested, it should be executable in both interactive and batch modes. Run-unit considerations include:

- Argument values
- Output report direction

- Output report formats
- Reuse of run-unit outputs
- Use of non-DBMS files

Argument values are critical to the development of general purpose POL run-units. In the interactive mode, these argument values are requested from the terminal user. For example,

SELECT CARS WHERE MAKE EQ &MAKE *ENTER THE MAKE OF THE AUTOMOBILE*

causes the quoted literal to appear on the screen so the user knows what to enter. In a batch environment, such data has to be provided by a specially created file, and the identity of the file has to be known to the POL run-unit. Such identity is often provided by a DATA statement that appears either at the start or the end of the procedure. For example:

DATA FILE IS <mydata>

Argument values are not just restricted to variable values. Operators, such as GE, LT, SPANS, etc., can be placed into arguments to make the POL run-unit more general purpose, for example:

SELECT CARS WHERE MAKE &OPER *PLEASE ENTER THE OPERATOR* &YEAR *AND ALSO PLEASE ENTER THE YEAR OF THE AUTOMOBILE*

Output destinations are another consideration in the effective use of POL run-units. In the interactive mode, the POL's output destination usually defaults to the input terminal. In the batch mode, the default might be the system printer, which is usually known to the system through file name conventions. If destinations other than defaults are desired, the POL should have the ability to specify names and devices. For example, FOCUS provides the ability to specify the destination of an output report through a SAVE command placed at the end of the procedure. For example,

SAVE on <filename> . . .

A number of languages also provide control over saved data formats. In FOCUS, if the command REPORT IS OFFLINE is provided at the start of the procedure, then the output is formatted to fit on a 66 line page rather than a 26 line screen. Additionally if the SAVE statement has a *FORMAT IS WP*, then the data is saved so that it can be used by a word processor. Other formats supported by FOCUS include the DIF format with a choice of value delimiters. Data in this format can be fed into other packages that can import delimited data. Harvard Project

Manager, for example, is a PC based project management package that supports this type of data importing. A database project's manager might for example, use PC/FOCUS for the staff's work product and time reporting, and then at the end of each week use a FOCUS procedure to generate an ASCII delimited file for input. Harvard can produce CPM and Gantt charts for the project.

Another batch processing consideration is that the POL can output data from within one run-unit, that can be immediately used during the execution of another run-unit against the same or different database.

A critical facility in any POL is the ability to manipulate data record instances from nondatabase files and invoke automatic IRDS editing and validation. Accepted data record instance can be written to a database, to reports, back to the file structure, or to other nondatabase file structures. With this facility, the POL supports nonDBMS files, as well as DBMS databases.

5.10.8 System Control

The system control capabilities normally available through a POL include:

- Audit trails for all updates
- DBMS message processing
- Backup and recovery
- Concurrent operations
- Multiple database processing
- Security and privacy
- Reorganization

The capabilities of each of these facilities are generally as described in previous sections on system control (see Section 5.7) and the HLI subsection addressing system control subsection (see Section 5.8.9) except as provided hereafter.

5.10.8.1 Message Processing

POLs usually have a fully functional message facility that is available through a program function key, for example, PF1.

Messages that are run-unit specific and intended for user response can be encoded right into the run-unit's language. Figure 5.32 illustrates a part of a POL program from a sports application that displays a message when there is an error situation. The run-unit has read the FAMILY-ID from an external file, and attempts to retrieve that family's data record instance from the database. If the family's identifier is not present, then the error message *Illegal Family Id* is written to an error file. These messages are reviewed after the batch of updates have executed and the erroneous data is corrected and resubmitted.

5.10.8.2 Backup and Recovery

Most often, backup and recovery is a function performed by the DBA. Some aspects of backup and recovery may be allowed to certain HLI users, but seldom is the control over backup and recovery allowed to POL users. If backup and recovery features are available through POL, they are usually automatic. If during the execution of a POL run-unit the database fails, the DBMS usually begins an automatic recovery cycle that restores the database to the last committed transaction of each active run-unit.

```
CASE FAMILY
   MATCH FAMILYID
   ON NOMATCH TYPE ON ERRFILE "ILLEGAL FAMILY ID"
   ON NOMATCH GOTO BIGERROR
   ON MATCH GOTO PLAYER
ENDCASE
```

Figure 5.32 POL Run-unit Application Message

In DBMSs that have sophisticated view facilities, transaction rollback and some aspects of backup and recovery may be encoded in the view facility logic to control the interaction between the run-unit and the DBMS.

5.10.9 Reorganization

Common to many POLs is some database reorganization capabilities. Typically available is the ability to create an entirely new data record type including data record elements, index indicators, etc. Once created, the POL run-unit causes the creation of an O/S file for selected records from the database. This store persists beyond the end of the run-unit's execution.

This kind of capability is especially useful for DBMS users that view POL as their only programming language. With the ANSI/SQL manipulation facilities a user can define, delete, and modify the attributes of any data record type. Such capabilities are subject to security controls that may have been imposed by a DBA and thus may not be available to all users.

5.10.10 POL Summary

A brief review of the capabilities contained in a POL quickly leads to the conclusion POLs are complete programming languages that often eliminate the need for other types of database access languages. For many years, users of FOCUS, Model 204, Nomad, and RAMIS DBMSs never used any other types of languages. These users designed, programmed, loaded, reported, and updated complete database applications with POLs.

5.11 REPORT WRITER

A report writer is usually the first language developed after the HLI by static relationship DBMS vendors. The majority of static relationship DBMS vendors have only lately developed POLs (4th generation languages). Except for the fact that report writers do not have database updating commands, the capabilities of POLs and report writers are very similar. Thus, references are made in this section back to the POL section (Section 5.10) for detailed explanations of most of the report writer's facilities.

In addition to the similarity between POLs and report writers, there is also a similarity between report writers of both static and dynamic relationship DBMSs, with the exception of data record instance selection and navigation strategies. Finally, report writers are often used as prototyping mechanisms for HLI programs.

The typical capabilities found in report writers include report titles, column titles, row titles, multiple levels of breaks, the ability to skip lines and pages, page headers and footers, output data editing such as floating dollar signs, selection clauses, page counting, logical and physical dimensions for report pages, left and right justification for alphanumeric data, setting and resetting of program variables and multiple report copies.

Sometimes, report writing capabilities do not exist as a completely separate language, but as an extension of one of the other natural languages. The execution alternatives also vary from interpretive, to direct, to compiler oriented.

Because report writer languages are not portable from one DBMS vendor to another, it becomes risky to create large quantities of reports intended to be large critical components of systems. Use of a vendor proprietary report writer is justified if the report formats change frequently, or if they are short lived. These risks would be eliminated if there was an ANSI standard language for report writers. There is, however, no committee working on such an effort.

The fundamental difference between static and dynamic report writers centers not on capabilities, such as footers, headers, and break totals, but on the fundamental nature of the DBMS. In a static relationship DBMS, the report writer output must mirror the basic design of the database through its already defined relationships among the data record types. In a dynamic relationship DBMS, report writer output can mirror any relationship that can be expressed between two union compatible data record elements from different data record types. Figure 5.33 contains an example of a report writer language program. It does not show the view used, and assumes that all database variables are automatically defined. The only variables defined are those *local* to the report writer program.

The following topics are applicable to report writers:

- Basic Capabilities
- View Access
- Schema Record Access

- Reporting
- System Control
- Error Control

```
COMPOSE:
     FOR REPORT SALES,
     PHYSICAL PAGE IS 55 BY 55:
     DECLARE SUM1 = RCOUNT OF ORDER-ID:
     DECLARE SUM2 = RCOUNT OF CONTRACT-ID:
     SELECT RECORD IF ORDER OCCURS:
     ORDER BY NAME OF CUSTOMER-ID, CONTRACT-ID, ORDER-ID:
     FOR CUSTOMER, SKIP TO NEW PAGE, SKIP 2 LINES,
     AT END, PRINT (15)$TOTAL NUMBER OF CONTRACTS$, R(45)SUM2:
     FOR CONTRACT, SKIP 2 LINES, COMPUTE SUM2,
          PRINT (15)$CONTRACT-ID$,    (30)$DATE-SIGNED$,(45)$MAXIMUM-COST$,
     AT END, SKIP 1 LINE, PRINT (15)$TOTAL ORDERS$,R(28)SUM1,
          (40)$TOTAL VALUE$,R(55)TOTAL-ORDER-COST.
     FOR ORDER, AT END, COMPUTE SUM1
     END REPORT:
GENERATE ACTIVITY WHERE CUSTOMER-ID EXISTS:
```

Figure 5.33 SYSTEM 2000 Example of Report Writer Program

5.11.1 Basic Capabilities

The basic capabilities of the report writer are similar to that of the POL except the report writer does not allow updating to the database. To accomplish sophisticated reports the report writer must support:

- Logic branching
- Looping
- Reading nondatabase files
- On-line reporting
- Off-line reporting

5.11.2 View Access

WHERE clause facilities have a definite impact on the requirements of any report writer program for the same reasons as with the POL. If there is not a sophisticated WHERE clause, the report will likely have to be written in COBOL. The previous sections on view facilities and WHERE clauses are discussed in Sections 5.8.9 and 5.8.10.

5.11.3 Reporting

Screens are seldom a critical requirement of a report writer as reports are generally destined for printing on a computer's high speed printers. If, however, a report is to be on-line, then the screen to which the printing is formatted might be defined by the DBMS's screen facility. It follows then that a necessary component of any screen driven report writer feature is controls for dialogue management. These are usually restricted to page up and down, and possibly side to side. The capabilities that must be present in screens and dialogue management are presented in earlier sections of this chapter.

The report formatting capability of a report writer falls into eight categories:

- User Prompting
- Statistical Operators
- Titles and Reporting
- Control Break Formatting
- Page Formatting
- Sorting
- Graphical Output
- Derived Data

All these capabilities are described in the corresponding section of the POL language (see Section 5.10.6, and its subsections).

5.11.4 System Control

The capabilities normally available through interrogation language programs include:

- DBMS message processing
- Multiple database processing
- Security and privacy

Since report writers are not able to update databases, most of the system control capabilities are not even of concern. Thus there is no need to be concerned about

- Audit trails for all updates
- Backup and recovery
- Concurrent operations
- Reorganization

The capabilities of each of the relevant system control facilities are generally as described in the earlier section on system control in this chapter.

5.11.4.1 Message Processing

Message processing in a report writing environment is primarily concerned with run-unit development. The only other place messages appear is during report execution when some aspect of the data cannot be found, for example, selecting a data record instance on the basis of a primary key when the data record instance is not present in the database. The messages are also generally not interactive. Rather, the report is executed, and then all possible messages are made available.

5.11.4.2 Multiple Database Processing

Multiple database processing is important in report writing because every organization is likely to have multiple DBMSs and also multiple databases. Sophisticated report writers can access multiple databases from the same DBMS. Given the wide scale acceptance of ANSI standard SQL, there are now report writers that can access both multiple databases from the same DBMS vendor and also databases from multiple DBMS vendors.

5.11.4.3 Security and Privacy

The only relevant aspects of security and privacy are those that affect views and view element instances values. If the security is not granted, then while a view may be permitted to be referenced in a report writer run-unit, it may be disallowed when first accessed. In addition to allowing/disallowing access to views, the security may also be used to further permit screening of view instances on the basis of view element values. For example, the security facility may prohibit access to all EMPLOYEE view instances that are managers or that have salary above certain levels.

5.11.5 Report Writer Summary

Report writers are a critical component of any database environment. Typically, they exist either alone or as extensions to either POLs or query-update languages. Most static relationship DBMS vendors have stand alone report writers. Most dynamic relationship DBMS vendors have report writers as extensions to either

POL or the query-update languages. Today, sophisticated report writers are being created by both DBMS vendors and by independent software vendors. These report writers can access data from multiple databases and from different DBMS vendors' databases. As this trend continues, and if one vendor's report writer becomes overwhelmingly popular, there may be a de facto standard for report writers just as FOCUS is the de facto standard for 4GLs (POL).

5.12 QUERY-UPDATE LANGUAGES

A query-update language interrogation program is typically constructed as a single sentence, while the POL and the report writer language interrogation may typically contain from 50 to 150 lines. The query normally consists of three types of clauses: output, sorting, and data selection. The output clause usually contains titles and a list of the data record elements to be printed. The sort clause specifies the fields for sorting, the sort order, and whether the sorting is to be high to low or reverse. The selection clauses specify the criteria for data record instance selection, which may include Boolean operations, relational operators, and the like. A typical query-update sentence might be:

```
PRINT <element-name> [, <element-name>,. . . ]

[ SORTED BY <element-names>,. . . ]

[ WHERE <element-name> <relational-operator> <value>

[ <Boolean operator>

<element-name > <relational-operator> <value>. . . ] ]
```

Query-update languages often contain less sophisticated formatting capabilities than report writers. Query-update languages also offer processing logic less complex than POLs. Query-update languages do not compete with POLs or report writer languages. Rather, they offer the ability to do something simple in a simple way. As a consequence, query-update languages are very popular with the ad hoc interrogator who obtains a simple listing of data from one or more data record types or who performs a single update.

The typical capabilities present in a query-update language include tabular reporting with titles, sorting by one or more elements, arithmetic functions such as MIN, MAX, and AVG, results of arithmetic formulas, and selection clauses that include arithmetic, relational, and Boolean operations.

Again, the fundamental difference between static and dynamic query-update languages centers not on capabilities, but on the fundamental static or dynamic nature of the DBMS. In a static relationship DBMS, query-update languages produce reports that conform to the structure dictates of the database. In a dynamic relationship DBMS, query-update languages can produce reports from

```
LIST/TITLE      L(5)CUSTOMER-ID, L(15)CUSTOMER-NAME,
         L(40)CONTRACT-ID, R(50)TOTAL-ORDER-COST,
         ORDERED BY CUSTOMER-ID, CONTRACT-ID
         WHERE CONTRACT-ID EXISTS:


ASSIGN SALES-PERSON-ID EQ 123-45-6789
     WHERE CONTRACT-ID EQ 76498:


REMOVE CONTRACT WHERE CONTRACT-ID EQ 76498:
```

Figure 5.34 SYSTEM 2000 Example of Query-Update Language Program

different record types that can be related through union compatible data record elements. Figure 5.34 contains three examples of SYSTEM 2000 query-update programs.

WHERE clauses are the most critical component of a query-update language as there are no other facilities available for data record instance selection or relationship navigation that are available in an HLI or a POL.

Query-update languages are understood through:

- Basic capabilities
- View access
- Schema record access
- Updating
- Reporting
- System control
- Error control

5.12.1 Basic Capabilities

Because of the very nature of query-update languages, that is, single sentence orientations, their basic capabilities are typically restricted to being able to

- Read nondatabase files
- Read and update view record instances
- Report and update on line
- Generate off-line reports

5.12.2 View Access

Since the view access capabilities needed for query-update languages are the same as those for all natural languages, the sections earlier in this chapter address these.

5.12.3 Updating

Updating is a very important component of the query-update language. It is critical that the updating facilities be more sophisticated than those in either the HLI or the POL because the query-update language run-unit's orientation is single sentence oriented, and does not contain the language facilities for looping. To be sophisticated, a query-update facility must be able to

- Allow for prompted user-supplied arguments in the update clauses.
- Add, modify, or delete a view instance(s) that maps to a single instance from a data record type instance.
- Add, modify, or delete a view instance(s) that maps to a multiple instance from a data record type instance.

Very sophisticated query-update languages can also:

- Add, modify, or delete a view instance that maps to a single instance from multiple data record types.
- Add, modify, or delete a view instance that maps to multiple instances from multiple data record type instances.

Without the first three update capabilities, the query-update language can be used only for simple reports, and for single data record type instance adds, deletes, or modifies.

5.12.4 Reporting

The report formatting capability in a query update language falls into eight categories:

- User prompting
- Statistical operators
- Titles and report headers
- Control break formatting
- Page formatting
- Sorting
- Graphical output
- Derived data

These capabilities are drawn from the same set as described in the section on POL. The only differences are usually related to the degree of sophistication allowed. As the query-update language adds sophistication, the *single sentence* language construct becomes stretched until the language becomes either a POL or a report writer. Neither IBI's FOCUS nor Computer Corporation's Model 204 contains separate and distinct query-update languages. Rather, they each contain a POL that can be used in a single sentence fashion to accomplish simple reports.

5.12.5 System Control

The system control capabilities generally supported by the query-update language are the following:

- Audit trails for all updates
- DBMS message processing
- Security and privacy
- Reorganization

The capabilities of each of these facilities are generally as described in the Sections 5.8.9 and 5.10.8.

5.13 CHOOSING THE RIGHT INTERROGATION LANGUAGE

Generally, the choice of an interrogation language should follow this sequence:

- Attempt to develop the report/query with the least amount of programming effort. That means using either the query-update language, report writer, or POL. What is being developed is a prototype of the task rather than a production report.
- Demonstrate the result to the person who requested the report/query to determine whether it satisfies the needs. If not, change it until it does.
- When the report or query is acceptable, determine the frequency of operations and estimate the amount of data to be processed, the expected amount of processing time, and the amount of required system control support. Then choose a final programming language for the interrogation that satisfies the combined requirements--assuming that satisfying them is possible.
- Leave the prototype report or query in place for use by the requestor--if its performance is tolerable--until its replacement can be created.

The following benefits are derived from this process:

- The prototype is created with minimal human resources.
- The design is refined with minimal resources.
- The final product is created only after the design has been validated.

5.14 INTERROGATION SUMMARY

No DBMS can report data it cannot model. Thus to compare the overall reporting capabilities of a static relationship DBMS interrogation language to those contained in a dynamic relationship DBMS to determine which DBMS is better is like comparing the turning radius of a bus to that of a sports car in order to determine which vehicle is better. The bus has one purpose and the sports car has another. Neither the turning radius of the vehicle nor the capabilities of a DBMS's interrogation language alone is sufficient to determine which vehicle or DBMS is better.

The languages available in a particular DBMS can only mirror those functions the DBMS performs in an acceptable manner. No vendor is going to issue a language that will constantly *break the DBMS's back*. Thus, the fundamental difference between static and dynamic interrogation languages centers not on capabilities, but on fundamental DBMS design. In a static relationship DBMS, these languages must mirror the basic design of the database. In a dynamic relationship DBMS, these languages define relationships that allow any combination of data record types to be used in the interrogation.

A well-engineered DBMS contains multiple database interface languages. Although there is a growing tendency to rely on natural languages, the compiler interface languages, such as COBOL and FORTRAN, are important for data loading and data update, for more complex multiple database processing, and for building DBMS-independent applications.

The point of having multiple languages is to be able to choose the most appropriate language for the job. If a DBMS has only an HLI or a POL, then its vendor cannot be too interested in providing a helpful environment to its users.

A final aspect of interrogation is interfaces between DBMSs. Because of ANSI/SQL it is now cost effective to access a high-speed production database, say run under IDMS/R, extract data and load the extract into a Model 204 database for very high speed ad hoc queries.

Figure 5.35 compares and contrasts the different types of interrogation languages available from static and dynamic relationship DBMSs. Figure 5.1 compares and contrasts the relative work efforts for developing the same result through each language type.

LANGUAGE	STATIC	DYNAMIC
Host Language	Well developed, good function and facilities	Poor to acceptable development
Procedure Oriented Language	None at all	Well developed, good function and facilities
Query-Update Languages	Under developed usually no update Constrained by database structure	If developed then done well
Report Writers	Used only as a short cut to HLI Still constrained by data base structure	If developed, usually an extension of POL or QUL.

Figure 5.35 Interrogation
Static and Dynamic Relationship DBMS Comparison

6

SYSTEM CONTROL

6.1 SYSTEM CONTROL COMPONENTS

System control identifies facilities provide for the protection of the database, the smooth operation of applications that use the database and the DBMS, and the effective use of the DBMS.

A fully functional DBMS's system control facilities include the following:

- Audit trails
- Message processing
- Backup and recovery
- Reorganization
- Concurrent operations
- Multiple database processing
- Security and privacy
- DBMS installation and maintenance
- Application optimization

The DBMS's audit trails capture update transactions according to criteria such as user, data record type, date, time, and program. These transactions are selectively reportable, and available during backup and recovery operations.

Message processing facilities provide sophisticated on-line help for investigating the cause of a user, database, or DBMS error.

Backup and recovery facilities permit unaffected users to continue work while backups are taken of production databases and to undergo minimum interruptions while the DBMS recovers a database from a DBMS, user, or computing environment induced error.

Reorganization involves both logical changes to the database's data record element and relationship types, and physical reorganization of the database's storage structure components.

Concurrent operations let a single run-time copy of the DBMS support multiple concurrent update and retrieval transactions from multiple interrogation language run-units to the same or different databases without any compromise to database integrity, and with automatic detection and resolution of execution deadlock.

Multiple database DBMS allows more than one database to operate independently under a single central version. This allows logical database changes to be isolated and applied without affecting any of the other databases that may be running under that central version. Furthermore, if one database crashes, then only that database is affected, and while it is being recovered, the others remain operating.

Security and privacy support the definition of a comprehensive set of users, profiles, and passwords to prevent and report on illicit data access and database operations. The DBMS security provides protection at the database, schema record, and schema record element level for at least update and retrieval access, and ideally also for select clauses.

DBMS installation and maintenance facilities, if sophisticated, enable the generation of special run-time versions that favor certain types of update or retrieval processing.

Finally, application optimization is the process of using DBMS generated statistics of its own database application access efficiencies to guide physical and logical reorganization, or to create special DBMS versions. Sophisticated DBMSs provide performance assessment aids that enable the physical database designers to tune the performance towards critical applications.

The principal difference between static and dynamic system control relates mainly to the domain of each system control facility. In a dynamic relationship DBMS, the domain is normally a data record type because a data record type is usually stored on one O/S file. In a static relationship DBMS, the domain is usually the database, as it is a large collection of interrelated data record types stored in a complex way across a series of O/S files. What this usually implies for a dynamic relationship DBMS is that audit trails, reorganization, and concurrent operations are isolated in their effect to the data record type. For a static relationship DBMS, these same system control facilities affect the large, complex database as a whole. This means that with a dynamic relationship DBMS, normally just a data record type is locked during reorganization. With a static relationship DBMS, normally the whole database is locked during its reorganization. In short, the difference relates to both scope and size. Figure 6.1 provides an overview of the differences between system control facilities in static and dynamic relationship DBMSs.

System control facilities range from a series of DBMS vendor supplied software capabilities, manual processes, activities, and lessons learned through classes and experience. Collectively, these facilities have to be enhanced with well-engineered and established procedures that are centrally controlled within a database administration department/group. These activities have to be centrally administered and controlled because sometimes their invocation can occur only after the entire database environment is shut down. This is especially the case in a corporate database that is under the control of a static relationship DBMS.

While the activities within system control are not normally a monolithic set of utilities accessible by a large menu, many of these functions do exist in menu driven mechanisms that are easily used by the database administrator. This ease of use is both good and bad, especially in a dynamic environment where the database administrator is the same person who designs databases, loads data,

System Control Facility	DBMS Type	
	Static	Dynamic
Audit trails	Poor to good	Poor to good
Message processing	Poor to good	Acceptable
Backup and recovery	Good	Good
Reorganization	Acceptable	Acceptable to good
Security & privacy	Poor to acceptable	Poor to acceptable
Multi-database processing	Poor to good	Good
Concurrent operations	Acceptable to good	Good
Application optimization	Acceptable to good	Poor to acceptable
Installation & maintenance	Poor to acceptable	Acceptable to good

Figure 6.1 Static versus Dynamic System Control Comparison

updates data, and is *chief cook and bottle washer*. It is good in that this person really controls all the DBMS facilities. It is bad because all these facilities are so easily--and irrevocably--controlled.

Before proceeding, the following must be stated about what a database and DBMS environment is like without these nine critically important facilities.

- Not having audit trails means that there is no accountability for database updates, reports, and other types of use.
- Not having sophisticated message processing will not stop errors. Rather users will become frustrated, and stop using the system.
- Not having backup and recovery results in total database loss as important update transactions are lost and critical databases are not recoverable after crashes.
- Not having reorganization ultimately causes the database to become antiquated and *freeze-up*. This is due to structural inefficiencies or because the database does not contain the right data record elements, relationships, and data record types.

- Not having security and privacy enables valuable corporate data to be stolen.
- Not having multiple database processing causes a redundancy of facts, which in turn causes errors through time, and an eventual breakdown in the usefulness of database projects.
- Not having concurrent operations capabilities and guidelines will--at some time--prevent the generation of an extremely important report because of some trivial, but database locking, operation.
- Not having database application optimization causes the expenditures for hardware to increase as a consequence of unimproved database designs, inefficient physical structures, and inappropriate DBMS configurations.
- Not having good installation and maintenance procedures eventually causes special software libraries to be lost, different versions of modules to be linked together, and databases to be lost due to corruptions caused by misconnected DBMS modules.

Although time consuming and seemingly nonproductive, the only thing more expensive than good system control is not having system control.

6.2 AUDIT TRAILS

An audit trail is a time-ordered and user-sequenced record of operations that have been executed against the database. Without an effective and complete audit trail, there may be no way to determine the source of a destructive update.

Audit trails are used to determine the source of an update, rather than fixing a damaged database. Since the audit trail capability can operate effectively from different run units and in different modes, such as batch, interactive, and exclusive or shared use of one or more databases, the audit trail file(s) represent a compete chronology of the activities against the database.

A sophisticated audit trail contains enough information to identify correctly the source of the update. Typically, each audit trail transaction contains:

- Time and date stamps
- Database identification
- User-identification
- The update transaction itself

Under the assumption that the audit trail records themselves are stored in a database, the various DBMS languages isolate a single user's transactions from within a multi-user environment, or report the activities by transaction type, database, data record type, time of day, and the like. Figure 6.2 illustrates the

```
Date = yyyymmddd (julian format)
Time = hh: mm: ss: 100
Submitter Id
Database Id
DBMS Version Id
Database Data Cycle Id
Actual Command
Record Type Name
Before Image
After Image
etc.
```

Figure 6.2 Transaction Content

typical record format for an audit trail file. As seen from this table, all the information should be present to completely reconstruct the environment of the update.

With sophisticated audit trails, transactions can be from

- All the databases operating under a central version
- Certain dates or time periods
- Specifically identified databases
- Specifically identified areas within a database
- Specifically identified schema data record types within a database
- Specifically identified views within a database
- Specifically identified interrogation language types, e.g., query-update, or procedure oriented languages
- A named application program
- A class of application programs

Audit trails are stored either on tape or disk. Each has advantages and disadvantages. Tape is safer in that it almost never crashes. However, a tape drive is needed for each central version of the DBMS. Another disadvantage is that when the tape runs out, another must be started and/or mounted. During that time, all updates under the control of that central version have to be suspended, locking out the users.

Disk is less safe because it is subject to head crashes. Over the last several years, however, disks have become almost as safe as tape. Thus, when audit trails are properly established, there is no difference.

Under either tape or disk, the writes must be direct, not buffered. This means that only one transaction is lost in the event of a DBMS, operating system, or hardware crash.

A sophisticated audit trail is used to follow the data value changes for the purpose of isolating either an incorrect data value that is added to the database, or to identify the source of a valid but inappropriate value. Given that the audit trail data record instances are in a DBMS central version database, then the DBMS typically supports standard reports of audit trail data record instances on the basis of

- User-Id
- Date
- Database
- Data Record Type
- Run-Unit-Id
- Language Type
- Error Message Type

Natural languages must also support ad hoc reports from audit trail logs.

Before learning about any particular DBMS's audit trail capabilities and declaring them to be either good or bad, a careful assessment of exact needs for database integrity, the type of update auditing, various legal considerations, etc., has to be made. Armed with these requirements, a careful examination of DBMS capabilities will be productive.

There is no real difference in audit trails between static or dynamic relationship DBMS. Audit trails within a DBMS are either sophisticated or they are not. Static relationship, DBMSs however, have been around for a longer time, and are likely to have a better developed approach to audit trails. Other than for evolutionary differences between static and dynamic relationship DBMSs, there are no real differences. Figure 6.3 tabulates these natural differences.

6.3 MESSAGE PROCESSING

In a database application there are many sources of messages, from the DBMS, the O/S, various systems software, and the application. The sources of these messages must be determined, and there should be a central scheme for their definition, maintenance, and issuance. A well-organized DBMS has all its messages categorized and summarized in an easy to read and understand language. Five typical types of messages are:

- Syntax errors of various DBMS languages
- Application generated errors such as incorrect data record element names
- Data generated errors such as incorrect employee IDs
- Database integrity errors that indicate that a database storage structure component is missing or damaged
- DBMS integrity errors such as missing DBMS subroutines, bad code, etc.

Audit trail aspect	DBMS Type	
	Static	Dynamic
Database definition	Many intercon-nected record types	Single record type per database
Database sources	Well developed	Acceptable
Transaction content	Poor	Poor
Transaction storage media	Ok	Ok
Reporting	Ok	Ok

Figure 6.3 Static versus Dynamic Audit Trail Differences

Figures 6.4 thorough 6.8 illustrate typical message types and a probable cause for each. These messages are intended to invoke some action. Typically, these actions require

- Nothing when the message is informational
- Reentry of the data or command when the DBMS doesn't understand
- User termination from thc run-unit or DBMS when a password is not acceptably provided
- Detaching all users from the database when damage has occurred to a storage structure component
- Termination of the operation of the DBMS due to a missing subroutine or a logic error

Example:

```
MODIFLY EMPLOYEE-NAME WHERE

<< syntax error >>
```

Source

DDL language

interrogation languages

system control languages

Figure 6.4 Typical Message Types
Type = 1: DBMS Syntax Errors

Example:

```
PRINT EMPLOYEE-MAME WHERE...

<< no valid field employee-mame >>
```

Sources:

DDL languages

- Duplicate field name
- Duplicate schema/subschema

Interrogation languages

- Illogical request
- Untrue selection clause

System Control language

- Illegal password

Figure 6.5 Typical Message Types (cont.)
Type = 2 Application Generated

Example:

MODIFY EMPLOYEE-NAME EQ TED CODD WHERE
EMPLOYEE-ID EQ 485927143

<< illegal employee-name value >>

Sources:

Data loading

Records out of sequence

Illegal data value

Interrogation

Insert records/elements

Modify records/elements

Figure 6.6 Typical Message Types (cont.)
Type = 3: Data Generated

Example:

Open sales (mike)

<< sales database damaged >>

Sources:

Damaged pointers

Unreadable dictionary,

index,

relationships, or

data

Missing storage structure components

Figure 6.7 Typical Message Types (cont.)
Type = 4: Database Integrity

```
Example:

     START DBMS

     <<unrecoverable error 123>>

Sources:

     Missing subroutines

     Time bomb expired

     Trapped logic error
```

Figure 6.8 Typical Message Types (cont.)
Type = 5: DBMS Integrity

```
Example:

     DELETE EMPLOYEE WHERE SSN EQ '184-86-7787'

     <<employee deleted>>
```

Figure 6.9 Severity Levels
Severity = 1: Information Only

Figures 6.9 through 6.13 illustrate a message from each severity type and an example cause of the message.

There is no real difference in the types, kind, and result of messages between static and dynamic relationship DBMSs, except that if a single dynamic database is damaged, others will most likely continue to process, and thus only a few users are affected. While in a static environment, the termination of a single database stops the activities of large groups of people, such as a nationwide network of order entry clerks.

Figure 6.14 presents these message types and severity levels in a matrix. Each cell indicates the probable effects of the message type and severity on a transaction, depending on whether the executing DBMS is operating in single user mode (local version) or multiple user mode (central version).

It is important that sophisticated DBMSs contain an on-line message database that is available during any one of the on-line sessions. The data record type description of such a messages database is illustrated in Figure 6.15.

Example:

```
PRINT <EMPLOYEE RECORD> IF SSN EQ '34-134-8618'

<<no records found>>
```

Figure 6.10 Severity Levels (cont.)
Severity = 2: Correctable

Example:

```
MODIFY SALARY = 100000 IF EMPLOYEE-NAME EQ 'ME'

<<update authority not allowed>>

<<run-unit terminated>>
```

Sources

Request for inactive database

Request for an already exclusively controlled function

Security violation

Figure 6.11 Severity Levels (cont.)
Severity = 3: Run Unit Fatal

Example:

A read to index that has bad track

<<databased damage>>

<<run-unit terminated>>

<<no database access allowed>>

Sources:

I/O errors

Memory failure

DBMS bug

Figure 6.12 Severity Levels (cont.)
Severity = 4: Database Fatal

Example:

An O/S read to a DBMS subroutine that is not present

<<session terminated>>

<<O/S prompt for next command>>

Sources:

Malformed load of DBMS software

Hardware disk failure

O/S loader error

Figure 6.13 Severity Levels (cont.)
Severity = 5: DBMS Fatal

Message type and source		Message severity				
		1 Info	2 Correct-able	3 RU fatal	4 DB fatal	5 DBMS fatal
1	Syntax error	N/A	Local CV	Local	N/A	N/A
2	Applica-tion	N/A	Local CV	Local N/A	N/A	N/A
3	Data	N/A	Local CV	Local N/A	N/A	N/A
4	DB integ-rity	N/A	N/A	Local	Local CV	N/A
5	DBMS integ-rity	N/A	N/A	Local CV	Local CV	Local CV

Legend:

local = local mode (single user)
CV = multiple users from batch or on-line
N/A = not applicable

Figure 6.14 Cross Reference Between Message Types and Severity Levels

Finally, it is important that certain classes and types of messages be logged to the audit trail. If this is accomplished, then user training can occur as a consequence of reviewing the message logs. The message classes that should be logged are those above class 2, and the message severities that should be logged are those above severity level 3.

Figure 6.16 illustrates the format of the message audit trail data record type. This data record type should be a fundamental component of data dictionary system's database, and the data record instances in this database are used to assist in understanding problem areas in a database application design. If there is a large number of data entry editing and validation violations, or a large number of query language syntax error entries, then there is a need for remedial training.

6.4 BACKUP and RECOVERY

Backup and recovery embraces two different concepts. Backup is the ability of the DBMS to make a copy of one or more databases that are under the control of an executing DBMS. Recovery is the ability of a DBMS to recover from a failure that may be user, DBMS, O/S, or hardware caused. Since some types of recovery

```
Access keys

    message number

    short name

    long name
```

Figure 6.15 Messages Database Data Record Format

```
    message number

    short name

    long name

    message explanation

    suggested remedies
```

Figure 6.16 Audit Trail Data Record Elements For a Help Transaction

involve database backups, both topics are often presented together.

6.4.1 Database Backup

Prerequisite to any safe backup and recovery facility is the ability to backup the database. That means the DBMS, through a command, copies all the files associated with all the storage structure components of a database from an on-line media to an off-line media. The backup facility should also have a similar facility to bring back the database copy from off-line to on-line, under the same database name, or under a different name. The ability to change a database name is important because it enables a duplicate database for activities, such as database comparisons and training.

The practicality of making a database backup is dependent upon the sophistication of the DBMS's storage structure, and the ability to operate multiple databases within a central version. If there are many different databases within a central version, then backing up any one database is practical. If, however, the DBMS only allows a single database within a central version, then it is quite impractical to backup a multiple billion character database.

In a simple database and DBMS environment, backup is simple. On a microcomputer there might be a relational DBMS and under its control a single database of only 20,000 data record instances from all types, totaling only about 2 million characters. To backup that database might require only a single command and a few minutes. However, in a large mainframe environment when the database application involves hundreds of users, a hundred or so data record types, and millions of data record instances, the problem of backups becomes more complicated and time consuming. Such a database might be 4 billion characters in size and take four hours to backup

In large database applications, backup needs to be a great deal more sophisticated than just locking up the database and sending all the employees home while database backup is underway. It should be possible to backup a database while only retrievals are occurring. It should even be possible to backup a portion of the database while update activity is occurring on other portions. Incremental backups should also be possible, that is, only backing up the data record types and/or O/S files that have been updated since the last backup. This type of backup is popular on large mainframe environments and even on PCs. Database is inherently more complicated, however, because there are storage structure components for the schema and subschema/view, the indexes, relationships (static only), and the data record instances. Because of these complexities, the following questions need to be asked of any DBMS vendor before arriving at a complete understanding of the DBMS' backup facility:

- Can a database schema data record type be updated while a backup of that same schema data record type is in progress?
- Is there a DBMS facility to prevent updates while a backup is in progress?
- Can an O/S file be updated while a backup of that same O/S file is in progress?
- Can a database be updated while a backup of that same database is in progress?
- Does the DBMS support incremental backup of only those schema data record types that were updated since the last backup?
- Does the DBMS have the ability to report information on the incremental backups?
- Does the DBMS contain parameters to maintain the number of backups that are to be stored?
- Does the central version need to be off-line when a backup of one or more databases is in progress?
- Does the DBMS include a backup copy utility?
- Does the DBMS have the ability to report information on the backup copies?

6.4.2 Database Recovery

Database errors occur mainly during update. An update may not be completed successfully because there has been a computer hardware failure, or because of a problem in the system software, the DBMS, or the application. In addition to these types of failures, there may have been updates that are mistakes (for example, a whole group of customers may have been assigned to the wrong salesperson's territory). Under any of these situations the database may have to be moved *back* in time to a state in which the errors did not occur. Recovery capabilities are usually a combination of manual and DBMS-based procedures performed by the database administrator. The transactions that the DBMS recovery processor uses are often stored on a disk or tape file called the journal.

Critical to recovery are the capabilities provided by the DBMS for on-line and batch users, and the role a central database administration function may play during certain database damage situations. For example, the DBMS should have the capability to invoke transaction rollback to purge an unwanted update while a run-unit is in operation. This capability should be available from either the host or natural language environment.

There are five distinct DBMS alternatives that are typically available to bring a database back to a consistent state:

- Rerun the job
- Roll-forward from a checkpoint
- Rollback the database from a current state to a prior checkpoint
- A combination of rollback and roll-forward
- Transaction rollback instigated by the run-unit

There are two expense components in any database recovery. The first is the resources consumed by the DBMS in anticipation of a database crash. The second is the resources consumed during the actual recovery process. In general, these two factors are inversely related to each other. That is, the more resources expended during the update operations in preparation for database recovery, the quicker and less expensive the recovery. And, the fewer resources expended during update operations in preparation for database recovery, the longer and more expensive the recovery. Figure 6.17 identifies six classes of failures, and the types of recovery that are possible under three scenarios: immediate, rapid, and slow.

Choosing the most cost effective method of recovery involves choosing the level of protection that is both the maximum affordable and the minimum necessary. Basically that means balancing the cost of database unavailability against the cost of database recovery. For example, if the application is an on-line order entry system, then for every minute the order-taking database is not available there is going to be the unrecoverable cost of lost orders. The real cost of recovery is the actual cost of recovery minus the value of the lost orders. In contrast, if a batch job is established to update the database, and the batch job has a whole weekend to run, then it does not really matter if the job is finished Friday night, Saturday afternoon, or Sunday morning. In this case, almost any expense incurred for rapid recovery is wasted. For either case, the cost of recovery is essentially

<table>
<tr><th rowspan="2">Cause of failure</th><th colspan="3">Recovery method</th></tr>
<tr><th>Immediate</th><th>Rapid</th><th>Slow</th></tr>
<tr><td>Run unit exception</td><td>Not possible except for transient failures (full redundancy)</td><td>Run-unit rollback</td><td>Run-unit roll-back or roll-forward and restart</td></tr>
<tr><td>O/S or DBMS failure</td><td>Not possible except for transient failures (full redundancy)</td><td rowspan="2">System roll-back: restart from checkpoints</td><td rowspan="3">System roll-back or roll-forward and restart
or
rerun</td></tr>
<tr><td>Failure to execute CPU instruction</td><td>Hardware redundancy</td></tr>
<tr><td>Database unreadable</td><td>Dual files</td><td>Dual files</td></tr>
<tr><td>Corruption detected by DBA</td><td colspan="2" rowspan="2">Impossible</td><td>Log analysis: DBA takes manual action</td></tr>
<tr><td>Corruption detected by user</td><td>Analysis of run log and results correction of applications. Rerun</td></tr>
</table>

Figure 6.17 Comparison of Causes of Failure and Revovery Modes

insurance premiums paid against a certain loss. Only the organization can determine the appropriate premium cost.

6.4.2.1 Re-run the Job

The re-run the job method of recovery has the least preparation cost and is thus the longest and most expensive to execute. For example, if a database backup is taken just prior to the execution of a job, and if the job crashes 99% from the beginning, then all the work is scrapped, the backup restored, and the database job rerun. The cost to prepare for this recovery is only the cost of the backup. The cost to execute the recovery is the cost of rerunning all the update transactions that are present in the job.

This recovery method is practical when the probability of a hardware crash is pretty low, and when there is a very large volume of updates against a good portion of the database. This typically occurs in overnight batch update runs.

Figure 6.18 illustrates the basic process of rerunning a database job as a method of recovering after a crash.

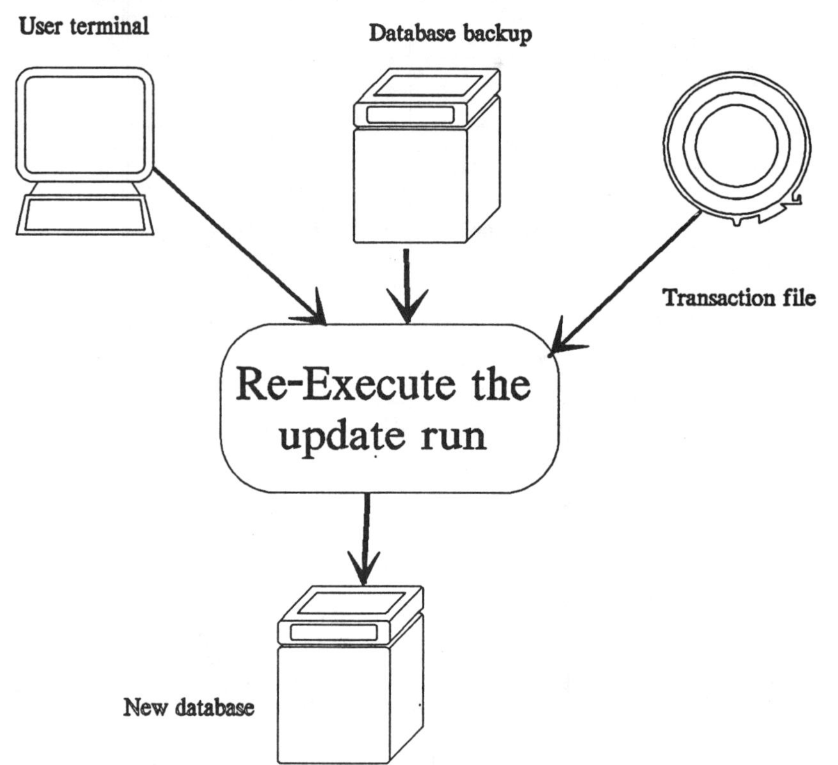

Figure 6.18 Single-user Recovery, Rerun the Job

6.4.2.2 Roll-forward

The roll-forward method of recovery comes in two variations. They are both similar in that they initially require a backup of the database, and write the update transactions to a journal file during the update run. In the event of a crash, the backup is restored, and the journal file containing a log of the update transactions is run against the database until the last successful update as been reapplied.

In the first variation, the journal file contains a form of the database update command. Something like: UPDATE FILE 5, PAGE 10, WORD 47 TO VALUE 88. The journal file contains a whole series of these spartan commands, and reapplies them very rapidly. The space required for each command is quite small, so the journal file may contain a large number. Each file and each DBMS record has to be located and brought into memory, the value changed, and the DBMS record written back to disk.

In the second variation, the journal file contains the actual image of the database DBMS record that is written to disk. The journal file contains a whole series of these DBMS records, and reapplies them even more rapidly than the first variation. This is because the only requirement of the recovery is to write these DBMS records directly on top of the corresponding DBMS records of the database.

Both roll-forward variations cost more than the re-run-the-job method of recovery, but less than the rollback method (next section). Both roll-forward variations take less time for recovery than the re-run the job method, but more than the rollback method.

The roll-forward recovery method is most appropriately used during single or multiple update runs against the same database, providing

- Those jobs have coordinated restart in the event of a crash while they were executing.
- The amount of time to recover to the point of job restart is not very critical.

Creating such programs requires careful design and programming, and then careful testing before they are put into place. Figure 6.19 illustrates the basic process of accomplishing database recovery through roll-forward.

6.4.2.3 Rollback

The rollback recovery method departs in philosophy from re-run the job and roll-forward in that it does not require a database backup, only the current database. As the updates occur, the before image of the database DBMS record (instead of the after image DBMS record) is written to the journal file. This enables recovery from the point of the crash back into time to a position in the database normally known as a checkpoint. A checkpoint is a marked point, or an instant when no updates are occurring to the database. The DBMS marks that instant as a point of database consistency, and uses that point of consistency as the *ending* place for a rollback. Figure 6.20 illustrates the basic process of accomplishing database recovery through rollback.

All update jobs running at the time of the crash also have to be rolled back to that checkpoint, and then be restarted. If a user has entered ten or twenty update transactions between the last checkpoint and the time of the database crash, then all those updates have to be reentered. For batch users, such program restarts, if properly programmed, cause all journal files to be reset and then reprocessed. Thus, careful design and programming are necessary.

A real problem arises whenever a job has started and finished between the last checkpoint and the time of the crash. A mechanism has to be created to identify those completed jobs from a job log, and to automatically re-execute those jobs.

The cost of preparing for rollback recovery is similar to the amount spent on roll-forward, and depending on how far it is to the previous checkpoint, the recovery can be faster or slower.

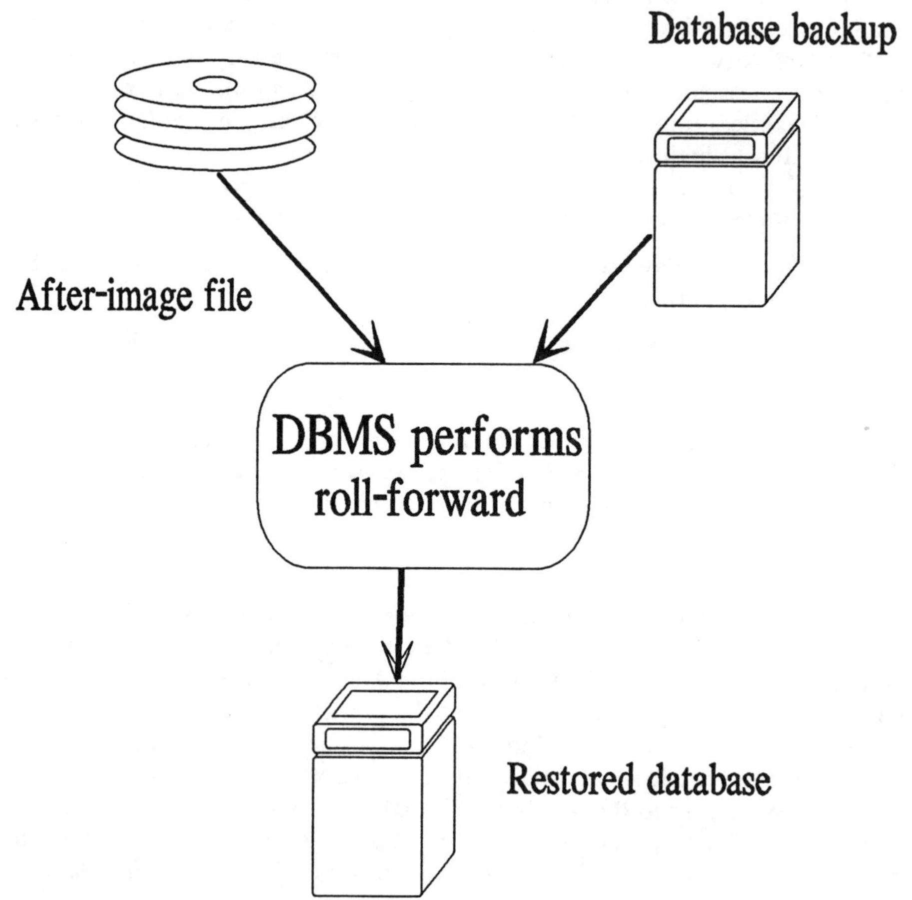

Figure 6.19 Single-user Recovery, Roll-forward (After image recovery)

6.4.2.4 Rollback with Roll-forward

The rollback with roll-forward recovery mechanism starts recovery at the point of the crash and moves backwards in time to the most recent checkpoint. The roll-forward method then recovers from the last checkpoint to the last successful transaction so that all jobs running at the time of the crash are recovered. The cost of implementing this capability is the most expensive because the journal file log must contain both the before images and the after images of database DBMS records that have changed.

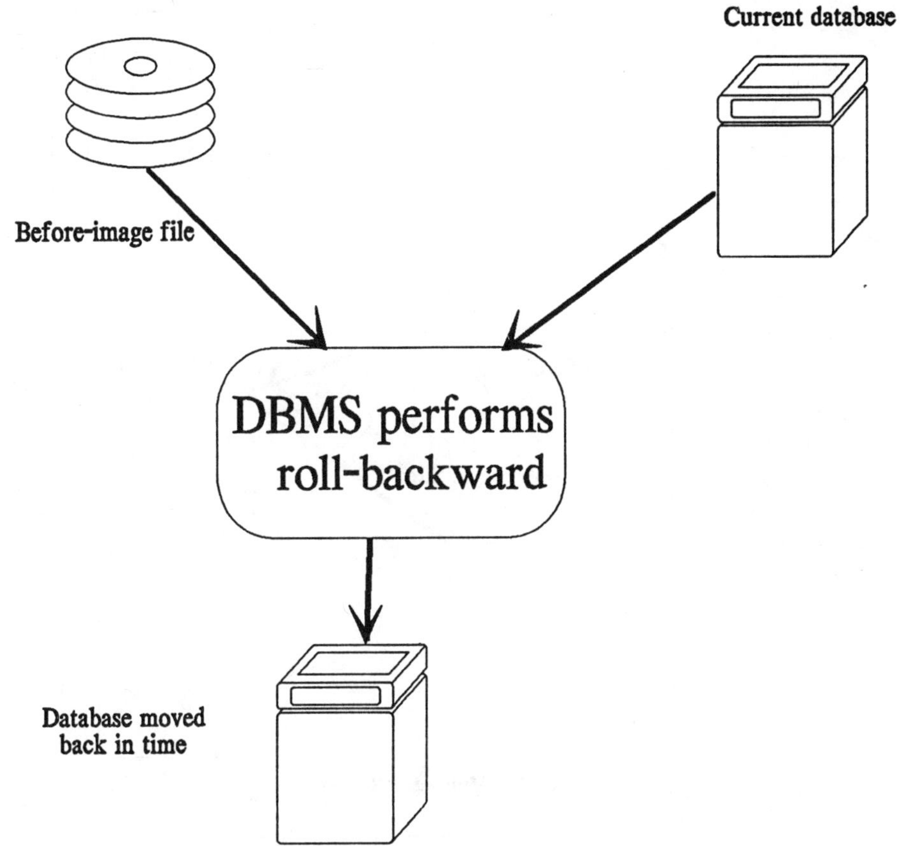

Figure 6.20 Single User Recovery, Rollback or Before Image Form

The most appropriate use of this recovery method is on-line applications that cannot tolerate long recovery periods. Even though the total cost of recovery is high, the cost of preparation plus the cost of recovery, the cost is spread over each transaction.

This method also has the advantage that transactions which occur earlier than the last checkpoint are moved off-line because they are not needed for recovery. This is in contrast to roll-forward recovery which requires all the after images from the point of the last database backup to the point of the crash.

Most modern on-line database update environments that use multiple databases under a central version with updates from different sources and languages make use of the combination rollback and roll-forward methods of recovery. During the time of such recovery, the database is usually locked out. Figure 6.21 illustrates this lockout and types of recovery.

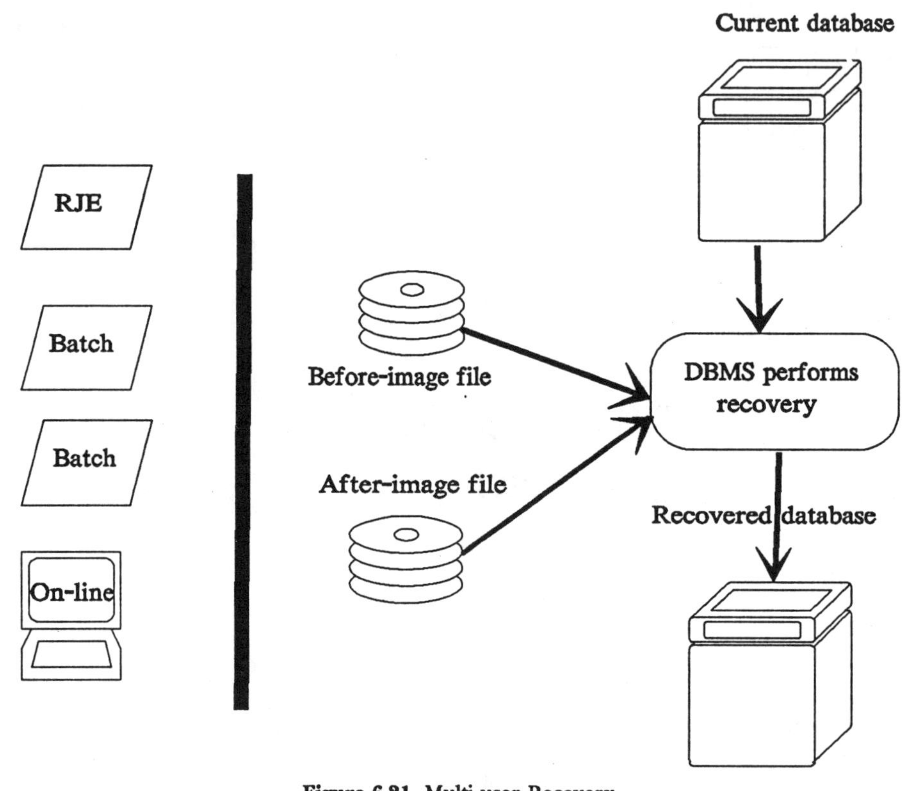

Figure 6.21 Multi-user Recovery

Another very important reason for having multiple database operations within a single DBMS central version is recovery. If one of the databases within a central version crashes, then that database undergoes recovery without impacting any of the other databases that are still operating under the control of that central version. If there is only one database within a central version, then when it crashes, everyone operating within its domain also crashes.

6.4.2.5 Transaction Rollback

If during an update, the user determines that the transaction is really not valid, a facility called transaction rollback lets the user reverse the transaction. It simply cancels the effect of the transaction on the database. There are two varieties of transactions: explicit and implicit. Figure 6.22 illustrates both these transaction types. When the transaction is explicit, then the run-unit issues a <START FRAME> command to the DBMS. The run-unit then issues one or more updates,

```
Explicit start and stop
     <start frame>
     Run-unit updates
     <end frame>

Implicit start and stop
     <start DBMS> (implicit open)
     Update transactions
     <finish> (commits transactions)
        (and opens next frame)
```

Figure 6.22 Transaction Rollback Alternatives

and if acceptable, the run-unit issues a <COMMIT> transaction. If, however, the run-unit issues a <ROLLBACK> transaction, the entire set of DBMS transactions is rolled back.

If the run unit is interrupted by a software or hardware failure, then upon recovery, the DBMS backs out all uncompleted transactions. The three versions of rollback are summarized in Figure 6.23.

The reason transaction frames are needed is that a business transaction seldom maps to a run-unit transaction. The pseudo code illustrated in Figure 6.24 illustrates this fact. From the user's perspective, the transaction is ADD CUSTOMER. From the run-unit's perspective, the steps within the transaction are

- Insert the customer data record instance
- Insert all the available contracts for the customer
- Insert for each contract each of the orders
- Insert for each order each of the order-line-items

The rule established for the user transaction is to add all or add nothing. The pseudo code reflects this with the inclusion of the explicit START and END TRANSACTION statements, and with the inclusion of the ROLLBACK statement at every subcommand within the user transaction.

From the DBMS's perspective, there are at least as many DBMS transactions as there are run-unit transactions. There are additional DBMS transactions for each index and/or relationship update, and for each recording of a before and/or after image update.

Since each type of business transaction is likely to contain a different number of run-unit and DBMS transactions, the business transaction must be carefully crafted to ensure that it is rolled back in its entirety rather than just some of its contained run-unit transactions.

```
Automatic

      Run-unit is interrupted during a frame
      DBMS restarts and finds uncompleted frame
      DBMS "backsout" all run-unit transactions
      Using the transaction rollback log


User-interrupted

      User interrupts a frame with <cancel>/<break>
      DBMS automatically backsout frame


User-instigated

      User finishes submitting update commands
        then determines there is a mistake
        then the user submits <rollback>
```

Figure 6.23 Transaction Rollback Alternatives (cont.)

If a transaction rollback facility exists, then what happens to other transactions that might have used its results for their updates? Are they rolled back? What of the user who has used the updated data for a report, and after the report is finished, a whole day's transactions are rolled back? These types of questions have troubled DBMS designers to no end.

The solutions seem to be partially user designed and implemented, and partially DBMS implemented. From the user point of view, each update requests exclusive control over the record instance or data record type (all data record instances) or database (the entire storage structure) that is being updated, thus ensuring that no other person interferes with the update. And when the person or program that submits the update is satisfied, the update's effects are committed to the database and then all the resources that were locked are released.

From the DBMS point of view, it imposes single threaded operation for all updates to the same database, and does not allow any other updates to occur until the submitter of the update has committed it.

6.4.2.6 Backup and Recovery Responsibility

Figure 6.25 identifies the different processing states through which an online transaction proceeds. As is seen, most states are the responsibility of other processors. Distributed processing complicates this chain even further. Distributed processing introduces additional processor state interactions between states 4 and 5, and between states 7 and 8. The complete set of these interactions is being defined by the ANSI X3H2.1 subcommittee for remote data access protocol

(RDAP). The X3H2.1 committee interfaces with the ISO committee for RDAP which is also a subgroup of WG3 (see Chapter 1).

```
START TRANSACTION
  DO WHILE CUSTOMER EXISTS
    INSERT CUSTOMER, IF FAILURE THEN ROLLBACK
      DO WHILE CONTRACT EXISTS
        INSERT CONTRACT, IF FAILURE THEN ROLLBACK
          DO WHILE ORDER EXISTS
            INSERT ORDER, IF FAILURE THEN ROLLBACK
             DO WHILE ORDER-ITEM EXISTS
               INSERT ORDER-ITEM, IF FAILURE THEN ROLLBACK
             END ORDER-ITEM
          END ORDER
      END CONTRACT
  END CUSTOMER
END TRANSACTION
```

Figure 6.24 Business Transaction, ADD CUSTOMER, Consisting of Many Run-unit Transactions

State	Action	Responsible
1.	User to TP monitor	User
2.	TP monitor response to user	TP
3.	Activation of TP processing module	TP
4.	TP processing module to user program	TP
5.	User program request to DBMS	O/S
6.	DBMS to database	DBMS
7.	DBMS response to user program	O/S
8.	User program to TP processing module	TP
9.	TP processing module response to user	TP

Figure 6.25 Processor States Responsibilities in On-line Transactions

Because of this complex and shared responsibility, it is critical to know which processor is in charge of a transaction in the event of a system failure to determine which transactions have to be re-entered. While that knowledge is clearly available after considerable research has been performed, it is more practical to research the data contained in the database after the environment has been recovered to determine whether transactions arrived there, and if not, to reprocess them.

6.4.3 Checkpoint and Restart

A checkpoint transaction is a special transaction that is placed on the journal file for performing database recoveries. The checkpoint transaction indicates that once a database is restored to that transaction, the database is consistent. A checkpoint transaction may be instigated by the DBA, or automatically once an hour. When the checkpoint transaction starts, it usually requests an update lock on the entire database and does not allow new updates to commence. When the exclusive lock is obtained, no other updates are in progress. At that moment, all buffers are cleared to disk and the checkpoint transaction is written to the journal, signaling that the database state is consistent. The checkpoint transaction generally requires specialized information to be sent to the journals so that the entire database environment is acceptably restored as of that checkpoint.

Checkpoints are needed for recovery methods that involve roll-forward. The opportunities for establishing checkpoints include

- The start of the first update job when it is bound to the environment
- The end of the last update job, when binding is terminated
- A DBMS data manipulation language commit point that may be implicitly or explicitly programmed into a run-unit
- A data manipulation language abort activity (rollback) that may have occurred within a job
- A data manipulation language *ready area* command (CODASYL)
- A journal file initialization
- During DBMS restart or recovery
- Job rollbacks that return the database to a consistent state (i.e., before the <start of job>)

6.4.4 Database Lockout

Database lockout is the DBMS process that precludes the execution of conflicting operations. In general, recovery instigates lockout by preventing the start of any new update run units. Eventually all the currently running update jobs come to an end, and the database is then locked from all updates. In some cases, retrieval jobs are also locked out from execution. For example, if the reason for the lockout is to add a new element type to a data record type then the DBMS might require that data record type and all its instances be locked out from all update or retrieval activity.

Static relationship DBMSs typically lock a larger portion of a database's storage structure than does a dynamic relationship DBMS. This is because the static relationship DBMS database is so much more complex. A static relationship database locks at least one O/S file, and if the file contains data record instances from many different data record types, then all those different data record types are also locked.

If the static relationship DBMS allows the instances from a single data record type to be spread across multiple O/S files then the lockout necessarily spans multiple O/S files.

In addition to locking the data record instances, any index structures associated with the data record type's data record elements are also locked out, if the indexes are built in a sophisticated way. For example, the index types described in Figure 6.10 that involve either DBKEYs or bit maps also have to be locked during any reorganization of data record instances as those addresses (a DBKEY or a bit map address) are also affected. The index organizations that only involve the use of primary keys in the multiple occurrence lists are untouched by any such reorganization.

A dynamic relationship DBMS, in contrast, typically only locks a single data record type and its associated instances as they alone may be contained in a single O/S file. Indexes associated with that single data record type are or are not locked depending upon the level of sophistication of the index designs.

Static relationship DBMSs have traditionally locked more of the storage structure than dynamic relationship DBMSs because their databases are used--most often--for corporate wide, large, complex databases. In recent years, these same use characteristics (corporate wide, large, and complex) are being imposed on dynamic relationship DBMSs. To acceptably fulfill these demands, the dynamic relationship DBMS vendors are making their database storage structures more complex. In short, they are starting down the same road traversed long ago by the static relationship DBMS vendors. At the end of that road will be broader locking domains and increased database reorganization times. That is the natural consequence of deploying sophisticated storage structures to achieve greater application performances.

A critical issue is the coordination of the recovery of a multiple database environment. Such an environment exists within the operation of a single DBMS instance or across instances of the same or different DBMS vendors in the case of a distributed environment. If the database is more simply structured in such environments, that is, if there is only one data record type to the O/S file, a minimum of indexes, and the indexes are all simply structured, then the required locking during any reorganization is minimized. However, those characteristics are typically the inverse of the characteristics of a fast running, corporate wide, complex database environment.

6.4.5 Differences between Static and Dynamic Relationship DBMSs

Generally, a database implemented through a static relationship DBMS is more complex than a dynamic database. It is likely to have more data record types (60 to 90 versus 10 to 15). It is likely to have larger quantities of data (billions versus millions of characters) and have many more programs (thousands versus hundreds) and more concurrent users (thousands versus hundreds) doing both updates and retrievals. Because of the multitude of complexities, the static relationship DBMS is likely to have more sophisticated backup and recovery that costs more per each update, and also takes longer to recover since the volume of transactions is greater. The recovery, however, is likely to be more reliable as recovery applies to the entire database of complex data record types.

In a dynamic environment, the DBMS is likely to restrict recovery to individual data record types, so it is important to design both the data record types and the updates to be as independent as possible. That is, one update, one data record type; or two updates, two different data record types; or two updates, two data record instances of the same type. Figure 6.26 tabulates these important differences.

Issue	Static	Dynamic
Inherent DB structure	Many record types	Few record types
Number of users per DB	Many	Few
Probability of damage	Higher	Lower
Time for recovery	Longer	Shorter
Recovery completeness	Greater	Lesser

Figure 6.26 Recovery: Static versus Dynamic DBMS

6.4.6 Disabling the Journal File

For certain databases operating within an executing central version of the DBMS, there may be a need to disable the journal file. This capability, if carefully used, leads to efficient processing of large volumes of transactions for which backup and recovery are more expensive than rerunning the batch job. If this capability exists, but only at the central version level, then the capability is not acceptable. It must exist at a level below that of the central version. That is, at the level of one or more databases within a central version, and preferably, at one or more separable subunits within a database, for example a CODASYL area or a data record type that is restricted to just one O/S file. In either case, if indexes are present, there must be a utility to regenerate them after the updates are completed.

To make this capability safe, database locks must be installed on the portion of the database that is not be recovered through normal recovery mechanisms. This exclusive area of the database can be updated through the batch run, and when the processes are finished, the unit is released for general use.

6.4.7 Backup and Recovery Summary

This very critical subject is too little understood by most database application groups. There is too little understanding of how to achieve serialization of transactions without requiring that all database update transactions occur in a serial mode. Serial mode requires single user update, and that is something user communities will not tolerate.

As stated above, the five types of DBMS recovery are

- Rerun the job
- Roll-forward from a checkpoint
- Rollback the database from a current state to a prior checkpoint
- A combination of rollback and roll-forward, and finally
- Transaction rollback instigated by the run-unit

Careful attention should be paid to evaluating the backup and recovery capabilities of the DBMS because recovery subsequent to a hard crash could take hours. For example, if there was only one database operating under a central version, and if the log files were collecting update images all week, then in the event of a crash on Thursday, the time to recovery could be hours. If, however, the DBMS could handle multiple databases under the central version, each with its own log files, then recovery only has to be performed on the ones that were *open for update* at the time of the crash.

In short, the least desirable option is that all users are locked out of a central version while the database is being backedup and/or recovered. More desirable is that users of individual databases within the central version--not undergoing backup--are free to perform updates and retrievals, and the retrieval users of the database being backed up are also free to operate. The most desirable option is the option just stated, with the addition that users who are not addressing the subunit of the central version database being backed up are free to perform retrievals and updates against other subunits of the database.

Sophisticated DBMSs enable the recovery mechanisms to operate independently against different databases within a central version. That way, if a specific database under a central version is damaged, others remain operational while the affected database is undergoing recovery.

As an extra measure of security, the DBMS should have the ability to *double* write the journal file. This greatly lessens the possibility of permanent damage due to bad writes to the journal file.

6.5 REORGANIZATION

There are two types of reorganization: logical and physical. In general, logical reorganization refers to processes the DBMS makes available to change the database's logical structure, that is, to add/delete a data record type, to add/delete/modify a data record element within an existing data rccord type, or to add or delete relationship type between or among existing data record types.

Physical reorganization, often automatically invoked through logical reorganization changes, also includes adding or deleting an index, reoptimizing the order of data record instances, and combining or separating data record instances from different types into one or more O/S files.

The greatest need for logical database reorganization is to accommodate new database application requirements. The largest quantity of changes happen during the first several years of a database application's lifecycle. If the database application is implemented with a static relationship DBMS then logical database changes always consume more resources to incorporate than do changes to a dynamic relationship DBMS. This is of course due to the very different nature of a dynamic and static relationship. Additionally, these differences are often due to the fact that a static database storage structure is often very complex, has many data record types represented in the same O/S file, etc. In contrast, the dynamic database storage structure is more simple, typically one data record type in one O/S file. But, as is stated in the previous section of this chapter, dynamic relationship DBMSs, in response to demands for greater performance, are allowing implementation of more complex storage structures, leading to the same reorganization impact as static relationship DBMSs.

Because complex storage structures are becoming a fact of life, regardless of whether the DBMS is static or dynamic, strategies have to be developed for database storage structure implementations to avoid the inevitable set of logical (and automatic physical) database reorganizations.

Two strategies are used. First, include generalized or restrictive data record element type clauses for data record elements that are not yet completely understood. For example, if EMPLOYEE SALARY is a data record element, then a picture of 99.99 can only allow up to a $99.99 salary, with the presumption that the salary is hourly. If an employee is hired and the salary is $75,000 per year, then that salary value is not be allowed until it is converted to a hourly rate. If the following two data record elements are included instead, the problem never arises:

- EMPLOYEE SALARY PIC 9,999,999.99
- EMPLOYEE SALARY PERIOD CHAR 2

In this case, the salary ranges from a very small number to a very large number, but its real meaning is defined by the second data record element's values:

- YR--yearly
- MO--monthly
- WK--weekly
- HR--hourly

It is unlikely that such a pair of data record elements would be subject to logical reorganization for a long time. A problem with this example, however, is that two data record element values are needed to fully understand the complete semantics of the value set.

The second strategy is to isolate the components of the database that are not yet well defined. These can be isolated into their own storage structure components so that when they are reorganized, there is either no impact on stable components or the input is minimized. For example, if the number of data record elements in the EMPLOYEE BIOGRAPHIC data record is subject to a great deal of change, but there is absolute certainty about the EMPLOYEE PAYROLL data record type, the EMPLOYEE BENEFITS data record type, and the other data record types related to an employee, then the stable data record types and all their data record instances should be stored in a single O/S file while the data record instances of the EMPLOYEE BIOGRAPHIC data record type should be stored in its own O/S file. When the inevitable logical reorganization occurs, only the storage structure component representing the EMPLOYEE BIOGRAPHIC data record type needs to be reorganized. The applicability of this technique varies widely among all the static relationship DBMSs, and should always be present in the dynamic relationship DBMSs. The inverse ability to design complex storage structures to enhance performance varies widely in dynamic relationship DBMSs.

These two techniques support DBMS's first principal: flexibility and performance are inversely related.

6.5.1 Logical Database Reorganization

As database applications evolve, there is always a need to add new database component types (data record element, data record, or relationship) to the database, to modify existing types, and to delete unnecessary types. The process of accomplishing these changes is called logical reorganization.

Logical reorganization includes the addition, deletion, or modification of

- Data record elements and subclauses
- Data record types and subclauses
- Relationship types and subclauses

Specifically, for data record elements, the changes are to:

- Add/delete data record elements
- Modify record element characteristics
  * Change its defined name
  * Change its defined length
  * Change its defined data type
  * Change its editing and validation clauses

When data record element clauses are changed so already stored data is no longer acceptable, it is very important to know what the DBMS's reaction will be before such changes are incorporated. One DBMS automatically invokes detailed checking at the data record element instances level, and if any of the values are not in conformance, the appropriate set of messages and offending values are printed along with the message at the end indicating rejection of the new set of rules. Changes for data record types include:

- Adding new or dropping existing data record types
- Modifying data record type clauses
    - Physical access clauses
    - Editing and validation clauses
    - Stored procedure references

Changes for relationships between data record types vary greatly between static and dynamic relationship DBMSs. For ANSI/NDL, the process is to add, delete, or modify set clauses or subordinate clauses. For ANSI/SQL, the process is one of data record element type addition, deletion, or modification. A very powerful subordinate clause within static relationship specification is the sort clause. When the sort clause component of the static relationship is changed, the data record instance references participating in all the relationship instances are automatically resorted. This resorting is done either all at once and immediately, or as the relationship instances are accessed.

Another critical issue is the effect of changing the definition of referential integrity. A quality DBMS examines--at the end of each referential integrity maintenance action--all the referential integrity definitions, rejecting those that could result in ambiguous INSERT, DELETE, or MODIFY situations. It is critical to know what the DBMS's reaction is going to be if the business rules are *tightened down* before a database reorganization begins.

Some DBMSs only accomplish the logical reorganization changes as the data record instances are touched (added or modified). For example, if a new data record element is added to a data record type, some DBMSs only add the space and the data record element value required as the data record instance is accessed. In the case of data record element deletes, some DBMSs merely mark the data record element as being deleted in the dictionary, and then return an appropriate message whenever the deleted data record element's value is requested.

While DBMS procedures vary widely in accomplishing logical database reorganization, the general process is:

- Access a special DBMS software module
- Input changes either interactively or batch

- Perform syntax checks
- If no errors are found, make changes, which in turn often commence some type of physical database reorganization

6.5.2 Physical Database Reorganization

Physical reorganization refers to the DBMS process to bring the physical order of the database back into close relationship with its implied logical order. Generally, when a database is initially loaded, its physical order closely matches its logical order. As record instances are deleted or added, the DBMS automatically rearranges the physical order of the database. Physical database reorganization is often invoked whenever logical database reorganization occurs.

Physical database reorganization involves the restructuring of one or more of the database's storage structure components:

- Dictionary
- Indexes
- Relationships (static only)
- Data record instances

Restructuring the dictionary is logical database reorganization, and is treated in an earlier section. Index reorganization might be to

- Reallocate the number of index levels to improve performance
- Change blocking factors
- Allocate padding to index DBMS records for extra values without reorganization
- Resequence index DBMS records to achieve optimum logical order

Relationship reorganization, applicable only for static relationship DBMSs, enables the resorting of the data record instances into an ordered set of relationship references for the primary relationship. In CODASYL, the primary relationship is called *stored via*. Data reorganization is employed to

- Reclaim deleted data record space
- Expand space in DBMS records for precise loading
- Change blocking factors
- Sort data record instances for specific processing improvements

Physical database reorganization is needed because the physical organization of the database becomes inefficient with respect to updates and interrogations. This means that programs are operating more slowly than when the database is *new*. Normally this is because the storage structure has become fractured. Physical database reorganization is the process of recapturing the efficiency that is in the database when it is *new*.

Physical database reorganization capabilities should include the ability to add or delete indexes, and reload data record instances to optimize data placement and increase index performance.

6.5.3 Impact of Reorganization

A very significant impact on logical database reorganization is whether the DBMS has a central version that handles multiple databases. If there is only one database within a central version, the effect of logical database changes is likely to be a complete user lockout. If the DBMS central version handles multiple databases, then only the users associated with the database being reorganized are affected.

A very valuable benefit of views, as described in Chapter 5, Interrogation, is that many logical database changes are accomplished without affecting operational programs. As stated in Chapter 5, the view becomes an intermediary between the program and the database's underlying schema structure. Changes to the database structure are shielded from affecting the program if they do not affect the view or only affect the view's navigation logic. In a static relationship DBMS, the view's navigation logic is accomplished with commands such as GET NEXT, GET MEMBER, GET OWNER. In an ANSI/SQL compliant DBMS, the view navigation logic is completely contained within the CREATE VIEW statement's SELECT clause. If, for example, a data record element is added to a data record type, then the programs using a particular view that do not need that newly defined data record element do not have to be modified in any way. Nor does that view definition have to change. If however, a new data record type is added in between two existing data record types, then the view's logic might have to change. Such changes should not affect the existing program, unless views are bound into load modules with the compiled programs. In that case all the programs using the affected views have to be recompiled.

6.5.4 Reorganization Locking

When reorganization occurs, locking occurs. The level of locking is typically dependent on whether the DBMS's storage structure is simple or complex. As the storage structure progresses from simple to complex, more and more of the storage structure is probably locked. With simple storage structures only the data record type, its instances, and associated indexes are locked. With complex storage structures, the entire database is locked from all users. With complex storage structures, database reorganization efforts must be carefully planned and timed to occur during the least important periods.

6.5.5 Static and Dynamic Differences

The effect of adding or modifying data record element types, data record types, and relationships differs from DBMS to DBMS. As the storage structure becomes more sophisticated, the complexity of making logical database changes increases.

Change	DBMS type	
	Static	Dynamic
Element	Reload at least an area	Reload at least a record type
Record	Reload at least an area	Reload at least a record type
Relationship	Add, delete, or modify relationship by writing a program to record relationship into data record instances	Change an element's value

Figure 6.27 Static versus Dynamic DBMS Logical Reorganization Comparisons

The difference between static and dynamic relationship DBMSs is striking. Figure 6.27 contrasts the types of logical reorganization changes with the static or dynamic nature of the database being reorganized. Logical reorganization in a dynamic relationship DBMS is easier and is accomplished more rapidly because the storage structure domain of the dynamic data record type is very restricted. Some dynamic relationship DBMSs even allow changes to the individual data record type without physical reorganization. The static relationship DBMS requires physical reorganization for all but the simplest logical database changes.

As might be expected, the domain of the affected data record types in a static relationship DBMS is much larger than in a dynamic relationship DBMS. Consequently, physical database reorganization in a static relationship DBMS is more extensive and consumes greater resources.

6.5.6 Reorganization Summary

Database reorganization is critical to the life of a database. Through its logical aspect, the database continues to be relevant to the needs of its users, and through its physical component, the DBMS can process user requests in an efficient manner.

As database structures become more complex, that is, as there are more and more data record types, relationships, and data record instances, sophisticated DBMSs provide utilities to monitor a database's performance so that physical reorganization is planned cost-effectively. It is cost-effective when the reorganization cost is less than the cost of running with degraded performance.

6.6 CONCURRENT OPERATIONS

Concurrent operations are the DBMS facilities that allow the DBMS to service multiple transactions--concurrently. There is a hierarchy of transaction types to consider: business, run-unit, and DBMS. A business transaction, the highest level, typically causes the execution of multiple run-unit transactions. A business transaction might be to ADD CUSTOMER. This business transaction is depicted in Figure 6.24. The run-unit effecting this business transaction, because of the looping implied in the business transaction, executes many run-unit transactions within one business transaction. For example, if there are 10 order-line-items for each of 5 orders for each of two contracts for only one customer, then there are 100 run-unit transactions. Each run-unit transaction typically consists of multiple DBMS transactions. For example, the run-unit transaction

INSERT ORDER, IF FAILURE THEN ROLLBACK

might involve (based on various data record type clauses) at least the following four DBMS transactions:

- Inserting the order data record instance only if all the appropriate data record elements are valued and all the data record elements pass editing and validation.
- Inserting the order data record instance only if there are no other orders with the same order primary key.
- Updating all the affected indexes associated with the ORDER data record type, for example, the index SALESMAN-ID-OF-RECORD.
- Updating all the appropriate relationships in which the ORDER data record instance participates.

If these same DBMS transactions are required to occur for each run-unit transaction then there are about 400 DBMS transactions for the 100 INSERT ORDER business transactions. Automatic DBMS rollback is at the run-unit transaction level. That means that if any of the relationships in DBMS transaction 4 were not able to be updated properly, then the entire run-unit transaction is rolled back. And then, according to the logic depicted in Figure 6.24, all the run-unit transactions are rolled back.

A key goal of DBMS is to keep the execution time of a run-unit transaction to a minimum. Prior chapters have addressed this from the point of view of index strategies, types of relationships, or the placement of logically related data record instances from the same or different types. There are also optimizations that are achieved by making sure that storage structure components are placed on different computer hardware I/O channels and in different O/S files. This section assumes that all that has been accomplished, and that the run-unit transaction execution time is as short as possible.

Concurrent operations are commonly viewed at the run-unit transaction level (INSERT ORDER, IF FAILURE THEN ROLLBACK). Since a run-unit transaction is broken into multiple DBMS transactions, a DBMS must be designed to handle that lower level of concurrency. As shown below in Section 6.6.3, a DBMS transaction can also be divided into subordinate transactions. Sophisticated DBMSs handle concurrency at all three levels.

A key component of concurrent operations is serializability. Serializability is the DBMS characteristic that enables a set of run-unit transactions (a business transaction) operating in a multiple user environment to produce the same results each time they are run in the same sequence.

When run-unit transactions execute against different data record types resident on different O/S files, then there are few problems associated with concurrent operations. However, when run-unit transactions affect the same data record instance, or when run-unit transactions submitted by different users affect overlapping data record instances, or when run-unit transactions each require/request complete locks of the database, then the DBMS needs to be very sophisticated to prevent unwanted effects or very, very long response times.

The term *concurrent operations* embraces two very different areas of conflict:

- Those between mixed data interrogation or update transactions to the same or different databases operating under the same executing copy of the DBMS
- Those between system control transactions, such as logical and physical reorganization, security and privacy, etc.

Generally, the second type of conflict is well documented and the effects on users are well known through messages from the database administration group:

Attention users, the database will be down between 0800 and 1200 for reorganization.

The remainder of this section deals with transactional conflicts among interrogations and updates against the same or different databases operating under the same executing copy of the DBMS.

There are three different concepts that exist in pairs and in various combinations contrasting the different types of DBMSs in the marketplace. The pairs are

- Single or multiple user DBMS
- Single or multiple database DBMS
- Single or multiple threaded DBMS

6.6.1 Single or Multiple User DBMS

A single user DBMS is one that only allows access by a single user to an executing copy of the DBMS. The database identified for use is then typically locked until the user session terminates. If another user attempts to attach the database, a *database in use* message is displayed, and no access is allowed.

A multiple user DBMS is one that processes multiple run-unit transactions from different run units concurrently. Such a DBMS configuration is employed in distributed processing, or multiple user micro, mini, or mainframe environments. Unless otherwise indicated, the run-unit transactions all process serially through the DBMS. Thus, the next run-unit transaction has to wait for the completion of the current run-unit transaction. Also, unless otherwise indicated, transactions from each run-unit only access a single database within a given user session.

6.6.2 Single or Multiple Database

A single database DBMS is one that permits one or more users access to only one database under the DBMS's control. If there are multiple databases concurrently being accessed, there must be one DBMS for each database.

This means that each user only accesses one database. Multiple users access that one database, but a single user cannot access multiple databases.

A multiple database DBMS is one that permits run-unit transaction access--from one user--to different databases that are under the control of the single instance of the DBMS. The DBMS processes to completion only one run-unit transaction at a time regardless of which database is being accessed. This configuration is typical on single user PCs.

6.6.3 Single and Multiple Threaded DBMS

A single-threaded DBMS only executes one run-unit transaction at a time and cannot service another run-unit transaction until processing finishes for the first run-unit transaction. A multi-threaded DBMS concurrently executes multiple run-unit transactions from multiple run-units against a single database.

Executing multiple run-unit transactions at the same time requires a computing environment that either has multiple CPUs to process more than one run-unit transaction at the same time, or multiple I/O device channels so that multiple channel control programs (I/O service routines) execute at the same time.

Key to executing multiple run-unit transactions at the same time is being able to decompose the DBMS transactions comprising a run-unit transaction into subtransactions. For example,

> Insert the order data record instance only if there are no other orders with the same order primary key.

can be divided into the following DBMS subordinate transactions:

- Employ the CPU to formulate the appropriate command to attempt to find an order data record instance that is already stored with the same primary key value
- Employ the I/O to determine that none is found
- Employ the CPU to formulate the store operation to actually place the data record instance on disk
- Employ the CPU to formulate a *success* message to be passed back to the run-unit

If the environment only has one CPU, but multiple channels, then an I/O request is issued to the channel, which in turn searches its mass storage devices for the data until it is found. When the data is found it is passed back to the computer's main memory for use by the CPU. While the channel is busy finding the data, another channel control program can be executing in another channel to find the data required by another DBMS subtransaction. Keeping all these DBMS subtransactions properly organized requires a very sophisticated DBMS design as well as a sophisticated computing environment.

6.6.4 Commonly Existing DBMS Combinations

The combinations that commonly exist are, in increasing order of sophistication:

- Single user, single database DBMS
- Multiple user, single database, single thread DBMS
- Multiple user, multiple database, single thread DBMS
- Multiple user, single database, multiple thread DBMS
- Multiple user, multiple database, multiple thread DBMS

These are depicted in Figure 6.28. The platforms that accommodate these different levels of sophistication appear in Figure 6.29.

DBMSs that are typically single user are also likely to be single database. These most often operate on PCs or time sharing services. DBMSs that are multiple user either are single or multiple database. Multiple database operations are clearly a level of sophistication over single database. Finally, DBMSs that are multiple user either are single or multiple threaded. Multiple threaded operations are significantly more sophisticated.

6.6.4.1 Single User, Single Database DBMS

The single user, single database is most common on single user PCs. However long waits are possible as the user submits one run-unit transaction and must wait

Increasing Level of Sophistication	User		Database		Threads	
	Single	Multiple	Single	Multiple	Single	Multiple
1	Yes		Yes		N/A	N/A
2		Yes	Yes		Yes	
3		Yes		Yes	Yes	
4		Yes	Yes			Yes
5		Yes		Yes		Yes

Figure 6.28 Sophistication Levels for Concurrent Operations Configurations

Typical Computer Platforms	User		Database		Threads	
	Single	Multiple	Single	Multiple	Single	Multiple
PCs	Yes		Yes			
PC Networks		Yes	Yes		Yes	
Mini Networks		Yes	Yes		Yes	
Mainframes		Yes	Yes		Yes	
Minicomputers and Mainframes		Yes		Yes	Yes	
		Yes		Yes		Yes

Figure 6.29 Typical Platforms for Concurrent Operations Configurations

until it is finished before starting another. In fast PCs, some DBMSs allow printing of one report concurrently with other activities. To achieve that the DBMS usually *electronically* prints the report to a spool file, and then *steals* cycles from the foreground job to send print records from the spool file to the printer. Simply put, there is a one-to-one-to-one relationship between the user, the database, and the DBMS.

Because of the speed of the Intel 80386 chip, multiple tasking operating systems are now viable on PCs. Even in the single user mode a multiple tasking operating system can start multiple jobs, each operating under different copies of the DBMS that run concurrently. Under this mode there is no concurrency control. Therefore the only safe run-units are reports against the same or different databases, or update run-units against different databases.

6.6.4.2 Multiple User, Single Database, Single Thread DBMS

A multiple user, single database, single thread DBMS configuration generally exists on PC networks, distributed networks, minicomputers or mainframes. In this environment, multiple users access only one database, as only one database is controlled by the executing DBMS. As a second user's run-unit transaction reaches the DBMS, it waits in a queue until the run-unit transaction currently executing is finished. Long waits are possible as the currently executing run-unit transaction might be performing updates to many data record instances.

6.6.4.3 Multiple User, Multiple Database, Single Thread DBMS

The multiple user, multiple database, single thread DBMS environment enables the DBMS transactions from the different users to access different databases all under the control of a single executing copy of a DBMS. Having multiple databases means that there are multiple sets of dictionaries, indexes, relationships, and data. Thus, under the control of one executing copy of the DBMS, the following transactions can occur concurrently to the different databases known to the single executing copy of the DBMS:

- One database is varied off-line through a DBMS backup transaction and then a O/S command is employed to delete the files from mass storage.
- A second database is accessed for retrievals, updates, etc.
- The third database is undergoing logical or physical reorganization.
- A fourth database is completely locked for special updating.
- Definition of a fifth database is occurring through DDL commands.

If the DBMS is single threaded, then all these run-unit transactions to the different databases queue up--as received--and are executed one at a time. A run-unit transaction from a user to the first database is executing at the time a run-unit transaction to the fifth database arrives. When the first database run-unit transaction finishes the run-unit transaction affecting the fifth database starts. During the execution of the run-unit transaction affecting the fifth database, a run-unit transaction for the third database might arrive and await in the queue. Then a run-unit transaction for the fourth database might arrive and also wait in the queue. After the run-unit transaction to the fifth database finishes, the first run-unit transaction in the queue starts. After it finishes, the next run-unit transaction in the queue starts. If all the run-unit transactions are short, the computing environment is sophisticated or fast enough, and the number of run-unit transactions in the queue is reasonable, then the waits are tolerable as the sophistication and speed of the computing environment overcomes the number of run-unit transactions in the queue. If the computing environment is neither sophisticated nor fast enough, then the queue becomes unacceptably long. Or, if the number of users suddenly increases, then the computing environment cannot keep up with the arrival rate of run-unit transactions and the queue lengthens.

6.6.4.4 Multiple User, Single Database, Multiple Thread DBMS

A multiple user, single database, multiple thread DBMS configuration is like the one described in Section 6.6.4.2 except that the DBMS handles the simultaneous execution of multiple run-unit transactions. Still, all the run-unit transactions must occur against only one database. Such a configuration requires a sophisticated computing environment found on either mainframes or multiple CPU database machines.

Since the typical DBMS transaction performs a minimum amount of CPU activity in contrast to the number of disk accesses (I/O requests), multiple DBMS transactions are serviced if the computing environment concurrently executes multiple I/O requests. Being able to have multiple and concurrently executing CPU processes is less important as database is typically I/O intensive, not CPU intensive. In the case of ANDing and ORing index lists, multiple CPUs enhance performance.

6.6.4.5 Multiple User, Multiple Database, Multiple Thread DBMS

The most sophisticated DBMS capability is a multiple user, multiple database, multiple threaded DBMS. In this environment the DBMS installation process often requires the definition of the number of threads (queues) and the maximum number of transactions allowed in each queue. Another installation parameter might allocate a service priority among the queues. There might also be a servicing algorithm for the queues that is affected by installation parameters. During the day time, query-update language transactions might receive a higher priority than batch requests. At night the reverse might be true. Thus, classes of run-unit transactions would be automatically allocated to certain queues. In this example, the COBOL batch jobs would take longer to execute during the day as they would be assigned to lower priority queues. Since query-update language run-unit transactions would be allocated to higher priority queues they would be serviced quicker.

In general, the dynamic relationship DBMS performs the multi-threaded, multiple database set of operations with less DBMS vendor software than is required for a static relationship DBMS. This is because in the dynamic database, the data record types are typically physically independent, and other aspects of their storage structure are physically and logically decentralized. As dynamic relationship DBMSs respond to demands for increased performance, their storage structures will become more sophisticated.

6.6.5 Complex Storage Structure Effects on Concurrent Operations

In general, the more complex the storage structure, the greater the likelihood that a lock imposed for one user's access will affect another user. In the Figure 6.30

PHYSICAL RECORD 1

ACCOUNTING	ABLE	BAKER
GRODMAN	KERR	PERKINSON
ADMINISTRATION	EDMONDS	CRITENDEN

PHYSICAL RECORD 2

FRANCIS	GIMBLE	HARRISON
JONES	ENGINEERING	APPLETON
QUINCY	RICHARDSON	ZIEGFIELD

Figure 6.30 Complex Storage Structure Effects on Concurrent Operations

example of two DBMS records, data record instances from DEPARTMENT and EMPLOYEE are stored on the same DBMS record instance. If a run-unit transaction performed a GET WITH LOCK obtained the ACCOUNTING department and if the locking strategy locked the entire DBMS record, then when another run-unit transaction attempts a GET WITH LOCK to obtain an EMPLOYEE data record instance for KERR, it will receive the message: DBMS RECORD LOCKED.

6.6.6 System Control Operation Conflicts

It is not safe to run certain operations concurrently with others. For example, logical or physical database reorganization transactions along with data updates. A Database backup can execute concurrently with updates if implemented in a sophisticated manner. For example, if a backup is started at midnight and continues through 9:00 A.M., and the on-line update queues are opened at 8:00 A.M., then the backup and after image journal records created after 8:00 A. M. are all that is needed to restore a crashed database environment at 10:00 A.M.

The effect of system control locks is greatly minimized through the use of a multiple database DBMS as described above in Section 6.4.1, Database Backup.

6.6.7 Concurrent Operations Locks

Certain DBMS operations impose locks explicitly or implicitly. An explicit lock is achieved when a lock command is issued. An implicit lock is one that is imposed as a consequence of the intensity of the operation. Locks often occur during:

- Massive data loads
- User-instigated DBMS locks
- Audit trail instigation, suspension, or modification
- As a consequence of messages with a severity 4 (database fatal), and severity 5 (DBMS fatal)
- During backups (sometimes) and recoveries (always)
- At the onset of logical and physical reorganization
- During security instigation and maintenance

It is critical to the acceptable operation of the DBMS that each of these locks be understood in terms of the resources consumed and in the elapsed time required. Armed with this knowledge, schedules can be created to minimize these undesired but necessary disruptions.

6.6.8 Deadly Embrace

Deadly embrace is a state in which two or more commands mutually await the other's locked resource. Deadly embrace disables only a poorly designed DBMS. A well-designed DBMS resolves the occurrence of execution deadlock by first terminating one of the conflicting operations, and then attempting to restart the terminated run-unit. Typically, deadly embrace is resolved in two steps:

- The DBMS stops one of the run-units.
- The DBMS rolls back all the stopped run-unit's uncommitted transactions.

Once the deadly embrace is resolved, the environment is recovered by either of the following:

- The DBMS requires the user to reinstigate the terminated run-unit.
- The DBMS automatically attempts a run-unit restart for a predetermined number of times or periodically for a predetermined wall-clock time before permanent abort.

6.6.9 Static and Dynamic Differences

The main difference between static and dynamic relationship DBMSs, in the area of concurrent operations, again reflects on the basic nature of the DBMSs and their databases. In a dynamic environment, any operation on any data record type can co-exist with any other operation on any other data record type so each data record type is completely independent. In a static environment, the storage structure is complex, and multiple users in fact are often using the same physical file even though they are dealing with separate data record instances. Because of this complexity, queues often result to prevent destructive competitive operations.

6.6.10 Summary

In concurrent operations, it is critically important to know where (storage structure) and when (user commands) conflicting operations can occur. Each must be verified by setting up tests to stop/slow processing via nonconcurrent operations. Finally, once these slowdowns are known, and when they are projected to occur due to required database operations, such as reorganizations, security and privacy installations, procedures must be established to notify users during scheduled and emergency lockouts.

6.7 MULTIPLE DATABASE PROCESSING

Multiple database processing is the ability of a single executing copy of the DBMS to know of and to support concurrent activities against multiple databases. This facility is not present in all DBMS products. With respect to two very popular, mainframe DBMSs, however, the vendor's typical response to inquiries concerning the existence of multiple database processing is *yes*. In fact, however, a single executing copy of these DBMSs knows of only one database at a time and thus supports only multiple user activities against one database. To know of, or to support, activities against another database requires stopping the DBMS's execution, changing the O/S file names that represent the name of the database in the DBMS's job control language, and restarting the DBMS.

Other DBMSs know of multiple databases through user database attachment commands. One user could be attached to 10 databases just as easily as 10 users could be attached to one database.

Multiple database processing implies exactly what the statement says, that the DBMS has the ability to process multiple, independently defined and loaded databases--concurrently.

To know whether a DBMS handles more than one database under a single copy of the DBMS requires a clear definition of database, how to recognize when only one database *can* exist within a single copy of the DBMS, and how to recognize when multiple databases *can* exist.

A database is that set of interrelated data that contains information about its own organization (dictionary) and data record instances (data). A database may include mechanisms for fast access (indexes). Finally, some DBMSs store pre-executed interconnections (relationships) between data record instances of the same or different types. A database cannot exist without a dictionary and data. Indexes and relationships, although critical, are optional. To have one database is to have one set of these components. To have multiple databases is to have multiple sets of these components.

A database is independent of other databases operating under a DBMS central version if it can be loaded, unloaded, updated, backed up, and restored independently from any other database also operating under the control of the same executing DBMS.

To have multiple databases within the control of a single executing copy of a DBMS requires, *a priori*, the ability to execute multiple schema statements. That is, the ability to state at least as many times as there are databases operating within the control of that executing copy of the DBMS:

SCHEMA NAME IS <database name>

Whether the DBMS allows concurrent access to multiple databases from within the various interrogation languages by a single user is another matter and is discussed in Section 6.7.6

To test the existence of multiple databases:

- Start a DBMS's execution, then
- Submit a DBMS command to attach to a database and then,
- While attached, execute a command that copies that database instance to off-line storage.
- Then submit another command to attach to another database.
- While attached to that other database, another user, not operating under the control of the DBMS, uses an O/S delete file command to remove the on-line instances of the O/S files representing the database that moved to off-line storage. If that O/S delete file action causes a severity 3 or worse message, then there is only one database.

Another key indicator that a DBMS permits multiple database processing is that a database can be moved from one instance of a DBMS central version to another instance of a DBMS central version without going through the process of data record instance unload and load.

Some DBMSs can only operate one database under the control of a single executing copy of the DBMS, while other DBMSs can operate multiple databases.

6.7.1 Types of Multiple Databases

A critical database design activity is the determination of its boundaries, that is, is the database restricted to well-defined subject areas such as human resources, customers, sales and marketing, etc., or is it restricted by fiscal year, calendar year, or by corporate divisions. Whatever boundaries are chosen, they are sure to exclude someone's data.

Two popular methods of setting the boundaries are by corporate level, and by *damage control.* The common corporate levels are executive or MIS, middle management control or administration, and operations. The *damage control* principle splits the data from one very large database into multiple databases, all having exactly the same schema. Thus, if a corporation had multiple divisions, each with their own sales and marketing force, there could be either one on-line database that is all operational or all inoperable, or there might be multiple databases, one for each division so that if one division's database is not operating, the other databases remain operating.

The five aspects of multiple database processing that need to be examined are:

- The DBMS's ability to operate multiple databases within a single central version
- The impact on physical database structures
- The ability of run-units in various DBMS languages to access data from two or more databases
- The impacts caused by a DBMS's system control facilities
- The differences imposed by the DBMS's static or dynamic character

A solution to not being able to handle multiple databases is to have multiple central versions of the DBMS. Central versions themselves consume considerable overhead with respect to computer and personnel resources. Since most database applications are interactive, that means attaching the central version to a teleprocessing monitor. The fewer there are of these connections, the easier the environment is to manage.

Each class of applications could be placed under its own central version. For example, to answer the needs of an on-line order-entry system there could be four central versions. Then there could be other central versions for the other different types of applications, that is, several for testing, some for manufacturing, personnel, financial applications, and the like.

In addition to the considerable overhead of handling multiple central versions, there is also the problem of consolidated reporting. Further, the more central versions there are, the greater the tendency to drift towards application databases.

Because of all the overhead there simply is a need for multiple databases under a central version. There is also a need for programs to interact with different databases under the central version, and between databases in different central versions.

6.7.2 Rationale for Multiple Databases

Not all applications within an organization require integrated data. For example, for a manufacturing organization, the need to integrate personnel data with manufacturing quality control is limited to probably just a few reports per year, or none at all. Consequently, the manufacturing and personnel applications could exist in their own databases. If a DBMS does not allow multiple databases, then these applications have to be contained in the same database. In that situation, the backup of one is the backup of the other, and the crash and recovery of one is the crash and the recovery of the other.

If there are multiple, different logical databases, then the database's definition can be developed and revised without affecting other databases operating under the central version. In a multiple database environment, a database development group does not have to wait until a specific time to perform logical database changes to one database that do not affect other databases.

The need for multiple databases extends well beyond separating different applications. For example, if there is a nationwide order entry system, the order entry hours could well be from 8:00 A.M. AST (Atlantic Standard time (1 hour beyond Eastern)) through 8:00 P.M. Hawaii time (three hours beyond Pacific). That includes Eastern Canada through Hawaii. The total order entry time is then 19 hours. That leaves only 5 hours for consolidated batch processing, reporting, and the like. If instead of a single database, there are three databases, each one representing 8 hours or less, there can be a database for the orders for the Atlantic time through Central time zones, another for the Mountain and Pacific time zones, and one more for the remaining time zones. As the on-line aspects of one database closes, it can begin its batch processing, including creating files for end-of-day sales reports. When the last database is *closed,* its batch processing is accomplished and all the batch transaction files previously created can be used for the final end-of-day sales reports. Each database has nonoverlapped time for detailed data editing and validating, summary statistics generation, backup, and the like.

What then of consolidated processing? There are several alternatives. The first is to write a file of data that is loaded into a central database. As the last database completes its processing, this consolidated database receives its last batch of updates. It could then be interrogated and the consolidated reports produced.

If a run-unit accesses data from multiple databases, then an HLI run-unit could produce the consolidated report. If the DBMS requires a one-to-one relationship between the view and the run-unit, these views and database accesses could be accomplished through properly defined subroutines.

The third alternative, assuming that some of these order entry databases are different central versions, is to have the consolidated reporting run-unit access these different databases through their different central versions, and then perform the consolidated report.

The need for multiple databases also arises from having multiple application databases that really belong to one subject area database. For example, there might be a database for all the personnel information, another for managing projects, and a third for personnel training and development. These three probably should all be a part of a single human resources management system, but for political, economic, or traditional reasons they are not. Naturally a problem arises whenever there is a need to develop a complete profile of an employee. One way to solve this problem is to ask for a complete print-out from each database for the employee, and then manually compile the report. While this might be faster for a few employees, it's not for hundreds or thousands. What is needed is a reasonably efficient mechanism to interrelate the data from many databases into single reports. Hence the need for multiple database processing.

If this is the only need, then a case can be made to consolidate the database into one. But as soon as this is done, someone is sure to want consolidated reporting on the financial data that is kept in decentralized systems, or if the financial data is centralized, to do longitudinal reporting for specific data over several years. The point is that no organization is ever without the need for multiple database processing.

6.7.3 Critical Issues

When accomplishing multiple database processing, the critical issues are:

- Schema commonality
- DBMS versions
- Required update coordination

Under some DBMSs, multiple divisions of a corporation employ different physical databases from the same logical design to accomplish the same application. Whenever these different databases need to be combined from these multiple databases, the schemas from each must be exactly the same with respect to the commonly accessed parts. To enforce schema commonality, a single group within the corporation must develop the schema. This group could be *real*, or be a joint committee from the decentralized divisions with the committee's chair elected or from headquarters.

Great care must be exercised in examining corresponding DDL. It must be the same for at least the following clauses:

- Data record
- Data record element
- Set (if ANSI/NDL)
- Edit and validation tables
- Table lookups
- Assertions and triggers

The second area of concern is DBMS versions. If, in a distributed environment, one division is running a database under the most recent version of the DBMS and another is running a version that is a year old, then a run-unit that has to access the two databases might not work because the storage structures of the different databases might be different. Coordination between the different sites with respect to DBMS releases and the application of interim updates by the DBMS vendor should eliminate this type of problem.

In a centralized environment there is never a concern over different versions of the DBMS for current data. Rather, the concern is over the different DBMS versions that are used to save databases for previous years. For example, there might be a set of corporate statistics for data in 1984 that were backed up with the 1984 version of the DBMS, and that data, due to the storage structure changes in the DBMS versions since 1984, cannot be restored with the 1991 version of the DBMS for use with data from 1990. To remedy such a situation, these backed up databases have to be periodically restored and rebacked up every time a DBMS release is made that affects the storage structure.

The third area of concern, update coordination, is especially important. If the multiple databases are multi-level, that is operational control, middle management, and strategic or MIS, there must be great care in the planning of update cycles. Batches of updates created for the lowest level database, then summarized for the next and top levels, must all be applied at the same time. There could be daily updates for the lowest level, weekly for the middle level, and only monthly for the highest level. Weekly summaries will always appear smooth as there are only five days in each week, except for holiday weeks. However, to create monthly summaries with only whole weeks in each month, some months have to be defined as four weeks while others are five weeks. The five week months are 25 work days, while the four week months are 20 work days. Quarters are four 13 week periods, not necessarily three calendar months. If the thirteenth week of the fourth quarter is in January, then that is when the year ends rather than on December 31. In computing corporate income and expenses on a monthly, quarterly, and annual basis, the figures will always look erratic unless they are smoothed to be truly monthly, quarterly, or annual.

When updates occur to the highest level database and fail, there must be well established policies about how to deal with the updates at the lower level.

Even more critical is the situation where information from a new employee is added to several different databases at the same time. A new employee might be added to the human resources data record types in the main corporate database for personnel, benefits, and payroll, but the appropriate updates to a decentralized division human resources database might fail. Before the new employee update is considered complete, both databases must be completely updated. In short, if the update fails on one database, there better be well established policies about dealing with the updates to the other databases to avoid partial updates. The reverse is also true if an employee leaves a division, or is transferred to another division, then the appropriate transactions must be generated to update all affected databases.

6.7.4 Logical Database Impact

The majority of the issues contained in the previous section address the logical database impacts on multiple databases. If there are relationships between data record instances from data record types in the different databases, then these relationships have to be dynamically based rather than statically based. That is because static relationship instances are usually based on DBMS record addresses that could change through various adds, deletes, or modifications. While the DBMS is expected to keep all those addresses straight within one database, it cannot do that activity across multiple databases, especially if one database is varied off-line and its disk space reused.

6.7.5 Physical Database Impact

Multiple database impact on the physical database affects mainly the operational mode of the DBMS.

6.7.5.1 Storage Structure

The storage structure impact from multiple databases is restricted to multiple sets of the storage structure components. If there are five databases, there are five sets of dictionaries, indexes, relationships, and data. Some operating systems impose an upper limit of O/S files known to a run-unit, which is the executing copy of the DBMS. In such cases, if the upper limit is 255, and each storage structure component is a single file, then there could be about 60 databases known to the DBMS. That number is actually too large because the DBMS often requires scratch and sort files, etc. Subtracting 50 files for that purpose, the upper limit of databases is about 40.

A real problem arises, however, if the storage structure requires a separate file for each data record element's index and each data record type. If the average corporate database is 30 data record types, and there are two indexes per data record type, and there are 20 files set aside for the dictionary and scratch files, the number of files required for just one database is 110. That leaves room for just two databases. In short, the impact of the storage structure design is significant.

Generally, DBMSs with sophisticated storage structures operate multiple databases. Multiple database processing must be designed into the DBMS product and its database storage structures right from the start.

6.7.5.2 Access Strategy

The multiple database impact on access strategies relates to transaction separation and buffer management. Keeping transactions from multiple databases separate is merely an extension to the problem of keeping user transactions separate in a multiple threaded environment. As the number of databases, users, and threads increases, the sophistication of memory resident buffers increases. The buffer management facility must *learn* from the transactions being processed. That is, it must keep in memory the most often and most recently used DBMS records from the various storage structure components of the various databases. If the buffer management facility is not properly tuned, performance suffers. It is certainly possible that one buffer configuration is highly tuned towards one set of databases, but is improperly tuned for another set of databases.

6.7.5.3 Data Loading

Multiple database processing affects data loading only because the name of the database has to be delivered by the run-unit to the DBMS. This enables the DBMS to know which database is the target of the run-unit's activities. If multiple databases are to be loaded then the multiple databases must be opened.

6.7.5.4 Data Update

Updates to a single database are likely to be faster in a multiple database environment as the databases are smaller. Thus, fewer data record instances are processed, smaller indexes are traversed, and smaller chains of relationships are scanned to update the data record type's instance.

If an order entry application is partitioned by region, resulting in ten regional databases, then to find the order for a particular product and customer is faster due to the smaller indexes and the smaller multiple occurrence lists that need to be ANDed (list processing indexes presumed). If the databases are statically oriented, summarizing the product orders to decrement inventories and to alert the regional shipping warehouses is faster because the length of the chains is smaller.

6.7.6 Interrogation Impact

Some application programs need to access data from two or more databases, simply because there is never one database schema that addresses all the data required by all the programs. Someone's data is always split across multiple databases.

Database access is either through a host language interface or through a natural language. Assuming the access is through views, then to access multiple databases requires either that the view definition language allow a view to be defined across multiple data record types from different databases, or that the run-unit allow multiple views from different databases.

The typical scenario for HLI multiple database processing is to read data from a nonDBMS file or input screen, and then STORE that data into one or more databases. When data passes from one database to another, the sequence is to GET data from one database and STORE the data in another. Such a scenario requires the manipulation of multiple sets of cursors, one set for each database.

In the natural language environment, there are several different existing strategies. One strategy, when data is required from two different databases that have the same schema definition, is to have a database attachment command that allows the inclusion of multiple database names. This strategy is most suited to the query-update natural language.

Another strategy is to develop a command language sequence that gets data from one database, writes that data to a dynamically created database, gets data from another database and writes that data to the newly created database. When all the gets and writes are finished, the program creates consolidated reports from the newly created database. This strategy is suitable to the POL and the report writer languages as these programming languages are capable of branching, looping, etc.

6.7.7 System Control Impact

The impact from multiple database processing primarily affects:

- Audit trails
- Backup and recovery operation, including transaction rollback
- Concurrent operations
- Security and privacy

6.7.7.1 Audit Trails

The multiple database impact on audit trails centers on obtaining a complete report of the activities that may have occurred on a particular business application. A financial application may, for example, receive transactions from various sources and store them in three journals, one each for the general ledger, receivables, and payables. Once the data is considered acceptable, summaries may then be derived from the payables and receivables journals and stored in the general journal. Summary data may then be retrieved from all three journals and stored in mid-level databases for business units or product lines that support weekly and monthly reports, and finally in high-level databases that support corporate wide reports, trends analyses, and the like.

If the DBMS stores transactions to each of these journals in different databases, then a consolidated audit trail report of financial activity is difficult. To create the audit trail, each journal based program would have to write to a consolidated financial transactions journal as well as to the individual journal databases.

Difficulty in this area does not, however, eliminate the need for multiple database processing. Rather, it increases the challenge to accomplish it in an acceptable manner.

6.7.7.2 Backup and Recovery

Most backup and recovery operations are restricted to all the databases operating within a single central version. Some DBMSs record all the transactions from all the different databases onto a single centralized journal, while others record the journal transactions onto separate journals, one for each database.

The critical issue is transaction rollback and recovery after a database crashes. If one database crashes and the only transactions backed out are those recorded against the damaged database, then what happens to the recorded transactions for the database(s) that did not crash? If user transactions span databases there is a failure in overall database consistency. In these cases, very careful planning must take place to ensure that the databases remain in synchronization.

6.7.7.3 Concurrent Operations

Multiple database processing affects concurrent operations only as it relates to backup and recovery, and audit trails. To ensure that a complete set of transactions is accepted by all the databases to which they were posted, there has to be a request for exclusive control over all the involved databases, and for the exclusive control to be maintained until all the multiple database transactions are accepted and a checkpoint transaction is posted.

6.7.7.4 Security and Privacy

Security and privacy affects the operations performed, the data record elements, data record types, and relationships processed, and possibly the actual data record instances viewed. Defining security and privacy on behalf of users is no easy task. DBMSs usually take one of two approaches: single database or user profile. In the first approach, the security is defined through the establishment of passwords and authorities allowed for those passwords from the viewpoint of a particular database. Thus, for a user to perform certain activities, the user must possess the password. Anyone possessing the password has the same access. While this approach is suitable for single database environments, it is unsuitable for multiple database environments.

The second approach starts from the viewpoint of the user, not the database. From the user viewpoint, certain processes and DBMS views are allowed into the user's profile. Whatever the user has permission to use is available, otherwise it is not. Thus, if a particular natural language allows access to multiple views (one for each database) or the run-unit accesses multiple databases, then the user can perform whatever the language or run-unit accomplishes.

6.7.8 Static and Dynamic Differences

Most dynamic relationship DBMSs have very well developed multiple database processing facilities because their databases are often designed with physically separate, simple storage structures. The dynamic relationship DBMSs allow multiple database processing in a variety of interrogation languages. Some DBMSs allow the user to open a list of data record types, and if they are all the same structure, the DBMS treats them as a single database.

In a static database, however, the database's storage structure is normally more complex, so these DBMSs usually provide multiple database processing only through the host language interface, or through POL and report writers.

The ANSI NDL, an evolution of the CODASYL model, does not prohibit multiple database processing. The current ANSI/NDL defines modules that are used by various programming languages. Even though a given module is restricted to a single <schema-subschema> pair, there is no restriction on the number of different modules that a program can call.

6.7.9 Multiple Database Summary

Multiple database capabilities are needed--always. That is because multiple database processing is the method of integrating:

- Database editions that are either time or volume based
- Distributed databases that are resident at different sites/computers
- Different applications such as personnel, engineering, etc.
- Multiple database levels such as operations, middle management, or high-level MIS applications

A minimally acceptable DBMS, whether it is static or dynamic, and regardless of data model, will offer capabilities to accomplish multiple database processing in its HLI. The more sophisticated DBMSs will additionally offer access through the POL and report writer natural languages.

6.8 SECURITY and PRIVACY

Security and privacy facilities are provided by the DBMS to define boundaries of allowable access, enforce these boundaries by rejecting attempts to penetrate them, and then report on the attempts to pierce these protections.

6.8.1 Rationale

Prior to the existence of database and DBMS, only the computer programs specially designed to access data files could make sense out of the data. In essence, security existed because the data structure's definition was fundamentally a part of the computer programs and not the data files. The data files and the programs were normally kept separated, providing additional security. The data files were on tape in a tape library, and the programs were kept in card trays at the programmer's work station. Since the separation of the data's definition from the data was a drawback to the generalized use of data by many different languages, technology came to the rescue and made the data's definition part of the data, giving rise to databases. Now, that solution is the problem, because anyone who has access to a generalized language can access a database since the database contains both the data's definition and the data.

In short, database use necessitates sophisticated security and privacy, since well organized collections of corporate data are readily available through easy-to-use, rapid-access, natural languages. To protect the database, security and privacy facilities must be provided.

6.8.2 Areas of Concern

There are more than just data record instances that need to be secured. In fact, the entire database environment including the logical database, physical database, interrogation, and system control needs protection.

6.8.2.1 Logical Database

The logical database, from the DBMS point of view consists of data record clauses, data record element clauses, and relationship clauses. Establishing a database should require prior authorization. With one DBMS, establishing a database's structure was so easy that within a few month's of the DBMS's installation there were hundreds of databases established, loaded, and being used. Of these hundreds of databases, some even had something to do with the mission of the organization. The databases proliferated to such an extent that the command allowing establishment of a new database had to be removed from the DBMS to bring the situation back under control.

Once a database is established, its definition needs to be protected from unauthorized changes, a topic addressed in Section 6.8.3.2.1.

6.8.2.2 Physical Database

Within the area of physical database, there are a number components that need to be protected. These are storage structure, data loading, data update, and backup.

6.8.2.2.1 Storage Structure

The storage structure of any database must contain a dictionary and data. It may also contain indexes and relationships. Dynamic relationship DBMSs do not have explicitly declared relationships. Since these components are really all O/S files, they need to be protected from unauthorized reading, copying, updating, and deleting.

The dictionary component of a DBMS's database contains a great deal of important information. While an uninitiated person is unlikely to decode its contents, someone trying to steal a database is unlikely to be uninitiated. Contained in a single database's schema are:

- Schema clause and subclauses
- Data record type clauses and subclauses
- Data record element clauses and subclauses

- Relationship clauses and subclauses

If the DBMS supports multiple databases, and if all the dictionaries for all the databases are kept in one dictionary, then that same information is available for all the databases. If that information is decoded and changed, then all these clauses and subclauses can be changed from what is intended. For example, the edit and validation rules could be changed to permit NULL values in an audit trail data record element USER-ID-OF-PERSON-MAKING-UPDATE.

As another example, the rules for record memberships could change. A payment could be made to a person without first checking the referential integrity rule that the payment be made only when there is a valid invoice.

Indexes can provide a great deal of classified information. For example, an index for SSN could provide all the social-security-numbers. An index for SALARY could provide all the unique salary values and the multiple occurrence lists of the primary keys (possibly the SSNs) of all persons earning specific salary amounts. The SSNs could also lead directly to the data record instances.

Relationships exist independently from the data record instances in the static-segregated form. In that form, a count of relationships implies a count of data record instances, and a count of the relationships within a relationship gives the quantity of data record instances within that relationship. In this form, or in the form where the relationships are embedded in the data record instances, changes could be made directly to those relationship pointers. For example, suppose all checks must be issued against approved invoices from an owning department. If the relationship instance between the invoice and its owning department is changed such that there is no owning department for the invoice, the checks attached to that invoice would be *lost*. When a report is run that shows paid invoices for the department these lost invoices would never appear.

The final storage structure component, data, consists of the data record instances. A utility could be employed to delete specific record instances, for example, the record of a written check in a payables journal, or the audit trail transaction identifying the person making a specific update.

How can someone find out how to decode such information from the storage structure components? Simple. All DBMS vendors internally publish detailed information about the exact structure of each storage structure file. These materials are needed for normal vendor programming and testing of the DBMS. They are also needed whenever a database crashes to such an extent that the only way to repair the damage is with an O/S utility that absolutely changes specific bytes. While these manuals are normally restricted to the DBMS vendor's employees, some client organizations have managed to acquire these books, leaving open the possibility of unauthorized duplication within the client's shop.

Because of all the information that can be gleaned from the files in a DBMS's storage structure, the site's operating system needs must prevent access to these files by any system software other than the DBMS.

6.8.2.2.2 Data Loading

DBMS vendor provided data loading utilities are often designed to bypass the carefully crafted editing and validation facilities that service the needs of on-line updating. Because of these bypasses, these utilities need to be protected from unauthorized use.

6.8.2.2.3 Data Update

Update security ensures that only authorized changes are made. Thus, there is a need to prevent

- Modification to particular data record elements and to particular values
- Adding new data record element values to existing data record instances
- Inserting new data record instances
- Amending existing relationships between data record instances

Changes to data record elements and data record instances are usually made either through views or subschemas. Thus, specifically designed views and the run-units using those views must be protected from unauthorized access.

6.8.2.2.4 Backup

Backups are copies of an entire database. It is almost useless to have highly sophisticated security on database access, the O/S utilities, etc., if someone makes a backup of a database and then hand carries the tape(s) out of the data center. Restrictions must be established on who makes backups and takes tapes out of a data center.

6.8.2.3 Interrogation

Interrogation, regardless of the language, consists of two components: the view/subschema, and the executing run-unit.

The view definition process must be protected because views are the primary method of accessing databases. Strict procedures need to be in place for verifying that the person requesting a view has the proper authority to perform whatever actions the view allows. A view has a data interface, operators and navigation logic, and select clauses. Each of these three components needs to be carefully examined.

In addition to view definition, view maintenance procedures need to be carefully examined to ensure that views are modified or deleted only by those with authority. Significant havoc could occur if someone deleted all the active views. Even though it may only take about one hour to establish one view, it would then take about 25 staff weeks to restore 1000 deleted views.

Run-units are programs written in one of the DBMS's languages that use a specific view to access a database. Some DBMSs require that run-units be registered with the DBMS so that only registered run-units are allowed to execute. When run-units are registered, their view is identified. When this is done, any change to the view or the run-unit requires a reregistration process.

The data uses to be protected are reading, updating, or selections. Data reads are for output directly or indirectly through statistical operations on the data record element, such as a count of SSNs. Updates to data include changing values to NULLs, NULLs to values, or values to different values. For a static relationship DBMS, changes also include relationship operators such as CONNECT and DISCONNECT. For dynamic relationship DBMSs, relationship changes are changes to data record elements involved in referential integrity clauses, and relationship operators such as JOIN and UNION.

View instance selection is an important component of any security scheme. Selection is either for updating or retrieval. For example, there might be a request to print the list of qualified candidates for job. To select candidates on the basis of a degree in electrical engineering and years experience of at least 10, the print clause might be:

```
PRINT EMP.FIRST_NAME, EMP.LAST_NAME, EMP.SALARY,
```

and the select clause might be:

```
WHERE BACHELOR_DEGREE EQ BSEE AND START_DATE LE 01/01/81
```

If the select clause is not protected from unauthorized modification, then someone in personnel might creatively add sufficient conditions to reduce the number of candidates. For example:

```
AND MASTER_DEGREE EQ MSEE
```

6.8.2.4 System Control

System control itself must be carefully protected. The areas sensitive to misuse include

- Audit trails
- Message processing
- Backup and recovery
- Reorganization
- Concurrent operations
- Security and privacy
- SDBMS installation and maintenance

Audit trail facilities sometimes allow the audit trail to be turned off. If for a large batch update to 50% of the data record instances, the normal audit trail mode is to capture both a before and after image, there are at least three times as much updating occurring. To reduce the activity's resource consumption considerably, the following sequence is undertaken:

- Backup the database
- Turn off the audit trail facility
- Run the large update job
- Backup the database
- Turn the audit trail facility back on

If such a scenario occurs, then the ability to turn the audit trail on and off must be protected, otherwise the following might occur:

- Turn off the audit trail facility
- Wire a big funds transfer
- Turn the audit trail facility back on

This, along with some of the other security areas identified above, might cause an untraceable transaction.

Security concerns in the area of message processing are also important to consider. All sophisticated DBMSs send security violation messages to a journal file, the computer center's operator console, or the DBA's terminal. If the data file in which these messages are stored can be penetrated, and the message:

SECURITY BREACH ATTEMPTED BY <user-ID>, <date>, <time>

is changed to:

OPERATION SUCCESSFUL <user-ID>, <date>, <time>

then the attempts at security breaches might go unlogged and/or unnoticed altogether.

Database recovery and transaction rollback provides another area of concern. Suppose a user wires a funds transfer, then instigates a rollback that returns the database to the condition prior to the funds transfer, would it be easy to trace the funds transfer? The ability of a user to instigate certain kinds of rollbacks must be protected.

Reorganization is an area that needs to be specially guarded. Logical reorganization causes data record element, data record types, and relationship types and associated subclauses to be added, changed, or deleted. In a static relationship DBMS, the MANDATORY clause could be changed to OPTIONAL.

In a dynamic relationship DBMS, the referential action could be changed from SET NULL to CASCADE DELETE, which is no small change.

Physical reorganization usually locks the entire database to reclaim unused space, optimize the indexes, and resort data record instances into an efficient order. In many respects, physical database is an unload and then a load. Physical database reorganization could well take hours and hours, so its instigation should be well planned and accomplished only by those in authority.

The extent to which a mixture of run-units operate concurrently depends on the types of run-units executing, and the installation parameters established for the DBMS. If an executing DBMS has eight threads with a queue of twenty for each thread, then the operations certainly will be disrupted if the DBMS crashes and is brought back up with only two threads and five users allowed in each thread. Another way to disrupt an environment through a processing slowdown is to start a series of jobs, one in each thread that touched every data record instance.

It should go without saying that the facility by which security and privacy is established should also be very well protected. The areas to be protected are all those discussed in this section.

The final area of system control security concern is DBMS installation and maintenance. DBMS vendors usually provide computer programs to perform various installation activities like applying bug fixes, establishing threads, lengths of queues, storage structure component absolute sizes, and the number and allocation of buffers. Since all these parameters dramatically affect the operation of the DBMS, access to the programs that change these parameters needs to be carefully guarded.

6.8.3 Definition Alternatives

There are two main alternatives for the definition of security and privacy: DBMS oriented and user oriented. The DBMS orientation views the DBMS as a fortress that needs perimeters of defenses. SYSTEM 2000 illustrates one example of this, and ADABAS illustrates another. With SYSTEM 2000, each data record element has three types of security: read, write, and select. A password is assigned to a matrix of these securities for all the data record elements in the database. Figure 6.31 illustrates the types of securities applied to four data record elements. The password ABLE provides access to components 1, 2, and 4. For the EMPLOYEE_ID, the password ABLE enables reading (display) of these data record elements. However, only the EMPLOYEE_ID data record element is used for selection. No permissions are given for updating any of the four data record elements. The ADABAS orientation to security is to establish concentric rings of ever-increasing power. The outside ring allows total control over all operations. As the rings get smaller, so do the permitted options.

The second alternative, user profiles, is typified by ANSI/SQL. In its implementation, specific privileges to facilities are granted to a specific user. In ANSI/SQL, the basic security privilege commands are GRANT and REVOKE. The

COMPONENT NUMBER	PASSWORDS			
	ABLE	BAKER	CHAD	DOG
1 EMPLOYEE_ID	r.w.	ruwv	r.w.	r.wv
2 FIRST_NAME	r.w.	ruwv	r.w.	r.wv
3 MIDDLE_INITIAL	r.w.	ruwv	r.w.	r.w
4 LAST_NAME	r.w.	ruwv	r...	r.wv

r = output authority

u = update authority

w = selection for purposes of retrieval authority

v = selection for purposes of update authority

Figure 6.31 System 2000 Security Illustration

ANSI/SQL, the basic security privilege commands are GRANT and REVOKE. The ANSI/SQL combines these commands with other components--for example, the commands SELECT, INSERT, and DELETE can be authorized for users such as FORD and SMITH on tables such as EMPLOYEE and PROJECT. Tables exist as either base or derived. A base table is one that is defined to be derived from no other. Thus, a base table holds the rows of data when they are first entered into a database. A derived table, called a view, materializes as a consequence of an operation on one or more base tables. Privileges are granted on either base tables or views (derived). Since a view can contain fewer columns (data record elements) than a base table from which it is derived, the ANSI/SQL view can be used to provide column (data record element) security. On the UPDATE and INSERT commands, a column list can be contained within parentheses to narrow the set of columns affected.

Additionally, a view can have fewer rows (data record instances) than its parent base table through the use of a WHERE clause. Consequently, ANSI/SQL also provides value based security. When views and select clauses are combined with the security commands, user names, and activity commands, ANSI/SQL contains sufficient security and privacy for most situations.

ANSI/SQL additionally allows privileges to be granted. That is, a user is granted the authority to grant security privileges to others. The process can become quite entangled. It might be well to have all the privileges stored in one database and centrally administered. Examples of ANSI/SQL security are

GRANT SELECT ON TABLE *myrek* TO *public*

GRANT SELECT, UPDATE (*salary*, *tax*) ON TABLE *stats* TO *nash*

6.8.4 Trapping and Reporting Security Violations

Enforcement of security and privacy is accomplished in a variety of ways. Some facilities are under DBMS control, others are integrated into the operating system. While the latter is more secure, it implies that the DBMS must be an integral component of the hardware vendor's system software.

Whenever a security violation is detected the most secure environments immediately terminate a covered function. Some facilities let the user immediately attempt a restart, while others prohibit restart for a period of time. A most secure facility prohibits the offending run-unit from being restarted until the run-unit is *manually* revalidated.

When a violation occurs, some DBMSs log various information concerning the attempt such as the user-ID, run-unit-ID, date and time, etc. A DBA can then review reports from this security log.

6.8.5 Static and Dynamic Differences

Over the years, the approach to security and privacy has changed from one of syntax clauses contained in a data definition language or clauses providing simple shielding to a security strategy of defining, deleting, and maintaining user profiles that grant specific privileges on specific database components to specific users. Since the majority of early DBMSs were static, and the majority of recent DBMSs are dynamic, the *older* DBMSs (static) are characterized by the former approach, and the *newer* DBMSs (dynamic) are characterized by the latter approach.

6.8.6 Security and Privacy Summary

Security and privacy is very easy to require, easy to formulate, but difficult to implement--effectively. Clearly, the weak link in any DBMS security scheme is the operating system. Through the operating system, the O/S files comprising the database can often be viewed through system editors, etc. Thus, the operating system must enable the DBMS to declare these O/S files secure from any type of access, except the DBMS.

The most useful security and privacy facilities are those that enable a profile to be defined, deleted, and maintained for specific users. Even though ANSI/SQL allows delegation of the granting and revoking of privileges to others, it is clear from the various ANSI/X3H2 papers on this topic that the delegation capability has problems. It is therefore best to avoid delegating delegations to delegators who. . .

Companies must publish their security and privacy policies in company handbooks and on bulletin boards just like notices of equal employment opportunity, sex harassment, and racial discrimination. Finally, there must be a sophisticated logging capability to capture various types of information about attempted violations. Once captured, the violators must be severely punished. For employees of a company, the penalties could range from personnel review for the first attempt to dismissal for a repeated attempt. For those outside the company, civil and criminal suits must be vigorously pursued. If security and privacy policies are not recorded and enforced, then it is all a farce.

6.9 INSTALLATION and MAINTENANCE

A sophisticated DBMS vendor provides well developed procedures for the DBMS's installation and maintenance. The activities included in this area are

- Initial installation and testing
- Special version configuration
- Interfacing with the operating environment
- Maintaining DBMS versions and upgrades
- DBMS--Telecommunications Monitor Interface
- Managing DBMS bugs

To help isolate DBMS bugs, the sophisticated DBMS vendor provides well-defined procedures that users can employ to determine whether the problem is with the user's program or with the DBMS.

A final component of any DBMS installation and maintenance activity is the inclusion of well-documented mechanisms for incorporating new versions of the DBMS and for transferring a database in the DBMS's old storage structure format to a new one.

6.9.1 Initial Installation and Testing

To accomplish DBMS installation, there should be complete instructions on its installation. These instructions should include

- Procedures for validating its correct operation
- A complete suite of test programs

With these procedures and test programs, an installation team can invoke these test programs to make sure that the installation was successful.

6.9.2 Special Versions]

Since most DBMS installations are large and diverse, a set of well defined procedures for creating special versions of the DBMS that improve the efficiency of certain applications is needed. For example, dramatic changes in application performances can be achieved by manipulating

- The number of buffer pools and their sizes
- DBMS subroutine overlay configurations
- Placement of storage structure components on different computer channels and drives, etc

As might be expected, DBMS changes that dramatically benefit one application often cause degradations to other applications.

When DBMSs are installed on multiple user systems, there are occasions when a special version of the DBMS needs to be created for just one very large job. For example, if an ANSI/SQL database is being transferred from one hardware manufacturer's machine to another, for example, IBM to DEC, the loaded database and the load modules created by the operating system from the application programs are not transferable.

The source statements of the schema, the data (in an unloaded format), and the source language statements of the application programs are transferable. Once these are moved to the DEC environment, the schema has to be redefined to the DBMS resident on DEC. If the application programs are written in COBOL, then certain parts of the application programs (e.g., the environment division) have to be converted. Then, if the DBMS vendor on DEC did not provide a generalized loader program, such a program has to be written.

The alternatives to accomplish the massive data loading required for a complete database transfer include

- A job within the multiple user environment, or
- A specially created single user environment, or
- A single user DBMS load job along with others on the computer, or
- Asking that the computer be reserved for this job alone.

The first alternative does not require a special version of the DBMS. The other three alternatives require DBMS versions specially configured for just one job, with special overlays and special buffer configurations.

For the purposes of this one very large job, the single user environment is preferable as well as exclusive use of the computer. Experience has shown that arranging for the exclusive use of the computer on the weekend, or a holiday, or late into the night is well worth the effort.

Another use of special versions is to remove certain sets of load modules to absolutely prevent an activity. For example, if the modules that permit security and privacy changes are deleted from the run-time copy of the DBMS, it becomes quite difficult to change these access controls.

Whenever special versions are created, procedures are needed for their maintenance, for example, the ability to segregate these versions by different names, or differently named libraries, so that they are invoked and maintained unambiguously.

6.9.3 Operating Environment Interfaces

Once installed, DBMSs interface with existing system software. This software includes the operating system, teleprocessing monitors, various access methods, job control languages, sort and print utilities, and the like. The specifications for these interfaces should be provided in sufficient detail that the DBMS's impact is adequately understood and normal everyday operations are carried out.

Many installations consist of combinations of mainframes and PCs, along with their disks and printers. It is not uncommon for an ad hoc query to be formulated on the PC, issued to the mainframe, and the response shipped back to the PC for printing or incorporating into other PC based processes.

Since PC-mainframe connections are quite common, it is important to know how the DBMS vendor handles these connections. If these are not adequately handled, another DBMS site may have accomplished it. Thus, membership in a DBMS vendor's user group often provides answers not available from vendors.

6.9.4 DBMS Versions and Upgrades

Throughout the years, DBMS vendors have traditionally issued new releases of the DBMS. On occasion these new releases require the saving of existing databases and restoring these saved databases through the new version of the DBMS in order to change the storage structure of the loaded database. One such change might be to install the count of the instances of a multiple occurrence array (indexing) at the head of the array. Such a change might be needed by a WHERE clause optimizer.

Whenever a new release of the DBMS is issued, the amount of time required for its installation is not just the transfer of a tape to disk. It also includes whatever saving and restoring has to be done to the existing databases. This activity also has to occur to all the archived databases that were created by the DBMS version that is being replaced.

Most DBMS vendors have a policy of repairing problems that are found only in the current released version and *one* prior version. That means if a site chooses not to upgrade as new DBMS versions are released, within one or two years there will be no support from the vendor--even if the maintenance contracts are in force!

If a site retires versions of a database, say the 1977 copy of its accounting data, through a DBMS SAVE, then that retired copy will have to be marched forward whenever a new release of the DBMS is issued to guarantee that the data is still accessible in 1991.

As a final precaution, every site should have one final backup of every database, and that backup should be in source (unloaded) data form. Included in this source form should be the

- Source language versions of the schema and all views
- Data in source format, preferably in third normal form
- The source language form of an unload and a load program

With these three sources, no database is ever permanently stranded. The data should be in third normal form because that forces all the relationships to be value based. If, for example, the relationship is arbitrary, then its loaded order is manifest through a data record element that serves as a sequence number.

When the DBMS software is re-released, sometimes all the software modules are released and other times only the changed modules are re-released. Accompanying each release, comprehensive documentation should be provided that has step-by-step instructions for modifying existing special versions. After the first installation of a mainframe or mini-computer DBMS, subsequent releases should be able to be installed by customer personnel, rather than DBMS vendor personnel. These releases should be installable in less than a week once the procedures for applying a new release are understood. Greatly assisting the process of installation is the use of a program that guides the installer through the process. This is quite common on PC products. Once installed, this program can be used to change installation parameters.

Between major releases of the DBMS, the vendor often provides temporary fixes to specific problems, often called program temporary fixes (PTFs). Whenever there are interim releases of PTFs, their accompanying documentation should instruct customers which PTFs are mandatory to apply and which are optional to apply.

Vendors of the more sophisticated and complicated DBMSs often offer classes and/or seminars geared to the needs of DBMS software installers and maintainers. The vendors also issue special newsletters and bulletins.

6.9.5 TP Monitor Restrictions

Whenever a DBMS is procured, there will always be the requirement to interface with one or more telecommunication monitors. Some DBMS vendors have these monitors as part of the operating system, and other vendors, such as IBM, allow multiple choices. Each of these choices has to be examined to determine the restrictions placed on specific DBMS features and on any multiple-user operations of the DBMS. A most critical issue relating to the interface between the TP monitor and the DBMS is the recovery process. That is, does either have to be brought down during the recovery of the other?

6.9.6 Managing DBMS Bugs

Every DBMS has software errors, popularly known as bugs. As an aside, the word *bug* is thought to have originated when one of the earliest computers (late 1940s) stopped working because a wasp got trapped in one of the electro-mechanical gates.

Included in the installed DBMS environment should be a series of vendor supplied test databases that are used to help isolate a bug. With this suite of databases, a member of the DBA staff should be able to duplicate the problem and then report it to the vendor.

A list of known problems should be provided with every release of the DBMS. These problems should be explained so they are understandable to the DBA staff, not just the DBMS vendor staff.

Whenever a bug is isolated at the client site, it should be centrally registered, and called into the vendor along with whatever information is required by the vendor. The vendor should then assign the bug an identification number to track its analysis and resolution.

It is important to keep sufficient information about each bug so that when new releases of the DBMS are received, the DBA staff can determine whether the bugs have been fixed.

6.9.7 Installation and Maintenance Summary

The installation and maintenance procedures for a DBMS only seem to get noticed when they are not working well, or when they are used too often because there are a large number of bugs that never get fixed.

It is important to know how to create special versions of the DBMS to achieve specialized performances, accomplish one-time jobs, and exclude unwanted features.

As new releases of the DBMS are issued it is very important to know how long it will really take to install because the DBMS's installation might require saving and restoring all the existing and archived databases, not just copying the load modules to disk.

Finally, since DBMS vendors typically only service the current release and one previous release, it is important to keep current on the DBMS releases because vendor service might only be forthcoming after several weeks to a month of backing-up, installing, and restoring databases.

6.10 APPLICATION OPTIMIZATION

Application optimization is the process of analyzing the operational characteristics of

- Databases
- Computer hardware support
- Systems software support
- The applications software

These analyses enable design modifications that can achieve:

- Performance enhancements
- Greater user satisfaction
- Improved corporate command and control

These performance improvements are achieved a number of different ways.

6.10.1 Logical Database Analysis

The logical database component of a database application is the database's design. There are a number of different areas to review when attempting performance improvements, for example:

- Adding derived data
- Denormalizing database designs
- Centralization versus decentralization
- Data record element specification

6.10.1.1 Derived Data

The initial design of a database should not have any derived data, and its data record types should all be in at least third normal form. This type of design contains the minimum amount of data, and has the most simple strategy for updating. Figure 6.32 illustrates the design of a database for a very large corporation that tracked product sales and competitor penetration within a specific product set. Within this design there are five main categories of data:

- Corporate headquarters
- Marketing headquarters
- Field unit
- National account
- Account

Within each main data category there is identification and address information, and for the national account and account data record types there are subordinate descriptive information. For NATIONAL ACCOUNT, there are:

- Discount Plans
- Key contacts

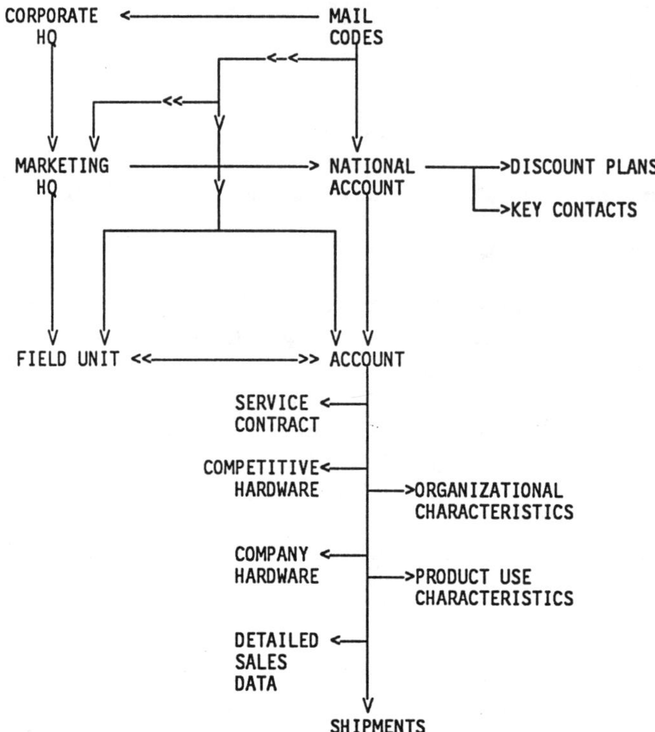

Figure 6.32 Sales and Marketing Database Design--Initial Design

Within the ACCOUNT there are:

- Service contracts
- Competitive hardware
- Company hardware
- Organizational characteristics
- Product use characteristics
- Detailed sales data
- Shipments

A MAIL CODES data record type was created to both standardize and centralize the type of mailings that each of the five main data record types is to receive. Each of the main data record types had a mail code that indicated which set of the mailings were to be received.

This design enabled the organization to know all the competitive hardware for a particular national organization by reviewing the competitive hardware for each of its members (accounts). The organization could know how each of its products is doing in sales by processing all the detailed sales data for each of the accounts. Finally, the organization could track the sales performance of its field units (regions, districts, and representatives) through the relationship between the field units and the accounts.

However, when the number of data record accesses were counted for reports that were more than listings of data record instances by account, the counts went into the millions. The creation of a third normal form database design caused retrieval efficiency to be sacrificed in the name of data nonredundancy and update efficiency. But since the database application was report intensive rather than update intensive, the trade-off was judged not acceptable.

The database design progressed through different redesign scenarios to achieve the maximum retrieval efficiency while still maintaining an acceptable level of update efficiency.

When the first scenario was completed, the redesign looked like the one in

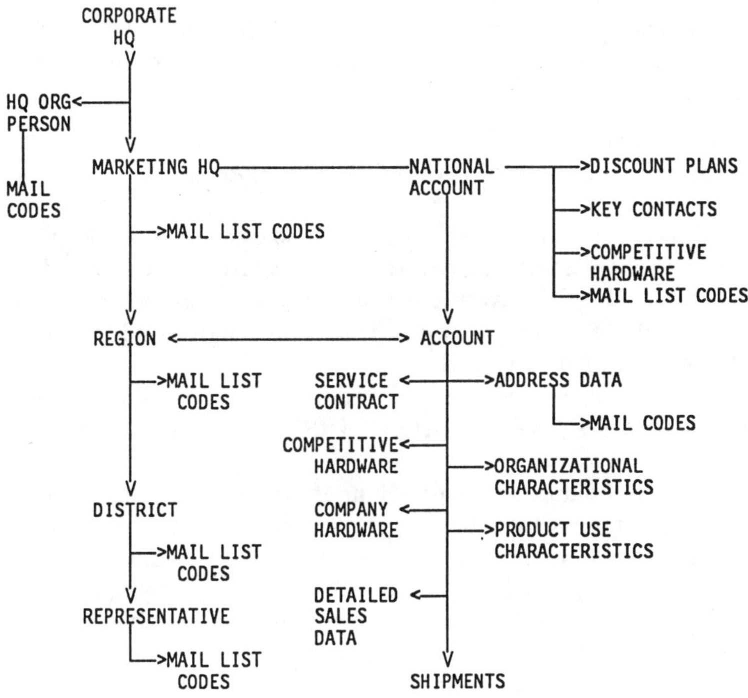

Figure 6.33 Sales and Marketing Database Design--Second Design

Figure 6.33. This redesign achieved a number of changes:

- Recognizing that FIELD UNIT is actually the nest of data record types: REGION, DISTRICT, and REPRESENTATIVE. This break out was done partially because the types of information kept at each node were different, and also because the periodicity of the data is different.
- Installing the data record type COMPETITIVE HARDWARE within NATIONAL ACCOUNT.
- Installing the ADDRESS data record type and relating it to ACCOUNT.
- Installing HQ ORGANIZATION PERSON and relating it to the CORPORATE HQ data record type.
- Installing MAIL CODES at each node. Multiple sets of mail codes were needed because each node needed to receive different types of materials.

These changes achieved two different benefits:

- Queries were created more simply as the data record type dealt with only one topic. As originally designed, only a sophisticated language could be used.
- The number of data record instances involved in each data record type was less as the data record types were partitioned.

These changes established new data record types and also expanded the scope of the data update programs from a few data record types to a larger number of data record types. The first set of derived data was from a summary set of COMPETITIVE HARDWARE information from the individual account COMPETITIVE HARDWARE data record type.

These changes did not, however address the millions of data record instances needed to be accessed to track sales by REGIONS, DISTRICTS, representatives, or by product.

The second major set of database design changes involved the creation of a SUMMARY STATISTICS matrix, which is composed entirely of derived data. These changes are in Figure 6.34, and are used to store a set of data about the sales data across a number of years. Included in this data are yearly, quarterly, and monthly sales by product for sixty months. Since there is a variable number of products, the data record instance is based on product, with the time periods as the columns. The number of columns is 85; that is, 60 for the months, 20 for the quarters, and 5 for the years. The data for these statistics data record types initially entered the database as new data record instances for the DETAILED SALES DATA. After this data is entered, it is sorted different ways, totaled, and appropriately entered in the various SUMMARY STATISTICS data record types. The benefit of these changes is that sales progress on a product by product basis

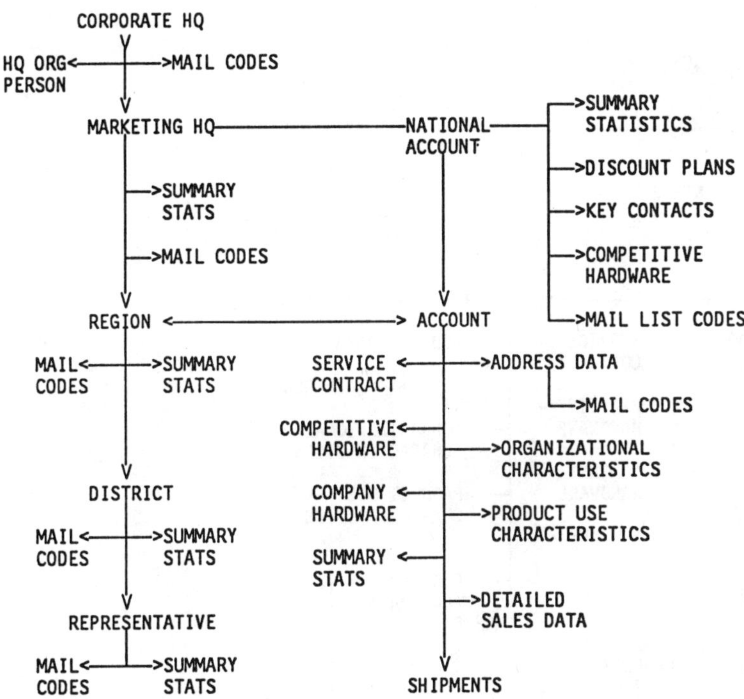

Figure 6.34 Sales and Marketing Database Design--Third Design

can be viewed within a relevant context. That is, within MARKETING HQ, REGION, DISTRICT, or REPRESENTATIVE, etc. Not addressed with this change, however, is the ability to track the progress of a particular product--directly. With the second set of changes, product sales performance tracking became possible, but only within the context of an ACCOUNT or REPRESENTATIVE.

The third design change specifically addressed the ability to track product sales performance. The database's design was required to view the description of data from three different vantage points:

- Account and national account
- Marketing organization
- Product organization

The first two view points are certainly handled by the database design presented in Figure 6.34. What is missing is the recognition of the existence of a third set of *clients* for the database: product developers. The first two clients, marketing and account managers, were handled but the third was forgotten. Serving the needs

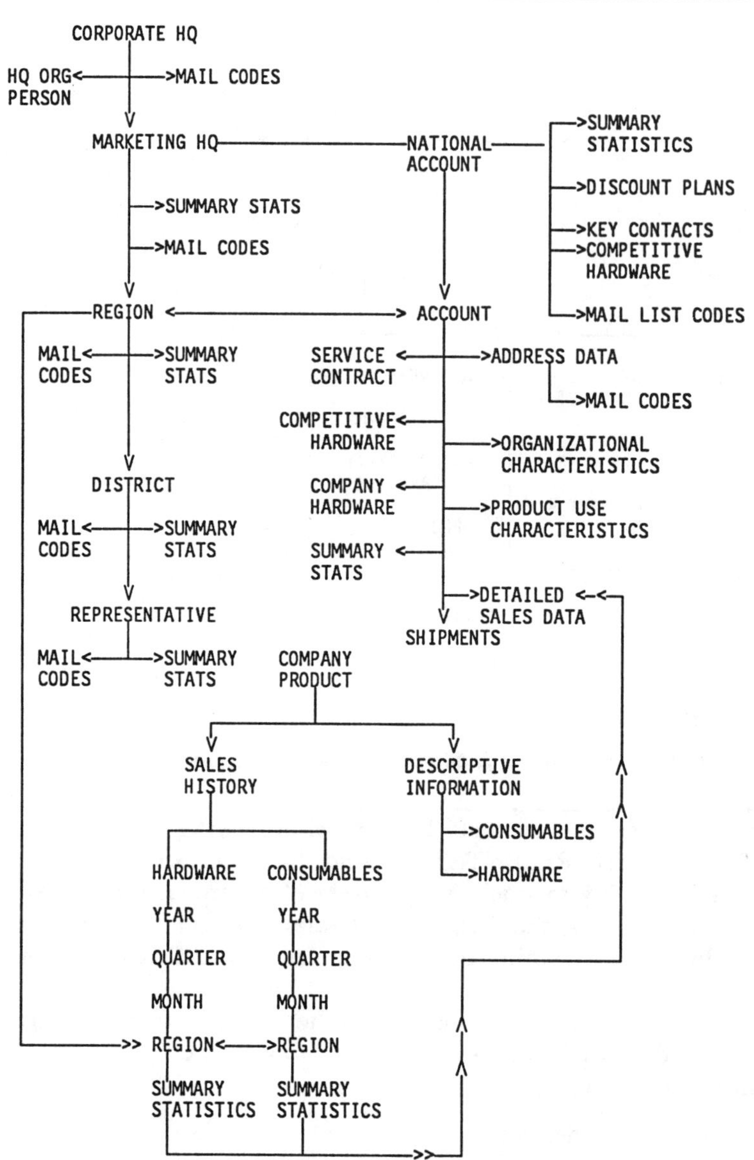

Figure 6.35 Sales and Marketing Database Design--Final Design

of this third client required an analysis of its retrieval needs, and the incorporation of the appropriate set of data record types. In the analysis of the clients, it became obvious that product is divided into hardware and consumables, and that these two sets of products had to be tracked independently. The set of data record types in

Figure 6.35 was created within the tree structure: COMPANY PRODUCT. In large measure, all the data contained in this tree is derived as it came from the DETAILED SALES DATA from the prior month.

These three sets of changes to the initial database design solved the majority of the retrieval problems. Managers, product, and market researchers were able to use natural languages efficiently to obtain the majority of the data needed for reports. These solutions were not free, however. The costs were of two types: data redundancy and increased update time. The amount of storage doubled. The updating time increased to the extent that the results of one month's sales were not available until the end of the second week in the following month. Previously, this data (Figure 6.34) was available at the end of the first week after the end of the month.

In summary, whenever a database application is designed and implemented, certain of its functions are apt to run slower than others. Most often, if the database is designed in third normal form, updating has benefitted at the expense of reporting. Bringing a balance between updating and reporting usually requires some level of database redesign of the kind described above.

There are other ways of tuning a database application. That requires a detailed understanding of the DBMS, the database, and the application.

Some DBMSs have special sets of utilities to produce statistics about the performance of their own operations. Included are input/output (I/O) counts, central processing unit (CPU) seconds, overlay swaps, structure navigation, etc. The purpose of these utilities is to learn how the DBMS reacts to a specific application configuration. This information can then be used to optimize the application code that processes the database, the design of the database, and the use of the DBMS.

Assessing the need for database application optimization requires that the DBMS have utilities to assess the performance of the database so as to identify bottlenecks, inefficient file structures, access methods selected, and database usage patterns.

Once a bottleneck is found, it is important that the DBMS be able to assess performance impacts on current applications resulting from proposed database revisions or on changes in application workloads.

6.10.1.2 Denormalization

Normalization is the process of designing data record type structures that are the most simple. Except for a redundancy of keys, when a database structure is third normal form, the updating process is minimized. There are additional benefits derived from fourth and fifth normal forms, but they are not addressed here. However, when third normal form structures are used for various types of reporting, the number of accesses are maximized. For example, in an order entry application an invoice data record type is likely have the following data record elements for each line item:

- Product item number

- Product weight
- Product unit price
- Product quantity ordered
- Extended price
- Extended weight

If this information is placed in an invoice line item data record type then its primary key is a combination of these three additional data record elements

- Customer number
- Order date
- Order number within date

If there were 10,000 orders each day and an average of three invoice line items per invoice, then the 120,000 accesses needed to create the invoices are:

- One access to obtain the product information for each product
- One to write the product, product and prices information for each invoice line item
- One to write the before image for recovery
- One to write the after image for recovery

There are also 30,000 accesses to obtain the invoice information to generate the invoices. For this application there are about 150,000 accesses. If the organization wanted to reduce the number of accesses, it might discover, through analysis that there has never been an invoice with more than 8 invoice line items. If the invoice line item were redesigned to include:

- Customer number
- Order date
- Order number within date
- Quantity of invoice line items ordered
- Product item number-1
- Product weight-1
- Product unit price-1
- Product quantity ordered-1
- Extended price-1

- Extended weight-1
- Product item number-2
- Product weight-2
- Product unit price-2
- Product quantity ordered-2
- Extended price-2
- Extended weight-2

through to

- Product item number-8
- Product weight-8
- Product unit price-8
- Product quantity ordered-8
- Extended price-8
- Extended weight-8

Then the number of invoices is greatly reduced. The total number of accesses is 60,000, as follows:

- An average of three accesses to obtain the product information for each product
- One access to write the product, product and prices information for each invoice
- One access to write the before image for recovery
- One access to write the after image for recovery

The number of accesses to print the invoices is an additional 10,000, bringing down the total number of accesses to 70,000 rather than 150,000.

This redesign process achieves significant performance improvements, but at the cost of denormalization. Because of the denormalization process the following problems arise:

- Reduced ability to use natural languages for simple queries and reports
- Having to add an additional invoice when there are orders having more than eight invoice order items

- The cost of having space for eight order items for each order when there is--on average--only three
- The additional programming logic that has to be installed to process a specific invoice line item

In short, the saved 80,000 accesses are not without cost. All the problems listed above have to be identified, enumerated, and analyzed to determine the real savings. If after the analysis there is still a net savings, then denormalization is beneficial to the organization.

6.10.1.3 Centralization Versus Decentralization

One of the largest factors in database application failure is the quest to build THE database. It is far better to design and build a database that has a too narrow scope than one that cannot ever be successful. In database, success is principally achieved through consensus and compromise. As the scope enlarges, the probability of consensus decreases. There are too many conflicts in the critical policies required for database success. Thus, it is better to restrict a database's scope to a well bounded area of corporate policy, for example, product engineering within one class of product lines. To attempt a single database across very different product lines is to court failure.

In the example contained at the beginning of this section, the product manager user was ignored in the drafting of the original database design. Until the needed reports were analyzed, the required changes in database design were not uncovered. The database project methodology must clearly identify all the relevant users, and capture their information needs in a comprehensive and correct manner.

6.10.1.4 Data Record Element Specification

Data record element specification is often over done. Database principles must apply to database application specification and building. That is, each fact must be defined only once.

A good example of over specification is telephone number. While there might be a home telephone number, an office telephone number, and a mobile telephone number, must all three be defined, or should telephone number be defined only once and then employed whenever relevant? There needs to be only one definition, not three. However, there are three data record elements: HOME TELEPHONE NUMBER, OFFICE TELEPHONE NUMBER, and MOBILE TELEPHONE NUMBER.

However, when data record elements have different semantics, they are different data record elements and their definitions must reflect those differences. For example, *order date, shipping date, invoice date,* and *payment due date* are really four different data record elements, each requiring a very precise definition because corporate policy behind each is different and the difference is critical to database applications.

Finally, data record element names should not be bounded by any artificial restrictions such as 10 characters, etc. Rather, they should be sufficient to convey to all knowledgeable users the same meaning.

6.10.1.5 Relationships

Relationships among sets of data record instances are methods of accessing specific sets faster than serial searching. In a dynamic relationship DBMS, relationships are implemented through indexes and are always value based. In static relationship DBMSs, relationships are value based or arbitrary, and are implemented through DBMS generated relationship mechanisms.

Establishing a relationship should occur only after a cost benefit analysis. To determine whether a relationship is cost effective, its creation and maintenance costs must be balanced against the savings derived from its use. The savings are the differences between the cost of finding a set of data record instances using a serial search versus using the relationship. The total savings are the savings for one use of the relationship multiplied by the frequency of its use. When the savings exceed the cost of creation and maintenance then the relationship is cost effective.

When there are too few relationships, performance improvements are achieved by creating new relationships. While the load and update program costs rise, the cost of retrievals, and the cost to find data record instances for the purpose of updating, lessen by a greater amount. Users of the update programs will have to be alerted that these programs take longer to execute.

Incorporating new relationships in the database does not automatically cause them to be used. In static relationship DBMSs, the language clauses within views that take advantage of relationships have to be changed. For example, if there is a serial search programmed into the view, that search language has to be changed to retrieve the data record instances according to the mechanisms provided by the relationship instances. In dynamic relationship DBMSs, the view has to be changed to select data record instances according to just one indexed data record element rather than having that data record element contained in a list of data record elements in the WHERE clause.

When there are too many relationships, that is, when the cost of creation and maintenance exceeds the access cost savings, then the relationship mechanisms have to be removed. In the case of static relationships, the programs that AUTOMATICally insert data record instances into relationships will not have to be changed because the operation is DBMS controlled and AUTOMATIC. If the mechanism is MANUAL, then the update programs have to be changed, otherwise the program logic will fail because the relationship mechanism is not present. All the retrieval views will have to be changed because they will attempt to use a facility that has been removed. In its place, serial search mechanisms have to be installed.

For dynamic relationship DBMSs that employ indexes, update programs do not have to be changed as indexes are usually automatically updated with every data record instance update. The views from the retrieval programs have to be changed to install the specially required logic to find the data record instances without the aid of the relationship.

When the relationships are too transitive, the volume of accesses can be too high. For example, to find a particular type of customer within a particular territory within a particular district within a particular region requires the following sequence of processing:

- Process the relationship region to find the particular region
- Process the various districts within the region to find the particular district
- Process the various territories within the district to find the particular territory
- Process the various customers within the territory to find the particular type of customer

If that processing occurs often, the relationships are said to be too transitive. All those relationship instances have to be processed to find the particular customer belonging to the required customer type. Rather, make the relationship more direct by placing all the customers of a certain type within a relationship of customer types.

As shown in Chapter 4, the mechanism of relationship processing differs widely between static and dynamic relationship DBMSs. In general, static relationship DBMSs process relationships much faster than do dynamic relationship DBMSs. Because of that significant performance difference, it should always be an alternative to consider changing DBMSs when all other performance improvement measures have been exhausted.

When an application is *young,* its design is more likely to change than when an application is *mature.* Dynamic relationship DBMSs enable relationship type changes much more easily and quickly than do static relationship DBMSs. Thus, it is almost always much *safer* to implement a database application with a dynamic relationship DBMS than with a static relationship DBMS. As the application matures, the quantity of relationship changes between and among data record types lessens, and so does the need to make these changes. When the application quiesces with respect to relationship type changes, the benefits of having a dynamic relationship DBMS disappear. Reimplementing the application with a static relationship DBMS at that time makes sense as the application will almost always run faster.

6.10.1.6 Model Transformation

Whenever a database is initially designed, it should be in third normal form. Once designed, it can be implemented relationally, or with an ILF or a network data model DBMS, and possibly even a hierarchical data model DBMS. Under relational all the relationships must be dynamic. With ILF, hierarchical, and network, some of the relationships are static and others dynamic. As the number of static relationships increases, the flexibility for relationship specification decreases. But, as the number of static relationships increases the performance associated with relationship processing increases. A database is transformed too much when it is both *specified* and *implemented* relationally even though the dynamic relationship benefits available--inherently--by the relational data model are not required by the application. Rather, what is required is implementation through one of the other three data models to accomplish performance requirements. A database that is under transformed is one that is specified relationally but is implemented through a static relationship data model DBMS in spite of needing the relationship specification and change benefit.

An important component of transformation is the ability to represent multiple third normal form data record types within one complex data record type. For example, in a personnel application there might be an EMPLOYEE data record type that has a series of subordinate data record types for

- Telephone numbers
- Skills and abilities
- Degrees, institutions, and dates
- Sick and annual leave transactions

If its third normal design is implemented relationally then the four sets of data subordinate to EMPLOYEE have to be implemented as four different data record types. In contrast, if the DBMS supports complex data record types then these four types of data can be implemented as one multiple valued data record element and three different repeating groups. Assuming that the candidate DBMS allows this data to be acceptably accessed through the natural languages (POL, query, and report writer) then it becomes difficult not to justify the use of complex data record types in this case. Complex data record types typically provide many of the static relationship DBMS benefits with the flexibility of dynamic relationships across different data record types.

The current ANSI/SQL language (SQL/86 or SQL/92) cannot, however, comprehend complex data record types. To overcome this, the DBMS vendor has to provide mapping between two dimensional tables and these more complex structures. Such a capability could be provided through the use of views where the user perceives a two dimensional table, and the SQL view language maps the view to an underlying set of base tables, where one base table is the apex of a set of tables, and the nested repeating groups are represented as underlying joins.

If only a relational DBMS is available then the database's design becomes overly fractured. To bring the database design back into an understandable scheme, denormalization might be the only solution. That is less preferable, however, than to change to an ILF data model DBMS that allows complex data record types.

6.10.1.7 Views

Views have one main value: they shield the application program from having to know the data model of the DBMS. If the view allows inclusion of the WHERE clause in the view's definition, the view facility additionally allows for a set of security that is not normally available from many DBMSs.

Views are defined at either extreme, one view for all, or a view for each. To retain complete control over the user-database interface, there should be a one-to-one relationship between the view and its run-units, and between the run-units and its users. In such a situation the database administrator, who presumably is the one who defines the views, could well become a bottleneck. Thousands of views might have to be created, maintained, and administered in a short amount of time.

The other extreme is to have one or a few views serve all the different users, run-units and applications. That alternative is undesirable because there is too little accountability and security.

A preferred approach is to allow decentralization in the authority to define views, and to allow wherever possible the users' inclusion of their own WHERE clauses. These WHERE clauses are in addition to those in the nested view logic that serve the needs of value based security. Without the ability to include WHERE clauses in the run units, the number of views grows with no real justification.

6.10.2 Physical Database Analysis

Database application performance can be improved without having to change the design of the application. The changes that are accomplished address the database's

- Storage structure
- Data loading
- Data updating
- Database maintenance

6.10.2.1 Storage Structure

Changes in the database's storage structure can affect its

- Dictionary

- Indexes
- Relationships
- Data

6.10.2.1.1 Dictionary

The dictionary typically contains the compiled schema, views, and other dictionary oriented information such as edit tables. Some DBMSs allow multiple schemas--one at a time--to control the operation of a given database. Performance improvements are achieved if different schemas are allowed to operate for different--exclusive use--jobs. For example, if a large volume of data is to be loaded, the presence of an extensive set of editing and validation rules exercised by the DBMS will consume significant computer time when compared to the same job without those rules. To have fast, large volume data loads requires external data editing and validation.

If the DBMS has an option to have multiple schemas, great care should be exercised in their use lest an uncontrolled schema remain operational after the data loading job is completed and the on-line access job queues have been reopened.

Alternative view constructions are also a source of performance improvements. The ANSI/SQL language provides several different techniques for accomplishing the same task. If each of these different techniques is encoded in the select statement contained in a view, then the different views are likely to perform differently.

6.10.2.1.2 Index Design

If a DBMS's DBA can choose among different index construction techniques, then an application might benefit from an alternative index design. For example, if the primary key data record element is solely for the purposes of unique access, then an index construction that enables both unique access and range searching is of marginal value. A hierarchical index construction for the unique value portion serves no purpose. It is better to switch to a hash/random unique value portion.

If an application's analysis shows that four secondary indexes are always used in combination to find a unique data record instance, then combining those values for the development of a candidate key (unique values guaranteed) certainly enhances performance. This change, however, requires changes in the views servicing the application programs.

An analysis of applications might show that many data record instances are being serially searched even though an index is used. An index cost benefit analysis should be performed to determine whether installation of another index is appropriate. This change also requires changes to the views servicing the application programs.

6.10.2.1.3 Relationships

The only relationships that can be changed without affecting run-units are the relationships that are stored as separated pointers. The only changes possible in this would be to change the relationship file's blocking factor or physical device location.

Other types of relationship changes such as reducing the length of chains by introducing intermediate data record types all require database design and application program changes.

6.10.2.1.4 Data

There are a number of changes that affect the data record instances. These changes include:

- Choosing fixed or variable formats
- Choosing fixed or variable length data record instances
- Clustering logically related data onto the same DBMS record instance
- Changing the blocking factors on the O/S files that store the data record instances

6.10.2.2 Access Strategy

Access strategy changes include many areas. Changes to the use of the dictionary, indexes, relationships, and data all affect the actual access strategy that is employed. The following are but a few of the access strategy changes that affect performance.

- If a schema data record type is assigned to different DBMS-required O/S files, there might be a difference in the locking mechanisms that can be installed.
- If multiple schema data record types are assigned to the same DBMS-required O/S file, then data record instances from different data record types are clustered to reduce the I/Os for certain retrievals.
- If a DBMS-required O/S file is assigned to only one memory buffer, then conflicts in the use of that memory buffer can be prevented.
- If a DBMS-required O/S file is assigned to multiple memory buffers, then the DBMS records from these files can occupy more of the buffers than is otherwise possible, increasing the application's performance.
- If the instances from a schema data record type are stored on different channels, there can be overlapping I/Os, thus increasing performance.

6.10.2.3 Data Loading

Changes in data loading affect performance. If an edit and validation intensive, large database load is in progress, all on-line programs will certainly suffer. Performance improvements are realized if those data loading efforts are isolated to just the night hours, or by keeping the on-line queues locked out during these loads so that already validated data is speed-loaded without the slowing effects of editing and validation.

If the DBMS supports an option that allows index adjustment at the end of a job rather than at the end of each transaction, performance can be greatly improved if all index maintenance is performed after all data record instances are loaded, rather than after each data record instance is loaded.

6.10.2.4 Data Updates

When a database is initially loaded, its organization is probably optimal. As updates occur, new data record instances are added, deleted, and modified, causing adjustments to the database's dictionary, indexes, relationships, and data. In short, the database's physical organization becomes different from its logical organization. As this difference increases, performance decreases, leading to a needed database reorganization.

A set of standard updates can be created and run periodically so that the degradation in the database's performance is tracked. At the point where the cost of degraded performance over a period of time exceeds the cost of reorganization, then it is time to reorganize.

6.10.2.5 Database Maintenance

Database backups are a integral cost of data processing. If there has not been a crash of a database environment for a long period of time, it is tempting to reduce the frequency of backups. A better approach is to vary the time between backups to reflect the immediate need for recovery. If during the month there are only ad hoc updates then maybe the backups could be every week or two. But towards the end of the month there may be a large number of updates reflecting end of month processing. During that critical period several backups might have to be performed in order to keep the recovery costs in line.

6.10.3 Interrogation

Natural languages offer an allure that is hard to resist: quick development and maintenance. This benefit is not without cost. If an entire organization develops hundreds to thousands of these natural language based run-units and if this language executes interpretively, then the overall performance of database applications will degrade rapidly in contrast to the same set of application run-units developed through a compiler language.

Natural languages are ideally suited for application run-units that have a short life span, or for components of an application that are not yet fixed in design.

For those applications that have a long life span it is an ideal strategy to develop these run-units with a natural language to take advantage of the quick development and easy maintenance, and then translate them to a compiler based language over time when the program design changes become lessened.

The cost of a run-unit consists of four parts:

- Cost of design
- Cost of development
- Cost of operation
- Cost of maintenance

Natural languages can dramatically affect the second and fourth components. As an application's life-span becomes longer the effect of the cost of development and maintenance becomes less in comparison to the cost of operation.

The cost of operation for an individual run-unit is basically the cost of a single execution times the frequency of execution. The cost of execution includes a number of factors, including:

- Data selection clauses
- Navigation logic
- Update effects on indexed data record elements
- The modification of relationships binding data record instances

Each of these four factors should be examined individually and then in combinations. For example, there are often a number of different ways to conform a select clause that employs different types of relationship logic while achieving the same effect. All the computed performances, however, will be different depending on the quantity of indexed data record elements.

The DBA group within each organization should maintain test databases that are of different sizes and designs. These databases can be used to test different combinations of select clauses, index combinations, and navigation logic.

6.10.4 System Control

System control performance assessment and improvements generally revolve around using or not using a particular facility.

6.10.4.1 Audit Trails

Audit trails identify the types of transactions that are captured. To improve a DBMS's performance only the update requests should be journaled. While such a change will improve performance, lost will be knowledge of when and for whom reporting is accomplished. Performance can be improved also by disabling journaling during a large data loading program. If the job fails then the job would be rerun from a database backup. That benefit would require that the database be exclusively used by the large data loading program.

6.10.4.2 Backup and Recovery

Backup and recovery costs can be affected by changing the method employed. If backups are performed only once every two weeks and if only after images are kept, then the recovery preparation cost allocated to the individual update transaction is lower than if the backup is twice a week and both before and after transaction images are captured. The cost of recovery, however, is much greater in the first scenario than in the second. If the number of update transactions is low, then the overall cost of the first scenario might be lower, all factors considered. The goal is to determine the most cost effective risk scenario.

6.10.4.3 Reorganization

Reorganization can dramatically affect overall database performances. If an index is badly disorganized the cost of reorganization is many times overshadowed by the savings realized in interrogation. The data record instances organization is affected through continued updates. If the access strategy is hash/random, and the distribution of the data record instances is by primary key value, the overall performance can fall dramatically as the volume of adds and deletes increases. If charts are carefully plotted, the DBA group can usually predict when database reorganizations should be performed. A sophisticated DBMS should have utilities to assist in determining the most opportune time to perform physical database reorganization.

6.10.4.4 Security and Privacy

Security and privacy is an important application optimization issue. Passwords should be centrally administered and changed on a regular basis.

While there is probably not a direct link between database efficiency and the quantity of passwords, there is likely to be real organizational efficiency in keeping these passwords well organized and centrally administered.

6.10.4.5 Multiple Database Processing

Multiple database processing generally provides faster access to the users of multiple, smaller databases than to the same users of a combined database. The three costs of multiple database processing are:

- The cost of the cross processing itself
- The cost of multiple database locks when a single logical update affects multiple databases
- The cost of maintaining more than one copy of some data

If these costs exceed the savings received by the users then the databases should be combined.

6.10.4.6 Concurrent Operations

The specification of the level of concurrency can affect database application costs. Locks are typically on the following levels:

- Data record instance (sometimes called row locking)
- DBMS record instance
- Data record type (that is, all its data record instances)
- O/S file
- Database

The cost of concurrency is examined with two cases. The first is the update whose select clause finds just one data record instance to change. The second is the update that finds thousands of data record instances to change.

If concurrency is maintained at the data record instance level, then for the first case, only one lock has to be posted. Under the second case, several thousand locks have to be posted.

If locking is at the DBMS record instance level, then in the first case, while only one lock is posted, data record instances from one or more data record types are locked. Under the second case, if there are 10 data record instances per DBMS record then possibly 10 times fewer locks have to be posted.

If locking is at the O/S file level, then in the first case only one lock has to be posted. Under the second case only one lock has to be posted, assuming all the data record instances are stored in the same O/S file.

If locking level is at the database level, then in either case only one lock has to be posted.

In all the cases, if the data record type includes indexed data record elements, then locks have to be posted on the index storage structure components as well.

Posting is only one part of the cost of concurrent operations. When the next update request arrives, the data record instances required by the second request have to be identified and all their locks attempted. If any of the locks from the first request conflict with the second set of locks then a decision has to be made whether to reject the second transaction, hold it in the queue, or partially process it. The effort to determine whether there are conflicts is easiest at the database and O/S level, and increasingly expensive as the number of locks to examine increases. The cost of examining locks increases as the number of update transactions grows and as the granularity of the locks becomes finer (DBMS record, data record type, or data record instance).

Careful tests have to be constructed to determine the costs (lock processing overhead) of concurrent operations as contrasted to the benefits (concurrent processing). These tests will produce different results depending upon the DBMS, the database, and the types of concurrent operations desired. When all these tests are performed, the tradeoff analysis can begin. For some databases and applications the most cost effective locking level might be the data record instance, while for other applications the locking level might be the DBMS record or even the O/S file.

6.10.4.7 DBMS Installation and Maintenance

Applications can be optimized by manipulating the configuration of the DBMS itself. The following are keys to DBMS performance:

- Whether the DBMS operates heavily overlaid, or flat
- Whether the DBMS's transactions receive appropriate priorities within the teleprocessing queues
- Whether there are sufficient numbers of appropriately sized buffers
- Whether the number, size and blocking factors of the various work files can be affected

6.10.5 Static and Dynamic Differences

As relational DBMSs attempt larger and more sophisticated production applications, their storage structures are becoming more complicated. Complicated storage structures are a fact of life for almost all the static relationship DBMSs, and many of the ILF data model dynamic relationship DBMSs.

The benefits of sophisticated and complicated storage structures are the performance improvements they bring to large database applications. However, these performance improvements typically require full time attention to database design, application configuration, and DBMS tuning. Many issues of database journals present articles that discuss tuning.

There used to be a great difference between static and dynamic relationship DBMSs in the area of application optimization. For static relationship DBMSs, tuning is a way of life for several professionals. For dynamic relationship DBMSs, the process is simple: there were no options. Now the options for tuning within dynamic relationship DBMSs are increasing dramatically, and that is supposed to represent progress.

6.10.6 Application Optimization Summary

If a database is designed in third normal form and there is only one user connected to an infinite size computer of blinding speed, there is no need for application optimization. Since the converse is true with respect to computer sizes and speed, tuning is a necessary fact of life. Accomplishing application optimization with the least disruption to existing applications is preferred. The following is a suggested sequence for attacking application optimization:

- Review and change the facilities that only affect the configuration of the DBMS.
- Review and change the database's storage structures for reblocking.
- Review and change the various system control facilities.
- Review and change the indexes, relationships, etc. and incorporate those changes into views.
- Review and change the database design through derived data and/or denormalization.

6.11 SYSTEM CONTROL STATIC AND DYNAMIC DIFFERENCES

The main difference between static and dynamic relationship DBMSs in the area of system control (see Figure 6.1) relates to the domain of the effects of the system control facilities. In a dynamic relationship DBMS, the domain is usually the data record type, while in a static environment, the domain is usually many interrelated data record types.

Since most system control operations affect a single database, a dynamic logical data record type reorganization is possible without physically affecting other data record types. In a static database environment, a logical data record type reorganization is likely to require the entire database operation to stop until the reorganization is completed.

In short, the principal difference between static and dynamic system control is the span of the various system control operations. The functions most affected by the difference are audit trails, backup and recovery, reorganization, and multiple database processing.

For example, if there is an operating system failure during the time an on-line, multi-user update DBMS environment is operating, a database recovery event recovers all databases that are active under a particular copy multi-user DBMS. In a static environment, all the data record types in all the active databases are recovered.

In a dynamic environment, the recovery might neither be as effective nor as complete as the static environment. For example, suppose all data record types are backed up over a weekend, and updates occurred on Monday and Tuesday to some dynamic data record types. On Wednesday, these updated data record types were removed from the on-line environment. A failure happens on Thursday. If the removed data record types are not on-line, then the Monday recovery cannot occur against those off-line data record types. In such a case, the DBMS has to issue a message indicating that the data record types are missing from the on-line environment, and until they are brought on-line, the recovery cannot be completed.

6.12 SYSTEM CONTROL SUMMARY

Even though the areas of system control have been presented separately, they almost always interact. For example, application optimization tests might indicate that the application is slowing. In response, physical database reorganization may be invoked to bring the database back into optimum condition. To accomplish database reorganization, the concurrent operations capability of EXCLUSIVE USE must be invoked. If the security and privacy facility permits user profiles with specification of database operational verbs, then only the DBA should be allowed to activate the REORGANIZE verb.

With respect to effects on database application design, system control is probably the second most critical DBMS function. The first is static or dynamic relationships. Because of the DBMS differences in system control capabilities, an in depth assessment of each DBMS and each application must be accomplished to determine the difference between DBMS capability and application need. If the match is good, then the amount of extra database application programming to overcome DBMS capability short-falls is small. Otherwise, it is large. Remember the risks of not having system control, which restated are:

- Not having audit trails means that there is no accountability for database updates, reports, and other types of use.
- Not having sophisticated message processing will not stop errors. Rather users will become frustrated, and stop using the system.
- Not having backup and recovery results in total database loss as important update transactions are lost and critical databases are not recoverable after crashes.
- Not having reorganization ultimately causes the database to become antiquated and *freeze-up*. This is due to structural inefficiencies or because the database does not contain the right data record elements, relationships, and data record types.
- Not having security and privacy enables valuable corporate data to be stolen.
- Not having multiple database processing causes a redundancy of facts, which in turn causes errors through time, and an eventual break down in the usefulness of database projects.

- Not having concurrent operations capabilities and guidelines will--at some time--prevent the generation of an extremely important report because of some trivial, but database locking, operation.
- Not having database application optimization causes the expenditures for hardware to increase as a consequence of unimproved database designs, inefficient physical structures, and inappropriate DBMS configurations.
- Not having good installation and maintenance procedures eventually causes special software libraries to be lost, different versions of modules to be linked together, and databases to be lost due to corruptions caused by misconnected DBMS modules.

Although time consuming and seemingly nonproductive, the only thing more expensive than good system control is not having system control.

Appendix A Keys and BNF Notation Definition

1. Key Type Symbol Detailed Description

PRIMARY--PK(subn)

One or more data record elements that compose a single unique logical key for record/row identification.

CANDIDATE--CKn(subn)

One or more data record elements that compose a single unique logical key for record/row identification that, for a particular design reason, was not designated the primary key.

SECONDARY--SKn(subn)

One or more data record elements that compose a secondary logical key (duplicates allowed), for purposes of selecting one or more record(s)/row(s).

FOREIGN--FUn(subn)

One or more data record elements that uniquely compose a UNIQUE logical key that directly relates to an existing primary key.

FOREIGN--FNn(subn)

One or more data record elements that nonuniquely compose a non-unique logical key that directly relates to an existing primary key.

Notes:

1. "n" represents a sequence number that allows differentiation between multiple keys.

2. "(subn)" represents a subscript to order parts of keys when a key is composed of more than one data record element.

Examples of Key Legend

DATA RECORD NAME : JOB TABLE

DRE NAME	DATA TYPE/LENGTH	KEY SPECIFICATION
JOB ID	PIC 9(04)	PK
JOB DESCRIPTION	PIC X(30)	SK1,SK2(2)
JOB SALARY START	PIC 9(05)	SK2(1)
JOB SALARY END	PIC 9(05)	

DATA RECORD NAME : EMPLOYEE TABLE

DRE NAME	DATA TYPE/LENGTH	KEY SPECIFICATION
EMPLOYEE ID	PIC 9(04)	PK
EMPLOYEE SOC SEC NO	PIC 9(09)	CK1
EMPLOYEE JOB ID	PIC 9(04)	FN1
EMPLOYEE NAME	PIC X(30)	

Notes:
======

1. JOB ID is the primary key.
2. JOB DESCRIPTION is the "first" secondary key, and is the second component of the "second" secondary key.
3. JOB SALARY START is the first component of the "second" secondary key.
4. EMPLOYEE ID is the primary key.
5. EMPLOYEE SOC SEC NO is the first (and only) candidate key.
6. EMPLOYEE JOB ID is the first (and only) nonunique foreign key.

2. BNF NOTATION

The syntactic notation employed in this book is used in the American National Standard for SQL. The notation is an extended version of BNF ("Backus Normal Form" or "Backus Naur Form"). In BNF, each syntactic element of the language is defined by means of a "production rule". This defines the element in terms of a formula consisting of the characters, character strings, and syntactic elements that can be used to form an instance of it.

The version of BNF used in this standard makes use of the following symbols:

<u>Symbol</u> <u>Meaning</u>

< > Angle brackets delimit character strings that are the names of syntactic elements, the non-terminal symbols of the SQL language.

::= The definition operator. This is used in a production rule to separate the element defined by the rule from its definition. The element being defined appears to the left of the operator and the formula that defines the element appears to the right.

[ ] Square brackets indicate optional elements in a formula. The portion of the formula within the brackets may be explicitly specified or may be omitted.

{ } Braces group elements in a formula. The portion of the formula within the braces must be explicitly specified.

| The alternative operator. The vertical bar indicates that the portion of the formula following the bar is an alternative to the portion preceding the bar. If the vertical bar occurs at a position where it is not enclosed in braces or square brackets, it specifies a complete alternative for the element defined by the production rule. If the vertical bar occurs in a portion of a formula enclosed in braces or square brackets, it specifies alternatives for the contents of the innermost pair of such braces or brackets.

. . . The ellipsis indicates that the preceding element of a formula may be repeated. If the ellipsis occurs immediately after a portion of a formula enclosed in braces, the repetition is of the whole of the formula enclosed within those braces.

-- Introduces normal English text. This is used when the definition of a syntactic element is not expressed in BNF.

Notes

Spaces and line breaks are ignored. Apart from those symbols to which special functions were ascribed above, other characters and character strings in a formula stand for themselves. In addition, if the symbols to the right of the definition operator in a production consist entirely of BNF symbols, then those symbols stand for themselves and do not take on their special meaning.

Pairs of braces and square brackets may be nested to any depth, and the alternative operator may appear at any depth within such a nest.

A character string that forms an instance of any syntactic element may be generated from the BNF definition of that syntactic element by application of the following steps:

1) Select any one option from those defined in the right hand side of a production rule for the element, and replace the element by this option.

2) Replace each ellipsis by zero or more additional instances of the object to which the ellipsis applies.

3) For each portion of the string enclosed in square brackets, either delete the brackets and their contents or change the brackets to braces.

4) For each portion of the string enclosed in braces, apply steps (1) through (5) to the substring between the braces, then remove the braces.

5) Apply steps (1) through (5) to any non-terminal syntactic element (i.e. name enclosed in angle brackets) that remains in the string.

The expansion or production is complete when no further nonterminal symbols remain in the character string.

Appendix B: Glossary

This glossary is intended to provide more than just brief definitions. Provided are detailed explanations, and where possible, synonyms are not defined, but reference a single term and definition.

4GL: Fourth Generation Language--A broad class of computer languages that are simpler, easier to use that third generation languages such as COBOL or FORTRAN. The capabilities of a typical 4GL are most like those of the natural language type: procedure oriented language.

Abnormal termination: An unplanned cessation of processing such that user control is not returned to the processor that was being utilized at the time the error occurred.

Access control: See security schema

Access method: A technique used to obtain data from or to place data onto a mass storage device; usually this refers to operating system software capability provided by mainframe manufacturers.

Access path: See view

Access strategy: The access strategy of the DBMS is that set of DBMS routines that analyze storage structure constructs to determine the access path in the database to find, retrieve, store, or modify any of the data contained in any of the storage structure components under the control of the DBMS. The access strategy typically involves DBMS vendor software and O/S vendor access methods.

After image recovery: See backup and recovery

Aggregate: See data element

Alias: An alternate identifier for a name (data element, data record, etc). Typically employed in different programming languages to avoid naming illegalities. For example, CODE-NAME is legal in COBOL, but means CODE minus NAME in FORTRAN. Consequently, an alias, CODNAM, would be required.

ANSI: American National Standards Institute. An organization of technical committees that standardizes many areas including data and information processing (committee X3). The following committees within X3 deal with database: SPARC, X3H2, and X3H4.

ANSI/SPARC, Standards Planning And Requirements Committee, determines whether standards are required, and recommends to X3 that projects be created, or abolished. The committee also resolves inconsistencies or problems between standards.

ANSI/X3H2 currently has four projects: Network, SQL (relational), and SQL2 (a significant extension to SQL), and distributed database protocol. The network (NDL) data model was accepted by ANSI as a standard in 1986.

The SQL data model was accepted by ANSI as a standard in 1986. It standardized the most commonly available SQL capabilities so that the maximum number of vendors can claim conformance.

SQL2 (Extended) is intended to incorporate additional relational features that could not be included in the first version of the standard. It is expected to be technically complete during 1991.

ANSI/X3H4 is the data dictionary committee. It has drafted a proposed American standard IRDS that is to serve as a specification for data dictionary systems for use with DBMSs and other data. The IRDS specification became an ANSI standard in 1988.

ANSI NDL: See NDL data model

ANSI SQL: See SQL data model

Application database: An organized collection of data designed to support only a specific application.

Application optimization: Those DBMS facilities for determining the overall performance characteristics of an installed database against a set of benchmark database operations. The DBMS application optimization facilities produce statistics that indicate such performance indicators as I/Os, CPU time, overlay processing, and the like.

Archival database: See backup.

Area: A CODASYL concept to identify a collection of data record instances. A particular data record instance is assigned to a single area and may not migrate between areas. For all CODASYL DBMSs, an area may contain occurrences from one or more record types. For some CODASYL DBMSs a record type may have instances stored in more than one area. In other CODASYL DBMSs all the instances from a record type may be restricted to just one area. In CODASYL DBMSs the relationship between an area and an O/S file varies. Because of these great differences in the AREA concept, the ANSI NDL does not contain a specification for AREA.

Atomic: An attribute of a data element indicating that it was not derived from within the system.

Attribute: See data element

Attribute name: See data element name

Audit trail: An audit trail is a log of all database activity in a format such that the audit trail data record instances are reportable through the various interrogation languages of the DBMS.

Authorization identifier: A character string that designates a set of privilege descriptors.

Automatic backout: Automatic backout is the process by which all updates performed within non-successfully completed transactions are automatically removed without outside intervention.

Automatic restart: The automatic restart is a process by which any inconsistency in the database caused by the partial execution of an update command during a previous session is resolved, typically through automatic backouts.

B-tree: A storage structure and access strategy for use in a storage structure that maintains its order by continually dividing the possible choices into two equal parts and re-establishing links (pointers) to the respective parts but not allowing more than two levels of difference to exist concurrently.

Backup: A database backup is a copy of the database. Database backup is also called a "save", or archival database. The database backup contains all the information necessary to transport a database from one computer site to another. A database is restored to operational status by recopying the database backup onto mass storage. A database backup is normally not accomplished through a database record unload, unless that is the only process that is available to accomplish a backup. Normally, the backup is instigated through a DBMS command or utility.

Backup and recovery: Backup has been described above. The converse to backup is a database restore. Restore is a process through which the backup of the database is copied from backup media onto mass storage to make it immediately usable by DBMS run-units. Normally, the restore is instigated through a DBMS command or utility.

Recovery is the process of either repairing damage caused to the database by a DBMS or computer failure, or the process of removing a specific update that was posted to the database by a run-unit.

There are two broad classes of recovery: database and transaction. Database recovery affects all current users of the database through after image recovery or before image recovery. Transaction rollback only affects the updates posted by a single user.

A quiet point is a state in which no update transactions are being processed against the database. The quiet point in a database, then, is a state of internal database consistency that is employed in after-image recovery, before-image recovery, or transaction rollback.

After-image recovery is the process of restoring a backup of the database and then applying the after-images of database records (that result from updates) to the restored backup until the most recent quiet point. This type of recovery is also called forward recovery because it moves an "old" copy of the database "forward in time."

Before-image recovery is the process of replacing current database records with their before-images until a quiet point is reached. This type of recovery is also called backward recovery because it moves the most "current" version of the database "back in time."

Transaction rollback is the process of removing the update transactions that have been made against the database on behalf of one user. Transaction rollback is typically started by the initiator of the transaction. The actual transaction rollback process is similar to before-image recovery, except that only one user's transactions are removed from the database rather than all user's transactions.

<u>Backus Naur form (BNF)</u>: A metalanguage used to specify or describe the syntax of a language in which each symbol, by itself, represents a set of strings of symbols. Synonymous with Backus normal form.

<u>Backward recovery</u>: See backup and recovery

<u>Base relation</u>: A relation that is not completely derivable (independent of time) from other relations in a relational database.

<u>Before image recovery</u>: See backup and recovery

<u>Benchmark test</u>: A test that uses a representative set of programs, procedures and data designed to evaluate the performance of the DBMS over a range of configurations.

<u>Blocking factor</u>: The blocking factor is the ratio between data record instances and DBMS record instance sizes. For example, if a DBMS record instance size is 20,000 bytes, and every data record instance is 200 bytes, then the blocking factor is 100.

The effective blocking factor is the actually experienced ratio between needed data record instances contained in one DBMS record instance. For example, while the blocking factor may be 100, if through a sequential search (see sequential search), the data record instances are found only 10 to the DBMS record instance, then the effective blocking factor is 10, not 100.

Buffer flush: A process in which all database DBMS record instances that are in memory and that have been updated are written out to the database (that is typically on disk).

CALC: See hash

Candidate key: See key

Cardinality: The quantity of rows (tuples) in a table (relation).

Central version: An instance of an executing DBMS that allows multiple user access to one or more databases. See also concurrent operations.

Chain: A linked list of data record instances that may be physically dispersed. Each link, representing a data record instance, typically contains a next data record instance pointer, a prior data record instance pointer, and an owner data record instance pointer.

Character: A letter, digit, punctuation mark, or other symbol. Each character is uniquely represented in the computer by a series of bits (1's & 0's). Patterns of 3-bit groups are represented by octal numbers. Patterns of 4-bit groups are represented by hexadecimal numbers.

Character fill: The process of inserting, as often as necessary into a storage medium, the representation of a specified character (normally a blank) that does not itself convey data. A character fill process displaces any other data already present.

Check clauses: There are three types of check clauses: data element, data record, and DML operation. See data element check clause, data record check clause, or DML check clause.

Checkpoint: In non-database processing, a checkpoint is a snapshot of all data and processes then currently active, such that in the event of a failure, processing can recommence once the snapshot is restored. In database processing, a checkpoint is a special transaction placed on the journal file that indicates that once a database is restored to that transaction, the database is consistent.

CODASYL model: A form of the network database model that was originally defined by the Database Task Group (DBTG) of the COnference of DAta SYstem Language (CODASYL) organization. Development of the CODASYL Model was stopped in 1980. The CODASYL model, after significant simplification, has been standardized by the technical committee of ANSI, X3H2.

See also the NDL data model

Collating sequence: A specified ordering sequence based on values, that is, numeric (1, 2, etc.), alphabetic (a, b, c, etc.), and special (!, ", #, etc.). Typically the concern is whether numbers sort higher or lower than letters, and where the special characters fall in the sort sequence: high, low, or where?

Column: A vertical set of data values from a relational table that are all from the same domain, and that are referred to by a common name. A column, by definition, is single valued. For example, BIRTHDATE, SALARY, or EMPLOYEE NUMBER. A column exists in the same role as a data record element. See also data element.

Command: The order or trigger for an action or permissible action to take place.

Commit: A process through which changes to a database are flushed from all memory buffers and placed within the appropriate database storage structure components such that these data can no longer be cancelled or rolled back, except as a whole by a later special command to undo the entire group.

Competitive updating: See concurrent operations

Complex data record type: See data record type

Component: A separate subordinate unit of a more complex facility.

Compression: The process of removing trailing blanks from alphanumeric fields and leading zeros from numeric field.

Computer program: See program

Concatenate: To link or connect two strings of characters, generally for the purpose of using them as a single value.

Concatenated key: Two or more data elements used together as a single key.

Conceptual schema: A term popularized by the ANSI/SPARC architecture. From SIGMOD Record (Volume 15 No 1, March, 1986), the conceptual schema "serves as an information model of the enterprise which the database is to serve, and as a control point for further database development. Information of interest to the enterprise is described in terms of relevant entities, their properties, and their interrelationships, together with various integrity, security, and other constraints." Typically, the data representing the conceptual schema is stored in the data dictionary/directory system.

Concurrent operations: Concurrent operations within a DBMS permit multiple run-units to operate against a single database--at the same time--in a manner that preserves consistency and integrity.

The following definitions apply to the different classes of concurrent operations within a DBMS environment.

> A single database DBMS is one that permits commands to access only the single database that is then under its control.
>
> A multiple database DBMS is one that permits commands to access different databases that are under the control of the single instance of the DBMS.
>
> A multi-user DBMS is one that can process commands from multiple run units.
>
> A single-threaded DBMS is a multi-user DBMS that can execute only one command at a time and cannot service another command until the processing is finished for the first command.
>
> A multi-threaded DBMS is a multi-user DBMS that can concurrently execute the multiple commands from the multiple run-units against a database.
>
> A multiple database processing DBMS is one that can concurrently access multiple databases during a single executing instance of a run-unit.
>
> A single-threaded, multiple-database DBMS is one that can execute only one command at a time while serving multiple users against multiple databases.
>
> A multi-threaded, multiple database DBMS is one that can concurrently execute multiple commands from multiple run-units against multiple databases.

Consistency: A database state in which there are no partially completed updates, nor are there any partially complete updates to any component of a database's storage structure.

Contention: A condition in which a user attempts to access a row of a table or data record instance that has already been locked by another user. Contention may be at the row/record instance level, or higher, that is, at the DBMS record instance level or even at the database level, depending upon the capabilities or options of the DBMS. If the lock is at a high level, more users are locked out. However, the locking process is simpler to manage. It the lock is at a lower level, fewer users are locked out. However, the locking process is very complicated to manage.

Cursor: An indicator that designates a current position relative to the ordering of the rows in a table for relational DBMSs or records from an independent logical file DBMS data record type. For hierarchical data model DBMSs, the cursor designates the current position relative to the ordering of each data record instance within the accessed hierarchical record structure. For ANSI NDL data model DBMSs, the cursor designates the current data record type, data record instance, and position within the set of data record instances that are "current" to the run unit.

Data (storage structure component): The data component of the storage structure contains data record instances. The complexity of the data storage component ranges from one O/S file for each record type to one O/S file for all the occurrences of all the record types.

Whenever the DBMS allows flexibility of storing more than one data record type's instances per O/S file, or storing just a subset of one or more of a data record type's instances per O/S file, the concept of an AREA is needed. An AREA is a definitional construct that indicates which data record instances (of one or more types) are stored in the same O/S file.

Data administration: An organization within a company that is charged with the definition, organization, management and control of data, not with its processing.

Data administrator: Data administration group head.

Data aggregate: See data element

Data analysis: The study of the definition and characteristics of data, and the relationships between distinct categories/classes of data. The emphasis is on data structure, not data flow.

Data definition: The process of creating the data definition language.

Data definition language (DDL, data description language): A DBMS processable language consisting of statements that provide the syntax of any one of the four schemas, that is logical schema, physical schema, views, and security schema.

Data dictionary/directory system (DD/DS): See IRDS

Data element: A distinct unit of data that represents values. A data element may be single valued, multiple valued (vector), multiple dimensional, group, or repeating group.

All the values from multiple valued and multiple dimensional data elements are of the dame data type. A data type denotes a specialized class of data values for a data element. The DBMS typically enforces the rules implied by the specialized class. For example, the double precision data type would automatically exclude alphabetic values.

If all the data values for the data element are defined to be the same length, then the data element is fixed length. If values are allowed to be different lengths, then the data elements are variable length.

If the data element is allowed to contain subordinate data elements, it is called a group. Each data element within the group may have a different data type.

If a group is multi-valued, it is called a repeating group. A multi-valued data element and a single or multi-valued group also known as data aggregate. Each data model allows only certain types of data elements.

A DBMS may reserve the definition of some of the more physical characteristics of a element, such a length and type, to the physical schema, leaving to the logical definition only the definition of the element name and a general type clause such as character and numeric.

<u>Data element check</u>: Data element check clauses restrict data characteristics such as length, type (numeric or character), editing and validation rules, and the like. The three types of check clauses are type, null, valid/invalid values. Once these clause are installed, only conforming data values are accepted by the DBMS for database loading/update.

A DBMS may reserve the definition of some of the more physical characteristics of a data element, such a length, type, and check clauses to the physical schema, leaving to the logical definition only the definition of the data element name and a general type clause such as character and numeric.

<u>Data element domain</u>: A collection of data from one data element. All the data has the same data type and fits within a prespecified range of values.

<u>Data element length</u>: A measure of length (size) of an element usually expressed in units of characters, words, or bytes.

<u>Data element name</u>: The name identifying a data element; e.g., "Date of birth," "Country of Citizenship," or "Age of Employee (years)."

<u>Data element type</u>: See data element

<u>Data file</u>: A data file is an instance of data used in a procedural manner to arrive at some result or conclusion. Data files can either be manual or automated. If automated they can be controlled by DBMSs or by defined strategies contained in

a computer program. A data file could be a computer system for testing DIRs, programs, modules, for training, and the like.

Data flow: A named representation of data that is passed between processes.

Data flow diagram: A graphic depicting processes and data flows.

Data independence: Data independence is a measure of the independence among the logical database, the physical database, and the application program. Changes in either the logical or physical database that do not relate to the program's record selection or processing should not require the program to change. Changes in the physical storage structure of a database should not require changes to the logical database. Changes to the logical database should only affect those areas of the physical database, and those programs directly affected by the program.

Data integrity: The data quality that exists as long as accidental or malicious destruction, alteration, or loss of data does not occur. Data quality implies that the data is correct, timely, accurate, complete, relevant, and accessible for the uses for which it was intended.

Data integrity model: The graphical and analytical representation of data and its policy through entity relationship diagrams, objects, elements, data integrity rules, and the like. A logical (rather than physical) picture of data. Normally, the logical database design is developed by data administration and is the foundation for the physical database designed by database administration. A logical database design is independent of the hardware of software incorporated in the DBMS.

The components of the data integrity model are described in the Whitemarsh database project documentation. Balancing the data integrity model is the data transformation model. Together, they form the business model, also know as the information model.

Data integrity rules (DIRs): A data integrity rule is a statement that must test true when no database updating is taking place. A data integrity rule may relate to data elements within the same or different data record types. A data integrity rule may also state a condition that must be true in a data record instance before an action can take place, for example, all data elements must be valued before the data record is accepted into the database.

A data integrity rule, acting as a referential integrity rule, can dictate the action after a certain class of update is attempted. The two referential integrity actions are: [CASCADE] DELETE and SET NULL (or SET DEFAULT). By implication if the conditions do not exist that permit either of those two actions to occur, then the initial action (ADD, DELETE, or MODIFY) is itself rejected. The types of match that are examined are: MATCH ALL or MATCH NONE.

While referential integrity is explicitly defined in ANSI/NDL and the ANSI/SQL, it also exists implicitly in varying forms in other data models.

ANSI/NDL referential integrity exists through the use of the INSERTION and RETENTION clauses in the schema set clauses that are specified on behalf of a member data record type.

ANSI/SQL referential integrity exists through the specification of the REFERENCES clause within the definition of a "child" table. The clause identifies a data record element (column) within the "child" data record (table) that is referred to as a "foreign key," and a data record (table) name and data record element (column) name of another data record (table) that is acting as the "parent" of the referential action. If no parent data record's data record element is specified, then its primary key is the default specification.

Data item: See data element

Data manipulation language (DML): The DBMS recognized syntactic representations of commands that access data within a database. The commands are broadly divided into three categories: record, relationship, and combination.

The record commands include: FIND, GET, STORE, and DELETE. The relationship commands for static relationships include GET OWNER, GET NEXT, GET MEMBER, CONNECT (a record to a relationship), and DISCONNECT (a record from a relationship). The relationship commands for dynamic relationships include PROJECT, DIVIDE, JOIN, etc. Combination commands include FETCH (FIND and GET), or MODIFY (FIND, GET, change, STORE).

Data record: See data record

Data record element: A data record element is a data element that has been allocated to a data record. The data record element may have a different or more localized name than the name of the data element. Further, the data record element may have a more restrictive set of editing and validation rules than the data element. When a data record element is simple (single valued) it can act as a relational column. See also data element.

Data record type: A data record type is a collection of assigned data elements that has a name and description. Among the assigned data elements there is typically a primary key data element; none, one, or more candidate keys; none, one or more foreign keys; and none, one or more secondary keys; and none, one, or more non key data elements. A data element that has been assigned to a data record is called a data record element. A data record is derived from the merger of objects and the data elements appropriate for representation through the object's property classes.

The data that represents a specific instance of all the elements is called a data record instance.

When the set of data elements that are assigned to belong to the data record are in third normal form, the data record instances are called simple data record instances. A relational table is thus a simple data record. And a relational table's row is a simple data record instance.

If multiple valued and multiple dimensioned data elements, group elements, or repeating group elements are assigned, then the data record is not in third normal form, and is called a complex data record. The relational data model cannot support complex data record types.

A data record in which all record instances are of the same length within DBMS record instances is called a fixed length data record. A data record in which the record instances are allowed to be different lengths within DBMS record instances are called variable length data record instances.

A data record check clause is a collection of data integrity rules that must test "true" before a data record instance is allowed into the database. Typical data record check clauses require that all the data elements within a record must be valued, or that duplicate records are not allowed.

Data resource management: See data administration

Data security: See security schema

Data storage description language (DMCL or DSDL): See physical schema

Data structure: An organized collection of record types. See data model.

Data type: See data element

Data view: See view

Data volatility: The rate of change of the data element values stored within a data record instance, or the rate of change of data record instance adds and deletes.

Database: A collection of interrelated data stored according to a schema. The data is stored such that it is independent of programs that use it. A database must contain information about its own organization and structure (dictionary), and of course, data record instances. A database may optionally include mechanisms for fast access, that is, indexes. Finally, some DBMS store pre-executed relationships between data record instances of the same or different types.

A database is able to be accessed by a DBMS, that is, loaded, unloaded, updated, backed up, and restored independently from those same activities that may be occurring to another database operating under the control of the same executing DBMS. See also physical database.

Database administrator (DBA): A person or persons given the responsibility for the definition, organization, protection and efficiency of databases for an organization.

Database key (DBKEY): A DBMS created mechanism used by the DBMS's access strategy to access a data record instance.

Database machine: A special purpose computer that provides data access and management through total control of the access method, physical storage, and data organization.

Database management system (DBMS): A database management system provides facilities in four areas: logical, physical, interrogation, and system control.

The logical database component enables the definition of data structures with a data definition language (DDL) according to the capabilities of the DBMS's data model.

The physical database component enables the definition of the physical structures (dictionary, indexes, relationships, and data) according to the scheme set down by a data storage definition language (DSDL). The physical database also encompasses the processes of data loading, update, and database maintenance (backup).

The interrogation component includes two main types of data access languages: host and natural. The host languages provide DML verbs that allow data access through COBOL, FORTRAN, etc.

The natural languages are of three varieties: procedure oriented (like BASIC), query-update (single sentence oriented), and report writers (control breaks, subtotals, etc.).

Natural languages are also called Fourth Generation Languages (4GL). The 4GL term is imprecise since there is no specification for this language such as exists for the ANSI/SQL, or ANSI/NDL. Further, the term 4GL is misleading as some natural languages were created prior to the Third Generation Languages (COBOL!).

The system control component includes facilities for backup and recovery, security and privacy, concurrent operations and the like. See also system control.

Database recovery: See backup and recovery

Database update: The process of adding, deleting, or changing data in the database. If the updates affect data elements that are supported by indexes, or other storage structure components, these are normally automatically adjusted by the DBMS.

DBMS data model: A logical (rather than physical) representation of the data record instances, AND the relationships explicitly definable between/among data record instances, AND the operations allowed on these data record instances and relationships. The data record structures allowed are either simple or complex. The relationships are defined under relationships below. The operations are cited under DML above.

The four data models are: network, hierarchical, independent logical file, and relational. Both network and hierarchical data models support static relationships. Both the independent logical file and relational data model support dynamic relationships. The network and independent logical file data models support complex record structures. The hierarchical and relational data models support simple data record structures.

DBMS record: A record instance that contains values of an index, pointers (owner, next, prior), or other storage structure components. When the DBMS record instance represents the storage of data record instances, it may contain less than one, one, or more than one data record instance from one or more than one data record types.

DBMS schema: See logical schema

DBMS subschema: See view

Deadly embrace: The state or condition that prevails when each of two or more application programs attempts to exclusively lock data record instances already exclusively locked by the other application program or programs. The attempted lock may also be at the DBMS record instance, area instance, file instance, or database instance level.

A deadly embrace is often resolved by stopping one of the run-units, rolling back all the run-unit's transactions that have already been performed, and then attempting a run-unit restart a predetermined number of times before permanent abort, or attempting a run-unit restart periodically for a predetermined wall-clock time before permanent abort.

Degree (of a relation): The number of data elements (columns) in a table (relation).

Delimiter: A flag that separates and organizes items of data. Also called punctuation symbol, or separator.

Derived data: Data elements that are drawn from the values of other data elements. For example, TOTAL-ORDER-COST could be computed from SUM (LINE-ITEM-COST + SHIPPING-COST + TAXES).

Determinant: A data element that is used singly or in combination with other data elements to uniquely select data record instances from a data record type. If only one data element is needed for the determinant, then it is a primary key. If multiple elements are needed, then the determinant is a part of a primary key.

Device media control language (DMCL): See physical schema

Dictionary (storage structure component): The dictionary component of the DBMS storage structure contains the compiled schema, all defined subschemas, and whatever other components that the DBMS vendor deems necessary to provide knowledge about the database's internal or external organization. That component of a database's storage structure that stores the database's names, integrity rules, pictures, etc. This storage structure component may reside in one or more O/S files, or may reside in the DBMS's integrated DD/DS.

Distributed database: A database that is physically distributed such that different processors control separate partitions of database data.

Division: An operation that partitions a relation, based on the contents of another relation.

DML operation checks: Records are added, deleted, and modified. For each such operation, there may be certain checks that should be done. The DML (ADD, DELETE, MODIFY) operations allow these checks to be defined and activated.

Document: This identifies the name of an external document that is retained as a more refined description of some aspect of the database system. This may relate to detailed diagrams, flow charts, detailed explanation of formulas, and the like.

DOS: Disk operating system

Dynamic backout: See automatic backout

Element: See data element

Embedded pointer: A DBMS relationship mechanism that is stored within the data record instance that points to another record. This pointer is usually available only to the DBMS.

Encode/decode tables: A table of codes and values employed to explain data that is contained in the database. For example, D.C. means District of Columbia.

End-user: A person, at any organizational level, whose occupation requires the use of a computer, but does not require knowledge of computers or programming.

Entity: An entity is a unit of data considered important by an analyst. In the Whitemarsh database project methodology, an entity is not intended to be well defined or precise. Rather, an entity instance (COMPANY, SALARY, CONTRACT, EMPLOYEE EDUCATION) merely becomes a data requirement that must be handled by the database application. An entity may transform itself into an object if and only if it "passes" certain tests. Entities that are not objects may become property classes (group of policy homogeneous data elements) or a data elements. In the example above, COMPANY and CONTRACT are likely objects. SALARY is probably a data element, and EMPLOYEE EDUCATION is probably a class of properties within the object EMPLOYEE.

Entity relationship diagram: A diagram that illustrates entities, and the relationships between entities.

Error recovery: The process of correcting or bypassing the effects of a fault to restore a computer system (software or hardware) to a prescribed condition. Error recovery means that abnormal terminations are not allowed to occur--by design.

Exclusive control: A lock applied to a data record instance that prevents other users from accessing that data record instance while the lock is held. The level of control may be broader, that is, data record type, area, O/S file, or database.

Extent: A list of unsigned integers that specify an array.

External document: An external document is a document that is retained as a more refined description of some aspect of the database system. This may relate to detailed diagrams, flow charts, detailed explanation of formulas, and the like. An external document may be free form text material, such as a policy or regulation that may be referenced as the basis for the definition of another IRDS (IRDS) component instance, such as data element, data record, data integrity rule, etc.

Fail soft: A class of system failure that results in a gradual shut down of database activity for subsequent restart.

Field: See data element

Field length: See data element

File: See O/S file

FIPS: Federal Information Processing Standards.

Fixed length element: See data element

Fixed length record: See data record

Foreign key: See key

Fully functionally dependent: A data element value that can only be identified via the entire primary key.

Functional decomposition: A top-down division of activity into lower levels of greater detail that can become defined computer software modules.

Group: See data element

Hash/calc logical: An access strategy in which the data element's value is used to locate a data record instance that has been physically stored in either primary key order or in an as-entered order. The hash/calc algorithm is employed as an alternative to a hierarchically organized index.

Hash/calc physical: An access strategy in which the data element's value is used by a formula to determine the physical location of the data.

When a hash routine is used to determine a physical address, the initial address determined is called the data record instance's home address. If that space is already occupied by a rightful owner of that home address, then the new data record instance is stored elsewhere, with a pointer in the existing home record pointing to the new data record instance (now called a synonym). When the home address is occupied by a synonym from another home address, that synonym data record instance is displaced to another location to make room for the address's rightful owner.

Heuristics: A method of obtaining a solution through inference or trial-and-error that uses approximate methods while evaluating the progress toward an acceptable goal.

Hierarchical data model: A data model consisting of tree structured data. Each data record type belonging to the hierarchy is simple. Further, each data record instance may have multiple descendants, but only one owner data record instance.

The data record instance operations allowed on the hierarchy are: FIND, GET, STORE, and DELETE. The relationship operations allowed are: GET OWNER, GET MEMBER, GET NEXT, ADD TREE, and REMOVE TREE.

Some hierarchical DBMSs allow indexes only at the top (root segment), while others allow indexing of any or all data elements.

Hierarchical index: An index that has its unique values organized into a series of levels. On each level are records of index values and the addresses (pointers) of the records of index values of the next lower level. At the lowest level, the index entries point to the data record instances.

Home address: See hash

Host language interface: The process of incorporating data manipulation verbs into a programming language such as COBOL or FORTRAN. Included in the interface are the specification of data to be obtained from or placed into the database, and the specification of the mechanism for receiving from or send messages to the DBMS. It is identified to the application programmer for logical and physical file manipulations. The tools are embedded in the host language (e.g., COBOL, PL/1) and are accessed usually through CALL statements, but sometimes by extensions in the language.

Independent logical file data model: A data model consisting of independently defined data record types (often called files). Each data record type may be complex, enabling each of its data record instance to look like a hierarchy of data. Some ILF DBMSs default to having all the data record instances from only one type reside on one O/S file, while other ILF DBMSs default to having all data record instances from all the data record types residing in one O/S file. Finally, some ILF DBMSs permit the mapping of a data record type's instances to O/S files to be defined in a physical schema definition language.

The data record instance operations allowed on the ILF are: FIND, GET, STORE, DELETE, and MODIFY. Relationship operations usually are limited to JOINs.

Index: See key

Inferential relationship: This type of relationship states that there is a relationship between two data record types, but neither relationship is dependent on the primary key of either. A typical example is PRODUCT-CONTAINER. The basis of the relationship is the dimensions of the product and that of the container. The relationship states that the product is likely to be able to fit in the container, but does not imply that it is actually stored there.

Information: Data evaluated in a specific situation, applied to solving a particular problem, or used in making a decision.

Information resource dictionary system (IRDS): At a minimum an information resource dictionary system (IRDS) contains metadata from the dictionary component of the storage structure of one or more databases that are under control of a DBMS central version. There are three types of IRDS: passive, semi-active, and active.

A passive IRDS is one that is loaded with data made available to it through specialized data loading programs.

A semi-active IRDS is one that obtains its data automatically whenever schemas, subschemas, or DML programs are compiled.

An active IRDS not only obtains its data at compile time, but it also is automatically accessed by executing run units for data editing and validation functions, security and privacy, valid use of subschemas, and the like.

A modern IRDS system contains all the data necessary to describe and control the corporate data structures, rules, policies, databases, programs, systems, subsystems, and the like. *The modern IRDS contains data sufficient for it to serve as an information model of the enterprise which the database is to serve, and as a control point for further database development. Information of interest to the enterprise is described in terms of relevant entities, their properties, and their interrelationships, together with various integrity, security, and other constraints* (SIGMOD Record, Volume 15 No 1, March, 1986).

Insertion: The process of adding a record to a database. For NDL DBMSs record insertion often involves the automatic adjustment of next, prior, and other pointers. There are three modes of insertion in the ANSI/NDL data model, AUTOMATIC, STRUCTURAL, or MANUAL. If AUTOMATIC, the DBMS automatically connects the record to all sets for which it is defined to be a member. For STRUCTURAL, the record is connected to the owner if and only if the identified field value specified in the member matches the identified field value in the member. If MANUAL, the record merely becomes a part of the database without being connected to any database set. The membership is established only through use of the DML verb CONNECT.

Installation and maintenance: Installation and maintenance activities relate to the actual installation of the DBMS at a computer center. These activities begin with an installation survey, software delivery, system generation, test database installation, problem resolution, and on-going DBMS patches and new release installation and testing.

Instance: A set of values representing a specific occurrence of an element or record.

Integrity: A state of database consistency.

Integrity constraints (DBMS enforced): Constraints on data values and their relationships.

Internal schema: See physical schema

Interrogation: Interrogation is the process of accessing data element values from the database through a user schema interface via any one of a number of different interrogation languages.

See also host language interfaces (HLI), and natural language.

Inverted access: A term that indicates a mode of processing that is the inverse (inverted) to that of traditional data processing. Traditional data processing locates and acquires contexts (data record instances) and then discovers data element values. The inverted approach discovers data record instances based on the values of one or more data elements. That is, from value to context, rather than from context to value.

ISO: International Standards Organization.

Join: An operation that takes two tables as operandi and produces a new table by concatenating the rows by matching the values of the columns stated to be the basis of the join. While the columns of values must be JOINable (same domain) the column names must not be required to be the same.

Journal file: A computer file that stores data record instances that can be used to restore a database subsequent to a failure. In some DBMSs, these data record instances are before and after images of DBMS record instances that result from updates. In other DBMSs these data record instances contain a highly condensed version of the update.

Justify: To adjust the value representation in a nonnumeric field to the right or left boundary (i.e., margin) ignoring blanks at the front or back.

Keeplist: A sequence of database keys maintained by the DBMS for the duration of the session associated with its creating module and referenced by data manipulation language statements.

Key: A data element that is employed by the DBMS to locate or store one data record instance. In general there are four types of keys: primary, candidate, foreign, and secondary.

A primary key is the designation of one or more data elements that can be used to locate one data record instance. Traditionally, the value set of a primary key is unique across all instances of a data record. In the event the DBMS does not provide for the enforcement of uniqueness, then there is no semantic difference between primary and secondary keys.

A candidate key is the designation of one or more data elements that can be used to locate one data record instance. The candidate key is not the primary key, by decision of the data analysts.

A foreign key is the designation of one or more data elements within one data record type (table) that is the primary key of another data record type (table). The purpose of a foreign key is to represent a relationship between two data record instances (rows) and to imply automatic actions whenever data value changes occur on the foreign key's value.

A secondary key is the designation of one or more data elements whose values are not required to be unique across the set of data record instances for which it is a key. If the DBMS enables the imposition of uniqueness on a secondary key, then there is no semantic difference between a secondary key and a primary key.

Key value: The actual contents of a key at a given time.

Language: A set of characters, conventions, and rules that is used for conveying information. The aspects of language are pragmatics, grammar, semantics, and syntax.

Line: Line is a term used to identify a specific telecommunications link.

List processing: List processing implies AND or ORing lists of data record instance identifiers (usually DBKEYs) together. Each list of DBKEYs is most often created as a consequence of a select statement, e.g., SELECT EMPLOYEES WHERE DEGREE EQ PHD AND JOBCODE EQ ENGINEER. In this example, two lists are built: the DBKEYs from the select DEGREE EQ PHD; and those from JOBCODE EQ ENGINEER. These two lists of DBKEYs are then ANDed together to find the set of data record instances that qualify.

When the data elements are from data record types that are not the same, but are relatable, then a normalization process must occur. That is, raise or lower one set of DBKEYs to the level of the other. Static relationship DBMSs that accomplish this, in the case of downward normalization, do so by utilizing the GET MEMBER operation with the pointers from the parent DBKEYs to determine the DBKEYs of the members of the selected OWNERs. Since the two sets of DBKEYS then relate to data record instances from the same data record type, the lists are then able to be ANDed. Upward normalization works the opposite.

List processing DBMSs typically allow other Boolean operations (AND, OR, NOT), relational operations (LT, LE, EQ, NE, GE, GT), and parentheses.

Load (data): Data loading is the process of taking data that is outside the database and bringing it into the data component of the storage structure. Included in data loading are all other processes that are necessary to build indexes, relationships (static only) and all other necessary components of the storage structure. A database is loaded when all these activities have been successfully accomplished. The loading process may be accomplished through a single DBMS command or a series of separate job steps.

A database unload is the process of returning data back to a DBMS independent format on some storage media for possible transport to another computer, or DBMS, or for use by another access method.

Lock: The situation that prevails when one run-unit program is granted exclusive access to data record instances and all the other run-units must wait until the first program releases the lock. The lock may be, depending on the DBMS, at the

DBMS record instance, area instance, file instance, or database instance level. Additionally, the run-unit can be in HLI, or any of the natural languages. Finally, certain DBMS functions may cause a lock, for example, logical database reorganization.

Log file: See journal file

Logging: The process of writing log records.

Logical and physical interrelationship: From the user's point of view, the database consists of data record instances. The DBMS sees the database from the same point of view, except that the definition of a data record instance relates to two different concepts. The DBMS dispatches or receives DBMS record instances to and from the O/S system software routines, which in turn dispatch or receive them to mass storage devices such as disks. The user obtains and puts data record instances to and from the DBMS. While a data record instance may be coincident with a DBMS record instance, normally it is not. In most DBMSs, a DBMS record instance contains multiple data record instances, and a data record instance is allowed to span multiple DBMS record instances.

The DBMS reads and writes DBMS record instances from all of its storage structure components. That is, from its dictionary, its indexes, its relationships (static only), and its data, while the user reads and writes data record instances. The DBMS, in support of the user's requests, reads and writes DBMS record instances to and from storage structure components. If a user writes a single data record instance to a database, the DBMS may place that data record instance in the appropriate buffer and not dispatch it to the O/S because the buffer is not full. It may further, in support of the user's write, have to create and store onto the database DBMS record instances in support of the user record's relationships to other records, the addresses for indexes that have been changed. In short, a single user write might generate no I/Os, one I/O, or many I/Os.

Logical data model: See data integrity model

Logical database schema: See logical schema

Logical file: See data record type

Logical record facility: See view

Logical schema: The logical schema is a linguistic expression of the syntax and semantics of the interface between the database designer's concept of the database and the DBMS. The rules specified in the logical schema apply to all users of the database.

<u>Logical terminal</u>: A logical terminal is an indirection facility that allows HLI programs to send or receive messages from terminals without precoding the terminal's physical characteristics.

<u>Logical user view</u>: See view

<u>Many-to-many relationship</u>: This type of relationship states that an owner data record type can have one of its instances relate to one or more data record instances of another data record type. The second data record type would be serving in the role of a member data record type. And at the same time, one of the member data record instances, now serving in the role of an owner, can relate to one or more member data record instances of the data record type that was formerly serving in the role of an owner data record type. A typical example for the relationship is DEPARTMENT-BUILDINGS. A DEPARTMENT may be located in more than one BUILDING, while at the same time a BUILDING may have multiple DEPARTMENTs located within it.

<u>Map</u>: A map is a general term employed to relate two entities, for example, data element positions within screens to data elements within record types.

<u>Member</u>: A data record instance that is owned by another data record instance of the same or different data record type in a CODASYL, ANSI NDL, or hierarchical data model DBMS.

<u>Message processing</u>: Message processing is that process of the DBMS in which information about the status of a command, the database and the DBMS is provided to the run-unit or the process that is currently accessing the DBMS.

<u>Messages</u>: Text statements that are able to be provided to users through various languages.

<u>Meta language</u>: A language used to specify itself, or another language. The specification of the ANSI NDL and the ANSI SQL is in a BNF format meta language.

<u>Metadata</u>: Data that describes other data. An IRDS database is metadata.

<u>Module</u>: The module is a self contained component of a program that retrieves, updates, or processes data. A module may reside in multiple programs.

<u>Multi-user mode</u>: See concurrent operations

<u>Multiple database processing</u>: Multiple database processing is a facility offered through the DBMS to allow a run-unit (host language or natural language) access

to more than one database. Access to each different database may be through different subschemas and/or views.

See also physical database.

Multithread: See concurrent operations

Multivalued dependency: A one to many (1:M) or many to one (M:1) association among data elements.

Natural language: A natural language is a language that is almost always invented by a DBMS vendor to provide access to the database. The program that results from a natural language is normally not able to be utilized on any other DBMS vendor's system.

There are typically three types of natural languages: procedure-oriented, query-update, and report writer. Not all DBMSs have all three. Some have only one, which may be either the procedure oriented language, or a combination of the query-update and report writer languages.

A procedure oriented language is a natural language that typically allows looping, branching, computation, print formatting, data record, selection, retrieval, storage, and modification. This language is sometimes called a fourth generation language (4GL).

A query-update language is a natural language that selects, retrieves, and either updates, or formats and prints (outputs) the data in one statement or sentence.

A report writer typically contains verbs to select, sort, and specially format data into reports. Special formatting controls usually include control breaks, subtotals, totals, headers, footers, column titles, page numbering and the like.

Natural languages typically execute in four different modes: HLI, direct, interpretive, and compiler.

HLI implies that the natural language expression is actually data to a HLI program, which determines the actions to be performed and accomplishes the activity, as if the natural language run unit had been written as a HLI program.

Direct execution natural language implies that the query expression is data to a computer program that directly executes against the database through subroutine calls, etc. This type of program is often written in assembler.

Interpretive natural language means that each statement of the natural language run unit is decoded, and then executed. If a loop is required to acquire successive records of data, then the natural language instruction is reinterpreted during each cycle of the loop.

Compilers executing natural languages translate the natural language statements into another language. That language is then compiled into a run unit that is executed. When the run unit is to be reexecuted without source code changes, the compile step does not have to be reperformed.

Navigate: A set of DML commands that are explicitly executed by a run-unit (GET OWNER, GET NEXT, or GET MEMBER), or are implicitly executed by the DBMS when data elements from different record types are printed with a query language.

Generally, the navigation logic for a static relationship DBMS is expressed explicitly in the run-unit DML. With the advent of logical user views, the DML logic has been moved to an intermediary processing interface between the run-unit and the DBMS (which accesses the database).

For dynamic relationship DBMSs, the relationship operations of PROJECT, JOIN, etc. are navigation commands. These too may be explicitly stated in queries, or executed through the logical user view intermediary.

Whether the DBMS is using indexes or embedded pointers is immaterial to the notion of navigation.

NDL data model: A form of the network data model standardized by ANSI-X3H2. NDL record types can have single- or multi-dimensional data elements. The record operations are FIND, GET, STORE, DELETE, and MODIFY. The relationship operations are CONNECT, DISCONNECT, GET OWNER, GET MEMBER, and GET NEXT. The combination operations supported are RECONNECT (DISCONNECT and CONNECT), and INSERT (STORE and CONNECT).

The ANSI network data language (NDL) specifies data record structures, relationships, and the operations on the structure. The specification provides the syntax and semantics of the schema and subschema. NDL specifies only the semantics of the operations, as the syntax of data processing languages is the function of other ANSI committees.

The relationships supported through the NDL's DDL are owner-member, owner-multiple member, singular single member, singular multiple member, and recursive.

Network: A set of relationships between owner data record types and their instances and member data record types and their instances such that a single member data record instance may belong to more than one data record instance from different owner data record types.

Next key (next pointer): The DBKEY of the data record instance which is the logical successor of the current data record instance.

Non procedural language: A high level language requiring very little syntax and few data format declarations and suitable for non data processing users to learn and become productive in a very short time.

See also natural languages.

Normal forms: First normal form: data that has been organized into two dimensional flat tables.

Second normal form: first normal form data that additionally has all its non-primary key data elements functionally dependent on the entire primary key.

Third normal form: second normal form data that additionally has no dependencies between any non-key data elements and any other non-key data elements.

Fourth normal form: third normal form data that additionally has its primary key related to all data items in the record such that it contains no more than one nontrivial multivalued dependency on the primary key.

Fifth normal form: fourth normal form data that additionally has the characteristic that if its primary key is a concatenated key such that none of the components of the concatenated key can be derived from another component of the concatenated key.

Normalize: The process of conforming to or reducing to a norm or a standard, such that all members of the group are commutative. Commutative means that the members of the group are able to be combined in such a manner that the result is independent of the order in which the elements are combined.

For example, the process of combining proper fractions is the process of finding the "lowest common denominator." It therefore is a process of normalization. Once the common denominator is found, the fractions can be combined.

As another example, if total salary of all departments is desired, and if the managers' salary were stored in the department data record instances, and the employees' salary were stored in the employee's data record instances, the DBMS could not simply select the department managers, then the employees, and then combine the salaries. That's because the DBMS does not "know" which department manages which employees. Consequently, the managers must be "normalized" down to the level of the employees before the appropriate manager's salary can be combined with the manager's employees.

Unfortunately, the term "normalization" has taken on a special meaning for the relational data model. That is because the relational data model only allows simple data record instances, that is, flat. In relational terminology, the process of removing multi-valued items, or repeating groups, that is, of adhering to a standard, is called the process of "normalization." Records that are "flat" are said to be in a "normal form." The gradations of normal quality range from one to five.

Notwithstanding the relational use of the term normalization, the process is useful for other data models. That is, each data aggregate within a data element of a complex data record instance should conform to at least the third normal form.

Normalized data: Data that has been placed into a structure that conforms to the fifth normal form.

Null: An item or record for which no value currently exists or may ever exist.

O/S file: A collection of DBMS record instances known to the operating system under a single name, and that are accessed by a single O/S access method.

One-to-one relationship: This type of relationship states that there is a one-to-one relationship between two data record instances from two different data record types. That is, there is one owner instance, and only one member instance. Further, the DBMS enforces the fact that there cannot be more than one member data record instance. A typical example might be PRODUCT-FACTORY. The relationship enforces the fact that one and only one FACTORY manufactures the particular PRODUCT.

Order: To place items in an arrangement specified by such rules as numeric or alphabetic order. Order is also a synonym for sort.

Ordered: Maintained in a sequence depending on the value of user specified data elements based on a collating sequence.

Outer join: An outer join is a relational operation that joins a tuple from one table to a tuple from another table when the columns, which are the basis for the join are NULL.

Overflow: A technique to store and then subsequently select or modify data record instances that are not able to be located in the normal location that the access strategy initially seeks to find them in.

Owner: A data record instance that has dependent data record instances. A owner data record instance may itself be a member data record instance in another set instance.

Owner key (owner pointer): The DBKEY of the owner data record instance.

Owner key (owner pointer): The DBKEY of the owner record.

Owner-member relationship: This type of relationship states that there is one owner data record type, and one member data record type. There may be one or more member data record instances for each owner data record instance. In typical example, for the relationship COMPANY CALENDAR, the YEAR would be the OWNER, and MONTH would be the member.

Owner-multiple member: This type of relationship states that there is one owner data record type, and more than one member data record type. There may be one or more member data record instances of each type for each owner instance. A typical example for the relationship is EMPLOYEES, where COMPANY is the OWNER, and PART-TIME-EMPLOYEES, FULL-TIME-EMPLOYEES, and RETIRED-EMPLOYEES are the members.

Packed decimal: A representation of numeric values that compresses each character representation in such a way that the original value can be recovered.

Padding: A technique used to fill a data element value instance, data record instance, or DBMS record instance, with dummy data, usually zeros or spaces.

Page: See DBMS record

Parameter: A data element or an array of data elements that specifies the data type of its values and assumes or supplies the value(s) of the corresponding argument in the call of a procedure.

Password: A character string that enables a user to have full or limited access to a system or to a set of data. See also security schema.

Physical attribute: See data type

Physical database: A physical database is defined as that physical occurrence of all storage structure components that result from the definition of all the records within a single database schema. Included in these resultant components are the database's storage structure, the DBMSs access strategy for storing and retrieving records, and the processes for data loading, update, and database maintenance.

A single database could be as little as a single computer file, or a large number of computer files. The number of files and the organization of each file is immaterial. A database is able to be removed from an on-line status to an off-line status by a backup command. That space is then immediately available for use by a different database. Further, if the backed-up database is desired to be placed on-line again, it may be restored onto different on-line storage space and accessed by the DBMS just as before without having to again go through the process of data loading.

Two or more databases are two or more physical occurrences of the components just described.

Physical record: See DBMS record

Physical schema: The physical schema is a linguistic expression of the syntax and semantics of the interface between the desired database (represented by the logical schema) and the computing environment's operating system's storage and retrieval.

Included in the physical schema is information about the database's storage structure allocation to storage devices, the physical organization of data record instances, the allocation of data record instances across O/S files or areas, DBMS record blocking factors and the like. The physical database schema is communicated through a data storage definition language (DSDL).

If the logical schema only contains general statements about data types for data elements, the physical schema must complete the definitions. For example, if the logical schema only contains the specification that a data element is numeric, then the physical schema would specify further that it is packed decimal, fixed, floating point, complex, and the like. In short, the complete specification is the combination of the specifications contained in both the logical and physical schemas.

Physical terminal: A specific type of terminal utilized within a telecommunications environment.

Pointer: A DBMS created addressing mechanism, typically a DBKEY, which relates data record instances of the same or different types. See also Owner, Next, and Prior keys.

Populate: See load

Precision: A measure of the ability to distinguish between nearly equal values.

Primary key: See key

Prior key (prior pointer): The DBKEY of the data record instance that is the logical precedent of the current data record instance.

Privacy: See security schema

Privacy key: See security schema

Privacy lock: See security schema

Procedural language: A language such as COBOL or FORTRAN that enables looping, branching, prompting, data reads and writes, and the like.

Procedure oriented language: See natural languages

Program: A program is an occurrence of computer code contained in the program's modules to accomplish a specific objective. The program's language may be natural, O/S command language, or compiler (FORTRAN, COBOL). Each program is described in the IRDS and in the program itself. Further, the program is described in external documentation to the extent that neither the IRDS nor the program listing provides sufficient explanation. A program typically contains one or more modules which interact with data from one or more views. For the purposes of this Glossary, the languages in which a program is written may either be host or natural.

Programmer productivity tools: A programmer productivity tool is a software facility provided by the DBMS vendor to enhance the development of a database application. These tools relate to the four components of database: logical, physical, interrogation, and system control.

Logical database productivity tools include for example an interactive, screen-driven facility that allows the building of a data definition language through the selection of various syntax units.

Physical database productivity tools include automatic or default physical schema generation, database size estimators, data loading utilities, and data update programs.

Interrogation productivity tools include interactive screen driven facilities for generic report generation. Additional facilities include subsets of DBMS facilities to prototype an entire database application in order to validate a database design.

System control productivity tools include facilities for determining database performance, default security schema generation and maintenance, and DBMS version default generation.

Projection: A relational data model operation that takes one relation as an operand and returns a second relation that consists of only the selected columns, with duplicate rows eliminated.

Pure alphabetic: A representation which is express using only letters.

Pure numeric: A representation which is expressed using only numbers.

Qualification: The selection of a subset of stored data.

Quality assurance: The policy, procedures, and systematic actions established in an organization for the purpose of providing and maintaining some degree of confidence in the data integrity and accuracy throughout the life cycle of the data, which includes input, update, manipulation, and output.

Query update language: See natural languages.

Queue: A queue is a telecommunications term indicating a temporary storage area for various items like data streams, messages, and the like.

RAM: Random access memory.

Random access: See hash/calc physical

Real storage: The execution space in a virtual storage system that is directly controlled by a central processing unit.

Record: See data record

Record check: See data record

Record-element: See data record element

Record layout: A description of the arrangement and structure of data in a data record. See also data record, and DBMS record.

Record length: A measure of the length (size) of a data record, usually expressed in units of character, words, or bytes. See also data record, and DBMS record.

Record type: See data record

Recovery: See Backup and recovery

Recovery file: See journal file

Recursive relationship: This type of relationship states that the owner data record type and the member data record type are the same name. For each instance of the recursive relationship, there is one owner data record instance, and one or more member data record instances. A typical example for the relationship is PROGRAMS, where a PROGRAM may be composed of (sub)PROGRAMs, which in turn are composed of other (sub)PROGRAMs. The depth is unknown.

Referential integrity: See data integrity rule

Referential integrity key: See foreign key

Relation: A table in which column entries are the same type and the rows (i.e., tuples) represent instances of the columns.

Relational algebra: A specification of the operations that manipulate relations. The basic operations of the relational algebra approach can be characterized as follows:

1. Algebraic operators refer to a fixed number of relations; selection and projection are unary operators, i.e., they operate on one relation. Binary operators are union, intersection, difference, join, and division as they operate on two relations.

2. Algebraic operators apply simple selection criteria: the selection operator applies a criterion that refers to constants and attribute values of individual tuples

in one relation only. The join operator applies a selection criterion that refers to two attribute values of individual tuples in two relations. The division operator tests sets of attribute values in two relations for set inclusion. This class of selection criteria can be defined formally by the expressions of the propositional logic.

3. Algebraic operators provide target transformations for tuple restructuring. Projection and division operators choose distinguished attribute values to form derived relations.

Relational calculus: A language that states the desired results of a relational database manipulation using first-order predicate calculus.

Relational database: A time varying collection of relation values of assorted degrees, each of which satisfies the properties defined by a relation scheme.

Relational model: A data model providing for the expression of relationships among data elements as formal, mathematical relations. Informally, a relation appears as a table of data representing all occurrences of the relationship among the data elements or attributes of the relation. A row of the table, called a tuple, comprises one occurrence analogous to a data record instance.

Relational view: See temporary view table, and view

Relationships (interrecord): Two data record instances of the same or different type can be related. Either the DBMS already "knows" about the relationship, or the user knows. In the "DBMS knows" case, the DBMS provides verbs to process the relationship instances that already exist among the data record instances. These relationships are called static because they are already known.

In the "user knows" case, the DBMS allows the user to specify the basis of the relationship, and then the DBMS, again through special (but very different) verbs, determines whether any data record instances belong to the user hypothesized relationship. These relationships are called dynamic because they are dynamically discovered during the execution of the interrogation. A static relationship DBMS has formally defined relationships. These formal definitions are needed so that the DBMS can create the pointers that relate data record instances. Static relationships typically have a name and a set of rules that govern the operations that process data record instances through the relationship. For example, ordering rules would govern the order of data record instance access for both retrieval and update.

There could be rules that prohibit duplicate data record instances within the relationship of employee and jobs, even though duplicates for job record instances might be allowed under some other relationship in the database. This is in contrast to a duplicates clause that prohibits duplicate employees. There could also be rules that govern participation of data record instances in the relationship on the basis of element values in one or more record types.

The definitional construct of the relationship is called a relationship type. If a relationship occurs between two or more data record instances then there is a relationship instance. Note, the relationship instance is the occurrence of the mechanism of relationship, not the data record instances that participate in the relationship instance. To say that the records are the relationship as in "the relationship is a set of records" has the same analogous logical consequence of having two people be their relationship, and when the relationship is dissolved, so too are the people.

A dynamic relationship DBMS, in contrast, does not formally define the relationships between/among data record types. Relationships for a dynamic relationship DBMS are defined either in the subschema/view that may be employed by multiple run-units, or in the run-unit itself.

Relationships are of two kinds: information bearing and value-based. An information bearing relationship is one in which the rules for membership are wholly contained in the run-unit that inserts and disconnects data records or view records to/from the relationship. A value-based relationship is one in which the rules for membership are required to be manifest as a data element's value belonging to the MEMBER record. Most static relationship DBMSs can have both kinds of relationships, while dynamic relationship DBMSs can only have value-based.

Notwithstanding, the eight types or kinds of relationships that are able to be defined (static), or created through DML commands (dynamic), are: owner member, owner multiple member, singular (singular member), singular (multiple member), recursive, many to many, inferential, one to one. Each of these are defined in the glossary.

<u>Relationships (physical)</u>: Relationships are the mechanisms of data record instance traversal. Relationships, either static or dynamic, have been defined above. For static or combination DBMSs, relationships are typically manifest through relative record addresses that are typically stored in the data record instances. Dynamic relationships are typically manifest through data values that are also stored in the data record instances.

<u>Relative addressing</u>: A method of data record instance selection from within DBMS record instances that is based on the location of the data record instance relative to the starting address of the first DBMS record instance. If a data record's address is 75, and if the blocking factor is 10, then the record would be the fifth data record within the eighth DBMS record instance.

<u>Reorganization</u>: Logical (database) reorganization is the process of making changes to the logical schema of the database through the addition, deletion or modification of data element types, data record or relationship types (static only) contained within the current database schema. Logical reorganization often automatically invokes physical (database) reorganization, to some extent.

Physical reorganization is the DBMS process of making physical changes to the organization of the database. Included, for example, would be the reorganization of logical database data record instances into a different physical order; the "repacking" of data record instances within DBMS record instances to eliminate empty space, etc.

Repeating group: See data element

Report writer: See natural languages

Representation: A number or symbol used to express a particular concept or meaning. It may be in the form of a name, abbreviation, code, or numeric value.

Restore: See backup and recovery

Retention: Retention is a subclause of the NDL set clause. The retention subclause specifies whether the data record type's membership in the database is FIXED, MANDATORY, or OPTIONAL. If the retention option for the data record type is FIXED, then a member data record instance must remain a member of some set instance from that set type until it is deleted from the database. If the retention option for the data record type is MANDATORY, then a data record instance must remain a member of that specific set instance or some other instance of the set until the data record instance is erased from the database. If the retention option for the data record type is OPTIONAL then a data record instance can be disconnected from a named set instance, and still belong to the database even though the data record instance belongs to no other set instance.

Retrieval: The process of obtaining stored data from a database. The process includes the operations of identifying, locating, and transferring the data.

Ring structure: A set of relationships among records such that the last next pointer points back to the beginning of the record.

RJE: RJE means remote job entry, which means that computer jobs done in batch are submitted for execution from remote locations.

Robust: A property that enables a system to continue error-free processing despite some failures.

Rollback: See backup and recovery

ROM: Read only memory is a form of computer memory that is not erased when the computer loses power.

Root segment: See hierarchical data model

Row: A horizontal set of data values from a table, one from each column. Rows are typically the smallest unit of data that can be stored into and erased from a table.

Run unit: A run-unit is the instance of a computer program that is accessing a database, normally through a subschema. The language of the run-unit is immaterial.

A run-unit command is a request for DBMS services that is transmitted to the DBMS by the run-unit.

A multiple database run-unit is one that is able to access multiple databases during a single executing session of an instance of the run-unit. A multiple database run-unit must, therefore, be able to access multiple subschemas, each from a different database.

A HLI run-unit is a host language program, typically COBOL, with the incorporated DBMS verbs that access the database.

A natural language run-unit is an instance of a set of natural language commands that access the database to effect data selection, reporting, or update.

Save: See backup and recovery

Scale: The negative power that a number is multiplied by, taking into account its base. For example, the value of 104 base 10, scale 2 is 1.04.

Schema: A schema is a term employed to describe a database organization. Typically, a schema is defined in terms of syntax and semantics. The syntax is defines the rules of valid construction. The semantics define the rules of operation that are allowed under the schema.

In actuality, the schema is the specification of an interface. The four interfaces typically present in a DBMS are: logical, physical, view, and security.

Secondary key: See key

Secondary storage: Direct access media, such as disk packs.

Security: See Security schema

Security and privacy: See security schema

Security schema: Security and privacy are those sets of DBMS facilities centrally defined and enforced that prevent inadvertent and/or unauthorized access to the contents of the database(s) under the control of the DBMS. In general, there are protections for data record type instances and data element value instances, and for database operations. The security and privacy are specified in a security schema.

The security schema is a linguistic expression of the syntax and semantics of the interface between the view and the user in order to allow or restrict user access or manipulation of specific data record instances and/or elements and/or other database operations that may have already been more globally allowed through a user schema.

In some early DBMSs, the protection offered for data record instances and data element value instances was implemented through subschemas. That is, if the data record instances and/or data element value instances are not contained in the subschema, then the user of the subschema cannot access these missing data record instances or data element value instances. Some other early DBMSs implemented security and privacy through clauses contained in the (logical) schema.

More modern DBMSs create security and privacy through a separately defined and compiled set of security syntax that is part of the overall database definition process. This security schema is analogous to but different from views.

Clearly, a view defines a specific window into the database. However, if multiple users accessed data through the same window, but were to access different collections of data record instances, then an additional filter, based on data element values in the data record instance, would have to be active in order to discern one data record instance collection from the other. In addition to data record instance collection screening, the security schema might specify passwords, terminal identifiers, and the like.

Database operations security enables certain database operations to be inaccessible without the proper key to unlock the prohibition against the operation's use.

Segment: A discrete portion of a complex data record type, usually relating to a repeating group occurrence. For example, if an EMPLOYEE data record type has a repeating group DEPENDENTS, then each occurrence of the repeating group is a segment.

Selection: Identification of a subset of stored data meeting specified criteria. See WHERE clause.

Semantics: The meaning to be attributed to a syntactical form in a language. The relationships of characters or groups of characters to their meanings, independent of the manner of their interpretation and use. The relationships between symbols and their meaning.

Sequential search: Data record access according to the order represented by a key field.

Serial search: Access according to the physical storage order of the records.

Serial storage: A data record instance storage strategy in which data record instances are ordered in sequence (sorted) according to the values of one or more key data elements in each data record instance, and in which the data record instances are physically stored adjacent to one another according to this sequence.

Serializability: The property in which the effects of a group of transactions are invisible to other groups of actions that are concurrently executing. The effect is that of serial execution of the groups of transactions. Further, as each group of transactions successfully completes (that is, after a COMMIT), the effects of the group can be rolled back as a unit.

Session: A transient state that is associated with each execution of a module.

Set: In a network or CODASYL database a set is a named logical relationship between data record types. See also relationships.

Simple record: See data record

Single thread: See concurrent operations

Single user mode: See concurrent operations

Singular, multiple member relationship: This type of relationship states that there is no owner data record type, and one or more member record types. There may be one or more member data record instances of each of the members for each relationship instance. A typical example for the relationship is again HIGH-ACHIEVERS, where PART-TIME-EMPLOYEES, FULL-TIME-EMPLOYEES, and RETIRED-EMPLOYEES are the members.

Singular set: See relationships

Singular, single member relationship: This type of relationship states that there is no owner data record type, and only one member record type. There may be one or more member data record instances of the member for each relationship instance. A typical example for the relationship is HIGH-ACHIEVERS, where FULL-TIME-EMPLOYEES is the member, and the data record instances that belong are those determined to be high achievers.

Snapshot: See backup and recovery

SQL data model: The specification of a language that defines two dimensional tables of data and allows access to the data represented by the tables.

The record structure of ANSI/SQL is simple. That is, all the data elements are single-valued. The relationships are value-based and are expressed only in DML operations.

The record operations are STORE, DELETE, and MODIFY. The relationship operations are JOIN, PROJECT, DIVIDE, etc.

Storage structure: The physical organization of a database. That is, its complete set of dictionary, indexes, relationships, and data. These data are organized into DBMS record instances. The storage structure is specified through the physical schema.

Subject database: A database and related system designed to support mission descriptions and their applications by managing the data for a particular subject area. A subject database often encompasses the scope of several application databases.

Subschema (external schema or user schema): See view

Subschema data definition language: A language that is used to define a subschema.

Subschema record type: See view

System: A subsystem is a collection of programs that accomplish a well defined class of actions. The system typically has a flow among programs with a job control language or driver program to govern this flow. A system may be decomposed into subsystems.

System control: The definitions included for system control relate to:

Audit trails

Message processing

Backup and recovery

Concurrent operations

Multiple database processing

Reorganization

Security and privacy

Application optimization

Installation and maintenance

Systems analysis: The combined activity of data analysis and process analysis in support of building business systems.

Table: See relational model

Table look up: A table is a list of codes and values employed to explain data that is contained in the database. For example, D.C. means District of Columbia.

Teleprocessing task: A teleprocessing task is a small unit of work that is accomplished by the teleprocessing monitor system whenever needed.

Temporary view table: A set of data derived by some an expression of relational operators applied to a collection of base tables. See also view.

TP: Transaction processing

TPM: Transaction processing monitor: A transaction processing monitor is a software package that interfaces with the end-user that is on-line. It receives and transmits messages that are subsequently processed by DBMS and standard access programs.

Transaction: A command, message, or input record that explicitly or implicitly calls for processing action (e.g., updating a record). A transaction is atomic with respect to recovery and concurrency.

Transaction backout: See backup and recovery

Transitive dependency: A nonkey data element that can be used to access (or identify) another nonkey data element.

Tree structure: See hierarchical data model

Truncate: To delete characters from a character string, usually from either end of the string.

Tuple: A group of related fields from a row of a table.

Unload: See load

Unordered: Not maintained in a user specified order.

Update (data): Data update is the process of changing data values within existing data record instances, adding new data record instances to the database, deleting data record instances from the database, or changing the relationships which relate data record instances.

Static and dynamic relationship DBMSs change data values in a similar manner. A data record instance is selected, retrieved, changed, and then restored.

Adding or deleting data record instances to a dynamic database involves merely adding or deleting data record instances to or from the appropriate data storage component. Adding or deleting data record instances to a static database involves the additional step of modifying the relationships which bind the data record instances together.

Changing the relationships which bind data record instances together differs significantly between static and dynamic relationship DBMSs. In a static relationship DBMS, the relationship modification process involves these four steps:

1) The data record instance must be found.

2) The data record instance must be disconnected from the relationship which binds it to other data record instances.

3) The new relationship context in which the data record instance is to be stored must be found.

4) The data record instance is then connected into that relationship.

The process of changing a dynamic relationship, in contrast, is the mere process of changing the data element's value that is used within the run-unit to identify the collection of data record instances that participate in the static relationship.

Data updates that change data elements that are indexed, or that change record membership, automatically invoke DBMS processes that adjust the indexes, or the pointers from "neighboring" data record instances.

User: See end-user

User interface: A system boundary at which the user issues commands.

User schema (subschema): See view

User view: See view

User working area or UWA: See subschema records

Valid, invalid, and range value tables: An enumeration of those data element, data record element, or data element domain values that are either valid or invalid, or are a valid and/or invalid range of values within a domain of values. The enumeration may be valid only, invalid only, discrete only, range only, discrete and range, or finally collections of valid and invalid values. In any of the combination cases, the IRDS must contain a processor to identify conflicts.

Variable length data element: See data element

Variable length record: See data record

Vector: See data element

View: A view, also called a user schema or subschema is a linguistic expression of the syntax and semantics of the interface between the database and one or more specific users' access of the database through any particular data manipulation language.

The view represents a logical partitioning of the database for an individual's access. In short, the user's window into the database. A view instance is created as a consequence of the execution of the view's components. These are: schema records, schema record elements, navigation logic that exercise the relationship among schema records, and schema record select clauses. When a view instance is constructed, it consists only of single valued elements called view elements.

To handle the requirements of different programming languages that must "know" about views, a view definition language typically has data element, data record, and set rename clauses. For example, in FORTRAN, the schema record element EMPLOYEE-JOB-CODE would be interpreted as the value of the field CODE subtracted from the value of the field JOB subtracted from the value EMPLOYEE. To avoid this, a view would have a renames clause. For example,

EMPLOYEE-JOB-CODE RENAMED TO BE JOBCDE

The view might also have conversion specifications to allow for translation of schema data types to program language data types.

A dynamic view may optionally contain the specification of relationships that are to be "executed" whenever the run-unit requests data record instances through the view.

The rules specified in the view affect only the run-units operating under the user schema's control.

Whenever a view is derived from other views, it must contain the specification of the navigation logic (access path) necessary to transport the database's data record instances from the different data record types to the view records in the correct sequence for the run unit. The run-unit perceives a view record instance to be a simple record, and uses commands of FIND, GET, DELETE, STORE, or MODIFY.

As used by Whitemarsh, the view takes on two levels of precision: specification and implementation. The specified view is the interface between the specified data model and the specified process model. As an interface, its view element relates to data record elements, and the view itself is employed by business events. The specified view is either an input or output view, and is either a base view or a derived view. A base view is decomposed only into view elements, while derived views are decomposed into other views, which may in turn be derived or base.

View element: A view element is a data record element that has been identified to be employed in a view. A view element may have a different name, but must contain the same semantics as a data record element.

Virtual data element: A data element whose value(s) is not stored in the database but is derived from stored data by means of user-defined operations.

Virtual relation: See view

Volatility: A measure of the number of data record instance adds and deletes over a period of time, as well as over the total number of database data record instances.

WHERE clause: A WHERE clause consists of one or more WHERE expressions. If there is more than one WHERE expression, then they are connected with boolean operators. WHERE clauses are included in at least data record check clauses, views, natural languages, and the host language interfaces.

WHERE expression: A WHERE expression is a set of syntactic units employed by the DBMS to determine whether certain criteria are satisfied. A WHERE expression is simple if it contains no subordinate select expressions. A BNF representation of the components of a WHERE expression consists of:

<complex where expression> ::= {<where expression>

[boolean operator] }...

<where expression> ::= [<left parenthesis>]
[statistical operator]
<data element name> <operator>
<value> [<right parenthesis>]

<operator> ::= <unary operator>¦<binary operator>¦

<ternary operator>¦<arithmetic operator>

<unary operator> ::= <EXISTS>¦<FAILS>

<binary operator> ::= <GT>¦<GE>¦<EQ>¦<NE>¦<LE>¦<LT>

<boolean operator> ::= <AND>¦<OR>¦<NOT>

<ternary operators> ::= <SPANS>¦<RANGES>

<parenthetical operator> ::= <left parenthesis> (nesting).

<arithmetic operator> ::= <+>¦<->¦<*>¦</>

<statistical operator> ::= <min>¦<max>¦<sum>¦<count>¦
<avg>¦< sigma>

Sophisticated DBMSs allow WHERE expressions that involve any variety of data record elements to be placed in the same WHERE clause.

Index

Note: commonly used words like DBMS, relational data model, SQL, etc. were not indexed as those indexes would not provide a discriminating alternative to a table of contents.